# Understanding the Media:
# A Sociology of Mass Communication

**THE HAMPTON PRESS COMMUNICATION SERIES**

Mass Communications and Journalism
Lee Becker, *Supervisory Editor*

American Heroes in the Media Age
   *Susan J. Drucker and Robert S. Cathcart (eds.)*

Media, Sex and the Adolescent
   *Bradley S. Greenberg, Jane D. Brown, and
   Nancy Buerkel-Rothfuss*

Understanding the Media: A Sociology of Mass Communication
   *Joel Smith*

# Understanding the Media: A Sociology of Mass Communication

**Joel Smith**
Duke University

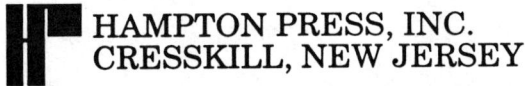

APR 24 '96

**HAMPTON PRESS, INC.
CRESSKILL, NEW JERSEY**

Copyright © 1995 by Hampton Press, Inc.

All rights reserved. No part of this publication may be reproduced, stored in a retrieval system, or transmitted in any form or by any means, electronic, mechanical, photocopying, microfilming, recording, or otherwise, without permission of the publisher.

Printed in the United States of America

**Library of Congress Cataloging-in-Publication Data**

Smith, Joel, 1925-
 Understanding the media : a sociology of mass communication / Joel Smith.
  p.   cm. -- (The Hampton Press communication series. Mass communications and journalism)
   Includes bibliographical references and indexes.
   ISBN 1-57273-004-8. -- ISBN 1-57273-005-6  (pbk.)
  1. Mass media--Social aspects. I. Title. II. Title: Sociology of mass communication. III. Series.
HM258.S538
302.23--dc20                                                95-3103
                                                               CIP

Hampton Press, Inc.
23 Broadway
Cresskill, NJ 07626

For Barbara, without whom . . .

# Contents

| | |
|---|---|
| Preface | ix |
| **1 Introduction: Mass Communication and Its Legacy** | **1** |
| Mass Communication? | 2 |
| The Legacy of Mass Communication for Contemporary Media | 5 |
| The Character of Media Study | 10 |
| Communication, Entertainment, and Influence | 15 |
| Communication and Entertainment Revisited | 19 |
| The Structure and Process of Communication | 22 |
| Communication, Mass Communication, and Mass Media | 27 |
| **2 Communication as a Social Process** | **31** |
| Communication Situations—Acts and Processes | 33 |
| Senders and Receivers | 38 |
| Information | 42 |
| Classifying Acts in Potentially Interactive Situations | 47 |
| Limitations on the Classification of Acts as Communication | 51 |
| Noninformational Acts and Messages | 53 |
| The Analysis of Noninformational Material | 56 |
| **3 The Structure and Processes of Communication Systems** | **61** |
| Elements of a System of Communication | 62 |
| Some Variable Qualities in a System of Communication | 66 |
| Alternative Models of Communication Systems | 82 |
| **4 Systems of Mass Communication** | **87** |
| Differentiating Systems of Communication | 87 |
| The Distinguishing Features of the Different Mass Media | 92 |
| The Context of Communication Systems | 125 |

## Contents

**5 The Social Role of Mass Communication and the Media** — 131
- Mass and Mass Communication — 133
- The Social Role of the Mass Media — 141
- Advertising as Influence — 153
- Media Effects Revisited — 157

**6 Control of the Mass Media** — 163
- The Nature of the Control Process — 164
- The Structure of Control of American Media — 166
- Control and Media Hegemony — 172
- Control and the Meaning of Media Material — 175
- The Varying Dynamics and Tactics of Control — 178
- Control and Public Policy — 182

**7 Public Policy and Control of the Media** — 187
- Locus of Control and Public Policy — 191
- Loci of Communication Policy — 193
- Public Policy and Self-Control — 197
- Public Policy and Individual Rights — 201
- Targets of Policy — 204
- The Range of Media Policies — 209
- Prospects for Policy — 212

**8 Development of the State and Public Communication** — 219
- Why Look Elsewhere? — 220
- The Nature of the State — 224
- The Development of the Modern State — 226
- Nation, State, and Country — 234
- States and Communication Policies — 239
- Rule and Communication — 244
- States, Media Systems, and Policy — 246
- State "Theories" of the Media — 251
- The Global Economy and National Media Policies — 257

**9 Contemporary Media Policy Issues in Comparative Perspective** — 265
- Public Broadcasting and Privatization — 266
- Cultural Imperialism and the New World Information Order — 274
- The Information Society and Wired Cities — 290
- The State and the Media — 295

**10 A Sociology of Mass Communication** — 311

References — 323
Author Index — 371
Subject Index — 381

# *Preface*

Research and commentary on mass communication and the media is now so widespread that probably few people are aware that the scholarly study of the media was formalized and nurtured primarily in sociology until the mid-1950s. I recall, as a college undergraduate in 1943, attending a meeting of the New York Academy of Sciences at the Museum of Natural History and listening to Robert K. Merton speak on his research with Paul F. Lazarsfeld (published later that year as "Studies in Radio and Film Propaganda"). Major contributions by other sociologists—Charles Horton Cooley, Robert Park, and several of the Frankfurt critical theorists—had appeared at least ten to more than 30 years earlier. Admittedly, seminal work on related matters had been done by others—Walter Lippman, George Herbert Mead, Edward Sapir, Benjamin Whorf—but most of the landmark research and few formal course offerings before the mid-1950s had been done, wholly or in part, directly or indirectly, by sociologists.

Since that time the study of mass communication and the media has migrated to many other disciplines as well as become a discipline in its own right. With these changes new issues and new approaches have come to dominate scholarship on the subject. As has often happened when sociological specialties have been colonized by scholars from other disciplines, sociologists lost interest and moved on to other topics. Consequently, although the study of mass media has flourished, the sociological project never has been brought to fruition. Analyses of the mass media as social systems embedded in and interacting with other social systems have not been pursued and, thus, this perspective has not been brought to bear on analyses of mass communication. This book returns to that project and applies traditional sociological concepts and analytic style to an examination of why the media operate as they do, hold their devotees, and engender the deep concerns that make them the whipping boy of the 1990s. Rather than being a conventional research monograph or textbook, it is a critical reanalysis of traditional basic issues in the sociology of mass communication.

*I*

One need not be a keen observer to be aware that the "mass media of communication" are pervasive. In cities it is obvious. Personal television sets, television antennas and dishes, newspaper racks, transistorized radios, and magazine stands abound. People everywhere walk around with earphones draped around their necks. They read, listen to, view, and discuss the media and the material they provide. Though in slightly less variety and quantity, mass media also are widely available outside cities and outside the core of developed countries. Not only are daily newspaper delivery, mail delivery of magazines, and radio and television reception common in rural areas, but the proliferation of dish antennas that dot the landscape indicates that the range and quantity of audiovisual material available in the countryside soon may equal urban levels.[1] Using television as an example, their presence "...cannot be confined to the periods when the [television] set is switched on. Television is not only part of the process of viewing, or reading or talking about it, but it is also part of our cultural lives when its presence is less direct, less obvious" (Fiske, 1989: 74). The media are intrinsic and essential to contemporary life.

Since the mid-1960s, scholarly interest in the study of the mass media and mass culture—first manifested in the 1920s and slowly accelerating for the next 40 years—has grown explosively. Without negating the significance of these pioneering analyses and studies, even a cursory glance would reveal how recent most of the literature is. The surge in scholarship—which, not incidentally, coincides with the resurgence of Marxism in the social sciences, major increases in nonindustry supported research, and the diffusion of postmodern criticism from literary and cultural studies to the social sciences—may obscure the fact that the central role of communication in human social life has never been at issue (Scott, 1990: 1). Indeed, as Luhmann wrote (1990c: 100), "The system of society consists of communications. There are no other elements, no further substance than communications. The society is not built out of human bodies and minds. It is simply a network of communication." There is no question that communication is essential for the adaptation of any social arrangement to changing conditions (cf. Allen, 1977).

## Preface

If we can paraphrase the poet, Allexander Pope, who wrote that "the proper study of mankind is man" and say that "the proper study of society is communication," it may be even more appropriate to say that "the proper study of contemporary society is mass communication," for the mass media originated with and are necessary—though not sufficient—to sustain today's complex societies. Ward (1989: 4) echoing this view, noted ". . . a growing awareness among contemporary historians of the importance of mass communications in understanding historical developments over the last hundred years." Given that mass communication and the media are 20th century terms that refer to the new nonpersonally mediated communication that differs from past systems and processes, it is useful to cite up front Raymond Williams' (1987 [1986]: 46) caution to avoid blindly drawing on the difference to understand the distinctive qualities of the media:

> The simplest response . . . [is] to separate off those new means and systems as a modern area, and by calling them mechanical and electronic and then mass communication convert all previous history of communications to their implied opposites: human, natural, and personal. But if there is one thing that the detailed histories show, it is that from the beginning the processes of communication have involved the use of both direct and indirect—human and non-human—physical resources. Similarly, the development of 'impersonal' communications—as distinct from the model of direct 'face-to-face' exchanges—is at least as early as the development of writing systems and indeed, in their graphic predecessors, much earlier. There is no future in trying to reduce the many problems of modern communications to falsely absolute contrasts.... On the other hand, to fail to realize changes in degree, in just this respect, would be to underestimate the problems quite hopelessly. . . .

This analysis heeds his warning by starting from the unique structural characteristics of the media rather than from contrasts with seeming opposites.

Although, as indicated, sociologists were early in recognizing the centrality of communication to social organization and in making lasting contributions to the study of mass communication and the media (Schudson, 1986; Wright, 1986b), they have produced few broad analyses (for exceptions, see McQuail, 1984, 1987a) and have varied considerably in their approaches and emphases (McCormack, 1986). Nonetheless, most still address the social role and impact of the media largely from a social problems or pathology perspective (Lowery and DeFleur, 1988). This is another reason for returning to a subject on which far too much may have been written already. Obviously, I feel that sociologists—not practitioners, communication scientists, psychologists, policy analysts, or any other "ists"—still have much to contribute if we eschew a social problems approach. This book is one such contribution.

The task is daunting. Making a cogent, informed statement about the field requires coming to terms with the diversity of theoretical perspectives, political viewpoints, and issues represented in a massive literature. Moreover, such a large literature inevitably is fraught with conflicts and disagreements. However, this can be an asset because accounting for them can enhance understanding. For example, in studies of whether outside interests shaped the content of classic Hollywood films, Wasko (1986 [1978]) concluded that financiers influenced the films of D. W. Griffith, whereas Buscombe (1986 [1975]) concluded that it is impossible to demonstrate that the interests of financiers and top management are detectable in the pre-World War II films of Columbia Pictures' top producers and directors. The seeming conflict over film financiers' influence arises because they try to exert influence in some circumstances but not in others. Control is not so simple that there is only one pattern. To understand control requires (a) being able to specify the factors that shape whether financiers try to exert influence, and (b) examining such related issues as whether film producers, directors, and financiers share the same tastes, values, and interests, and, if so, why. In another case, three sharply divergent accounts and interpretations of the history of mass communication research have been produced by Gitlin (1978), Morrison (1978), and Dennis (1989 [1988]). That three such different accounts can be produced without serious errors in scholarship is understandable—Gitlin takes a neo-Marxist, Morrison an academic history, and Dennis an industry perspective. The different interpretations of events do not indicate errors in the accounts; they reflect different perspectives.

At a minimum, the presence of divergent perspectives and conclusions in the work of reputable scholars is a warning against resolving disagreements simply by citing seemingly valid and reliable work in support of a particular view. More important, they indicate that there are no single "right or wrong" alternatives on many matters, that competing positions may all be supported by data that derive from different circumstances. The problem in media research is not to find *the* correct answer to a question but to specify the different conditions that lead to what appear to be conflicting assertions.

These cases suggest that no adequate analysis of mass communication or the media will be simple. It may start with a few simple concepts and propositions, but it will not remain simple. Simple models will not suffice because communication is not simple. The boundaries of communication acts are amorphous and those of episodes so ill-defined that direct, precise observation is hampered. Postmodernists are correct in contending that the nature of communication makes it impossible to observe key elements of the process directly. The complexity, amorphousness, and intractability of the process obscure the possibility that mass communication is not communication at all—if it is not, then it ought not be treated as if it is and, instead, the mass media rather than mass communication ought to be the object of study. At the least, I argue that the structural features of the media are ill suited to communication and, consequently, that it is unlikely to occur and unreasonable to expect it in the media. The most interesting questions—Why are the media so popular? What do they accomplish? Why do they so routinely appropriate the identity, apparatus, and terminology of communication? Do media professionals, let alone members of the public, know the difference? Why and how do media systems give a special status to materials that they would not have in other venues?—surface in trying to understand how the structure of the media permits a counterfeit process to use the appurtenances of communication to mimic it.

The analysis of mass communication and the media is hampered not only by their complexity but also by the fact that many scholarly treatments mirror lay discussions by neglecting four matters that are basic to understanding: (a) the process—mass communication—and the system in which it occurs—the media—are not the same; (b) even though the same stimulus simultaneously can elicit a sense of being both informed and entertained, the two experiences, as well as information and entertainment and the experience and the material that provides it, differ fundamentally; (c) the transfer of an idea and what may happen subsequently are not necessarily contingent events, and both may be unrelated to the basic difference between a sender's intentions to communicate and to influence; and (d) the present spate of interest in the meaning of media texts only encourages a one-sided emphasis on producers' intentions, consumers' roles, or textual features in giving them meaning, in total disregard of the fact that understanding any attempt at real or simulated communication—and, certainly, a successful attempt—requires examining the interaction and conjunction of all three. Neglect of that interaction is what moved Fiske (1989: 57) to complain that "...we have now collapsed the distinction between 'text' and "audience."' This analysis builds on these neglected distinctions.

Conceptual sloppiness encourages the conflation of mass communication and the media with communication and the neglect of fundamental differences. However, even if they are different, communication can be a useful analogue for mass communication. Indeed, the parallels are what led me to use the words *mimic* and *counterfeit*. Specifying the differences can help in identifying the distinctive, significant qualities of mass communication and the mass media. Thus, communication can be a useful point of departure for understanding both.

Perhaps what is distinctive about the analysis is my preference not to dwell on the media as simply a social problem, but, rather, to (a) analyze mass communication by using the communication process as an analogue (for a similar approach, see Severin with Tankard, 1988), and (b) examine media systems at many levels—in themselves, as related to other systems, and as embedded in larger social systems. Given my sociological orientation, I largely ignore individual behavior and individual effects. Thus, I do not analyze the media's role in cognitive change or the psychological processes involved in encoding or decoding messages. Moreover, I treat specific features of individual media only to clarify a point, preferring, instead, to look at the structures, problems, and social roles of the several media from the perspective of the larger social context and the minimum requisites for any social system to be viable.

## II

Fiske's use of the term *text* reflects the strong influence of postmodernist discourse on contemporary media studies. The relevance of postmodernism to the media is obvious. Postmodernists look to the media for ready evidence of the aspects of contemporary life that they consider crucial in differentiating it from the modern—in particular, to the fast cuts and discontinuities in music videos and television commercials, and, more generally, to the ways in which media technology cuts people off from direct experience with the world and encourages them to accept media representations as the world. Although most analyses of postmodernism emphasize the diversity of viewpoints that share that rubric, they also agree that the essence of what all postmodernists identify as the significant break from modernism is the stylistic fractionation, discontinuity, and incoherence of today's culture as compared to the rationality, coherence, and integration that are said to be the hallmarks of modernism. Thus, although postmodernists may disagree on details of the role of the media in bringing about cultural incoherence, they agree that cultural incoherence now is embedded in and reenforced by the media. Indeed, for postmodernists one essential aspect of the postmodern world is the definition of reality by the media.

## Preface

In view of these arguments, it is important, in situating my work, to explain the absence of discussions of postmodernist perspectives. Although it simply could reflect age or inertia, at the risk of appearing self-serving, I consider it an appropriate response to what I deem to be fundamental problems with a critique that encompasses much more than today's media culture. As postmodernists' concern for the loss of direct, authentic experience suggests, it is a commentary on all of contemporary society. Its critics consider its extreme forms to be nihilistic. If they are correct, it is not just another faddish literary theory but a serious challenge and concern for scholars in all fields rather than only for sociologists interested in the media. Moreover, it is particularly important that I discuss the omission, not only because I may appear to be out of step with a major approach in contemporary media scholarship, but also because the inescapable uncertainties in analyzing communication are at the heart of both the postmodernist argument and my discussion of communication in Chapter 2.

The uncertainties that limit analysis relate particularly to the treatment of communication as purposive or intentional action. The problem does not have to do with what the intent is and whether an act of symbol production must have a particular type of intent to be communication, issues whose centrality to an understanding of communication I do emphasize. Rather, it has to do with whether it even is possible for anyone, including the communicator, ever to be certain what the intention behind an intentional act is. The problem inheres in the fact that, although receivers of messages may infer intentions behind them, corroboration for these inferences can come only from the senders, who can provide it only by issuing new messages about past intentions. Because there is no way to validate whether new expressions represent original intentions accurately, attempts at corroboration produce only a spiral of uncertainty.

Postmodernists vary in the conclusions they draw from this, but most suggest that messages must be treated as texts with no fixed or primary meaning, and that any meaning anyone who perceives a text attributes to it is equally valid. This is taken to legitimate the issuance of any sort of text and of any interpretation placed on a text. Radical postmodernists, a group that Rosenau (1992) refers to as skeptics, extend the analysis to suggest that disorder rather than order, disintegration rather than integration, uncertainty rather than certainty, unpredictability rather than predictability are the natural conditions of social life. By implication, society, viewed by most sociologists as structurally ordered interaction within a group, rather than being a necessary condition for species survival, may be only a legitimizing concept used by groups whose political project is to control people by enticing them to regularize and control their actions. Obviously, many sociologists find it difficult to accept such a viewpoint.

It will be clear that I assume that action occurs in a structured framework. Although, like postmodernists, I always have acknowledged uncertainty and imprecision in, and even the impossibility of, identifying the intentions of communicators, unlike postmodernists, I also argue that actors find sufficient corroboration in the outcomes of ongoing sequences of action to be satisfied to continue behaving largely within the framework of a system's rules and understandings. Sociologists tend to view uncertainty and imprecision as posing manageable, but not ultimately resolvable, problems for systems. Postmodernists tend to the view that all people are isolated because they cannot get beyond one another's framework of assumptions, that this shields the interpretations that guide their behavior from others, and, consequently, that disorder is normal and order abnormal. Sociologists, like postmodernists, vary widely in their emphasis on these issues and the extremity of the inferences they draw from them, but, unlike postmodernists, they rarely conclude the impossibility of communication, the absence of any sharing, or the inevitability of disorder in social reality.

There are several other serious questions about the postmodernist critique. For example, is the evidence adequate that modern social life is characterized by disorder, nonintegration, and unpredictability? How is it that people are able to get along and even improve their life expectancies and average circumstances of life if these are the conditions? Why even bother producing and expressing the critique if a text has no assured meaning and all interpretations of it are equally valid? The important point, though, is that sharing a position on the irreducible uncertainty that afflicts any analysis of communication does not require accepting all or any part of the postmodernist position. Indeed, I believe that much can be learned about mass communication as an orderly process and system by accepting the irreducibility of the imprecision and uncertainty in communication. Consequently, I do not accept many assertions of postmodernists about mass communication and the interpretation of media texts. Relatedly, the cultural studies approach to the media as central elements in the production and distribution of popular culture also receives little attention in this treatment.

### III

Having distanced the analysis from most of the approaches that characterize discussions of the media in critical literary and cultural studies, it may help the reader situate it more precisely if I now respond to a good friend who, when I complained about how much time and energy the manuscript was taking, asked me what important theses I was examining. At the time, I told him that I could not specify them because I could not decide whether I had any theses in the conventional sense. However, there are several propositions about the nature of communication, mass communication, and the media that I consider important and useful and that serve variously as presuppositions, definitions, truisms, and, perhaps, theses. Mostly I assume them to be valid or to be propositions whose validity should be tested. I believe they can enhance understanding of the media as constituent elements of contemporary society:

1. Pure communication is rare; pure communication through the mass media is even rarer.
2. Ongoing communication requires the existence of a system that can persist beyond its immediate use or success. The functions of such a system, once developed, need not be limited to communication.
3. The concept of mass communication, taken literally, is a contradiction in terms that interferes with understanding both the mass media and what transpires when the actions referred to by the term occur.
4. Although the referents of the terms mass communication (process) and mass media (system) initially were inseparable, they are now only partially contingent inasmuch as the former still requires the latter but the latter no longer require the former.
5. Forms of mass communication and the media vary in the context of each society and its culture.
6. Both mass communication and the mass media are intrinsic to large modern societies and developed in conjunction with them. It is misleading to treat them as appurtenances that happened to develop as modern societies developed.
7. Control of mass media systems is diffused throughout their components and many elements in the larger environment. How systems operate reflects the balance in the exercise of this distributed power.
8. As states became the form of ultimate control for all areas of the globe and the people living in them, governments developed a deep and inescapable interest in national and international communication systems. The distinction between the two is disappearing.

It takes a sense of history to appreciate how radical these propositions and the ideas behind them are. They would not have occurred to me when I first offered courses on mass communication and the media. The few graduate courses I had taken and the research in which I had participated did not provide a systematic sociological perspective for organizing, synthesizing, and understanding the available material. There were no textbooks to suggest such a perspective. Scholars were fascinated by mass communication—not the media—as an empirical phenomenon. Their attention was on the ability to reach vast numbers of people simultaneously and quickly with the same material, not on the sociologically relevant differences among the media through which the material was conveyed, nor on the fact that technology mediated the relationship of sender and receiver.

This is not to say that there was no awareness of the importance of media as such. Print and film long had been available, and the fact that they attracted different types of people and, hence, may have had different significance for their audiences was appreciated. Nonetheless, mass communication emerged as a sociological topic only with the spread of radio. The capacity of radio to grip people's interest and imagination and to produce instant, reflex-like responses was seen as ushering in an entirely new social epoch. The shift in people's relations among themselves and with the larger environment was considered as substantial as the shifts in the nature of social reality that contemporary postmodernists attribute to the introduction of new media technology.

Hitler's use of radio, film, and print to mobilize German support for the Nazi cause and Roosevelt's reassuring radio "fireside chats" to help Americans get through the privations of the worst modern world economic depression had dramatized the potential of the media for having a quantum impact on social organization and change. In this environment scholars focused on the effects of rather than differences among the media. Except for devotees of progress, social scientists had not widely accepted change as the normal state of society; thus, they tended to treat the media as intrusive, new forms likely to destabilize society rather than as intrinsic to society. Moreover, they focused on individuals (e.g., whether and how people would vote, whether and what they might buy, whether they knew about and what their opinions were on issues) rather than on the structural accommodations and alterations that inevitably would occur as the new media became integrated into societies. Lazarsfeld and Merton's (1943) studies of the conditions for effective propaganda through the media typified such interests.

Sociologists consider communication, if not mass communication, central in their analyses of societal organization and disagree, if at all, only on whether it is *the* or *a* basic social process or, simply, an important but not basic process. Nevertheless, even in the days when it was a budding sociological specialty, there was not, nor has there since been, a systematic sociological analysis of mass communication. Consequently, when I offered my first courses in the area I organized them around the then popular "Who say what to whom through what channels with what effect" paradigm, even though, in using it for a synthesis of magazine audience studies that became my Master's thesis, I had found it wanting because most questions interesting enough to generate research crosscut and violated the categories. It was all that passed as theory at the time. Only when I offered my first graduate seminar on mass communication was I forced to confront its inadequacies and find something better. An unusually able group of students insisted that we examine whether mass communication should be distinguished from other types of communication—that is, why not just a sociology of communication, a topic already theoretically grounded in social psychology, rather than a sociology of mass communication? They insisted on addressing two questions. Is mass communication anything more than the sum of a great many acts of individual communication? If so, in what respects is it different? The answer to the first clearly is yes, but it was not so obvious at the time. The answer to the second still is not obvious.

The seminar participants argued that these questions could best be addressed by specifying what communication is and assessing what transpires in mass communication by that standard. The results of that approach are reflected in Chapters 2 and 3 and reveal that (a) much that is communication from a sender's or a receiver's perspective is not communication from the perspective of both; consequently, (b) much of the activity in ongoing communication is not information sharing but repeated attempts to assure that intended efforts succeed. It includes trial-and-error attempts to correct failed efforts and exact and varied repetitions to assure retention of successes. Initial failures are not necessarily consequential because there usually are opportunities to remedy them. Senders and receivers draw on other aspects of their relationship to sustain their efforts until communication occurs. This is what fundamentally distinguishes mass communication from the generic process. It lacks the qualities that ease the strain of communication in other settings. It is particularly difficult to monitor success as the effort proceeds, and, because entire message sets usually are prepared before anything is sent, senders cannot adjust for the performance of receivers in the course of the process, even if they are able to monitor it.

Because the information sharing that is possible in most communication is highly improbable in mass communication, the ties that hold face-to-face, or acquainted-but-separated senders and receivers to one another do not exist for the media. The attraction of media sources and their audiences must have some other basis and must be able to withstand the frustrations of frequent failures. Moreover, material transmitted in mass communication is unlikely to produce the same quantity and quality of communication possible in most other sending-receiving situations. Because mass communication often produces deep bonds of loyalty of receivers to senders even though very little, if any, successful communication occurs, this raises a host of questions that cannot be answered by treating mass communication as if it were the same as other forms. What binds receivers to disembodied, socially distant senders? What is happening in the process if very little communication occurs? How does social life accommodate the media consumption that increasingly takes people's time and energy?

Such questions are addressed throughout the book, particularly in Chapters 4 and 5, in which the conceptual approach developed in Chapters 2 and 3 is applied to the structure of the media and the nature of their social role. It is not necessary to have answers, however, to realize that the very fact that questions arise that cannot be answered as they would be for more direct interpersonal communication means that there is a place and a need for a sociology of mass communication. If, as I contend, there is very little, if any, communication in mass communication, then to speak of the sociological study of the mass media as the sociology of mass communication is misleading. Rather, it is the study of the institutionalized activities that potentially may be communication but that almost always is something else. Given the rarity of communication in the mass media, the sociological study of mass communication is primarily the sociology of the mass media, the institutionalized arrangements in which communication-like activities are pursued, rather than the sociology of mass communication.

It has taken me many years to appreciate the importance of these distinctions and to develop their implications. Despite its many costs, being slow has provided an opportunity to test and adjust the concepts and propositions as major innovations have changed the character of the mass media. When I was a graduate student taking the only courses available, for all practical purposes there was no commercial television. When I first taught the subject, the community in which I lived could not access a national network, and direct broadcast satellites and dish antennas were the stuff of science fiction. Had I rushed though this analysis at that time it could not have accounted for today's media. The mass media were almost exclusively public and remained so until the 1980s. That has changed with new media technology capable of public and private access, storage and transmittal, and interaction and one-way sending.

With these changes have come a host of issues that, because Americans tend to be exceptional in their perspective on the social role of the media, rarely make the public agenda in the United States. The roots of this unawareness and disinterest lie in a tradition, unlike that of most other countries, of valuing the individual more than the collectivity. The difference is reflected in media history. In most countries the media developed under state surveillance with partial or complete state involvement in the claimed interest of collective national goals. Market factors were secondary. In the United States, although often justified as information providers, the media developed as private, market driven enterprises supplying barely distinguishable entertainment (primarily) and information (secondarily) to individual consumers.

Reflecting the value difference, as compared to others, Americans are more prone to render judgments primarily in terms of their beliefs about the effects of the media on them and the people close to them. Typically, Americans fail to distinguish between information or entertainment, accuracy or inaccuracy, and fact or fiction in making these assessments. Public efforts at media control are usually responses to wide concern about what is provided or its presumed consequences. I consider all these matters in Chapters 6 and 7. There is little awareness of several issues that have arisen with the capability of new telecommunications technology to manipulate and control information and access to it. Where the view that the media should serve the country dominates, these matters receive equal, if not greater, attention. The concern is that how those issues are resolved will determine the country's economic and political conditions and its position in the world for at least the next century. Americans are uninformed on and uninterested in these matters, even though they are equally at risk. I discuss these issues in Chapters 8 and 9.

The analysis, then, has two distinctive features. First, it addresses systemic features and relationships that characterize the media generally rather than specific media at specific times, thus continuing a strategy that marked my approach to mass communication more than 25 years ago when I presented a paper with the essential core of Chapters 2, 3, and 5 and even earlier when I organized my first courses. Second, it covers a broad range of media phenomena from the most specific—a single communication act—to the most wide ranging—mass media systems in relation to entire societies, the state, and the functioning of a world economic system. Thus, at one level I explore the anomaly of the term *mass communi-*

*cation* by applying standard sociological conceptions of interactive social behavior to the activities of the participants. At another level I examine how the facts that only one actor can initiate activity and that access to and operation of media technology is asymmetrical lead to the unbalanced power that pervades sender-receiver relations in media systems. At still another level I examine how the stability of media systems reflects the consonance between behavioral regularities and expectations in people's central social activities and the behavior required of them as media consumers. In short, every aspect of the media from their constituent elements to their systemic qualities to their relations with the broader environment is examined.

There is no single powerful theory with which to address these many aspects of mass communication and mass media. The Meadian approach that I apply to the actions of senders and receivers has no clear relation to the structural approach with which I address such issues as what is required for media systems to persist successfully or why media system users and personnel do not come into conflict more often than they do in light of their divergent interests and power inequalities. Except for the behavioral models, the perspective is basically structural. It treats the media as social systems in their own right and as components of more inclusive systems, such as society, the state, and global corporations. It applies principles that pertain to the conditions that affect how such systems operate and survive, the internal conditions that must be met for them to be viable, and how they constrain the behavior of participants. The inconsistencies and lacunae are characteristic of sociology generally. This is, as the subtitle says, *a* sociology of mass communication.

## IV

The book begins with an extended discussion in Chapter 1 of some of the confusions in our thinking about mass communication and the media. It is placed in the context of the period in which mass communication began to be analyzed and studied and the term came into general use. Although the implied conclusion is that the phrase *mass communication* is an oxymoron, the fact that no change in terminology is imminent suggests that it is more useful, instead, to develop a clear understanding of both terms. Accordingly, after briefly discussing and defining *mass* (considered in more detail in Chapter 5), I define communication. That concept is explicated in Chapter 2 with a schema that specifies the communication characteristics of any identifiable situation that potentially is interactive. The schema clarifies what communication is and sets the domain of the discussion. In Chapter 3, a general model of a communication system based on that of a social system is postulated, its qualities are specified, and differences between mass communication and other communication systems are examined. This leads to a discussion in Chapter 4 of the implications of differences among the individual media. In Chapters 5-9, questions about the process and systems of mass communication as institutions are considered in more detail—for example, to what extent does communication occur in systems of mass communication? In what sense are they "mass"? What is their social role? How is their operation controlled? What policies might help resolve some of the problems we associate with them? How do American concerns with the media compare with those of other countries? And why the differences, if any?

Although, as mentioned, my interest in and studies of mass communication stretch back to my college days, it probably is accurate to say that this book began with the work of a Michigan State University graduate seminar that I offered in 1956 and that was elaborated in a paper published in 1962 and developed further in a long paper prepared for the 1969 meeting of the Southern Sociological Society. I then kept making small increments to the 1969 paper in order to clarify or explain certain points. Eventually, the manuscript became so long that there was no choice but to see if I could turn it into a book. Almost until the end of this process I had had no intention of writing a book. Indeed, I did not know that I had done so until it was accepted for publication. Had I thought that I was becoming committed to writing a book, almost surely I would have dropped the project. Much of the work during this gestation was supported by grants from the Duke University Research Council, for which I express great appreciation and thanks for encouragement in what was, at the time, a labor of love and interest rather than a commitment to a product.

The most substantial cost exacted by an almost endless project is that it becomes very difficult to remember and thank all those who helped along the way. I know that I could not name all the students who have had to live with the many iterations of the manuscript. Their term papers, examinations, and classroom comments have all contributed to the direction and content of the discussion. The Michigan State University graduate students who participated in the 1956 seminar until all hours of the night and sometimes over several days are listed in footnote 1 of Chapter 2. They deserve special acknowledgment for the clear thinking and analysis that produced a schema—one that differs very little from that in Chapter 2—for specifying the communication character of any potentially interactive situation. All the teaching assistants who provided me with feedback from their sessions with students struggling to figure out what I meant made especially valuable contributions. They include Margaret Glasgow, Beth Rushing, Chris Ellison, Kevin Kresse, Darren Sherkat, and Dina Rose. Beth Glennie provided invaluable assistance by testing my ideas on the state and media policy against a literature that would have been too difficult to access while I was in the throes of writing. I also want to give special thanks to those former students who years later have told me how useful they found some of these ideas when, as adults in the "real world," they came to understand them more clearly. They—and the scholars who have produced a voluminous literature that does not yet include a book that comes close to covering the points I think must be dealt with from a perspective that I feel is adequate—are the ones most responsible for my having persisted with this project.

My dear friends, Allan Kornberg, Thelma McCormack, John Thompson, and Charles Wright all have helped me situate my work. I wish that I could have applied more of the particularly helpful advice they provided whenever I asked. Finally, I want to acknowledge the support of Barbara Vorsanger Smith, who always seemed to be the one left waiting when I decided that another 15 minutes at the office would see me to the end of some endless task. She has been an unerring consultant who never hesitated to let me know when I had doubts that they were well founded and that I was not writing in the English language. Without her kindly patience and constructive criticism, the project would never had had an end.

## NOTES

1  Hudson (1987) carried this observation further and applied it to the availability of the entire spectrum of new telecommunications technology.

# 1

# Introduction: Mass Communication and its Legacy

The tools for this analysis are the concepts of communication and the ideas they generate when applied to mass communication. They provide a perspective for examining the social roles and control of the mass communication process. However, the path to that point is long and meandering, so it may help to review some key ideas and suppositions that shape and motivate this work. I begin by proposing that there no longer is—indeed, may never have been—mass communication. I then note that, despite the strong reasons for taking this position, mass communication and the media were thought of as communication when they first drew scholarly and critical attention and suggest that it will aid our understanding of modern media if we recognize that those ideas still influence current thinking. I offer several examples of this influence to support the argument. In considering why this line of thought has not had wider appeal, I suggest that early media scholars were working in circumstances that did not require them to define communication precisely, and that this led to neglect of the distinction between communication and its consequences, on the one hand, and among communication, entertainment, and influence, on the other. This neglect has become habitual and, I argue, accounts for confusions that hamper contemporary understanding of mass communication and the formulation of media policies. This chapter provides a preliminary overview of matters that are treated more thoroughly throughout the remainder of the book.

## MASS COMMUNICATION?

Although the rapid diffusion, universality, and impact of the media might lead one to expect an emphasis on the prevalence and dominance of contemporary mass communication, these are not my primary interest. Admittedly, no examination of contemporary media can ignore these matters—all the more noteworthy in that, for all practical purposes, in 1900 only print was widely available. Nonetheless, my orientation is "the end of mass communication," for, their pervasiveness notwithstanding, media products and their delivery are becoming increasingly specialized, and content specialization is the antithesis of mass communication (Austin, 1986: 108). Furthermore, this trend is not an aberration but, I would argue, intrinsic in the relations among mass communication, the media, and the social, economic, and political contexts in which they developed and now operate (Cantor and Cantor, 1986b).

Actually, this wording misstates my position. More accurately, it is that there never has been mass communication. I do not claim that the institutions and processes to which the term usually is applied are not major forces. Rather, I accept a compelling argument that very few events ever fit all the specifications of both concepts that form the phrase and that the few that may fit are likely to be so brief as to be ephemeral. The analysis employs long-established formal concepts of *mass* and *communication* that differ from popular usage. To take the concepts in any sense close to their connotations in social science usage would imply that true mass communication would require substantial expenditures to survive in any type of economy. The analysis suggests that the nature of the media as communication systems and the conditions of their development and operation inhibit them from being systems for conveying "mass communication." This does not deny the importance of what media systems provide or how they operate. Rather, failure to understand that both the concepts of *mass* and *communication* are idealized constructs and not descriptions of real phenomena results in important misconceptions of reality. Recognizing that the entities we ordinarily have in mind when we think of the contemporary mass media always differ in some ways from the image implicit in these concepts enhances a more realistic understanding of them.

If there are cogent reasons to argue that there is no mass communication, how did the two constructs ever get joined in scholarly use? In addition to erring by disregarding differences between concepts and reality, how could scholars also have ignored the implicit contradiction in the two terms? There is no easy answer. It probably was not pure blindness or mere stupidity. More than likely, the concepts seemed to fit the character of the media at a time of major social disruptions that were considered harbingers of complete social disintegration. Modern communication technology was being developed and its use spreading in the same social, economic, and political environment that was producing *mass men*—people cut off from social anchorages and restraints and without ties to traditional society (cf. Mosco, 1984). Because media expansion coincided with the proliferating demagogic totalitarian movements and full-scale world depression that were indicative of mass society—the concept for those political, economic, and social conditions—it would have been easy to consider the media integral to that process (cf. DeFleur and Ball-Rokeach, 1989: 145-167). Only after World War II were significant differences between the mass communication concept and actual media operations recognized.

In addition to the sheer force of logic, two essays should have led to a reconceptualization of mass communication no later than 25 years ago—Friedson's (1954) critique based on observations of media operations and audience behavior, and Sears and Freedman's (1967) analysis of the inconsistency between the concepts of selective exposure to media by consumers and of audience members as passive consumers, addicted to whatever media material happens to come their way. The exercise suggests three propositions that undergird the thesis that mass communication, if indeed it ever existed, is improbable, at best:

1. By definition, there can be very little communication, in the sense of purposeful information transfer, in mass communication.
2. Because a mass is unorganized and maximally heterogeneous socially, it neither can be identified by communicators to target nor is it an attractive audience for media entrepreneurs to sell to clients, most of whom wish to reach select markets.
3. Technological innovations that lower the cost of both sending and receiving equipment make it feasible to target materials to relatively small, homogeneous population sectors.

The first proposition expresses a transmission rather than a ritual view of communication (Carey, 1988: 14-23). I think it useful to treat it as an intentional process—one in which senders knowingly select others to receive informative messages constructed so as to maximize the chance that they will be received and understood as intended. Moreover, if the outcome is to be communication and not a variant, the messages must be received and understood as intended. Furthermore, as Cherry (1978) cogently noted, the appropriate term to describe the process is *sharing* rather than *transferring*, for the material remains with the actor even after transportation is successful (cf. also Lowenthal, 1984: 292; Luhmann, 1990a: 32). However, sharing emphasizes the terminal state of the participants and tends to ignore both the transmission process and the act of reception that must occur before the outcome is an issue. Therefore, although material is not relocated in communication, I use *transfer* to call attention to the other processes (e.g., conception, externalization, transmission, perception, internalization) that must precede sharing.

This concept of communication is more restricted than most usage and employs several potentially ambiguous concepts (e.g., message, sender, receiver, intentions, information), therefore, I develop it in some detail in Chapter 2. It leads me to emphasize communication system development and activity as a social process rather than the role of the media in cultural production and the consequences of that process. However, I also argue that the former is fundamental to the latter and that the media are understood best by viewing them as social systems (the position is developed and applied in Chapters 3 and 4).

The second proposition follows from the implications of the use of *mass* as a modifier to denote a distinct type of communication. The evolution of the phrase is problematic, but early usages suggest that the social science concept of *the mass* is the referent of the first word (cf. McQuail, 1987a: 29-31, who employs Blumer's analysis but not Blumer's full definition). Rather than vaguely connoting a large group, that concept specifies details that are integral to the theory of mass society (McQuail, 1987a: 62-63). As Ward (1989: 8-9) put it,

> Early social thinkers, concerned with the development of industrial societies at the end of the nineteenth century, became convinced of the persuasive power of the forms of mass communication which developed in the period. They perceived of urban societies as consisting of individuals, divorced from their roots, who were susceptible to the messages and ideas produced by newspapers and films, and eventually broadcasting.

This connection helps explain perennial concerns about the social impact of mass communication, for the mass society is an inviable social form that contains the seeds of its own demise. However, *mass* in that sense in tandem with *communication* is a paradox, a contradiction in terms that suggests the antithesis of communication—sending noninformation only to hold the attention of unknown, unselected receivers. Unlike communication, mass is a formally specified concept that derives from a more comprehensive theory. As such, it is especially useful for identifying the distinctive features of certain rare and unusual cases of message sending to numerous others. It is only by contrasting the concept to features of the microstructure and selectivity of contemporary media that it may be helpful for understanding an institution whose existence depends on attracting and holding the attention of those large, dispersed, anonymous groups called *audiences*.

The last proposition, in contrast, has an empirical basis. The quality, portability, and cost of both transmitting and receiving technology have improved and continue to improve constantly. New electronic technologies are obliterating the differences in technology that originally separated the five established media. Intended to increase audience size by increasing accessibility, improving quality, and lowering the cost of receiving equipment, these innovations could create more mass-like audiences. In fact, though, they have had just the opposite effect. Less expensive transmission equipment enables senders to target smaller, more homogeneous groups with more specialized materials and to charge more for the service. Miniaturization, in particular, has facilitated the development of less costly, more accessible electronic equipment. From specialized cable television to desktop publishing to CD-ROMs, new technology has enabled and encouraged exclusive private rather than inclusive public communication, thus promoting movement away from rather than toward mass communication.

## THE LEGACY OF MASS COMMUNICATION FOR CONTEMPORARY MEDIA

These considerations lead me to argue, as did Lee Thayer (1988), that the mass media and mass communication should be distinguished rather than treated as synonymous. If it is largely true that mass communication is no more and that the media are a product of but no longer tied to a process with many but not all of the attributes denoted by the term, is mass communication no longer of interest? Or is there no significant residue from the period when the phrase *mass communication* may have come closer to fitting the image of transmitting mass culture for a mass audience? Of course, it is of interest and, of course, there is a significant residue. Indeed, one could argue that the legacies rather than the fact of mass communication are what make the media a major social concern, or, to take it a step further, that the media are the legacy. If we could recreate the media constrained only by the capacity and potential of current technology and the interests, needs, and capabilities of contemporary senders and receivers, the media surely would be very different than they are today. The discrepancy between what they might be if they could be created anew to take maximum advantage of current conditions and what they are reflects the impact of yesterday's mass communication on today's mass media.

Despite the fact that contemporary media retain many traditions and practices of the past, technological innovations are expediting several developments that lend credence to the claim that the media are diverging more and more from their early image. In addition to the shifts from distinct media to integrated telecommunications systems and from larger, more heterogeneous to smaller, more homogeneous audiences, these innovations facilitate several related transformations that already are or soon will be under way. These include shifts from one-way action to interaction, from exclusive to inclusive to exclusive audiences, from relatively hard form (e.g., print copy) to relatively soft form (e.g., passing sounds and images) products, from immobile to mobile production, transmission, and reception, and from national to international systems.

Cumulating changes are having two opposite effects on media material. On the one hand, the ability to reach small, homogeneous audiences inexpensively makes it possible to provide more highly focused materials of special interest to particular groups. On the other hand, the proliferation of inexpensive means to reach the public creates an almost insatiable demand for material to fill these new vehicles. Consequently, much of the expanded capacity is used to convey nonlocal material from sources and with meanings that are novel or alien to many prospective receivers. Thus, media materials are increasingly diverse, spanning a range from meaningful "local" to ambiguous "alien."

A description of the mass media in the five- to ten-year periods bracketing World War II would have depicted four (i.e., newspapers, magazines, radio, film) and then five systems (i.e., adding television) that attracted large, heterogeneous, inclusive audiences to predominantly hard materials delivered by immobile, relatively local systems. Although none of this fits the emerging new media, their qualities are being shaped to some extent by this image and the related conception of mass communication. That legacy conditions our expectations and perceptions of and responses to today's media. As Ward wrote (1989: 9), "A concept of a 'mass society' created by the products of the mass media . . . dominated critical thinking for well over fifty years, and is still found in public discussions about the mass media in the 1980s." His observation continues to apply.

An illustration of how the mixing of past and present media concepts and practices impacts on how we try to use and control the media is provided by a starkly contrasting pair of news items that appeared shortly before this was written. The first item (Anderson, 1991) reported that Britain's Open University was using the latest media technology to bring students scattered in homes throughout the country into a common "virtual world" in which they can see and interact with instructors and classmates as they would in a classroom. A little over a month later a second item (Heller, 1991) reported that 7,000 Michigan State University students were protesting a decision to teach a required History course by what was referred to as television. The plan was to divide students into groups of 50, have each group watch a video for a half hour, and then have a graduate assistant lead a discussion in the remaining time. The Open University plan was employing the latest media concepts of virtual reality, the Michigan State University plan simply applied traditional concepts.

Other cases are less dramatic. Thus, unpopular or insecure governments still censor media, exile dissidents, and otherwise try to prevent the importation, production, and distribution of suspect material, despite the proven inadequacy of such measures—which only have been partly effective when applied to traditional media—to control the entry and spread of videocassette recordings and miniature radios. In Iran, for example, although Khomeni had been exiled and domestic media placed under close surveillance, the Shah's government was overthrown by an uprising sparked, in part, by videotaped messages from Khomeni smuggled into the country for viewing on VCRs (Ganley and Ganley, 1988). In Canada, during the 1970s, government officials debated policy for what could be carried on the burgeoning cable systems—basically a technology that can increase but still control the program supply — while people were buying dish antennas to access anything available via satellite. In these and other cases, control measures were and are undertaken as if there had been no significant changes from earlier media forms despite evidence to the contrary. The stubborn and pervasive influence of early concepts of mass communication also helps explain several other varied and otherwise inexplicable characteristics of today's media. They are exemplified by the following.

(a) The mediating technology in media systems—and this was particularly the case in the past—shields senders from receivers. Moreover, most receivers, being unable to access or have any direct experience with this expensive equipment, find it incomprehensible. Despite the fact that sending equipment has become increasingly accessible and requires less skill and training to operate, the idea that equipment is inaccessible and that operators require special skill and training continues to lend a mystique to those who are assumed to be skilled in their use—particularly those who personify media organizations. Those whose roles the public is most aware of (e.g., actors, newscasters) have been able to use the prestige they accrue from that mystique to personal advantage and power in other sectors (e.g., government, business). The derivative prestige also helps explain current high levels of media consumption and media effectiveness (if not trust in media) as agenda setters, entertainment providers, and validators of messages as information.

(b) For reasons subject to ideological debate, at least since the 1920s, the media routinely have provided glimpses of otherwise inaccessible celebrities and exotic settings (Lowenthal, 1944). Today, however, this practice has much wider ramifications than simply giving celebrity status to its subjects. Because modern technology can easily and fully access almost any private or public locale, the media now provide much more detailed private and intimate information about people, processes, and places than ever before. Such recent trends as an accelerating decline in privacy, a loss of respect for the status of leaders, and a blurring of lines between gender, age, and class statuses, have been attributed to the impact of this coverage (Meyrowitz, 1985). The old media image contributes to the conferring of celebrity status on its subjects; today's media demystify the celebrity status of their subjects. Growing public resentment of the media for intruding into personal and private matters in conjunction with a growing belief that one has the right to know everything about public figures is a related inconsistent consequence.

(c) Rigid time and space conventions carried over from early media practices that bore little relation to real-world structure and process (e.g., program scheduling in multiples of 15-minute chunks beginning on the hour as in the halcyon days of network radio, print news media copying old television news formats) increasingly shape social reality (e.g., they influence the scheduling, organization, and presentation of events as diverse as sports contests and political conventions). Similarly, the long association of the media with entertainment affects material selection and presentation; witness the charge that "hard news" is selected and presented to meet standards for entertainment.[1]

(d) Most measures to limit the availability of media material (e.g., audience membership restrictions, censorship) were developed to deal with hard copy and relatively limited distribution channels. Modern media, however, rely less on hard copy (e.g., magazines, films, books) and employ technology that is much more difficult to monitor and regulate. Only radio once posed special problems for control. Now almost any material can be sent to wherever appropriate receiving equipment is available, be it a printer, VCR, fax machine, television screen, or audio monitor. Transnational corporations can use this capability to avoid local control (Elliott, 1986; Morley, 1992). This applies to receivers as well. People with the necessary equipment and desire can access media from anywhere without regard to local rules and standards and can choose the time and place of consumption (e.g., home video, earphones). Control methods, however, largely extend past practices and fail to adapt to these innovations.

(e) The early concern that the media isolated people and helped them escape to a fantasy world raised questions as to the responsibility of the media. Many argued that the media should inculcate the norm of rational participation in democratic society and provide the information required to practice it. These continue to be major criteria for evaluating media performance (Keane, 1991), despite the fact that the media now operate for different purposes in a different political world. Targeted media materials tailored to special tastes, wants, and needs tend to separate groups and end conformity to a single standard. At the same time, previously inaccessible, exclusive information increasingly is available. Thus, the media simultaneously splinter and homogenize society. Although the net effect may be to redefine the core of shared information and create new social divisions based on common interests that crosscut older class, economic, or biologically based ties, except for concern with their possible impact on children, evaluations of the media and discussions of control policy continue to emphasize these early goals (cf. Elliott's, 1986, critique).

(f) Early debates over what and how much is available and who may work in media industries were shaped by the view that media control was lodged with powerful owners (e.g., Louis B. Mayer, William Randolph Hearst, William Paley). Consequently, regulatory efforts focused on the upper echelons of media organizations and neglected other forces that shape the media. Despite current concerns over the absorption of media enterprises by corporate conglomerates, this perspective persists. Control still is viewed as a top-down process rather than an outcome of interaction among all the elements that comprise and influence communication systems. Telecommunications deregulation might seem to be accounted for by that concept insofar as its proponents argue that consumers interact with owners as equals in a competitive market, but the related claim that competition makes owners respond to public interests really continues an owner-centered approach to regulation. Owners are still treated as the final arbiters of content and, hence, as the chief agents of control. Government is relegated to a role of a monitor that reacts only to the most flagrant excesses.

(g) In early analyses, scholars tended to treat the media not as an integral part of society but as alien elements that impinge on society. This view persists despite the inroads of postmodernism. Most modern scholars still frame their questions in terms of the influence of the media *on* society rather than their role *in* society. The former implies that the media are not intrinsic to society and ignores the fact that the media could only develop in a congenial social setting and, hence, are not alien. It also implies that there could be society more or less as we know it but without the media. Implicit in the use of *on* is the idea that some aspect of society (e.g., politics, education, or recreation) would differ if that were the case. It impedes understanding that critical questions about the media and their social role are critical questions about society in its entirety.

These examples are chosen to reflect the scope of the current impact of earlier prevalent perspectives on mass communication.[2] Those perspectives shape the characteristics of contemporary media that fuel complaints that the quality of media materials is far too low, that the materials are socially harmful, and that controls in place do not address these deficiencies—issues that generate the fascination with and intense concern about the media that permeate both the general public and the scholarly community.

## THE CHARACTER OF MEDIA STUDY

It is relatively easy to understand that the heavy hand of the past continues to shape practices in the public communication industries. In capitalist economies industries usually avoid major changes unless profits are severely threatened; the media industries generally have been profitable since the 1920s. It is equally easy to understand the persistence of past approaches to governmental treatment of the media; by and large, regulators and administrators are drawn from the industries themselves or from a consuming public that has been conditioned to the industries' conventional practices. It is somewhat more difficult to understand why media scholarship has not had a substantial impact on industry practice and public debate. Admittedly, the

# Introduction

social sciences tend to be discounted as ivory tower activities with little connection to the real world. They usually are not taken seriously. However, other factors also contribute at least as much to their marginal influence on the use, operation, and control of the media.

Two aspects of the environment in which serious scholarly study of the media began may help explain the long-term effects of that period on how the specialty has developed within the social sciences and why its contributions have not been more impressive. One was the influence of the disturbing social, economic, and political events of the period. They fostered a conception of the media as systems of mass communication rather than systems of widely accessible public communication. Once established, that concept has persisted more than in name only; it has implied a priority for certain approaches to research and action. The other was that the media, in addition to generating growing audiences, generated public interest and discussion that usually treated them as something new being added to society. Scholars, being members of that world, apparently bought into that view. It leads to the aforementioned "affect on" rather than "role in" line of inquiry and directs scholarship toward certain issues and neglects others.

Both factors contributed to uncoordinated scholarship that lacked a guiding paradigm to set an agenda. Scholars who were engaged in empirical research seem to have chosen subjects largely in response to public interests of the "affect on" rather than the "role in" sort. They included such questions as whether the use of media detracted from constructive uses of leisure, the viewing of crime movies by youth increased juvenile delinquency, the provision through the media of information about elections increased voting, or the devotion of time to the media contributed to the alienation of unemployed workers. Scholars also conducted research to meet industry concerns, such as how to identify and measure the size of real audiences or assess the effectiveness of advertising. Analytically oriented scholars generally had other concerns. They were more interested in reasoning out the larger, more diffuse impact of the media on modern societies and tended to be much more speculative. Not surprisingly in view of political and economic developments in the period between the two World Wars, their analyses were influenced by events in their immediate environment. Without a dominant paradigm, let alone one that might indicate the full range of important issues, neither research nor theorizing directly came to grips with the nature of the media as social systems or their social roles.

By current standards, publication was light, and most of the material did not contribute to an overview of the field that helped establish a useful paradigm. Syntheses of research, critical analysis, and speculation published since the end of World War II vary in focus. Thayer wrote (1988: 52) that "... what we do have is sterile," perhaps because the "... mass media [have] proved to be the most fiercely resistant to adequate theoretical formulation—indeed, even to systematic discussion" (Carey, 1988: 69). Because theories address limited phenomena, key propositions can be inconsistent or illogical (Sears and Freedman, 1967). The failure to describe many aspects of mass communication adequately continues to impede our understanding of it as an institution and social process. Indeed, until the mid-1970s, the only social science textbooks devoted to the subject were "readers" and handbooks (e.g., Schramm, 1954b; Dexter and White, 1964; Berelson and Janowitz, 1966; Pool, Schramm, Frey, Maccoby, and Parker, 1973) and a few brief, original syntheses (e.g., Wright, 1959, 1986a; DeFleur, 1966; Mendelsohn, 1966; McQuail, 1969). Even now, most texts deal only with specific systems (e.g., motion pictures, Jowett and Linton, 1980; television, Comstock, 1980) or limited, albeit important, sectors of systems (e.g., soap operas, Cantor and Pingree, 1983; film finance, Wasko, 1982; news production, Gamson, 1984). During the past 25 years, there has been a quantum increase in scholarship and publication, but the spate of productivity has not markedly increased the coherence of the field. It has, however, affected the emotional fervor of the scholars who are involved. Previous differences over analytical perspectives are now intense disagreements. They plague the field without showing any sign of resolution (McQuail, 1987a) and do not seem likely to wane in the near future.

None of this is surprising in light of the early days of media scholarship[3] and its subsequent progression. Harold Lasswell (1948), an innovative political scientist who, with Paul Lazarsfeld and Wilbur Schramm, was a leader in media research during its formative years, invoked his schema for the analysis of politics—who gets what, when, how—to suggest that the study of mass communication be guided by a paraphrase—who says what to whom, how, and with what effect? The *who* called for control analysis, the *what* for content analysis, the *whom* for audience analysis, the *how* for media analysis (i.e., it also stood for "through what channel"), and the *what effect* for effects analysis. Berelson's *Content Analysis* (1952), Klapper's *The Effects of Mass Communication* (1960), Lazarsfeld and Kendall's *Radio Listening in America* (1948), and Bogart's *The Age of Television* (1956) were among several works whose topics or organization reflected Lasswell's conception of media inquiry.

When there was not much research, Lasswell's formula was a workable guide for syntheses. However, its ad hoc, purely descriptive character was mechanical and restricting and tended to lead to almanac-like record keeping. It was not a guide to theoretically relevant research. Moreover, it usually was ignored when pressing issues arose (e.g., Why did a radio dramatization of H. G. Wells' *War of the Worlds* create a panic? How did motion pictures affect children?). Although this static framework largely has been superseded by three more dynamic foci—the social role of the media, addressing the links among control, content, and effects; the impact of commercial aspects of the media on audience composition, media forms, and effects; and, from a conflict theory perspective, analyses of factors that have shaped media study—there still is no dominant paradigm. Materials simply accumulate unevenly as interest in various topics (e.g., children and the media, television in politics, the meaning of entertainment material, how media meet needs of and gratify their audiences) waxes and wanes.

Lasswell's paradigm also has fallen into neglect because it is not relevant to the interests of the increasing numbers of critical and Marxist scholars who have become interested in the media.[4] In their view it obscures the role of the media in the hegemonic processes of modern society. It is misleading in that it emphasizes changes in the behavior and attitudes of individuals as effects and media personnel and the material they produce as the agents of change. Instead, they consider the media to be an integral element in a system that reinforces, reproduces, and manages the established order of class, power, and control by monopolizing the production and distribution of culture and information, thus obviating the need for coercion (Gitlin, 1987 [1982]: 241; Rachlin, 1988: 24-29). Rachlin (1988: 24) quoted Gwyn A. Williams in describing the hegemony that results as a situation ". . . in which a certain way of life and thought is dominant, in which one concept of reality is diffused throughout society in all its institutional and private manifestations, informing with its spirit all taste, customs, religious and political principles, and all social relations. . . ." Gitlin (1987 [1982]: 241) added that it ". . . encompasses the terms through which the alliances of domination are cemented; it also extends to the systematic (but not necessarily, or even usually, deliberate) engineering of mass consent to the established order" (also see Good, 1989; Goldman and Rajagopal, 1991). The consequence of hegemonic processes is that the favored way of life is not only dominant and sustained, but also seen as natural.

Despite its volume, fragmentation, and diversity, however, the social science literature on mass communication probably can best be described as in large part reflecting one or the other of two perspectives. One treats the media as providers of news and information, as a means of education in large, complex societies. Its focus is newspapers, nonfiction magazines, public television, and news. The other treats the media as providers of entertainment, instruments of cultural production that deal in fantasy and fiction. Its focus is film, commercial television drama and sitcoms, the comics, and magazine fiction. Rogers (1985) sketched a similar distinction in discussing what he called the empirical and critical schools of communication research. Carey (1988: 13-36) employed a congruent distinction in suggesting that two concepts of communication have dominated scholarship—transmission, paralleling the first emphasis, and production, paralleling the second. Rachlin (1988: 14-19) reviewed and noted differences among several versions of an administrative research-critical research dichotomy, but in the end adopted a distinction much like those of the others for his analysis. I would suggest that these distinctions all reflect an underlying difference between an information and transmission approach to the media that emphasizes communication and views it as a process that can be, but may not be, informative for a receiver by some standard, and an entertainment and production approach that downplays the communication aspect and information potential of the media and emphasizes instead their potential as instruments of manipulation of the social order through cultural production (cf. Tuchman, 1983; Garnham, 1986, Gitlin, 1987 [1982]).[5]

Scholars who are primarily interested in the media as instruments of cultural production tend to be identified with critical theory (as Marxists or neo-Marxists of some type), postmodernism, or semiotics. They tend to argue in some way that popular culture maintains the established social order by deadening people's critical faculties and legitimizing present social institutions and power arrangements. They consider the media to be among, if not first among (Madrid, 1986), the instruments that create and deliver popular culture. However, I would suggest that, although they rarely use the term, scholars who rely on empirical studies of what is produced, who consumes it, and its consequences, implicitly are equally critical. They, too, are concerned that information is not provided equitably by the media and that people cannot learn from them (see Tichenor, Donohue, and Olien, 1980, for a study of how local newspaper performance in different American communities bears on their residents' ability to take positions on local issues). The difference is grounded in the politics of the approaches, in their views of what societies can be and how to achieve it. Empiricists tend to subscribe to liberal pluralism; critical theorists to humanistic socialism.

These ideological and political differences are important for they suggest very different understandings of the nature of communication and information. In the course of this discussion there will be frequent acknowledgments of and references to these differences, differences that are so deeply rooted in values that they are not going to be resolved in the short run. What is important is to employ the contrast between information and transmission, on the one hand, and entertainment and production, on the other, to clarify the character of the media and to formulate appropriate responses to the concerns they cause us. Given that these differences in perceptions of what primarily occurs in mass communication derive from deeply held political positions, if one wishes to say something useful about mass communication and the media and relate it to the vast literature, one simply must stake out one's position on communication and information and adhere to it. It should serve as a criterion for interpreting what is transpiring as the media operate, and that, in turn, should give a more precise understanding of their social roles. Ultimately, this should help to resolve disagreements on policies to address issues that may be far more serious than such matters as who should be permitted to read what sorts of magazines or who should be permitted to view which films or television programs.

## COMMUNICATION, ENTERTAINMENT, AND INFLUENCE

I opt for a narrow conception of communication, even though this may give a false impression that I view the media as appropriate to convey only information and not other types of symbolic expression. Obviously, though, my concern is that they convey precious little of the former and primarily provide the latter. Perhaps more important is that differences among various types of symbolic material disappear when it comes to meaning, for all symbolic production can be meaningful to those who perceive it. The meaning of any symbolic expression emerges from an interaction among conventions (i.e., the rules of symbolic use and discourse), action, and the context of action (i.e., the conditions under which the activity proceeds).[6] The appropriate conjunction of the three helps maximize the receiver's confidence in having understood the symbolic production correctly. When the rules are observed, the preconditions for communication as information transfer are present.[7] But the fact that there are rules also opens the way for other possibilities. Humor, for example, involves purposely violating rules and settings to create bizarre and unexpected mismatches, such as with a play on words (i.e., using a word improperly in a statement) or saying the wrong thing in the wrong place or time (i.e., violating the rules of context). We know such humor to be humor only when we know the rules that are being violated intentionally.

It is because humor takes the form of symbolic expression that it can be meaningful, but that alone does not make it communication. It could be communication if the primary intention is to convey information, but it would not be if that purpose is solely to produce amusement. Obviously, both intentions might be present simultaneously in the mind of a producer, and in this case it is quite possible that the two could not be distinguished unless they were quite unequal and/or the producer was quite clear as to the weight of each. This ambiguity is characteristic of almost any issued symbolic product and is addressed by Jansen (1988: 196-198) in discussing how those she fondly calls "epistemological criminals" avail themselves of techniques like irony to subvert the efforts of censors. She attributes the availability of such techniques to the fact that all discourse requires a double reading because language has a dual nature, being ". . . *both univocal and equivocal*" (p. 197; emphasis in original). I would rephrase her analysis slightly only to suggest that *almost all* discourse requires a multiple reading. First, I would argue that there are minimal messages that do not suggest a duality or multiplicity of meanings (e.g., SOS, 1+1=2), although admittedly they are rare in normal discourse. Second, I would note that the rich connotative meanings of words enable us to convey more than two meanings with one message and all may be informational. The possibility of humor or irony is a reminder that it is easier to formulate clear and decisive definitions than it is to apply them easily and reliably to the stuff of everyday life.

The more general point is that symbolic expression need not be informational in the sense used here to be meaningful, for as Luhmann (1990a: 27) has pointed out, "[t]he function of meaning . . . does not lie in information. . . . If it is repeated, a message or piece of news loses its information value, but not its meaning." Meaningfulness is not the equivalent of communication. All communication is meaningful, but all that is meaningful is not communication. If all communication is symbolic expression but not all symbolic expression is communication, types of symbolic expression must be differentiated by criteria other then meaningfulness. I propose relying on a combination of the purposes that motivate the symbolic expression and the end state of the (intended) receiver to accomplish this. The fundamental sociological questions about mass communication from this perspective include: (a) Whose conventions shape the participants' actions, and (b) how are contexts defined? Addressing such questions about social process can provide the richer understanding of mass communication and the media necessary to design and implement appropriate, effective policies for addressing situations in which the media are involved.

# Introduction

Scholarly differences in interests and ideologies, by themselves, are a secondary factor in the theoretical disarray in media analysis. I continue to hold to the position I took more than 30 years ago when, writing with two colleagues (Smith, Bealer, and Sim, 1962), I attributed the situation primarily to the failure to distinguish communication from its consequences. We argued that, because the factors and conditions that affect the former necessarily are very different from those that shape the latter, the failure to differentiate the two in accounting for the outcome of communication at any time after it has occurred results in confusion. In this regard, too, early perspectives continue to shape scholarly practice. Little has changed since we wrote that piece. The focus continues to be more on the consequences of mass communication than on its structure or process. Now, as then, both usually are treated as indistinguishable parts of the same reality,[8] and whether systems are communication mechanisms is not considered problematic. As Scott (1990: 12) has remarked, "... we are so habituated to the fact of communication ... that we do not notice the process, only the results."

Our habituation to communication owes not only to its pervasiveness as an activity but also to the fact that symbols, the basic materials employed, structure and give meaning to every experience we have and to our entire understanding of reality. Indeed, Peters and Rothenbuhler (1989) have argued that the very phrase, "talking about," implies a false dichotomy and that our symbolic capacities are our experiences and reality. In their view, speech and that to which the speech pertains are inseparable and indistinguishable parts of the same symbolic activity. Regardless of one's position on that argument, it emphasizes that for humans there is no unmediated experience or reality. I agree that there is no unmediated experience; there is, however, experience that is not mediated by the mass media. A more productive study of mass communication, then, would start from the distinction between communication as a general phenomenon and the media as a distinct institutionalized form in which symbol production, transmission, and reception occurs, and add several other distinctions, concepts, and propositions. Because this analysis adheres to this distinction, it devotes much more attention to communication generically than do most discussions of the media.[9]

It helps put these matters in perspective to distinguish systematically not just communication and entertainment, but three processes that exclusively, or almost exclusively, employ symbolic production—communication, entertainment, and influence. Any episode of symbolic production may involve only one, any two, or all three. Moreover, each tends to be associated, though not exclusively, with different social systems. Indeed, one reason that media activities are conflated with communication and communication conflated with the other two processes is that the media are associated with all three as well as with the institutions primarily involved with only one of them.

As behavior and experience, communication, entertainment, and influence may be indistinguishable. All three can involve the production and exposition of symbols for transfer. Moreover, for reasons to be discussed in the next chapter, all three are likely to be present in varying degree in any episode of interactive symbolic behavior whose primary purpose is communication. They differ in terms of the criteria producers use in selecting the symbols to be employed. Success at any of them, at a minimum, also requires that those targeted be exposed to the material. Their fundamental differences, then, are not obvious—although the symbols used and the media in which they are embedded may be distinctive to each. The key distinguishing factors are in the psyches of the participants—in the goals of producers prior to and while acting and in the condition of target persons after reception. With respect to producers, the goal in communication is to resolve known or suspected uncertainty or confusion in targeted others. In entertainment (including art), the goal is to have both a satisfactory experience of self-expression (although this may be minimal in some cases) and a nontrivial affective impact on any receiver(s). In influence, it is to sustain or introduce some particular belief, attitude, or behavior in targeted receiver(s). For receivers, communication and entertainment have complementary and analogous psychic outcomes; in communication, receivers feel that uncertainties have been resolved, and in entertainment that they have had a worthwhile affective experience.

There always is an element of pleasure in having had a worthwhile affective experience, so entertainment is, to cite Morley's (1989: 31) interpretation of Bordieu and Ang, ". . . first and foremost a pleasure of recognition" for the receiver. Recognition need not involve reduced uncertainty from the receipt of intentionally sent information, but it can. There must be reduced uncertainty for communication to have occurred. Because receivers derive an element of pleasure from recognition in both communication and entertainment, that aspect of the experience does not differentiate the two. The reduction of uncertainty that defines the occurrence of communication does. In many modern democratic societies, influence by symbolic means is confused with communication for a different reason. The emphasis that often is placed on individual responsibility encourages people to believe that they have chosen their opinions, attitudes, goals, and behavior of their own free will rather than acquired them by giving in to the wishes of others. Consequently, influence, when it is experienced (and often it is not even perceived), is more likely to be interpreted as having been helped by being informed. That interpretation of the experience is much the same as in communication; thus, it also may generate its own sense of pleasure. Finally, it may share with the other two a sense of pleasure that derives from no longer feeling uncertain.

Given the similarities among the three—the employment of symbols, media, and dependence on both producer and consumer roles—and the fact that in order to distinguish them we need to understand the motivations of producers and the meaning to receivers of experiencing the symbols, confusion among the processes is not at all surprising. Moreover, although generally each process is associated with different social systems—information with research organizations and schools; entertainment with art, literature, and the theater; and influence with advertising, public relations, politics, and cause organizations—the media are associated with all three. "Why" is one of the most hotly debated questions in modern media studies (cf. Madrid, 1986).

One factor obviously is structural. All three processes involve a transfer of something from inside persons to inside other persons and, hence, require what is being transferred to be externalized and, if necessary, transported in some tangible form. The mode of representation and channel of transportation is a medium, and all three employ similar media. Another factor is organizational. Influence and entertainment may be undertaken indirectly, using real or seeming information, or directly without it. Relatedly, communication may be undertaken to influence or, at least hypothetically, simply as an end in itself. Moreover, because communication is work and receivers' attention cannot be guaranteed, producers also may feel it necessary to be entertaining. Professors like to believe that teaching and learning are ends in themselves, but there are impelling reasons why few, if any, acts of communication are exclusively that. In life there is little pure communication—even less in the mass media.

## COMMUNICATION AND ENTERTAINMENT REVISITED

Communication and entertainment differ in both the nuances of symbolic production and the impact that a producer intends to have on the mental condition of a receiver. Influence, in contrast, differs from both in that its focus is to affect a subsequent course of events. A targeted receiver's immediate experience of an influencing stimulus is secondary or irrelevant to a source. In political campaigning the object is to secure a vote regardless of whether the voter becomes more informed by the campaign material or enjoys the experience of being exposed to it. In product advertising the goal is to create sales and/or product recognition and acceptance, again without regard to whether targeted persons are informed by or enjoy the ads. Symbols may be a preferred medium of influence, but influence can take such extreme forms as physically pushing or hitting. It need not involve any symbol production and transmission.

All three processes are subject to evaluation in terms of how they accord with cultural norms, so there is constant assessment as they occur. There are proper and improper ways to communicate, entertain, and influence, as well as acceptable and unacceptable reasons for doing each. Because the activities of the media are considered synonymous with all three processes, the institution as a whole as well as particular instances of its performance also are scrutinized and judged continuously. When those judgments are negative and mobilize concern, the concerns expressed almost always imply a presumption of influence, that is, it is believed that the media have or are likely to have undesirable consequences. If concerns become public, they are likely to be expressed as demands for new, state-mandated regulations or restrictions for the media. However, in most modern countries, state entry into the private sphere requires a rationale to legitimize any seeming intrusion into citizens' personal affairs. Those rationales are based on a postulated societal consensus as to the nature of the state and its appropriate functions and are articulated in a charter or implicit contract (e.g., the U.S. Constitution). These understandings and their ultimate implications for the sorts of policies that can be implemented in responding to the presumed influences (or consequences) of mass communication relate to the fundamental differences between communication and entertainment, differences that are particularly pertinent in countries that guarantee freedom of speech and the press but also try to control what is available in the mass media. They may help in resolving that apparent conflict.

If we accept as legitimate a state's right to implement the roles it claims on a legal-rational basis, we can apply the differences between communication and entertainment to understand the limits on a state's communications policies. The implications of this right and the relevance of the difference between communication and information is quite clear in the United States. Like all states, the American state is obligated to protect the country against external and internal threats to its integrity and survival. Accordingly, it is responsible to develop and maintain an infrastructure that enables it to monitor the domestic and international situation and to mobilize the resources to meet any threat. In an electronic age, this obligation requires it to assure its access to state of the art equipment and the frequencies needed for unimpeded transmission of audiovisual signals. Therefore, the state may become a party to international agreements that assign exclusive frequencies and that promote the development of equipment. Similarly, it can allocate frequencies and set and maintain equipment standards for domestic use.

With respect to what can be transmitted, the state seeks to fulfill its responsibility for sustaining the country by determining the sorts of information that can and cannot be publicly available through administrative and legislative actions that follow prescribed procedures. Declarations of war or states of emergency are instructive for understanding what is involved in setting legitimate state communication policies. Such declarations are sanctioned means for indicating that normal constraints on the state are suspended in the national interest. A suspension is also a reminder of the state's normal jurisdiction over the flow of materials. By definition, all the material over which the state legitimately may exercise this responsibility is information. That is, it is material that, in the circumstances in which it is received, reduces the uncertainties of the receiver (cf. Luhmann, 1990a: 27).[10] If the receivers are state functionaries responsible for meeting and overcoming threats to the country, state policies are directed to acquiring and transmitting informational material. If enemies of the country could be recipients, policies are meant to deny them information, for example, by classifying, hiding, or censoring material.

States vary with regard to how they define their legitimate rights and those reserved for persons. Thus, a state may be enjoined from instituting policies to control the provision and transmission of information. The United States and its first amendment guaranties of freedom of speech and of the press provide an example. The American system is premised on the right of citizens to choose their officers and even to change the structure of the system. Further, it is understood that to exercise these rights responsibly citizens need to be able to exchange and receive information pertinent to the options. State officials are forbidden to take any action that would hamper citizens' exercise of these rights. The material involved is information in the sense that it contributes to reducing citizens' felt uncertainties about the choice to be made on these matters.

The right of the state to set policies for communication, then, derives from more inclusive prescriptions and proscriptions. The areas delineated in this way generally happen to require rational action based on adequate information. None of this involves entertainment, which is primarily distinguished by both a sender's intention to produce a particular affective experience for a receiver and success in doing so. Entertainment is only entertainment if it produces the intended affective experience in a receive—unless one is satisfied to entertain oneself, in which case no exchange or transfer occurs and, therefore, there is no action that even remotely resembles communication. Entertainers are not satisfied that they are doing what they mean to do if they are laughed at but do not intend to be, or if their audiences respond to comedy seriously. Stimulating a particular affective state is the primary purpose in entertainment; any informative role is accidental, incidental, or secondary.

Despite the definitional distinction, people may feel that they have learned from entertainment or that what they have heard or witnessed merits imitating. If so, and if the consequences are undesirable (e.g., copying crimes seen in films), there may be a demand for the state to control such material. In such cases, there is no state interest and therefore no clear indication that the state may have a role. However, if the state's responsibility to protect the country is broadly interpreted, the public nature or consequences of the activity may sanction its being treated as a matter of state interest. Whether states have that option is a central controversy in state theory that is addressed in more detail in Chapter 7. In the case of entertainment, however, the issue is not to locate it with respect to a line that delineates the state's authority to exercise its power, but rather to determine the public or private character of the experience or its consequences. Most theories of the state suggest that a democratic state's interests and legitimate authority are only in the public realm and that it can act in that realm only when it can be demonstrated that there is a public threat or collective consequences from the target of its action.

## THE STRUCTURE AND PROCESS OF COMMUNICATION

Given the many public processes that utilize symbolic production, why the primary focus on communication? Communication is a central social process because ours is a species that depends for its survival on the ability to organize and reorganize quickly. To organize on other than biological bases we must be able not only to think but also to externalize and convey our ideas and knowledge. This requires us to be able to convert thoughts, requests, questions, and information to external representations that others will be able to apprehend and comprehend reliably and accurately. From the viewpoint of one with something to share, the intertwined work of representation, projection, and externalization is the essence of communication. From the viewpoint of those who wish to understand what others project, recognition, internalization, and interpretation of what is proffered is its essence. The work includes conception, perception, and externalizing and internalizing tasks, and it is difficult because there are no a priori limits to the meaning of a message. This is a consequence of the facts that (a) experience and the language used to express it continuously evolve (Carey, 1988: 71-86), and (b) receiving involves at least as much creative as automatic activity (Lowenthal, 1984: 291-301).

Communication, then, is the basic work required for sharing. It is the essential process for validating Luhmann's (1990a) assertion that meaning is sociology's basic concept. There are many ways to share meanings. The varied forms that communication takes depend largely on who and how many participate, their physical and social locations vis-à-vis one another, and what is to be shared. Like most work, the more enjoyable or crucial it is, the more likely are the workers to keep at it. How the conditions translate into the different forms of communication is a direct outcome of social forces.

In communication, structure and process interact in many different ways. Two examples are particularly pertinent to mass communication and the media. First, the larger and less selective a group, the smaller is the portion of each member's symbolic stock that is shared by all its members. Consequently, a communicator is more limited in transmitting information to everyone in the group and finds it necessary to rely more on widely recognized and understood affective symbols to hold everyone's attention. Second, the larger or more dispersed a group, the greater the need for supplementary technology to reach all its members. Such mechanisms, in turn, limit and shape the actors' range of expression and reception. Moreover, because relationships between senders and receivers who are not in direct contact are less likely to be supported by extensive personal knowledge, strong ties, and mutual obligations, the pleasure or gratification in the activity becomes increasingly more important than its informative value for sustaining such relationships. This helps explain the emphasis on entertainment in the media. The implicit argument is in accord with a comment I came across long after I wrote this:

> The basic dynamic in the phenomena of mass communication, the pivotal mechanism out of which all else evolves, is not the technology, awesome as it has become. Nor is it the "message," or the implicit culture implied in the "content" of the media. Nor is it the "effects" which the media are purported to have. The basic mechanism inheres in the *social and personal*

> *uses* to which people put the media and its fare. (fn., This was the gist of Katz's paper on mass communication research in 1959 . . .) It is this basic dynamic which any relevant theory of mass communication will have to be based upon. (Thayer, 1988: 63; emphasis in original)

Pleasure and gratification rank high among most people's social and personal uses.

These two examples emphasize the importance of specifying what is being transmitted in communication for understanding how the structure of the media impinges on the process, that is, what distinguishes technologically mediated communication. This approach clarifies why there is so little communication and so much other activity in mass communication. It also helps in identifying the strategic distinctive features of the mass media collectively and individually. The concepts and propositions employed are used to specify the necessary conditions that shape the distinctive features that all mass communication systems share and, less directly, also apply to the constraints on, operation of, or consequences of particular systems. The general forms of systems matter, however, for they bear directly on their consequences.

An analysis of the media in their societal settings does not account for individual consumption patterns, nor whether, how, or why those patterns influence people's information, beliefs, or attitudes. Those explanations involve theories of cognition, learning, personality, attitude change, and the like. These concepts and propositions treat communication as social exchange in emergent systems. The impact of the structural features of such systems on the process must be distinguished from the impact of particular participants. The concepts and propositions are abstract because the specific rules, norms, and knowledge that shape and constrain the components of communication systems vary widely among and within societies (Shimanoff, 1980; McLaughlin, 1984: chap. 3; Lull, 1990 [1982]). That diversity accounts for the great variety of real systems. Hence, the analysis emphasizes the common more than the unique features of all communication systems. It focuses on the unique only to the extent that it deals with the distinctive features of the five traditional media. Differences among particular operating units (e.g., television networks, newspapers, magazines, radio stations) or media products (e.g., films, television programs, newspaper articles) are noted only in the context of more general principles.

A discussion of communication in the mass media context is difficult. For many reasons, some already suggested, much activity and material that seem to be communication may not be. Events that may fit a common abstraction and may appear to qualify as members of the same class of activity vary in many ways. Consider, for example, the differences between a solitary speech rehearsal and its delivery before an audience, viewing an instructional film seen for the first time and a teen horror film seen twice before, or a first grade teacher introducing pupils to sums and reading a familiar story to the same children at the end of a long week. Clearly, many complex factors (e.g., the presence and absence of receivers, the sender's purposes, the type and familiarity of the material) must be taken into account in developing a useful concept. There must be some standardized usable criteria for distinguishing communication from communication-like activity. If not, any potentially symbolic expression and every instance of growth or change in knowledge or attitude—and therefore, by implication, nothing—is communication. Consequently, ". . . the study of communication . . . appears to be about almost everything" (Scott, 1990: 5). Certainly this is a position that would appeal to postmodernists, who see the world as being constituted by potential texts.

Definitions, because they specify the essential criteria that distinguish a phenomenon from everything else, provide focus. However, scholars often disagree on criteria (i.e., on definitions) because their selection and specification have been shaped by a broader theoretical or ideological position and/or by their usefulness in a particular piece of research. In disciplines that lack consensus on an overarching theoretical paradigm—and this certainly characterizes sociology (Eisenstadt, with Curelaru, 1976; Wilson, 1983)—there often are inconsistent or even conflicting definitions for a term. This is the case with communication. Therefore, any definition I employ is likely to engender criticism and disagreement.

In this analysis I employ a definition that includes at least two elements as criteria—information and the intentions of senders—that other scholars explicitly reject (cf., e.g., Thayer, 1968: 14-15 [intention], 189-190 [information], Maruyama, 1980: 28-31 [information]). Nonetheless, an incisive definition is essential, especially if the mass media are to be understood, for they involve much symbolic activity and many instances of mental change or reinforcement whose status as communication would be questionable by any definition. In fact, a pervasive and probably unresolvable issue that motivates this project is why scholars, media professionals, and laymen alike seem compelled to refer to so many activities and materials as communication when they would not do so if those activities and materials were to be evaluated by any reasonable standard.

In addition to the effects of ideological differences among scholars and their seeming aversion to using a single, rigorous, consensual definition of communication consistently, improved understanding of mass communication and the media also is hampered by the tendency to treat them as synonymous. I have referred to mass communication as a process and the media as a social system or institution. The difficulty in any analysis is that the two are so intertwined that definitions alone cannot make people distinguish them. Although processes do not recur frequently without a system developing, and systems or institutions do not persist without a process occurring, each is possible for a while without the other. That is why clear distinctions between them are imperative.

A process is a course of activity with an intended outcome. Differences in intended outcomes distinguish processes and organize the activities involved. Construction, for example, is distinguished from demolition not by its constituent activities (e.g., wielding a hammer, using a saw), but by its purpose and outcome and the course of the activities involved. A social system, in contrast, is a bounded set of relationships among people who regulate their actions to take account of the other(s) involved according to rules that previously existed or that emerge through trial and error. Unlike processes, bounded ongoing relationships rather than a specific purpose or a fixed course of activities are fundamental to a social system. The satisfactions of interaction and/or coercive constraints on the actors, not the achievement of any purpose for which the relationship(s) developed, sustain the system. Operating factories are social systems regardless of the quantity, quality, or nature of their products, or regardless of whether their workers also are friends, date, or attend the same church. Social institutions are the abstracted ideas of structures and norms derived from wide experience with social systems with the same intended functions. Personnel is secondary in the sense that it is interchangeable. Institutions transcend personnel. Schools are social systems and teaching, learning, socialization, and training are processes, but education is an institution intended and expected to facilitate the development of social systems in which those processes can occur. A process is that process only if it succeeds as intended at some acceptable level. Both social systems and institutions, however, may survive for extended periods without succeeding in their ostensible purpose or without the putative process even occurring.

Because human action sequences recognized as processes are complex and may include action sequences and resources that also are put to other uses, they may have multiple functions that go beyond their ostensible purposes. As evident in the construction-demolition example, any tangible component of a process is subject to a variety of uses. The independence of function and purpose is even clearer in a social system. A group of boys and girls who team up at first to study but who eventually date and marry simply moves through a series of activities, although their relationships as a social system are stable. Institutions fall between the two, for though their ostensible function is never lost, clearly it may be secondary, as is true of many businesses, churches, schools, and families. Achievement of an explicit purpose for which the arrangement was legitimized, then, is increasingly key to the survival of social systems, institutions, and processes, in that order. In each case, however, it is quite possible, even likely, that other purposes may be served. The variety of those other purposes and their lack of relation to the explicit purpose generally decreases in that same order. In light of these distinctions, the infrequent occurrence of communication (a process) in the mass media of communication (an institution) is not surprising.

## COMMUNICATION, MASS COMMUNICATION, AND MASS MEDIA

At a minimum. the literature on the media and mass communication is chaotic because they rarely are distinguished. Tuchman's (1988) assessment of the sociological study of mass media institutions is a rare exception. However, even her project of relating current media studies to early studies of mass communication, British cultural studies, and American studies of cultural production results in some misplaced criticism. What is more typical are references to any aspect of the media that involves any element of communication as mass communication even if there is no intention to communicate. Systems developed as communication systems are treated as such regardless of whether they communicate, and institutions so named are treated as if communication is dominant regardless of what goes on in them. Communication, entertainment, and influence do intermingle in the mass media, but analysis is facilitated by distinguishing them.[11] If television commercials are claimed to be informative, that does not make them so. If communicators say they failed to communicate when they failed to influence, that does not mean they have not communicated. Understanding aspects of social reality may require imposing frameworks that are not used by those involved in them.

Study of the media and mass communication will remain confused so long as these differences are not recognized and are not employed in analysis. The media and their constituent elements are tangible and, because they are, can be put to various uses—only one of which may be their ostensible purpose. When that purpose is as crucial to any social group as communication is, it is important to know how much communication occurs in the institution, what else occurs, and the consequences of the balance and interaction among these several processes. Moreover, that other things occur or even replace the ostensible primary activity does not mean that the latter does not occur or could not be revived. This point is germane to this entire analysis. The original print media were used to inform a large population, and the expression and reception of information has always been a (not the) fundamental purpose of symbolic activity. All the media can accomplish transport-for-sharing, and all symbols have an information potential. Whether they merge as communication or as entertainment and influence is at the heart of a sociological understanding of mass communication and the media.

## NOTES

1. This is not to ignore the charge that most news on television is entertainment. That development is not surprising given the hard work most viewers otherwise would have to do to attend to and assimilate news. In this regard, Eason's (1988) analysis of the Janet Cooke episode in which a story about child drug addiction was manufactured is most instructive.
2. In a very similar argument, Garnham (1992) attributes several major failures in understanding the media not only to the influence of outmoded "institutionalized practices of mass communication" (364), a phrase synonymous with the term *media*, but also to outmoded theories of communication.
3. Morrison (1978) used the occasion of the death of Paul F. Lazarsfeld, considered by Berelson to be the only "founding father" of mass communication research to have concentrated on mass communication problems per se, to recount the early history of the field. In an account reconstructed from the archives of the Rockefeller Foundation—the supporter of the major early noncommercial research in the area—and information from the major players, one of his main themes was the un- and disorganized character of the work originally undertaken. He repeatedly noted Foundation concerns about the lack of coherence and order in the overall project that sponsored most of the original conceptualization and research. He attributed this to Lazarsfeld's intellectual interest in methods rather than to his politics. Indeed, he made a point of referring to Lazarsfeld's Marxist background (351), a quality that Gitlin (1978) did not consider to have had a major impact. (In his analysis of the same events, Gitlin interpreted them as an effort by capitalists to maintain their hegemony.) Morrison's account helped me come to terms with my impression as a student in Lazarsfeld's courses that, although they could be stimulating and exciting, they were disorganized and inconsistent.

## Introduction                                                29

4. Ward (1989), however, did use it to organize his recent historical study of the role of the media in the modern world.
5. Even this distinction conveys a somewhat biased view of the large body of media research because it is oriented to the American and Western European scene. Szecskö (1977) described a very different way of organizing the communication research undertaken in Hungary, a Soviet bloc socialist country at the time.
6. The context of action is used in the same sense as Goffman's concept of "situation" as respecified by Meyrowitz (1990). Goffman's concept has the handicap of having been formulated largely to deal with his observations of interaction among parties who were all present during the event. Meyrowitz (1985), because he already had dealt extensively with mass communication, understands the need to adjust it for circumstances in which the situations of the sender, the material itself, and the receiver may all differ.
7. It must be emphasized that these are only preconditions. As Luhmann has noted (1990a: 27), meaning and information are not equivalent. The former is a preexisting structure, the existence of which is a necessary condition for the latter—as well as for the comprehension of all other types of symbolic material. As such it functions to structure all perception. In the case of symbolic material, inasmuch as we easily recognize and understand material we already know, all such material does not constitute information, even though it may be meaningful.
8. The burden of that analysis was that factors not only not integral but perhaps even irrelevant to the communication process often may account for a particular consequence. We identified serious confusions that may result from failing to recognize and maintain this distinction in a comprehensive theory.
9. It is not unusual for significant analyses of mass communication and the media not to take communication in the general sense as a point of departure (Wright, 1986a; McQuail, 1987a; DeFleur and Ball-Rokeach, 1989). Even Budd and Ruben (1988), who did treat it as such, only discussed communication in their sixth chapter after extensive discussions of the media.
10. Defining information in this way is very useful for purposes of analysis but it does not alleviate the problems in formulating policies to control information. In fact, it may not be useful at all for policymakers, who face a situation that Braman (1989: 23) has captured in noting that "[t]he abundance and diversity of definitions bewilder." This is because policymakers feel that they need to be able to identify information by examining the material being transmitted without considering the participants in the process. Policies tend to focus on information as independently existing material that can be identified as such by any expert or experienced person. Research, in contrast, can deal with material in the social context in which it is produced, shared, and retained. Skeptical postmodernists (Rosenau's term) would deny even the possibility that textual material could be identified unambiguously as information.

11. Classification, because it is based on representation, is an operation that postmodernists would reject (cf. Rosenau, 1992: 92-95). This is one of the many fundamental differences between this and a postmodernist analysis of the media.

# 2

# Communication as a Social Process

In its typical forms, the process of mass communication involves the mediated transmission of material by an anonymous organizational source or an identifiable individual who, despite not being personally acquainted with most receivers, represents the organizational source. The transmission is directed to a dispersed, loosely organized group whose members rarely are in the same place that the sending acts occur. Moreover, in every case but live radio and television, the sending act occurs some time before it is executed for the receivers. The mediation always involves the physical separation of senders and receivers and their linkage by means of some technology.

    This description of the mass communication process specifies several details that merit brief comment because they help shape the features of modern media and our concern with them. Taking them in the order of the preceding statement, first, transmission is mediated. Contact is not direct, rather it is accomplished through some intervening technology. This has at least two important consequences: (a) the material being transmitted is vulnerable to being reshaped by the mediating mechanism, and (b) the continuously adjusting behavior by both participants that normally occurs in direct exposure may not occur. In short, mediated transmission can change both what is being transmitted and how the parties involved interact.

Second, the initiator of the process and the participant who monopolizes the action is a surrogate for an organization. Thus, (a) the real initiator is not a human being but a corporate person, and (b) this makes for a substantial power imbalance between senders and receivers because, as Coleman (1974: 57) has noted, corporate persons tend to escape the control of their human creators. They amass more resources than almost any person can and are not subject to the same motives and emotional responses as humans. The fact that there is a human surrogate for the corporate source compounds the imbalance because receivers tend to be misled into attributing human qualities to the source.

Third, mass communication is described as a process of transmission "to," indicating that there is only minimal, if any, exchange between sender and receiver. Fourth, the targets of the transmission are dispersed, loosely organized groups, not individuals, even though individuals do the receiving. This has several implications: (a) the material cannot be personalized for its targets because every individual in a group is different in at least some respects; (b) because they are dispersed and, as individuals, have different interests, motives, and goals, the targeted persons have difficulty in organizing to influence the sender; and (c) for the same reasons, receivers are unable to help each other come to a common understanding of the transmitted material and, thus, to share reasons for and a common interest in organizing.

Last, though no less important, the statement mentions neither communication nor media. With respect to the first omission, the statement refers to a process of transmitting material. The implications are that (a) transmission by itself is not communication, and (b) material transmitted in mass communication need not have any intrinsic communicative potential. Indeed, I would argue that the primary reason for the choice of material often has nothing to do with communication. More than likely, the primary concerns of the senders are to influence and/or to entertain. The omission of any reference to mass media is purposeful. It emphasizes the fact that mass communication and the mass media are separable, not one and the same thing. The former is a process, the latter a context that has become a social system and an institution. The two are dependent, but they can be separated. All mass communication must occur through the mass media which, in turn, also can process other communication and material having nothing at all to do with communication.

## COMMUNICATION SITUATIONS—ACTS AND PROCESSES

In order to put some of its more important features in proper perspective, it helps to place mass communication in the context of communication generally—the wisdom of which is now becoming evident in such proposals as Heeter's (1989) to adjust theories that do not do this so that they take account of innovations in interactive technology—and to distinguish communication from its consequences. As already has been indicated, to study communication in order to understand it is no simple task. In addition to the fact that it is so easy to confuse communication with other forms of symbolic expression and with learning, Scott (1990: 1-9) has suggested that the project of understanding is hampered in two other ways: (a) we employ the elements of communication in order to understand it, and this puts us at great risk of circularity or regression; and (b) communication is so pervasive and universal an element in every aspect of social life that the analysis of communication would seem to entail the analysis of everything. The appropriate way to resolve such difficulties is to formulate and adhere as closely as possible to a rigorous definition.

I have found it particularly useful in analyzing mass communication to define communication as "... the process through which a set of meanings embodied in a message is conveyed to a person or persons in such a way that the meanings received are equivalent to those which the initiator(s) of the message intended" (Smith, Bealer, and Sim, 1962: 12). Baudrillard (1988 [1985]: 207-208) has added to a very similar definition a responsibility to reciprocate when one engages in the process, but I see this as more of a value position than a necessary element in a definition. Our definition, in the symbolic interaction tradition of George Herbert Mead, elaborates a more concise definition (i.e., an interactive process involving the exchange of significant symbols), recognizing that the exchange is a transition from individual possession to sharing. It emphasizes both the intent of the initiator of a message (or communicator) and the equivalence of meanings sent and received. Full clarification of the concept of a "significant symbol" requires that several other concepts be elaborated on (Engelkamp, 1983), but the only aspect that need be noted here is that its meaning is tied to the conventions of a specific group. It is a symbol for which the members of a specific group share an understanding of what the appropriate response to it is (i.e., when used within the group it evokes the same response from any member). That response is its meaning (Potts, 1977). The definition also implies that the primary purpose and outcome of the exchange must be message transfer.

In addition, the analysis is informed by three propositions:

1. Although that which is being transferred among participants in a human communication process may be conceived of as a single unit of meaning (in the sense of the information theorist's concept of a bit of information), normally it is a complex set of meanings composed of many bits.
2. Behavior and/or objects that appear to be communication are not necessarily communication.
3. Information new to an individual need not necessarily have been obtained through communication.

The concepts[1] derive from the notion of a social act—an actor with a goal- or end-orientation employing means under a set of conditions. A social act is distinguished by the orientation of the actor to ends that transcend the immediate situation. A social act is not a reflex response; it involves conscious anticipation of future states and requires symbol-using skills. Whether the outcome is as intended does not bear on whether the act is social. What matters is that the actor is oriented beyond the activity. Mead noted that all interaction processes occur within the context of the social act (Miyamoto, 1959: 51). Finally, the concept of a social act implies the possibility of *a* single unit of behavior; social action suggests a continuing sequence of units with features similar to those of acts.

The uniqueness of communication as a form of social action cannot be overemphasized (Habermas, 1979: 209). First, it is always potentially interactive. Second, the goal, whatever else, always includes the reception and sharing of intended meanings by targeted persons. In fact, if an act succeeds, it does so *only* in the sense that it produces a congruent set of meanings in the minds of recipients (cf. Delia and O'Keefe, 1979). In this sense, communicating as intentional behavior may have either of two outcomes—it may be communication or noncommunication. The former indicates action with both the intent to transmit and the intent to mean that results in congruent reception and comprehension; the latter indicates either the absence of one or both intentions on the sender's part, or the targeted recipient's failure to receive or to comprehend as intended. Because more than one intention on the part of the sender and more than one activity on the part of the receiver are required, any communicating act may be any one of the several types, although ultimately it can turn out to be one and only one of these alternatives.

Many definitions of communication and the communication act go beyond the intention to transmit selected meanings that will be received and understood as intended. They stress the usual inten-

## Communication as a Social Process

tion of senders to create an effect beyond this. Newcomb (1953), for example, recognized that the "communicative act" is simply a transmission of information about an object to another person, but suggested that communication also is a means to bring about symmetry in the orientations of A and B to some object Z. Communication, in his view, does not occur unless the receiver's perception moves toward that of the sender as a result. Berlo (1960: 11-12) also has said that the purpose of communication is to affect another: "Our basic purpose in communication is to become an affecting agent, to affect others, our physical environment, and ourselves, to become a determining agent, to have a vote in how things are." Thayer (1968), after arguing the inadequacy of a definition (14-16) as compared to a fundamental understanding (16-26), credited earlier work by Berne as his basis for specifying communication as occurrences in which ". . . an organism (an individual) took-something-into-account" (26). Moreover, he meant that phrase to apply in the broadest sense, for the "something" includes "something someone did or said or *did not do or say*, whether it was some observable event, some internal condition, the meaning of something being read or looked at, some feeling intermingled with some past memory—literally anything that could be taken-into-account. . . ." (27; emphasis in original). Ward (1989: 5), who initially seemed to avoid including effects in saying about communication that it ". . . may be simply described as a communicator sending a message to a receiver," slipped into a similar usage two paragraphs later by adding that ". . . the information which . . . (the message) . . . contains, presumably requir(es) a reaction from the receiver."

This analysis explicitly excludes the intent to affect as a component of communication per se. If one distinguishes three types of intent of an initiator of communication—an intent to transmit, to mean, and to affect—only the first two are relevant in analyzing communication as such, although, admittedly, the last is what usually motivates the initiator. Circumstances in addition to information transfer are omitted for two reasons. First, regardless of whether message transfer succeeds, in one sense some effect always occurs after an attempt to communicate. Thus, the occurrence of an effect, by itself, does not distinguish kinds of outcomes. Second, whether the additional effect is that desired by the sender usually involves more factors than whether senders transmit messages as they wish to and receivers receive them as intended. Both considerations may be illustrated.

The first point is particularly appropriate to election campaigns in a democracy. For an election to serve the purpose intended, the underlying concept is that citizens have full information about what to expect of each prospective regime in order to make rational choices. The essential mechanism on which the system rests is information acquisition; the campaign is expected to provide the information. Ideally, the individual's choice is determined by rational evaluation of the information received from each candidate and is not shaped by accompanying emotional baggage. This requires all candidates—as senders—to succeed in communicating. If they do, all will have contributed to the effect when a decision has been made. However, in each voter's case, only one candidate can achieve the motivating goal they all share—receiving that person's vote. One candidate's success is the other candidates' failure. In the ideal election, then, whether communication has occurred is not measured by who gets elected but by whether voters understand the messages as the candidates intend. Who gets each voter's vote is a function of how each subsequently evaluates all the information and acts on it on election day—or so it would work ideally. The voter has three burdens—to know, to decide, to act.

In most campaigns, polls play a major part. Their ostensible role is to let people know how the electorate would decide if they had to do so on the basis of the information acquired by the time of the poll. However, critics of preelection polling are concerned that information as to who would win at that time creates a bandwagon effect—that choices are changed only because voters wish to be associated with a projected winner or do not want to waste their resources on a projected loser. But it is equally plausible for supporters of projected losers to respond to the same information by working even harder. Still another response is to ignore polls as irrelevant or unreliable. Given these several possibilities, it should be clear that information acquisition by itself has no necessary or intrinsic tie to any particular subsequent consequence.

With respect to the second point, an Indian student in one of my classes was extremely upset by a speaker he had heard during the previous hour whose thesis was that failures to achieve desired changes indicate failures to communicate. The speaker had used as an example a demonstration to farmers in an Indian village of the advantages of tractor over animal power. When there was no change a year later, the speaker concluded that he had failed to communicate. It was because my student, who happened to have been in the village for the demonstration, knew that the farmers had understood, had badly wanted tractors, simply could not pay for them, and were terribly frustrated—that nothing had happened because the farmers were poor and not because they had failed to receive or understand the message—that he was extremely upset. Clearly, in this as in the previous case, the outcome indicated nothing about information transfer. Rather, both cases dramatize the fact that there is no necessary relationship between communication and a specific effect, and, hence, that *neither can be a reliable index of the other*. Thus, I emphasize only the intent to mean and to transmit and the reciprocal responses of receiving and understanding in deciding whether the outcome of communicating is communication.

The concept of a social act is broad and includes that of a communication act as a subtype. The latter, by definition, is distinguished by an actor's prior intent to transmit a bit of information successfully; the former only by being oriented beyond the present situation. Real and apparent communication acts differ in the fact that only in a real communication act does the actor intend both to mean (i.e., to formulate a message) and to transmit (i.e., to make it available to the other). Whether an intended act of communication, in turn, is communication or noncommunication depends on whether the information it embodies is received by the intended receiver(s) with the meaning intended by the sender.

The communication status of a single act is an either/or matter, not one of degree. In contrast, everyday understandings of success in communicating usually include one or both of two different matters—how much information in a series of communicating acts is received and understood as intended (this implies degrees of communication in an episode or extended process), and, irrespective of this, whether the desired subsequent state of affairs was achieved. The first is consistent with my usage, the second is not.

The contrast with the social act directs attention to several other matters. If the intentions of the sender and the pre- and postact mental condition of the receiver are crucial in determining the status of potential communication acts, then there are several irreducible uncertainties in the empirical study of communication. What is the sender's intention, or are there several intentions prior to execution of the act? And how much prior? If these intentions are dynamic, some continuing and others changing through time, when is it necessary or best to ascertain them? Do actors know their intentions consciously? Are they clear enough to communicate to analysts? What if senders do not wish to share their motives with observers, or simply err in doing so? Because intentions must be communicated to investigators and cannot be observed directly, at best there can be only meta-inquiry—analysis of reports of intentions rather than of the intentions themselves.[2] Determining the status of the intended recipient of the act presents similar difficulties. At what point subsequent to the act should we look for the presence of the intended meanings in the mind of that actor? What if the receiver already knew the communicator's intended meaning? If the receiver knows the sense of the act but is unable to express it precisely, how can an observer be sure there is an equivalent meaning? How long does it take for the meaning of the act to become clear to the receiver? And how soon does it begin to dissipate?

There are, of course, no single acts with single meanings. Human action is extremely complex; it is not a collection of discrete acts. Humans do not transmit single bits of information with a single intent. This makes it difficult to apply these concepts to real events. In mass communication, the application of the communication act metaphor is even more problematic. Whose intentions in a sending organization matter, and whose actions and responses in an ill-defined targeted receiver group need to be determined? Nevertheless, the concept is useful for highlighting the importance of (a) senders' intentions, (b) congruence between *what is intended to be sent and received* and *what is received* for success in communicating, and (c) the intractable obstacles to an accurate determination of the communication status of any situation of potential social interaction.

If single acts could be observed and the problems of accessing necessary information overcome, the data could be used to determine the communication status of all the acts in an episode (i.e., a finite time period in a defined setting). That would require deciding whether communication had occurred and, if not, in what respects the act was deficient. Episodes that could be analyzed would include any that met either of two common conditions: first, the presence of two or more actors in circumstances in which communication appears feasible, or second, prior knowledge that a setting ordinarily is meant for communication (e.g., an empty seminar room on a weekday afternoon). To do this within the framework provided by our definition, of course, would require knowing the intentions and actions of the actors and whether the message was informational as well as meaningful. Therefore, I first discuss (a) the meanings of "sender" and "receiver," and (b) the sense in which messages are informative as well as meaningful.

## SENDERS AND RECEIVERS

In analyzing social communication, the concept of senders refers to people who either intentionally act to transmit meanings or occupy the role conventionally understood to control sending. Persons are considered receivers, however, for only one reason: They are selected for or accepted in the role by the sender (e.g., invitees to a lecture, anyone who hears a cry for help). They are not people who receive messages that are not meant for them (e.g., spies, overhearers, eavesdroppers, observers).

In mass communication the sense of the concepts is clear and their referents (e.g., television newscasters and their viewers) are easy to comprehend. However, empirical determination often is not easy in specific cases. Many people may participate in preparing and executing sending acts; there may be a sharp disjuncture between those whose intentions are being executed and those who perform the acts. In effect, the latter are proxies for the former and for some purposes may be ignored. However, depending on the medium, these proxies may alter an intended message by dint of personal style or by consciously or inadvertently changing it. For such reasons, task specialization in complex sending organizations may compound the difficulties in identifying senders.

There are comparable difficulties in identifying receivers. First, there may well be a gap between senders' ideas as to who they would like to reach as receivers and the qualities those groups actually have. The current practice of media sellers and buyers is to identify desired audiences by so-called "demographics." This involves defining strata of intended receivers by combinations of a few demographic attributes (e.g., gender, age, race) on the assumption that the selected two or three attributes are highly correlated with some other desired but unknown attribute (e.g., high income, above average intelligence, special tastes or interests). The actual correlation often may not be sufficiently high or may even be nil. Thus, even when sellers deliver the desired audience to buyers, the buyers in their role of senders may not be addressing the group they would prefer to reach.

An even more serious source of difficulty is that the public character of media material makes it extremely difficult to prevent unwanted people from receiving. People with some but not all or even none of the characteristics of intended receivers often may consume the material (cf. Ang, 1991: 40). Audiences of selected issues of women's magazines, for example, include as much as 20% or more men. Exclusionary techniques like the motion picture rating system are meant to prevent unintended receivers from consuming media material, but there are no foolproof methods. What complicates matters even more is that, generally, after material has been distributed and media enterprises estimate audience size to set advertising rates, no one will be disclaimed as a receiver—intended or not. The confounding tendency of media enterprises to disregard the distinction between intended targets and actual consumers in identifying receivers adds to the ambiguity (cf. Ang, 1991: 17-41).

Several distinct intentions are involved in each actor's participation—the sender's to transmit, to mean, and to affect, and the receiver's to receive, to understand, and to be affected. To identify the status of a potential communication act, however, I have argued that it is sufficient to consider only the sender's intentions to transmit and to mean and to ignore any other intentions of the sender and all those of the receiver. However, to know the *outcomes* of situations in which sending acts can occur, it is essential to know whether receivers receive and understand as intended. Although receivers' intentions in playing their role are irrelevant for ascertaining outcomes of an episode, they certainly may affect the probabilities of alternative outcomes as well as the sender's expectations for the future of the relationship. A disinterested receiver is less likely to understand as intended and, perhaps, even less likely to remain in the role for the sender's next efforts. Receivers' intentions normally will be taken into consideration by senders because, when interacting, we define situations by taking account of the intentions of others in interpreting their behavior. An unintentional killing is an accident, an intentional killing is first degree murder. Experienced senders know that the problem of being received and understood is less acute and different in kind when targeted receivers intend to receive and understand than when they do not.

Knowing whether there is a sender role, who occupies it, and a sender's intentions is essential; that person's behavior is secondary, useful mainly in dealing with unexpected acts or inactivity. An identified sender who acts with both intentions can be said to be engaged in a *communicating interact*. Normally, having both an intent to mean and an intent to transmit assures the occurrence of transmission that potentially can be successful. In the absence of both, normally the designated sender is inactive. Even if that person's inaction is perceived and correctly interpreted as meaningful by the receiver, it cannot be part of a communicating interact. In short, the minimum conditions for communication to be possible include (a) an acting sender (b) with both an intent to transmit and an intent to mean.

Although it might seem natural for both intentions to be either present or absent in any potential communicating situation, a sender may intend only to mean (e.g., "I wish I could tell that so-and-so what I think of him."). In becoming a member of a social group, one learns when to keep things to one's self—not to speak out of turn or place. Nonetheless, unintended transmission of messages that probably never would have been transmitted can occur. If one loses patience and blurts out information one would never have considered sharing (e.g., telling that so-and-so what you do think of him or her) or inadvertently shares a secret with a person who should not know it, sending acts that meet these conditions occur. This can happen even to media professionals (e.g., in what almost certainly is an apocryphal story, it is said that many years ago, Uncle Don, host of a popular children's radio program, thinking that he was off the air and that the microphone was dead, was heard by everyone tuned to his station to say, "That ought to hold the little b——ds."). Unless the sender announces the error, the receiver may find these acts indistinguishable from communicating interacts—normal behavior that can be received and understood. However, because the sender did not intend to share that meaning, in this analysis such an event is referred to as an *acommunicating interact*. The opposite combination—having an intent to transmit but not to mean—is an anachronism. It implies wanting to perform the act of communicating without any substance—a contradiction in terms. When it does happen, as it may, we think it pathological.

Such acts as singing to one's self or schizophrenic babbling also are not communicating acts. They exemplify externalized, possibly mindless symbolic behavior (i.e., transmission without an intent to mean) because they lack intentional meaning for others. Although perceivable and interpretable, they are not sending acts in that context because they may not employ significant symbols and are not intentional in at least that one respect. Regardless of whether the actor would have been recognized as a sender in a conventional communication setting, they are not sending acts. Whether they are treated as such by a receiver also is irrelevant, that is, a correct interpretation of what is happening does not make a difference.

To summarize, whether the sender is acting as a normal occupant of that role is key in distinguishing otherwise indistinguishable sending and nonsending acts. Because only the sender's intentions determine whether an act may be sending and, if so, communicating, the actions of the receiver—whether reception occurs, whether what is received is understood, whether such an understanding is as intended by the sender—are purposely ignored. Those reactions, however, are critical in judging the outcome of the sender's performance, regardless of what it might be.

In considering the receiver's role, it is extremely important not to rely only on that role occupant's subsequent actions and mental state (i.e., was the message received and how was it understood) in analyzing the outcome of communicating situations. To treat any situation in which a receiver derives information by observing a sender as communication, and not to emphasize that sender's intentions to transmit and mean, would be to argue, for example, that poker players whose habits reveal their bluffs to their opponents mean to "tell" the other players that the bet is a bluff, that liars who are not believed mean to be found out, or that persons overheard singing mean to inform others of how they feel. This confuses communication and learning. Acts that can be perceived, interpreted, and treated as message sending are not communication if they are not fully intentional (i.e., if there is no meaning in the sender's mind or no meaning that the sender wishes to share with the receiver). This position is taken in explicit disagreement with Thayer (who argues that intention is not necessary [1968: 14-15]) because the fact is that receivers also may learn by other means than the purposeful transmission of information by others—thoughtful analysis and observation of the environment being two other important possibilities.

## INFORMATION

An implicit aspect of communicating that often is ignored in classifying acts is whether a message contains information. In the same sense that communication is a sine qua non for organized society, information is central to communication. As Scott (1990: 1) has put it after asserting the centrality of communication to ". . . self and society. Both live on information . . . just as surely as they subsist on a material base." In several previous references to the material that senders make available to receivers, the term *information* was used interchangeably with *message* and *meaning*, although by now it should be clear that meaning refers to a more inclusive framework and message is a "packet" of symbols that may or may not contain information. This loose wording reflects our tendency in everyday usage to treat the three as synonymous and is not intended to override the basic proposition of this argument that in its essential form communication is a process of intentional information sharing (Dua, 1990: 113-117).[3] There are several reasons for this assertion. One is technical; an analytic approach that disaggregates the process to act units becomes meaningless for material other than information. More important, however, is the assumption that the main immediate objective of receivers in attending to senders is to obtain information. Such an approach is not inconsistent with Langer's surmise (1948: 83-116) that language development may have been promoted by the opportunity early humans were afforded to indulge in the luxury of exuberant expression once they were able to exist above a level of mere survival. She suggested that prior to this communication was necessary for species survival and, using italics in her text (89) for emphasis, refers to ". . . the pragmatic use of vocables. . . ." She later quoted approvingly Bühler's assertion that the need for "empractic" uses was among the major factors that promoted language development (110).[4]

    The assumption that information receipt is a prime factor in receiver participation in communication does not require an overly narrow conception of the communication process. It does not imply, for example, that senders are always primarily motivated to provide information. However, it does suggest that regardless of senders' reasons for wanting to engage receivers, it is important for them to seem to be providing information. Moreover, although Langer did not suggest it in an analysis intended primarily as an explanation of language development in humans, its essential information-providing aspect would help account for communication being such a widely accepted form of interaction and for the related tendency to designate almost any symbolic expression as communication. Furthermore, it does not imply that noninformational symbol transmission and reception do not occur. Rather, it identifies such practices as essential components of basically pragmatic communication relationships despite being, by this definition, counterfeit or pseudo-communication.[5] As will be seen, they play essential roles in the communication process.

An important consequence of the proposition that communication is a process of information sharing and the definition of information as that which reduces uncertainty for the receiver is that receipt of a message already known by the receiver is not communication. It is confusing, or meaningless, or repetitive material that can reenforce, emphasize, reassure, or, eventually, bore, but it provides no information. However, because information is novel to a receiver,[6] for whom, by definition, it is unfamiliar at first,[7] it is very difficult to transmit information successfully without also providing familiar markers to help the recipient recognize, understand, and relate it to other knowledge. Therefore, all but the briefest effort to communicate consists of message "chunks" that include orienting material. As in metaphor, only small portions of messages are novel. As Luhmann (1990a) has suggested, the meaning of information is present because the meaning of the symbols used comes from a grounding of the symbols in experience. None of that is new. Communicating interacts that give no information to receivers are not communication. However, most informational message "chunks" must contain noninformation to help the receiver apprehend, understand, and retain information.

Information receipt and transfer is difficult for the participants. They experience it as hard work and frequently need relief. It is this fact that led Luhmann to speak elsewhere of "the improbability of communication" (1990b: 86-96). He observed ". . . that a multitude of problems and obstacles have to be surmounted before communication can come about" (87). For this reason, most communication episodes contain "breathers" that provide a great deal more noninformational material than just the contextual material needed to make information understandable. In order to make an episode enjoyable enough to balance the discomfort associated with the work of making it valuable, humor, emotion, repetition, and other types of more easily comprehended symbolic expression are included as well. The skilled communicator knows how to minimize such extraneous material without sacrificing maximum effectiveness, and, at his or her best, is able to work such material into the message flow in forms that are indistinguishable from the information components.

Information is not a synonym for accuracy or truth. Indeed, even though Scott (1990: 7) introduced the term in the context of knowledge—by which is generally understood material whose "truth value" is in its having met certain technical standards of reliability and validity that exist beyond the individual—his elaboration of the concept emphasizes that ". . . ideas, facts, opinions are 'informative' to the extent that they add to, or somehow affect, *our* state of awareness and knowledge" (27; emphasis added). It is because news need not be accurate or true that it is treated as information throughout this analysis. This is not to reject well-documented critiques that argue that news may be selective, incomplete, biased, and inaccurate (Tuchman, 1978; Gans, 1979; Bagdikian, 1987; Herman and Chomsky, 1988)—not the window on reality it is conventionally considered to be (Connell, 1980). Information is relative to the mental situation of the receiver; it reduces his or her disorder or uncertainty at and for a time, a fact echoed in the comment (Luhmann, 1990a: 32) that ". . . information has its identity as something occurring at a particular point in time and not as something that endures in time. . . ." There is one important condition, however. When a receiver accepts an untruth and acts on it as information, in the nontrivial case (i.e., when correct information matters for subsequent events) the consequences of that action would show the message to be misinformation. More generally, not only is information defined by the actor's response in the immediate time frame of an act, but, from the perspective of communication in an ongoing social situation, information is information only so long as an intended receiver feels that it reduces his or her uncertainty. News, despite its distortions and inaccuracies, generally meets this standard.

There are other reasons for not equating information with truth. First, to do so would imply that the information in messages is forever valid, when, in fact, knowledge changes. Second, even if senders know their messages are untrue, the criterion for success in transfer is that they be received and understood as intended. Were that not so, there could be no successful lying. Third, because communication requires only receipt and understanding of messages as intended and because the receiver's view on whether a message is informative hinges only on whether it diminishes his or her uncertainty in that setting, the message must be understood for its informational potential and need not determine subsequent beliefs or action. Thus, fourth and last, people can receive, understand, and be satisfied with inconsistent explanations, assertions of fact, and advice. No one could accept any message as information, and, hence, there could be no communication, if guarantees of the permanent truth of every statement also were required. Mistakes are corrected as they are identified.

Admittedly, the third point concerning informational potential is in slight disagreement with Postman (1985: 67-68), who emphasized the fact that most news, although it may be quite accurate, is context-free and therefore cannot guide people's actions. He referred to that material as irrelevant information that produces an information glut and criticized television news for having a poor "information-action ratio." If, instead, as argued here, action need not follow from information, the status of "irrelevant information" depends solely on the subsequent mental state of the receiver. This usage is consistent with Lazarsfeld and Merton's (1948: 105-106) discussion of the "narcotizing dysfunction" of the media, in which they suggest that the sense of being well informed about an issue that comes from following it in the news, if it is equated with being adequately engaged, may be substituted for action on the matter. That possibility is feasible only if people consider news informational. From this perspective, if the material has psychic value in the short run, it is not irrelevant.

Just as a message need not be true or accurate to constitute information, information (or misinformation) acquired in potentially interactive situations need not have been transferred by sending acts. Indeed, that is just one of the three possibilities for a variety of recognizable potentially interactive situations (see Figure 2.1), in some of which no action even faintly resembling communicating or information acquisition may occur. Four types of inactive situations meet the conditions for being potentially informative in socially interactive situations: (a) there is a receiver, but someone expected to be in the sender role is absent (e.g., a scheduled speaker fails to appear); (b) receivers anticipate statements from senders who do not send, even though they are present and able to perform (e.g., the designated speaker says nothing, the suspect refuses to answer questions); (c) there is a sender and receiver, but the sender only emits familiar symbols with no intent to mean or transmit (e.g., singing to one's self); and (d) there are no actors, but the setting is socially defined as appropriate and normal for communicating (e.g., an empty college classroom on a Tuesday in October during the most popular hour for classes, cancellation of an episode of a regularly scheduled TV series unknown to some loyal fans who were unable to watch that particular evening).

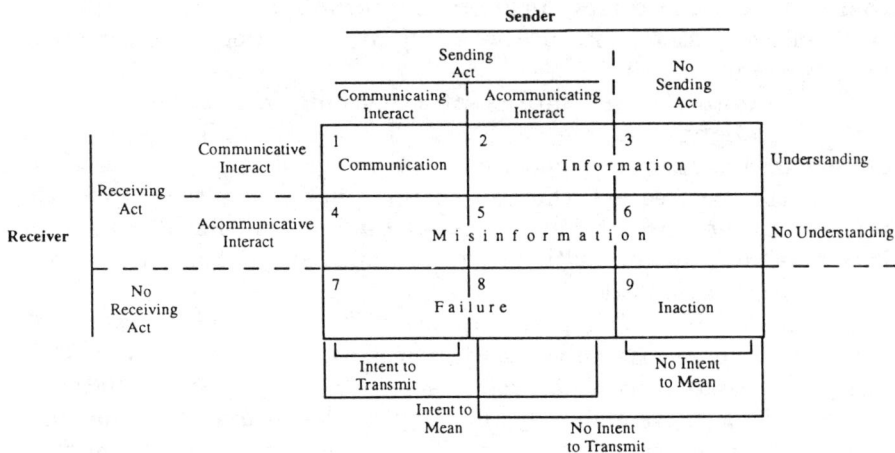

**Figure 2.1. Socially interactive situations in terms of their communicative character**

To identify and interpret cases in which there is a sender role but no sending act requires independent knowledge of the rules and norms that apply to situations.[8] For the first three of the situations just specified to be informative and not trivial, the receiver's inference eventually must be verified. The possibility, then, of gaining information from situations without sending acts requires only defined receivers who know that a sender role is not being played and who make correct inferences from that fact; indeed, to satisfy the conditions the sender must not even have wanted to try to convey anything. These situations add justification for the proposition that receivers can acquire information without communication.[9] Cases of the fourth type can only be informative to a nonparticipant observer or analyst.

## CLASSIFYING ACTS IN POTENTIALLY INTERACTIVE SITUATIONS

The universe of situations to which Figure 2.1 applies (i.e., situations in which there are people who appear to be senders and receivers and/or in which communication activity is expected) is defined by one or the other of two criteria—action and social definition. The assumption is that these criteria could be applied reliably by trained observers (i.e., they would agree that a situation meets those standards), and it is only for their use that Figure 2.1 is developed. In order to decipher particular situations, it is important to understand that the two are conceptually independent. Although many cases qualify as communicating on both grounds, analyst-observers must be aware of which takes priority. Unlike the empty seminar room used in an earlier example, an empty parlor, an unused public telephone, a half-full newspaper rack in a shopping mall, two silent family members, or a household television set that is not turned on do not define situations sufficiently for analysis. Only action can give them meaning for an analyst.

Because the absence of action can be meaningful to an observer of communication, Figure 2.1 includes a Cell 9. Much social activity is expected to but may or may not occur in situations defined as communication settings. The classroom provides a good example. In these cases, how action and social convention inform analysis depends on the question being asked. In formally structured cases, for example, the question of who occupies the communicator role usually can be answered by referring to known conventions. In contrast, questions about what is transpiring during specific exchanges place the priority in analysis on what is actually happening. In all cases, however, to the extent possible, observation is informed by an a priori understanding of the structure of the situation.

Is the priority on action or on structure in analyzing mass communication? In the abstract general sense, mass communication is conventionally and situationally defined. Nonaction should be meaningful because both senders and receivers have well-defined expectations that lead to mutual dependencies and compelling guidelines for interpreting action and inaction. Moreover, the physical mechanisms of reception (and sometimes transmission) tend to shape and define the settings and occasions for communicating. Scheduling and role exchange conventions are well established, widely understood, and enforced. Failure to enact either role is serious. It follows that analyses of mass communication should require at least as much emphasis on the norms and rules that govern established relations as on action. How would it actually work?

To determine the communication status of a given media episode (e.g., a television program, a film, an issue of a newspaper), the situation of each person exposed to the material plus those who were intended to be but were not reached would be summed for each act that constituted the episode. Despite the importance of structure in interpreting cases, however, the emphasis may have to be on action either because the targeted group is poorly defined or because many actual receivers may not have been targeted (e.g., 13-year-olds watching R-rated films) and media entrepreneurs usually will not exclude actual recipients from a claimed audience. In either case, it is extremely difficult to know what to make of many individuals' inactivity or actions. If media producers cannot target or exclude either specific individuals or very clearly demarcated groups as intended receivers, analysts and actual and would-be participants must rely on what happens in the situation to define it.

Figure 2.1 depicts all the possible outcomes of potential communication acts when these factors are applied. It includes the minimum set of categories needed to identify any unit of potential social interaction (i.e., a social interact) in this regard and derives from the relation of the intentions and actions of senders to the actions of receivers. It applies only to (a) acts whose end or goal orientation *can* involve transmitting meaning to others, or (b) a receiver's perception that such an act has occurred. It does not apply to any acts in solitary not meant to be shared, even if they are social acts (because the actor took general social norms or the imagined reactions of others into account [e.g., eating with silverware or dressing for bed when alone]).

Because any normal communication act requires both a sender and receiver, one axis—the horizontal—is assigned to the subject (the sender) and one—the vertical—to the intended object (the receiver). The three situations of potential senders depicted in the columns differ only in terms of the role occupant's intentions as to meaning and transmission. They set the potential communicating character of the situation at the instigation of an act; the rows indicate its communication outcome.

The three cells in the first column describe the possible outcomes of unambiguous efforts to communicate. Cell 1 refers to pure success; an actor has a message, wishes to transmit it, and does so in a way that gives intended receivers exactly the same idea. The two lower cells indicate the only possible types of failure in attempted communication—misunderstandings of messages by active receivers (Cell 4) and failures of intended receivers to receive messages, regardless of the reason (Cell 7).

The middle column also refers to situations in which there is a sender. That person also has clear messages in mind but, for whatever reason, does not intend to transmit them. Regardless of whether the sender slips and actually sends them unintentionally or they are never sent, if designated receivers are present, the sender's unintended actions or inaction may either be received or inferred and interpreted correctly (Cell 2) or incorrectly (Cell 5). Cell 8 refers to similar situations in which those in the receiver role miss or forego the opportunity to perceive the situation and, therefore, draw no conclusion from it. Both this column and the first are distinguished from the third by the fact that there is a person in a sending role who is contemplating sending a message. Therefore, there is no question that receivers are correct if they perceive that person's actions as meaningful symbolic activity.

The right-hand column applies to situations understood as appropriate for communication that lack an actor in the sender role or to situations with a known sender who is playing neither aspect of the role. They may take three forms. One is rare and unusual. An identifiable sender engages in irrelevant sending actions (e.g., sings, talks to self aloud). Designated receivers may observe the behavior and interpret its significance correctly (i.e., it informs them) or incorrectly (i.e., it misinforms them), but it is trivial from a communication perspective because there is no intentional effort at information transfer.

The more common types of nonsending have already been identified. In one, senders are present but inactive. Receivers consider this informative when they feel either that they perceive interpretable cues from the sender or that they know why the sender is not acting. The former is the case, for example, when receivers infer what might have been but was not sent from gestures or so-called body language (e.g., facial expressions, physical mannerisms). This may happen with senders who inadvertently gesture whenever they attempt to deceive. The distinction between Cells 3 and 6 rests only on whether the receiver's inference matches the facts of the sender's case. A very different instance of information acquisition from an inactive sender who has neither intention and gives no cues is that of a sender who is considering but has yet to select one of several possible messages. An experienced receiver might not wait and, instead, might infer which of those messages will be sent (e.g., an automobile salesman who anticipates a customer's rejection of a quoted price). Indeed, this is often what facilitates rapid exchanges and unexpected role changes during conversations or negotiations.

The other possibility is that of absent senders in situations in which people who might legitimately be receivers draw inferences from the inaction. Cell 3 (information) applies to instances in which the receivers draw inferences that are the same as reality (e.g., viewers conclude that a television station is off the air because of a power outage, which is so; students decide that the instructor is absent because he or she is delayed at a doctoral oral, which is the case) and Cell 6 to cases in which the inferences are incorrect (e.g., viewers who conclude there is a power outage are wrong because the station is off the air due to transmitter difficulties; the students' instructor is caught in a traffic jam). Deciding whether a case meets the criteria of Cell 3 or Cell 6 requires information that must be obtained independently of the situation. Cases that fit Cell 9 can only be identified by observers who are not participants and who, by drawing on independent information, understand that the absence of all activity in that setting is meaningful.

To summarize, any intentional act by a sender to transmit a message thought to be informative for a selected target is a communicating act; it is communication when the target receives it, understands it as intended, and considers it informational (i.e., when it reduces that person's uncertainty or confusion). Whether other configurations of unintended action or inaction in situations structured for communication are informational depends on how well targeted receivers diagnose the meaning of the situation.

This analysis should help clarify a major confusion that arises from using the terms *mass communication* and *mass media* as synonyms—on the one hand, treating the media as information sources because they are involved in symbol production and transmission or, on the other hand, considering them noninformative if they do not communicate. These distinctions clarify how they may be highly informative without communicating. The independence of information from communication in communicating situations also suggests why and how participants may feel satisfied with interactive situations in which little communication occurs, for they still can come away feeling that they have learned. The partial dependence of the two, in that communication always involves both symbolic expression and information gain, also may help explain why people treat (a) any symbolic expression as both communication and informational, and (b) the occurrence of either as indicative of both.

If there were single acts and the data collection problems could be resolved, any act could be identified as being of one of the nine types, and each act in an episode could be assigned to a cell. All communicating acts that are communication would be in Cell 1. All others would be distributed among Cells 2 to 9. With respect to *whether* communication had taken place, their exact location would not matter. With respect to *why* communication had not taken place, their location would be crucial. Successful communication requires that the proportion of all acts in an episode that fall in Cell 1 be sufficiently high relative to expectations that neither the sender nor the receiver is so frustrated, discouraged, or disappointed as to leave the role or terminate the arrangement. Disappointment and frustration with attempts to communicate are, of course, socially influenced. Among the more important of these influential factors are the importance placed on the message and/or the parties involved and actors' expectations of the situation.

The possibility that poor performance may cause actors to leave their roles calls attention to a critically important condition in communication that has been assumed in developing this schema. The assumption is voluntarism—actors are free to play or leave their roles. The bottom row and two right-hand columns of Figure 2.1 are especially useful for established systems in which participation is voluntary. Not all systems are voluntary (e.g., in dictatorial or highly controlled environments); social situations differ in how much choice they allow actors in communication systems. In countries like the United States, however, the mass media are almost totally volitional. In the long run, their survival depends on how actors accept and play their roles and on how they respond to the other and the other's role playing. From a sociological perspective, this is, perhaps, the central point about the media as interactive social systems.

## LIMITATIONS ON THE CLASSIFICATION OF ACTS AS COMMUNICATION

It is relatively easy to define the nine different statuses of potential acts but difficult to provide comparable illustrations of each. The reason is that, to keep things simple, the same schema has been used for two basically different types of situations—one defined by action, the other by social convention. Action-defined situations are not otherwise recognizable as potential occasions for communication. Therefore, they provide few instances of extended meaningful inaction, and Cell 9 is largely irrelevant for them. The actions of people observed in a park facing each other and apparently conversing can be sorted out in terms of communication. There is nothing to sort out if no one is there; the situation does not even suggest communication-related possibilities. The absence of people makes it meaningless in those terms. Even Cells 3 and 6 are not useful unless an analyst has observed an episode long enough to understand its unique structure. Episodes that are not conventionally structured exist only when defined by action and, even then, they permit the participants only short periods of inactivity for thought or comfort. When action ends, both the episode and the analyst's ability to understand it end.

The third column in Figure 2.1, then, applies almost exclusively to widely understood or predefined situations in which there is no action. When there is action in such situations, the analyst has a choice of assigning sender and receiver roles on the basis of either conventional definitions or what rare activity occurs and does so according to the purpose of the research. Ordinarily, there is no choice in unstructured situations. Roles go with action.

These differences are important for mass communication. The mass media are highly structured message production and distribution systems in which continued activity depends on the probability that some portion or segment of the population will be exposed to the product at some later time. Paradoxically, however, the communication status of the situations that occur in them is defined only by action. Television, radio, film, magazines, and newspapers certainly set the form of the consuming act, and in the first three cases also may set the locus of consumption, but none of them determine who, if anyone, consumes or what is consumed or when it is consumed. Moreover, in contrast to action-defined communication situations in which roles are set by behavior, roles in media systems are highly structured. Publishers and producers are considered communicators, even though audience members may occasionally write letters of appreciation or turn off television sets in fits of pique or dissatisfaction. The total freedom of actual and potential receivers largely to do as they please when they please makes for unpredictability in the media and, hence, the paradox and uniqueness of mass communication.

To apply the schema to all the acts in an episode would require a chart for each participant who performs a sending act. For most unstructured situations, it would be sufficient to include only the first two columns and all three rows for each participant's chart. For a structured situation, however, the full nine cells would be needed for the actor in the sender role (e.g., an instructor in a college class). In either situation, accuracy would require a chart for each possible sender-receiver combination. So, for example, an analysis of acts in a college class with 20 students would require 20 instructor-student charts for the instructor and 19 student-student and 1 student-instructor chart for each student. A conversation on the street would require just two charts, a 2 column x 3 row chart for each conversationalist. A media situation would require so many charts that only a sampling of actual and intended recipients would be feasible. Without knowing beforehand who constitutes these groups, representative samplings are probably impossible. Any entire episode in any of these cases would be described by the distribution of tallies summed across all the necessary charts.

## NONINFORMATIONAL ACTS AND MESSAGES[10]

The emphasis on information gives a distorted image of what is being shared in an episode of communication. Messages rarely are, nor are they formulated to be, purely informative. Why is this? Why the need for "orienting" material in informational messages? Although significant symbols are necessary for social communication, with a few rare exceptions (e.g., emergency signals), one or a few of them in isolation could not be informational because, by definition, they already would be known by the receiver. Instead, new information is conveyed in two forms—novel combinations of significant symbols or symbols that are not yet "significant" to the receiver. Therefore, when information is transferred both sender and receiver usually must work—the sender to create an effective informational message and the receiver to decipher and understand it correctly. Often, these are difficult tasks.

In episodes of any length or stringency, therefore, and particularly if participants are free to discontinue and/or it is imperative to succeed, it is important to facilitate and ease the work. To facilitate it, the messages contain orienting material—familiar material that alerts the receiver that there also is something novel and that provides guidance in how to understand it. To ease the stress of executing a difficult task, other noninformational material that relaxes, rewards, or satisfies the workers—both sender and receiver—also may be introduced. Such materials may make the work more enjoyable by providing release (e.g., humor) or recognition (e.g., flattery, encouragement, reminiscence) or a sense of satisfaction with accomplishment (e.g., the proverbial "well-turned phrase") or other pleasing experiences. Because communication episodes vary greatly in character (e.g., short to long, able to inept actors, easy to difficult information), the ratio of information to noninformation in them also varies widely. Generally, the more novel and concentrated the material, the less adept the participants, or the longer the episode, the higher will be the ratio of noninformation to information.

In the case of most media (newspapers and newsmagazines being exceptions), however, this proposition is often confounded because they emphasize noninformational components to such an extent—primarily in response to the extensive but largely unknown dimensions of heterogeneity that characterize their relatively large audiences—that they have acquired reputations as entertainment sources. Consequently, their audiences often do not expect or recognize information as such. I recall a high school student, who was interviewed after the first broadcast of a United Nations meeting, saying that future sessions should not be broadcast because they are so important and they would not be taken seriously if they were on the radio. The proposition, then, can be expected to hold only within a medium, for that takes account of any differences in the reputations of the various media as sources of information.

To be more specific about what is emitted in communicating-like behavior, it helps to identify three types of material by their function: information representation, reinforcement, and aesthetic expression. The first is normally the stuff of communicating and, if things go right, communicates. In the language of metaphor, it includes both the novel—the new, or that which is informational in our sense—and the ground—the orienting material that enhances comprehension. To accomplish communication, Cherry (1978: 243-252) implicitly argued that signals must have some surprise value or degree of unexpectedness but also be familiar to the receiver. Even more to the point is his explication of the assertion that cognition also entails recognition.

The third is also like an information message in form but *primarily* serves to provide satisfaction for sender or receiver and, by doing so, makes the work more tolerable. Often, it is entertaining. Although it also may give pleasure, the second type, reenforcing material, *primarily* encourages actors to continue in their roles. It enhances the receiver's sense of self to be recognized as a person or to have his or her virtues acknowledged. Although it satisfies the criteria of communication in terms of sender intention and receiver equivalence, it does not by itself reduce uncertainty for receivers. Such messages may include greetings, small talk, and redundancy. Although the exchange of "Hi's" between passing coworkers could be new information of the sort, "Well, this is still a different time that we have seen each other and it is the 3,486th such occasion," this is tortured and trivial. The lack of information is even clearer in redundancy, in which, to raise the probability of successful transfer, the same meanings are repeated in the same or varied form or the receiver is reminded of what he or she already knows.

Noninformational material comprises a major portion of what is exchanged in human communication systems. However, it is not waste material; it reinforces the ties between system participants[11] and/or, by doing so, facilitates information transfer. Not the informational stuff of communication, some of it sustains relationships that facilitate communication. Some of it has intrinsic value because the successful use of, or similarity to, effective communication arrangements gives a sense of accomplishment or satisfaction. It eases the work. Indeed, as an indication of the importance of such acts for communication, it could be argued that we cannot account for the great effort put into communicating by attributing it only to the need to satisfy an altruistic commitment to share information or to the desire to achieve some personal goal.

Despite the emphasis on communication as behavior that employs significant symbols to produce nontrivial intended changes in the knowledge state of the targeted receiver(s), the analysis of systems also must attend both to these necessary reenforcing and facilitating materials embedded in the process and to their concurrent expressive and aesthetic uses. The presence of expressive utterances, for want of a better term, in communication reflects its central social importance. The importance of achieving communication (i.e., a high rate of communication acts) with ease is indicated by the honor and respect we accord the feat and those who can accomplish it. That respect eventually diffuses to systems in which it occurs, as well as to their components. Viewed in this light, it is not surprising that people derive obvious pleasure from self-expression that employs highly valued communication processes and systems and their components. Nor, for that matter, is the interest and respect accorded the mass media, media personalities, and even the equipment surprising.

The lack of attention to the second and third types of material reflects the emphasis on communication as an interactive process intended to lead to new and congruent mental states in designated others and on single communication acts as purposive attempts to transmit successfully a bit of information in a sense akin to formal information theory.[12] Why dwell on the difference between communication interacts and all other sender and receiver activity? Many definitions of communication do not even distinguish them. They do not specify that meanings sent and received be equivalent for an interact to be communication; for them, any interactive situation that results in knowledge acquisition constitutes communication. McDonald (1961: 58), for example, defined a communication act as ". . . any observable behavior by which information is transmitted from an information source to a human recipient." Such concepts treat all *potential* communication as such. I use the term only for interacts in which meanings sent intentionally are understood as intended by those targeted because it helps explain why communication systems fail or disintegrate. It shifts focus to the variable qualities of the process that eventually inhere in communication systems (e.g., redundancy, noise, capacity, compatibility) and enhance or hinder their rates of communication.

There are other reasons for adopting an information-oriented approach. The importance of information for problem solving, training group members, and enhancing group cohesion and organization all contribute to the view that information sharing is the primary function and task of communication. It is no accident that all governments, in executing their obligation to maintain the state, reserve control of and maintain surveillance over their communication systems. The 30-year-old films being rerun on television, of course, have more than economic significance. Entertainment relieves the hard work of receiving and, thereby, ties receivers to systems. However, this is not paramount in understanding the mass communication process and the development of the media. Nonetheless, although not geared to the analysis of such material, this approach helps explain its presence and role. Moreover, an information-oriented perspective also helps resolve such questions as why people do or do not pay attention to some or all of the news or why they prefer it in smaller rather than larger chunks. To understand mass communication, how it operates, and its role in modern societies, an information-oriented perspective is strategic.

## *THE ANALYSIS OF NONINFORMATIONAL MATERIAL*

Opting for an information-oriented analysis of communication does not obviate the fact that there is much important noninformational material in almost every episode of communication. How is it to be handled in analyses? Most of it could be fitted to one of the nine categories of the schema without requiring the schema to be changed, assuming, of course, that reliable data on intended meanings and the understandings of intended receivers were available. However, to do only that would be to ignore most of its more important aspects. Indeed, to consider using the schema on noninformational messages directs attention to several fundamental problems that confront such an analysis. It also suggests several important questions that the schema is not geared to address.

It is much more difficult to include noninformational material in an analysis of disaggregated communicating acts because it requires dealing with the possibility that one act generally has more than one meaning and, thus, may have more than one function. To include such material requires first determining whether each act is, in fact, a synthesis of a number of acts with distinct roles in sustaining the process—reenforcing and pleasure giving as well as information bearing. To disassemble multifunctional acts is extremely difficult, if not impossible, and exacerbates the problem of ascertaining intended meanings.

This is not a trivial matter. There is much more noninformational than informational material in most communication episodes. In addition to multiple intentioned acts, as discussed, almost any ongoing process includes material with no informational role. Indeed, a skilled communicator will be sure to include such supporting and facilitating materials. Because they lack an information component, the analytic schema in Figure 2.1, although it can be applied, will not explain failures. Thus, to analyze this material in information terms may well be an empty exercise. Nonetheless, the material cannot be ignored. Misfiring of these messages can have the same devastating effects as failed communicating interacts for an established communication system or social relationship.

Although there may be little to gain from analyzing the noninformational components of a communication episode from the perspective of the schema, the idea of success in achieving a purpose may be useful when the purpose of each noninformational act can be specified. Most elementary school teachers know that they have their students recite the pledge of allegiance not only to learn it but also to instill patriotism and loyalty. Although these are affective states, and the idea of information gain does not apply, the notion that there may be a measurable change in a desired direction does pertain.

Many elaborations on information transfer are not so obvious, however. Stylistic mannerisms, for example, may give senders pleasure but may have an unspecifiable impact on receivers. A joke told to reduce strain on the sender may increase it for the receiver. Unlike intentional information acts, these materials need not even be produced with the receiver in mind. Indeed, their initial purposes often are not clear to the sender. In such cases there would be no goal against which to assess receiver response. Despite these problems in using the schema on such material, it cannot be ignored given its obvious importance for both senders and receivers' willingness to enter and remain in their roles. Without it, mass media audiences, which usually do not develop on an information basis, would never build or decline.

Communicating, in its informational sense, implies prior intent, but the communication-like activities that facilitate it and help build systems need not involve prior intent. Even if they did, what matters from a communication perspective is not the sender's intentions for these noninformational messages, but how they affect the receiver. Equivalence between intended purpose and outcome is less important for these materials than whether the process is facilitated or the system strengthened, and the latter requires very different analytic strategies. Treating them as conventional acts of communication provides little guidance for developing such new approaches.

Aside from the problems that arise if noninformational materials are to be treated in the same analysis, just to contemplate doing so shifts attention to other, equally important issues. For one thing, if the fundamental importance of communication as communication derives from information sharing, the proportion of noninformational material must remain below some critical level or the arrangement would lose its identity as a communication system. This, in turn, would strain the bonds among participants. If so, the distribution of acts in an episode between information and noninformation could be more important for understanding communication than the outcome of noninformational acts.

In addition, because the main point in classifying all the acts in an episode is to understand how success levels sufficient to sustain a system are achieved, we must understand the role of noninformational acts in producing that condition. This raises several specific questions. For example, what is the effect of strong reinforcement when information transfer is already very efficient, or of an emphasis on aesthetic pleasure when information transfer is nil? In short, even if an ongoing episode could be disaggregated and the outcomes of its informational and noninformational acts identified, the significance of the amount of the latter material for successful communication remains a question.

For these reasons, only the one schema has been postulated and examined. At least the implications of the proportion of communicating acts that are communication for understanding and analyzing communication processes and systems are clear. The questions that pertain to noninformational materials do not require the same act-oriented approach as do information-based potential communicating interacts. The concepts for addressing some of them are available, however. Their application depends on the particular question being addressed.

## *NOTES*

1. Most of the ideas in this section derive directly or indirectly from the work of a seminar group led by the author in 1956. I am particularly indebted to Robert Bealer, Howard Ehrlich, Donald Halsted, James Harkness, and the late Francis Sim.
2. Dua (1990: 115) summarized these difficulties briefly more than 30 years after they were identified by the members of the seminar group to which I have referred in the Preface and the preceding footnote.
3. The unfortunate practice of treating the terms as synonyms leads to their being used interchangeably. This everyday practice probably has developed from the fact that information derived from others almost always is formatted as messages in forms that carry meaning (i.e., composed of significant symbols, in Mead's sense).

4. Thayer's (1968: 14-15) strong position that communication need not be intentional seems to follow from his emphasis on the receiver rather than on interaction and his tendency to equate learning with communication.
5. Thayer's (1968: 189) assertion that "... Shannon specifically disavowed any pertinence of his mathematical communication theory ... for human communication" is difficult to understand. Shannon (Shannon and Weaver, 1949: 96-97) did emphasize his concern with what Weaver called the technical problem but, as Weaver pointed out, human communication is only to be understood when the constraints of the technical situation are resolved. Moreover, Shannon's references to natural language suggest that he saw the theory as pertinent to human communication. Unlike Thayer, I find no disavowal of such an interest.
6. In identifying communication with information, Luhmann has said (1990a: 32) that "...it is a shared actualization of meaning that is able to inform at least one of the participants." Why he opened the possibility that more than one participant may be informed is not clear. Aside from the obvious possibilities that he may be thinking of multiple receivers or the role exchanges that characterize conversation, he also may be accepting the possibility that the act of communicating informs the communicator. If so, the definitions we both use would imply that this could only happen when the communicator misperforms, an event that can occur in a communication situation but that I would not consider to be communication because it violates the required conditions of intentionality. This issue is discussed in the following section. Incidentally, Luhmann added a footnote that grounds his interpretation, as ours, in the thought of George Herbert Mead and his intellectual predecessor, John Dewey.
7. It is after making this point about information and identifying communication with sharing information that Luhmann wrote (1990a: 32) that "... communication, then, is not the transfer of things but the allotment of surprises."
8. Argyle (1977: 74-76) is unusual in emphasizing the importance of understanding situations, or what I have called contexts, for the analysis of communication. Lull (1990 [1982]) has suggested that rules can be the focus around which the study of television and society can be organized.
9. Drawing the conclusion that it is likely to rain upon witnessing a display of thunder and lightening provides an even clearer illustration of this possibility. To place this in a communication framework would be tantamount to describing the display as nature telling us it is going to rain. This position is in sharp contrast to that of Thayer (1968: 26-27), who argued that the concept encompasses anything that a person takes into account.
10. Thayer (1968) devoted an entire section of his analysis to several functions other than information transfer—command and instructive functions (205-219), influence and persuasive functions (220-238), and integrative functions (239-250). With the possible exception of the last,

which I address here, they are what I have distinguished as consequences.

11. Scott (1990: 21) has commented on this explicitly, noting that "(r)elatively redundant structures in social interaction are well illustrated by the phenomenon of phatic communion. . . . This takes place when interlocutors have nothing in particular to say but maintain a sense of a living relationship by 'talking for the sake of talking.' Where this is desired all around,. . . (a)rchetypal stories will be re-told, old nicknames, idioms, and catchphrases and other ways of speaking resurrected. . . ." Note that he carefully referred to these occasions as communions rather than communication.

12. By this point it should be clear that my approach to the process of communication is oriented by and borrows heavily from the concepts and processes that constitute information theory. In this I am not alone as a social scientist. Scott (1990) and Luhmann (1990a), among others, also do. Scott (1990: chap. 2), in particular, has provided a strong defense for this strategy.

# 3

# The Structure and Processes of Communication Systems

Because an ongoing social system requires successful communication for organized action by its members, over time (a) a sufficiently high proportion of communicating interacts must fall into Cell 1 of Figure 2.1, and (b) system maintenance requirements will lead to the preservation of arrangements for communicating that have satisfactory success levels (i.e., the proportion of communicating interacts that are communication). In fact, the occurrence of episodes of communicating interacts with a sufficiently high proportion of communication suggests that a system probably already exists, for arrangements with satisfactory success levels tend to be preserved. Sufficiently or satisfactorily high is a relative standard that varies with situations. It means that the participants are satisfied; whether they are relates to their expectations and the importance of the message. SOS signals are sent and searched for without fear of boring anyone until the emergency is ended. In this chapter I discuss the basic structure of communication systems, the minimal conditions and processes required for them to work, and how the approach taken here compares with some alternatives.

## ELEMENTS OF A SYSTEM OF COMMUNICATION[1]

Whenever the arrangement of components involved in a sequence of related social acts persists, it can be said to constitute a social system. The process of communication is a sequence of related social acts of a particular sort. The arrangement in which such actions occur constitutes a communication system. The distinction essentially is that between what must be present (system) and what must be happening (process) for communication to occur. A general description of the components and their relationships that are common to all such systems is a model of a communication system. An adequate model should be applicable to any type of communication system, be it conversation or one of the mass media. A useful model should be as simple as possible. Although that is my goal, it will be necessary to operate at a rather complex level, for "[t]he mass media system is...a rather complex social system consisting of actions carried out within the context of the external social conditions of the community and the society in which it operates" (Mowlana, 1990: 91).

The model of a communication system I employ is derived by analogy from the model of the social act. To highlight some of the major differences, both are diagrammed in Figure 3.1. Not only does the actor become the communicator and the goal orientation (a changed information state on the part of) the communicatee, but also the nature of the relationship alters. This is indicated by the change from the single-headed arrow of the act to the two-headed arrow of the communication system. Means and conditions are altered as well. Of all the means that might be involved, the focus is placed on the two that are of primary importance in human social communication: the symbol system that represents the message, and the physical apparatus that embodies, transmits, and apprehends it. Together, the two are a medium. In mass communication of various sorts, they are what have come to be called *the media*. The conditions are indicated by the enclosure around the system. It serves as a reminder that all such systems exist in a wider context of social, economic, political, legal, and physical forces that influence their operation. This chapter addresses features of the components to help clarify the model and demonstrate its usefulness.

In contrast to Figure 2.1, the terms *communicator* and *communicatee* are used, respectively, for *sender* and *receiver* to reflect the primary concern with social communication. Moreover, in this model the terms designate the socially defined predominant function of the role rather than the incumbent's actual behavior at any moment during an episode under scrutiny. Hence, a communicator is one who has

# Structure and Processes

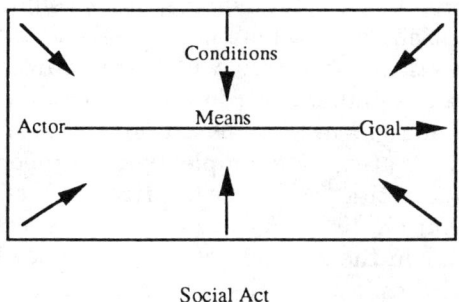

Social Act

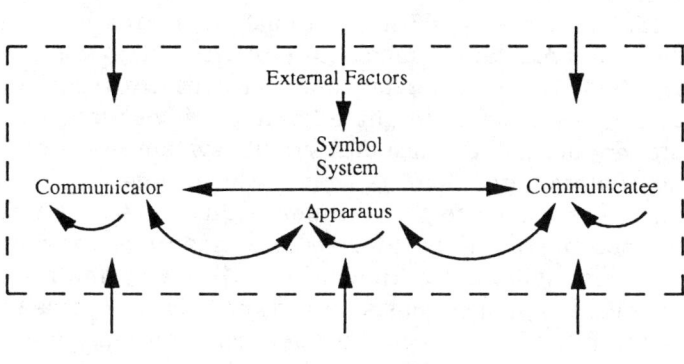

Communication System

**Figure 3.1. Models of the social act and communication system**

the status of primary initiator of messages in a system. However, in all systems that persist for any appreciable time, communicatees must reciprocate. The balance of acts initiated by communicator and communicatee—it could more properly be called the rate of role reversal—will vary from system to system. For example, contrast two university learning situations—lectures to large classes with a minimal amount of student (i.e., communicatee) comment, and seminars in which students play major roles in message initiation and the instructor may only initiate for a small portion of the time. Media systems do not permit communicatees to send to communicators as easily as does either learning situation.[2]

It should be clear from these examples that, although the status of communicator in an established system usually is defined by established conventions as to who has the legitimate right to control the flow of information, in certain widely recognized systems (e.g., conversation), the assignment of communicator and communicatee roles to the actors may have to be based on who seems to be in control. This may be indicated, for example, by the proportion of acts initiated by each actor that control the direction of the discourse (McLaughlin, 1984: chap. 3). By making the arrowhead pointing away from the actor in the communicator role somewhat larger than that pointing toward that actor, the diagram reflects the tendency in most systems of communication for one actor to occupy a role that dominates the initiation of action.

All social communication requires a system of material representational entities which, in Mead's terminology, are *significant symbols*, that is, symbols whose meanings are shared by their users. The system of significant symbols is, par excellence, a language (cf. Edwards, 1984: 16-22). Languages are essentially vocal, a circumstance that gives them a unique advantage. Speakers hear as and when listeners do. The essence of a symbol system in a working system of communication, then, is that its meanings, in the sense of appropriate responses to the symbols that serve as stimuli, are shared by the participants. Most of the meanings conventionally attached to any symbol are known by both the communicator and communicatee. Languages consist of the symbols, the forms they may take, and the rules that govern their use, combinations, and relationships. All people who speak a language do not and need not know either its total vocabulary or all its rules. Indeed, knowledge and use of the vocabulary and grammar of any language usually varies over the geographic areas in which the language is spoken and along lines of significant dimensions of social differentiation (e.g., age, gender, social class, race) within the group for which the language is native. Particularly relevant to an understanding of the media is that languages also adjust to the settings in which they are used, a phenomenon captured in Bell's (1991) study of media language. The effective symbol system for the participants in a specific communication system, then, is something less than the entire symbol system of the larger social group to which they belong. Moreover, members of subgroups who have associated for some time also may invent and share new symbols that are unknown to others in the larger social group (e.g., the private expressions used in such intimate and exclusive groups as courting couples, families, gangs, fraternities).[3]

The *physical apparatus* is a term I use to refer to all the mechanisms employed to externalize ideas as messages, convey them between actors, apprehend them, and internalize them. They include both parts of the body (e.g., mouth, eyes, ears) and any of the mechanisms that have been contrived to extend the body's range in time and space (e.g., radio transmitter, television receiver, movie projector, printing press).[4] They also include the materials in which the symbols are embedded after they are externalized and at least until they are internalized (e.g., air, paper, film, video screen). As distinguished from the symbol system, for which sharing and equality in use are the essential features, the physical apparatus is characterized by specialization and differentiation. Ordinarily, occupants of the two roles do not use the same apparatus for the same purpose at the same time. The speaker speaks with a mouth and the hearer listens with ears; the writer uses hands and a pen or a word processor and the reader uses eyes; the telecaster operates a transmitter and the viewer a receiver or monitor. Even when the acting units are people in a face-to-face situation with all their physical equipment intact, each uses that equipment in a specialized and differentiated fashion when playing the communicator and communicatee roles. The same applies to the telephone.

One important variable dimension of this functional differentiation is whether actors have access to both the sending and receiving apparatus employed in the system. In many common systems they do, and specialization is exhibited only in the fact that who uses what is determined by the role being executed (e.g., both participants in a conversation have a mouth and ears, but each uses only the complementary organ at any given moment). In others, and the media generally fit this category, the apparatus is inflexibly tied to only one of the participants and restricts people to their roles. That type of differentiation is a major reason for the important power differences among system participants. Recent innovations in electronic technology that facilitate interactive exchanges are, in part, responsible for the thesis that mass communication, as it has been conceived traditionally, is coming to an end.

The failure to note or develop the significance of apparatus specialization has been an important constraint on the development of a more powerful theory of mass communication. For example, one major source of both social distance in communication and inequities in power among persons who might otherwise be equals is the differentiated nature of the physical apparatus and, relatedly, the differences in skills and resources associated with its use. Skill and knowledge differences breed differences in power. The technology for message formatting and transmission in all mass media systems has been particularly expensive and esoteric. The implied wealth and expertise this has lent to mass communicators help contribute to their social influence by giving them an aura of glamour and prestige that their actual activities might not give them if understood by average people. For similar reasons, this helps lend a mystique to the entire system.

## SOME VARIABLE QUALITIES IN A SYSTEM OF COMMUNICATION

A simple enumeration of the minimal components that comprise an adequate model of a system of communication does not provide a basis for analysis. Other concepts that specify critical attributes of working systems must be introduced. Among those it is useful to consider are activity-passivity, feedback, noise, redundancy, messages, capacity, and compatibility. Feedback, noise, redundancy, and capacity are adapted from information theory usage.[5]

### Activity-Passivity

The characteristic way in which a system of communication normally operates can be referred to as its state. Changes in that state can originate from forces outside (exogenous) or inside (endogenous) the system. Exogenous factors that can change a system are innumerable. Some that have major roles in shaping the mass media will be considered in more detail later. Endogenous change is possible because all but one of the components of a system is capable of self-generated change. If the term *active* is applied to components that can change their state without outside intervention and the term *passive* to those that change only through the intervention of other agents, then the communicator, communicatee, and apparatus are active, and the symbol system is passive.

Although communicator and communicatee role occupancy and the predominant behavior expected of them remain unchanged over relatively long periods of time, role execution does change as the actors' behavior changes. This is the case regardless of whether roles are preassigned in institutionalized situations or established by the patterned behavior of actors in previously unstructured relationships that have become routine. In addition to the fact that playing a role is an intense activity that is performed differently by different persons as well as by the same person over time, for relatively brief periods role alternations usually are independent of external factors. Of course, in communication situations that are not yet governed by predefined roles or in which patterned behavior has yet to develop, behavior alterations that signify role changes also are actor instigated. Moreover, conventional behavior may vary either at the whim of actors or through inadvertent errors in performing roles.

The importance of the communicatee in this regard, especially if role incumbency is volitional, is crucial. In view of the fact that in democratic systems individuals need not play roles in mass communication unless they wish to, people's unwillingness to accept or continue in the role of communicatee is a major factor in the failure of media systems. Often overlooked is the fact that frustrated or disillusioned communicators also are free to leave that role with similar consequences for the system. This is not to deny that various combinations of social, economic, and political forces converge to reinforce role occupancy, but that is not unique to the communicator role in communication systems. Such pressures apply to all social roles—spouses, parents, employees, employers, students, teachers, and so on. The point is that there is no general requirement to retain those roles in communication systems and usually no significant enforceable sanctions for leaving them. Moreover, this applies even more to media systems, whose audience members are completely free to desist and whose producers are equally free to discontinue (e.g., newspapers that cease publishing often give only one day's notice).

The physical apparatus is also an active component of a communication system. Although it is tempting to treat human and technical transmission and reception equipment as passive—as controlled and operated by the actors—actor control is only partial. Involuntary changes in the nerves and muscles, for example, occur without the actor's control. Mechanical equipment changes as parts wear out or malfunction, and such changes may occur without either manipulation by persons in the system or the intervention of other agents. Parts wear out, and a radio transmitter or receiver no longer works. A linotype machine malfunctions and "shrdlu" appears. Sound engineers push to the limits of their knowledge and still the equipment adds elements that distort sound. In the dynamics of a system, the quality of performance is at least to some degree a function of the extent to which the physical apparatus deviates from standards set and/or anticipated by the actors involved. To that extent the apparatus and its contribution to the communication process is self-controlled rather than controlled by other factors. In this regard it is appropriate to note how quickly telecasters attribute the loss of sound or picture to changes in the state of the equipment (e.g., mechanical failures or breakdowns) beyond their control rather than to human error.

The symbol system is the one inert element in a communication system. It is incapable of self-generated change. It can neither add nor delete nor alter the meanings of symbols. It can never introduce an unexpected quality to performance to which other elements must respond or adjust. It can only be used or changed by its users. In monitoring the performance of a system, then, activity by a symbol system can be ignored. During relatively short periods it is a constant. The potentialities of symbols vary from system to system (e.g., compare the impact of a frown on the telephone or on television), a fact for which knowledgeable actors adjust their behavior. However, symbol meaning in a context never changes without either changes in one or more of the other three elements and/or consensual action by both the communicator and the communicatee to change symbols and their meanings. As a consequence, internal self-regulating feedback mechanisms may exist or be created for three of the components but not for the symbol system.

## *Feedback*

No system can persist without feedback mechanisms. A feedback mechanism, in much the same sense in which it is used in information theory, is any element in the structure of a system that functions to monitor or regulate the performance of any part of or the entire system. Feedback mechanisms are identified by their role in adjusting performance within the system—not by any distinctive structural features. An audience rating, for example, is such a mechanism if it guides program changes, but it is not if it is used only to plan program promotions. It is axiomatic that systems with no feedback eventually collapse because they are unable to adjust to changes in their environments. Similarly, systems that devote all their resources to feedback fail because they produce nothing. Energy and activity are used up in self-regulation; there is no product. To survive, systems must achieve an effective balance of resources between feedback and production.

Feedback mechanisms and levels vary markedly among types of communication systems. This is obvious from the contrast between the amounts and types of feedback in mass communication and interpersonal conversation. Time and space relations in the systems and the feedback opportunities they afford clearly differ. Feedback is instantaneous and almost unavoidable in face-to-face conversation. The communicatee need do nothing intentionally to provide feedback; the communicator can use the communicatee's facial expressions or other gestures. Furthermore, speech gives the communicator the opportunity to hear the message as the communicatee hears it, which may not be the case when the message is channeled through an intervening mediating apparatus. Johnson and Klare (1962: 158) noted that, "As the audience becomes further removed from the speaker the standard measurement becomes more obscure and so does the application of the feedback analogy."

Very low feedback is the rule in mass communication and creates severe problems for media systems. This condition has several sources. First, the differentiated and specialized apparatuses isolate communicator from communicatee. Ordinarily feedback cannot be channeled back through the same apparatus used to receive the original communication (although some receiving mechanisms now also can be used to send). Except in special cases (e.g., QUBE-like systems, viewing panels), television viewers cannot contact telecasters with responses to their shows quickly. A viewer's main alternative is to find another means to convey a response. More generally, mass media systems provide no readily available, rapid, institutionalized means for communicatees to respond to communicators. Although many media provide some mechanism for a few communicatees to respond to their performance (e.g., "letters to the editor" sections in newspapers and magazines, "talk" shows on radio stations), the large majority of communicatees either do not have this opportunity or are not aggressive or motivated enough to take advantage of what is available.[6] Often the only type of feedback that is truly effective is the mobilized public opinion that develops on matters that become general public issues.

A second factor that affects the feedback potential of the mass media is the characteristic qualities of a mass (later considered in more detail). Because members of the mass come from all social strata, true mass media must cater to a wide variety of interests to survive. But this necessarily reduces feedback potential. Because a mass does include such diverse backgrounds, interests, and goals, the increase of feedback beyond a certain point (given that it is used to make adjustments) may introduce so many complications and competing demands on the system that its costs may far outweigh its benefits.

Finally, because mass communication systems do not readily allow an easy give and take and the heterogeneity of the mass maximizes the diversity of the few responses, there is always uncertainty as to which messages have value as feedback. Are ten letters to the editor enough to force a change on the part of the communicator organization, or does it take something more, or less? It was said that in the early days of radio soap operas a single letter from a loyal listener was sufficient to trigger a plot change. As a result of the felt need of mass communicators for some reliable standardized type of feedback, various indirect measures of the quantity of "consumption" of each medium and responses to the material have been developed. Magazines, newspapers, radio, and television all rely on various forms of such media research to measure the size, composition, and reactions of audiences.

Media research that provides a sampling of responses to the material being produced is the only standardized means so far available for this purpose. At best, however, it is only partially adequate for getting useful feedback owing to the tendency to focus on what communicatees dislike so much that they may ignore or actively avoid the material (e.g., program, feature column, motion picture, advertisement). Because media research typically tends to provide communicatees with information on what to avoid, it has not been a vehicle for learning what would be well received. In the absence of such clues, media decision makers characteristically tend not to innovate but simply to avoid material similar to what is failing and to copy successes.[7] Media research may become a much more effective feedback tool as the techniques that have been developed for rapid telephone surveys during political campaigns are adapted and practical receiving equipment with interactive capability for the audio-video media becomes more widely available.

In addition to the feedback mechanisms available to the communicator and communicatee roles, the physical apparatus usually has internal feedback devices that employ self-adjusting and self-regulating servomechanisms. Printing presses count the number of copies printed and turn themselves off when they reach a designated total; self-regulating devices are built into radio and television equipment; camera lenses adjust to changes in light and distance; and so on. Feedback relationships also exist for any combination of active elements in the system, as well as for the system as a whole. Feedback in a system, then, is not simply present or absent but varies in kind, quantity, and quality. The assessment of feedback quality requires the identification of all the points in the system potentially available for or amenable to feedback and an evaluation of performance. The crucial feedback mechanisms for systems of communication are usually those that involve the interactive adjustment of two or more components rather than those that self-regulate, for the persistence of systems usually depends less on the ability of a component to perform than on the ability of each to adjust to the others.

### *Noise*

The concept of noise also is borrowed (from information theory) and refers to intrusive factors that impair the transmission or reception of messages during communication. Weaver (Shannon and Weaver, 1949: 99), for example, defined *noise* as those things added to the signal that were not intended by the information source. Communicators may unintentionally introduce noise by their own performance. They also base that performance on how they expect other components of the system to perform. Sources of noise may be found throughout the system. In addition to arising from defects within a system (e.g., static caused by a faulty part in a radio receiver) and external sources (e.g., sun spot interference with radio reception), noise may arise from the very character of the information being conveyed (Klapp, 1986: 81-103). Weaver (Shannon and Weaver, 1949:110) said that any residual uncertainty after the signal is known is ". . . undesirable uncertainty . . . due to noise." He described the capacity of a noisy channel as equal to the maximum rate at which useful information can be transmitted over the channel (111).

Levels of noise vary in systems over time and among systems. Probably no system is noise-free. Indeed, the presence of some low level of noise may be beneficial for a system, for it may force the actors to be more alert and careful in their roles. Nonetheless, like other imaginary concepts (e.g., the friction free machine, absolute zero), the concept of a noise-free system is useful as a standard against which to evaluate performance. The seriousness of impairments created by noise is, of course, relative to generally accepted standards of performance. Expectations for quality art reproductions are much higher than for pulp comic books; expectations for cheap transistor radios are considerably less than for FM-stereo multiplex receivers. Although there are absolute limits beyond which the level of noise may totally incapacitate a system, much of its destructive effect occurs within a range that would not be totally impairing if expectations for performance were different. Schramm (1954a) reflected this thought in his concept of the "fraction of selection," which he represented as "expectation of reward/effort required." A person who expects a reward for being a communicatee in a system is much more likely to strain to receive despite noise than if this reward were not available (129). Study of the jamming of foreign broadcasts and the lengths to which people go to listen would be instructive in this regard.

The term noise immediately brings to mind such noise-like phenomena as audio static. However, other distracting elements are even more likely to be detrimental to effective transmission. Any facet of the environment of the communicatee that impairs appropriate and effective role performance induces noise in a system. From this point of view it also is useful to consider as a source of noise the fact that symbols have several meanings, for the more the meanings associated with the symbols employed in a message, the greater the likelihood of not understanding it accurately.[8] Given its many possible sources, the reduction of noise requires a multifaceted approach that simultaneously deals with technology problems, improvement of actors' role-playing skills, clarification of language, and the like.

## Redundancy

A common antidote to noise or other causes of faulty message reception is to repeat the message in the same or varied format. *Redundancy* refers to this repetition. It indicates the fraction of the message meant to represent a meaning that is unnecessary, in the sense that, were it missing, all the meaning still would be provided (Shannon and Weaver, 1949: 104).

Different types of communication systems are characterized by different levels of redundancy. It is apparent, for example, that relatively little redundancy is called for in a conversation between friends and that much more may be required during a lecture to a large economics class. The relation to feedback and noise levels is evident. When friends talk the communicator has immediate sources of feedback and there is no need for redundancy unless the communicatee indicates that the intended message has not been received, whereas the lecturer cannot monitor all of the class members' responses and they, in turn, are subject to students' norms against raising questions in class. The mass media lack even such inadequate feedback mechanisms as are provided by after-class questions or periodic examinations for large lecture classes.

Noise potential (and the associated need for redundancy) ordinarily is lower when there is no intervening technical apparatus and higher when there is. In accord with this principle, the mass media—with their low feedback rates, high noise potential, and heterogeneous aggregates of dispersed people in communicatee roles—tend to have higher redundancy levels than other systems. Furthermore, the various media (e.g., radio, newspapers, magazines, television) differ from each other in this respect. For example, sound media are more redundant than print media, because the latter enable communicatees to create individual levels of redundancy by rereading passages, whereas broadcast sound is ephemeral.

One requisite skill of professional communicators is the ability to draw on knowledge of appropriate levels of redundancy for different systems of communication. Too much redundancy creates boredom and eventually results in the loss of communicatees. Too little redundancy generates frustration and anxiety; would-be communicatees become uncertain as to whether messages were as they thought them to be. Frustration develops and the eventual outcome is the same. The effective communicator knows, to the extent possible, how to achieve the proper level of redundancy for the situation. Klapp (1986: 71-80) dealt with this issue in a more inclusive sense in his analysis of "good" and "bad" redundancy. Among the factors to be considered in arriving at an appropriate level of redundancy are the sources of noise—possible noise in the apparatus, distractibility of the communicatee, and the use of vague, new, or esoteric concepts in the messages.

The importance of success in message transfer may override concerns about too much redundancy. SOS and other emergency calls are repeated as long as help may be needed without any concern that redundancy will breed inattention or confusion. Aside from such critical material, however, redundancy may not be a viable way to assure that meanings transmitted through the mass media are received as intended. For the many reasons cited, too much redundancy can be as detrimental for them as too much feedback. An alternative solution that media critics sometimes charge them with is the avoidance or simplification of difficult material. Both tactics run severe risks of misrepresentation—the former by omission, the latter by distortion.

## *Messages*

Communication systems traffic in messages. These last paragraphs have employed the idea of a message, but not clarified what a message is. From the point of view taken here, a message is a byte of information, and messages in a social system of communication consist of chains of such bytes. To restrict the idea of the message to its information component, however, ignores some of its more important features, for the message is not just the substance of information in the ideational sense, it also is the physical embodiment of the idea in a form characteristic of a communication system. Just as the thought might be represented by other symbols, the literal message "Wish you were here" on a postcard can carry an entirely different meaning than the same words expressed directly in speech.

The physical embodiment of a message includes more than the symbols that comprise it. The symbols comprise the text, but no text exists in a vacuum. Each message exists in and is inseparable from a context. Aside from such institutionalized contexts as religion and science that prescribe their own ritual forms for messages, there is no standard message form for most ideas. Communicators create ideas and then represent them in ways that express personal styles. Different orderings of the same words, punctuation, or differences in emphasis, by themselves, may alter meaning (Doherty, 1985: 3-13, 189). It is misleading to conceive of meanings as fixed in texts that can be abstracted out of the contexts in which they are produced and consumed. For receivers, contexts include (a) sources, (b) the media in which messages are placed for externalization and conveyance, and (c) the situations in which they are received.

With respect to sources, terms such as *trustworthy-untrustworthy* exemplify the many qualities of communicators that shape how receivers treat otherwise equivalent messages. People are likelier to take as "fact" an article in *Time* than the same material in an entertainment film. As to media, Carpenter (1954) reported that he and his colleagues found it impossible to use exactly the same symbols in the same sequence when they tried, for purposes of an experiment, to construct ideationally equivalent messages to transmit through different channels. Certainly, had Orson Welles filmed "The Invasion from Mars" instead of adapting it for radio, the Mercury Theater production would never have had the same memorable impact. Finally, the circumstances of reception vary in innumerable ways. The importance of noise-generating distractions has been noted. Of more sociological relevance is the likelihood that messages will be interpreted differently if received alone or in the presence of others (e.g., a comment by a boss at a party or in the privacy of the office). Because a message is a functional product of the interaction between idea, symbol, and context, it is unlikely that any two messages are ever precisely the same.

Other aspects of the information component of the message also are conceptually troublesome. If information is taken in the strict information theory sense of a received signal that decreases uncertainty, and most of the material transmitted in social communication is not information, then most of what constitutes a message is not informative. The important roles of reinforcement, metaphor, and redundancy have been noted. Indeed, because most of the material helps participants enjoy their roles, it serves complementary system maintenance rather than communication functions.

If the definition of information were to be loosened so that the newness of each byte is relative to the needs of the participants in the system or to social standards of acceptability—that is, the criterion is whether the message is stupidly meaningless, repetitive, or trivial from the point of view of the recipient—the question would remain as to whether there is much or, indeed, any information in the message-like material conventionally transmitted in systems of mass communication. What, for example, is the information in a painting reproduced in a popular magazine, particularly if the artist claims not to know what it means and only to have responded to an impulse to paint; or what is the message in the fourth television rerun of a 25-year-old fantasy movie? In these instances communication systems are employed noncommunicatively (inasmuch as informative message transfer is absent). They simply are cases of structural equivalence in which a unit (i.e., the mass media of communication) serves something other than its ostensible function (i.e., communication). Because such uses are so common, the sociological study of communication systems must deal with both the communicative (e.g., transferring information successfully) and noncommunicative (e.g., providing status to participants) functions of communication systems, even though theories and concepts useful for understanding the former may not be useful for the latter (and vice versa).

## Capacity

Reference also has been made to the capacity and compatibility of a communication system. *Capacity* refers to a concept of quantity of system product and *compatibility* to a quality of system structure. The two are not independent but, for purposes of discussion, it is somewhat easier to begin with capacity. Capacity refers to performance limits that are manifested in several different ways. For example, each system is limited in such respects as the speed or rate at which messages can pass through it, number of messages that can be conveyed simultaneously (e.g., levels of meaning, number that can be transmitted simultaneously on the same apparatus), types of messages that can be conveyed, and length of time messages can be preserved.

The capacity limits of a system inhere in each of its components. In a communication system, the communicator, communicatee, apparatus, and symbol system each has its own capacity. System capacities also are affected by the relations among these capacities. For example, a communicator and communicatee each may know half of their group's symbol system, but their ability to exchange messages is limited by the proportion they know in common. Because system capacities are, in part, a function of these fits among parts, any system has a maximum capacity which, unless its components match perfectly, is never a simple arithmetic function of the capacity of each element. An upper bound for the maximum capacity of a system can be estimated; it can be no greater than the capacity of the weakest component.[9] For the nontechnician, this emphasizes the importance of the relational aspects of capacity. In communication engineering it leads to an emphasis on matching components with like capacities to minimize wasted potential. The nonprofessional communicator is usually more concerned with matches that accomplish message transfers and less concerned with wasted potential.

Communication systems usually operate even below the limits set by mismatches in their components simply because the capacities of the components, particularly those of the actors in the communicator and communicatee roles, are not known. In many respects it is the human element that is most difficult to estimate. Not only do individuals differ in their capacities to play those roles, but the same person's ability to perform can vary considerably through time. The limits of apparatuses and symbol systems conceivably can be known through study and experience. It is even feasible to consider measuring the capacities of communicators in systems that control access to that role and to monitor the performance of its occupants. However, except for the few systems that tightly control access to the communicatee role (e.g., highly selective colleges and universities), it is extremely difficult, perhaps impossible, to determine the capacities of all potential communicatees. When capacities are unknown, the option is not to operate at all or to operate on the basis of safe guesses. The latter, of course, depresses performance below capacity.

The impact of ignorance of capacities on the relationship between level of capacity and level of performance is especially relevant for understanding mass media systems. The media can estimate and control communicator capacities through hiring practices, performance monitoring, and training. Skilled personnel know what the equipment can do and understand the potential of symbols. However, media systems have little control over who joins their audiences. When they do acquire such information, it usually comes after the fact of message production and dissemination. Moreover, uncertainty remains as to the composition of the next audience. Therefore, members of the communicator organization must guess as to communicatee capacities. Because system survival requires attracting and retaining as many people as possible for the audience, the tendency is to estimate each potential audience member's capacity as being low. It used to be said that the Hollywood studios made films for people with a mental age of 12. Regardless of the accuracy of this assertion, the point is that ignorance of communicatee capacity in media systems usually depresses performance far below what it might be. This ignorance is exacerbated by the fact that there is so little formal training for media consumption. Given the factors that encourage drastic underestimates of the capacities of audience members, the media usually operate at even less efficient levels than the low limits caused by technical mismatches would permit.

Finally, it should be noted that being called on to perform below capacity may discourage participation in much the same fashion that too much redundancy does. Such expressions of dissatisfaction as feeling that one is being talked down to or that one's interests are not being satisfied are common expressions of the sense that one's abilities are not being recognized or challenged. Thus, as capacity estimates are deflated to attract more potential communicatees at the bottom, others may be lost from the top. From the perspective of the media, identifying the estimate that maximizes audience size is a real problem. Even if an optimum audience capacity were to be found, however, it would not alter the fact that the popular media operate far below their capacity for what might be transmitted to and understood by a skilled audience.

## Compatibility

Unlike capacity, which is an attribute that basically inheres in each component, compatibility is an attribute of the relationships between components and refers to the quality of their fit in a system. Poor fits in capacity are one example of low compatibility. Systems with four components involve 11 relationships—six between pairs, four among triplets, and one among all four. In analyzing a working system, the identity of the units involved in particular relationships may be as important in explaining how it works as the fact that the compatibility in other relationships varies. Thus, for example, spouses are much more willing to strain to hear each other over a bad telephone line than are strangers involved in an attempt at a blind sale.

This example indicates that compatibility depends on the quality of fit between each of several different attributes of the components involved. The attributes of each component of a communication system that bear on compatibility are too numerous to specify. In technologically complex systems, each relationship among the many pieces of equipment has compatibility aspects. The matching of hi-fidelity components is an appropriate example of how aspects of compatibility are recognized in the creation and maintenance of a stable and effective system. For sociologists, the relationship whose compatibility is of most interest is that among and within the actor roles and their occupants. Accordingly, the qualities that affect the relationships between participants in a communication system are of major importance. They must be central to a sociology of mass communication, which, viewed in this light, may only be a special form of a sociology of social interaction.

The importance of identifying attributes that affect the compatibility between actors cannot be overstated. They are central to hypotheses about success or failure in volitional systems of communication. In such systems there is little to constrain actors to participate should they be inclined to reject their own role, the other role, and/or the actor in the other role. What we know about interaction indicates that such attributes as personal value systems, the reference groups and self-conceptions of each, and the image each has of the other critically affect how participants interact.[10] However, an understanding of mass communication requires consideration of other factors as well. Two that are illustrative and that receive little attention are the numerical size of the groups of individuals playing the roles and the structures of those groups.

Number is particularly salient because for most people it is the large numbers of people in communicatee and communicator roles that characterize systems of mass communication.[11] These systems typically include sending organizations with tens to thousands of employees and audiences ranging from thousands to millions of receivers. It is axiomatic that mass communication systems eventually collapse when there are imbalances in the numbers playing each role. An obvious example is the failure of magazines, newspapers, television programs, and theaters when their audiences are too small. System survival requires adjustments for numerical imbalances. One person can speak to one, two, three, ten, or a hundred. At some number, however, human physical equipment becomes inadequate to the task, and some supplementary means of reaching others must be employed. The supplements eventually require more communicator personnel to serve as additional senders and/or technicians to maintain and operate the auxiliary equipment.

To explore how flexible these numerical relationships are in media systems, I have had students twice investigate the association between the number of newspaper employees and circulation. One study examined a sample of large metropolitan dailies in the United States and the other a sample of North Carolina and Virginia dailies. The relationship in each sample was linear and the correlation well over .9. Although such data show the relevance of sheer numbers of role occupants for understanding varying compatibility in the communicator-communicatee relationship, they do not begin to reveal all its nuances. For example, are all numerical ratios comparable, or are there different balances for different kinds of messages, systems, social situations, and so on? Can a teacher teach the same number of students regardless of the nature of the material? Because judgments of social value enter (e.g., we differentially evaluate the costs of message transfer for such different purposes as education and advertising), we need to know more about the relationship of values to numerical ratios that are stable because they are accepted as compatible.

Another quality of the actors in a communication system that has a major effect on whether they sustain their roles derives from their accumulated experiences in other significant social activities (e.g., family activities, work, shopping) in which they are engaged. Each of these also is structured in such respects as whether the individual can impact the process, how extensive and rapid that influence may be, the degree of completeness and formality of the relationships involved in the activity, and the norms as to appropriate styles of behavior. From these other structured relationships, communicators and communicatees bring habitual behavioral styles and expectations of others that shape their initial behavior and expectations in their roles in the new systematized relationship. That behavior and those expectations may or may not be appropriate.

These broad orientations to others and to how to behave bear directly on compatibility. Anyone who participates in a communication system must maintain at least two sets of structured relationships, one within his or her role component of the system (e.g., the employee of a television network, the member of a class, a member of a movie audience) and the other in the relationship between the two actor roles that must exist for there to be a communication system.[12] The actors' styles must permit them to get along with each other. Therefore, how well the behavioral habits and expectations derived in other key social roles fit the new situation within role groups and across roles is another factor that contributes to overall system compatibility.

Several aspects of the mass media have major impacts on how well styles derived in other important structured relationships may fit their particular communication process. First, media materials are produced in highly structured production systems. The communicator role, in effect, is occupied by a more or less bureaucratically structured organization. Therefore, the personnel generally must adapt their performance to the requirements of the organization rather than the reverse. For people who see their work as creative or the task performance requirements as unpredictable, continued participation can create great stress. Second, the media create a highly structured product. At the time of consumption, media texts are fixed. Media consumers cannot alter them, raise questions, or request more or less. Thus, occupants of both roles must be comfortable adjusting their behavior to the material, rather than the reverse. Third, role relationships between communicators and communicatees are highly structured and almost inflexible. They have all the attributes of a classic secondary relationship. Each actor participates in such a highly segmented and socially and physically distant fashion that, with few exceptions, they are unable either to learn anything about each other as whole persons or to respond to one another directly. Moreover, the system is so structured that receivers cannot enter the sender's role. This can disaffect people whose other significant activities permit or even require very different types of interactive styles. Fourth, media systems generally—film being an important exception—lack rigorous norms for communicatee behavior, whereas most other communication systems have such norms (e.g., not speaking when others do, not making noise in libraries, student norms against asking questions in class). Thus, there also may be inconsistencies when people who are in the habit of being in rule-governed communication environments lack rules as media consumers.

What makes these matters generally relevant to communication—and this is particularly pertinent to receivers—is a strain toward consistency. Most people are more comfortable when their significant relationships have similar characteristic structural features,[13] are governed by similar rules, and require similar behavior styles. If people are free to choose, they tend to disengage from or sever relationships whose requirements differ markedly from or conflict with most of their other relationships. If disengagement is difficult or impossible and the rules governing behavior are not stringently enforced, they may act in a manner appropriate for a particularly dominant or important role, regardless of its appropriateness to other settings. That latter type of adaptation is exemplified by a term such as *bureaucratic personality*, coined to describe persons who indiscriminately behave like bureaucrats in all their roles regardless of whether any particular role is a part of a bureaucracy. Most sociological conceptions of organizations summarize, among other things, the qualities that characterize the organization's key role relationships. For example, some relationships may be segmental and involve only limited aspects of a person, and others may be complete in that they engage the whole person; some may be functionally specific and others general and undifferentiated; some may be formal and others informal.

If an individual's willingness to perform successfully in an optional role is affected by its consistency and coherence with the behavioral style required by important roles in other relationships, then potential receivers who have a choice are most likely to remain in roles that call for a behavioral style consistent with that characteristically called for in their other important relationships. Analogously, the greater the consistency between the structural features of the communication system and other salient organizations, the greater the likelihood that the communicatee will persist in playing that role.[14] It is the alien character of the behavioral style of that structure for most other situations, for example, that leads to the use of the term *bureaucracy* as an epithet. The styles and behavior requirements of media systems generally are less varied and flexible than those of most other social arrangements. Because this suggests lower compatibility, it also suggests that media systems must compensate to sustain receiver participation. Simply participating, in and of itself, may not be intrinsically rewarding.

For the sociologist, then, the compatibility of the relationship between communicators and communicatees is central to understanding the workings of communication systems. The compatibility of other relationships, of course, also is important. Obviously, it matters whether the equipment fits together, calls for scarce or unavailable operator skills, or can accommodate features of the material (i.e., symbol system) to be transmitted. Nonetheless, because all communication systems are social systems, their components also are governed by formal rules and informal norms. These standards are at least as important as physical capacities and constraints in determining such aspects of system performance as who can use what equipment for what purpose, who can use what language, how loud one can play the radio, or whether certain words can be printed. Taking all these matters into consideration, it would seem that among the most important contributions sociologists can make to understanding communication generally and mass communication specifically would be to identify those qualities of the four components of these systems that significantly affect the compatibility of their relationships. Not infrequently, both the failure to communicate when an effort is made to do so and failures to produce intended effects as a consequence of communication result from communicator-communicatee incompatibility.

Compatibility between communicator and communicatee is somewhat like noise, feedback, and redundancy in that too little may lead to system failure and too much to such satisfaction that the participants relax and cease to put out the effort required for system maintenance. In this respect, viewing communication systems from a human rather than a technological perspective leads to different assessments of how these four system attributes impact on system efficiency and survival. Technologically, the relationships are simple. When there is less noise, more feedback (up to a point), less redundancy, and more compatibility in the several systemic relationships, then the system is more efficient, viable, and stronger. From a human perspective, however, each of the four has a curvilinear relationship to system efficiency, viability, and strength. Feedback is a help up to a point and beyond that it is a hindrance; some noise helps keep the participants alert, too much impairs their abilities; some redundancy eases the strain on them, too much destroys their interest; and too much compatibility may distract participants from the communication purposes of the system, but too little destroys their commitment to it. An important task for those who study communication systems is to identify the optimum level for each of these four systemic features and the relationships among them. Relatedly, are the optima the same for the many different types of human communication systems? More specifically, are the optimum levels for the four the optimum combination for a system, or is some combination of below optimum levels for some or all of them optimum; and is the same combination the optimum for any system, or does each type of system have its own optimum?

## ALTERNATIVE MODELS OF COMMUNICATION SYSTEMS

This model of a communication system may be compared with several others in various respects, for example, how their basic components differ, whether they attempt to deal with all the major factors that affect the communication process or emphasize only one or a few, their potential for defining communication systems and generating hypotheses, and whether they can be employed to differentiate among systems of communication. Among the models considered in these respects are those of Schramm (1954a), Shannon and Weaver (1949), Berlo (1960), Riley and Riley (1959), Westley and MacLean (1966), and Hartley and Hartley (1952), as well as several others. They are treated here as formal models, although they are not all offered as such.

Of the models surveyed, none are comprised of the four components used here—communicator, communicatee, apparatus, and symbol system. Schramm, for example, identified source, message, and destination as the prime elements. Berlo identified these same three and added the channel over which messages are carried. Neither treated the symbol system as a separate component. The Hartleys, although they did not posit a full model, identified the communicator, communicant, and communique. The Rileys concentrated on the communicator, receiver, the feedback between the two, and the larger social system of which they are a part. Shannon and Weaver identified the information source and destination and then elaborated what I term the *apparatus* into transmitter, channel, and receiver.

Each model identified different components of a system of communication as basic because each developed from different notions about the important factors in communication success or failure. A number looked specifically to the human behavioral component and emphasized explicitly or implicitly the importance of encoding and decoding processes and, more broadly, the processes of conception and perception. For example, Schramm suggested that the source and receiver must encode and decode messages, but that they can only do this within the limits of their own experience. Implied is that communication success is a function of the extent to which fields of experience overlap. This is but one facet of communicator-communicatee compatibility in my conceptualization. Berlo also included an encoding and decoding component. His conception of communication "fidelity" led him to look to the skills, attitudes, knowledge levels, and sociocultural systems of the communicator and communicatee to explain communication success or failure. These, too, are facets of communicator-communicatee compatibility. Without explicitly discussing encoding and decoding processes, the Hartleys suggested that the major problem in communicating is to translate one's experience into symbols that can be perceived accurately by a communicant. This same problem has been a central concern for Johnson (1953) and Hulett (1966). Shannon and Weaver had quite another emphasis. They attributed the success or failure of communication to qualities of the transmission and the information value of the message. Problems are not specifically related to the roles of the communicator and communicatee (or source and destination in their terms), although low information value can result in system breakdown, in the terms used here, if it disaffects participants from their roles.

Most of these other models neither identify nor develop the implications of the variable qualities of communication systems systematically. Some consider feedback, noise, redundancy, capacity, or compatibility, but only in passing, and, when they do, relate them only to one or two components of the model. Schramm, for example, briefly mentioned feedback and redundancy, but only in relation to the roles of the source and destination. Shannon and Weaver developed concepts of noise, redundancy, and capacity more completely than did the others, but only with respect to factors employed in actual message transmission. They did not note that communicators and communicatees also might have capacities. Berlo briefly discussed feedback and then rejected it for the concept of "empathy," which makes it even more clearly a process involving only the communicator and communicatee. He did not develop the idea that the apparatus might also have feedback mechanisms essential to the functioning of the system.

All conceptual systems, including this one, are models and, therefore, partial and distorted. Their value depends on their utility. Obviously, the potential utility of this model should be at least as great as that of these others if, as this brief overview emphasizes, these other models share two weaknesses that this one addresses. First, most simply failed to identify or deal with all the major elements involved in the process of communication. As a consequence, hypotheses to account for communication success or failure are restricted unduly. Second, none of the models considered provided a basis for distinguishing among systems of communication. For example, they offered no means to differentiate face-to-face conversation from the mass media as stable types of systems. Westley and MacLean came closest when they suggested adding to Newcomb's ABX notion a C who plays a "gatekeeper" function between A and B in the situation of mass communication. In short, most of the models catalogued components deemed essential in all communication systems, but omitted features that would help differentiate among the various types of them systematically, a potential of this model that is addressed next.

## NOTES

1. If not already apparent, it should be clear that this discussion has many features in common with Habermas's (1979: chap. 1) elaboration of "communicative action."
2. Motivated by the emerging possibilities of such role reversals in newer machine-mediated systems, Rafaeli (1988) has proposed "interactivity" as a concept to describe this aspect of all systems, feeling that it varies sufficiently among systems to be a major dimension on which to classify them. In essence, his concept captures what I have called role reversal. Rafaeli's concept is deficient from a sociological standpoint, however, in that, although it does serve to focus on role changes during a course of action, it fails to draw attention to the socially defined statuses that give their incumbents the attributes that often define how systems work. Knowing that a person is a publisher and that a letter writer to the newspaper is a reader tells us much that is in addition to what the two are doing in a particular instance reveals. How statuses in a system shape public recognition and acceptance is as important as the behavior of incumbents for understanding the contemporary media, a point that merits repeated emphasis.
3. Because of its brevity and its purpose of highlighting certain features of the media, this discussion of language obviously cannot begin to convey the richness of scholarship on the subject. For two particularly insightful and suggestive discussions that consider aspects of language that are pertinent to important mass communication issues, see Elias (1991) and Jansen (1988: chap. 9).
4. Most analyses do pay at least some attention to technology. For example, Thayer (1968: 261) equated media with "hardware," and Postman (1985: 84) said that ". . . a technology is a physical apparatus. . . ." In contrast, Thayer called a "medium" in use a "channel" and Postman called a technology in use a "medium." In using the term *medium* for a system, I am closer to Postman. Thayer (1968: 253-254), incidentally, used *technology* as an all embracing term that even includes language. Here, language is referred to as the *symbol system*.
5. A succinct and clear discussion of most of these qualities in the more technical language of information theory and engineering may be found in a review chapter by Maley (1979).
6. The disproportionate influence of television ratings on programming is a symptom of the desperately felt need for feedback in the absence of communicatee response. Ratings exemplify the sorts of extraneous mechanisms that may be grafted onto communication systems to compensate for the absence of natural or intrinsic feedback mechanisms.
7. Turow's (1984b: 77) analysis of unconventional television programs began by characterizing most programming as "patterned and derivative."
8. Metaphor is the classic technique for reducing noise inherent in such symbols.

9. In a sense, the chain is no stronger than its weakest link.
10. For a discussion of the importance of some of these phenomena (especially reference groups) to editors of newspapers in small cities and towns, see Breed (1955a). It is easy to see in his discussion how such factors affect compatibility. Davis and Robinson (1989) have attributed disinterest in and apathy toward the news to major discrepancies in education between news professionals and the general public (see also Becker, Brewer, Dickinson, and Magee, 1985; Schudson, 1988; Thayer, 1988: 72-73 and fn. 38).
11. The impact of numbers on the stability of relationships was a topic of early sociological interest (cf. Simmel, 1950: 87-104) that had a brief resurrection with the flurry of interest in small groups during the 1950s. Recent interest in organizational ecology and the work of Blau (1977) have brought a renewed awareness of number as a group attribute with a critical impact on structure and the stability of relationships between groups.
12. A group dynamics T-group exemplifies a communication system with the most unstructured role relationships possible. Almost any other social system appropriate for communication is more highly structured, but all will differ in formality, frequency of role changes, extent of exposure, and the like.
13. This applies to other people as well as to situations. As Meyrowitz has noted (1985: 28), "Even with our friends, we expect some general consistency of style and behavior."
14. For further discussion of the notion of structural consistency, see Lazarsfeld (1948: 219) and Merton (1949: 47-53). For a research application of the principle, see Smith (1954).

# 4

# Systems of Mass Communication

An analytic model is an abstracted description of a segment of reality that should be useful for engineering, generating hypotheses, and elaborating definitions. With respect to engineering a workable system of communication, it identifies the necessary components. It does not state the form these components must take—only those that are minimally necessary and the minimum conditions that must be met. To explain system limitations or failure, hypotheses about minimum conditions that may not have been met can be specified (analogous to an engineering function). An apt analogy is a mechanic diagnosing a problem by running through a checklist.

## DIFFERENTIATING SYSTEMS OF COMMUNICATION

A model serves a definitional function in two ways. First, it defines (in its terms) a system of communication. It says that any entity with those attributes is a system of communication, and, conversely, that any system of communication has those features. As Mowlana (1990:

91) put it, "To distinguish a mass communication system from other social systems, we need to identify its main units." That essentially is the point of the discussion in the two preceding chapters. Second, by specifying the "values" of the variable components, the model also defines various *types* of communication systems. Thus, it distinguishes public lectures, radio programs, and telephone conversations in terms of the variable qualities of common components. Table 4.1 illustrates this with communication systems at three different levels of size and distance: interpersonal or face-to-face conversation, a seminar situation (as with a professor and students), and mass communication systems generally. A similar exercise also distinguishes among the several mass media.[1]

The cases in Table 4.1 are at different levels of generality. Seminars, for example, are only a type of instructional system; in contrast, all the media are treated as a single case. In fact, each term for a component element or variable quality of communication systems (left-hand stubs of Table 4.1) can refer not only to general types (e.g., mass communication), but also to such increasingly specific phenomena as a medium (e.g., newspapers), a unit in that medium set (e.g., *New York Times*), a specific instance of the unit (e.g., the *New York Times* of June 12, 1969), or an approximation of an act (e.g., a sentence or paragraph in an item). Differences in the level of generality of units being considered clearly are a major problem in formulating general propositions about mass communication (particularly for synthesizing propositions about effects).

Although each type always could be differentiated further, here they are treated only at very general levels. The fact that the media column in Table 4.1 is a generalization for the several media already has been noted. But this applies to the other two columns as well. Two-person conversations are only a special type of all small group conversations, but two-person conversations between friends, strangers, or family members are all somewhat different. Seminars also may be only one type of the more general class of teaching-learning situations, but seminars in different fields, for participants at different levels of training, or on different topics, all differ. Hence, the entries in the cells of the table must be seen as estimates of weighted averages across all the subtypes beneath the level selected to sharpen the contrasts.

Different systems need not vary in every feature specified by the model in order to be distinct (e.g., both conversations and seminars typically have a communicator role occupied by only one person). With respect to definition, if this process of specification were to be applied to all conventionally recognized types of communication systems, we would have both compiled definitions of each system and

## Systems of Mass Communication

**Table 4.1. Differentiation of Sample Types of Communication Systems**

| | Two-Person Conversation | University Seminar | Mass Media of Communication |
|---|---|---|---|
| **Communicator** | One | One | Structured group (not necessarily integrated except for business purposes) |
| **Communicatee** | One | Small Group | "Mass" (heterogeneous, non-interacting, etc.) or audience (homogeneous, etc.) (?) |
| | —Numerical relationships fixed by definition— | | |
| **Apparatus** | Human (ears, eyes, voice) | Human | Human and electronic or mechanical |
| **Symbol System** | Relatively personally esoteric | Relatively topically esoteric | Common to nearly all; simple; general |
| **Feedback** | High potential from many sources (language, gestures, expression); has incapacitating potential | High, but not as dependent on individual; collective feedback is more important | Low; largely through indirect channels; relatively few are involved |
| **Noise** *Message* | Low, or else termination of communication | Varies by communicatee | Relatively low because of redundancy check |
| *Technical or transmitting* | Only human physical handicaps | Only human physical handicaps | Infrequent transmitter or receiver failures |
| *Environment* | Variable | Low, except for infrequent and uncontrollable external sources | Varies with medium: low for film; variable for others |

## Table 4.1. Differentiation of Sample Types of Communication Systems (cont.)

| | | Two-Person Conversation | University Seminar | Mass Media of Communication |
|---|---|---|---|---|
| **Redundancy** | | Low; use only as needed | Moderate amount (potentially high feedback reduces need) | High (print somewhat lower) |
| **Capacity** | | High | High | Low (open nature of system permits many mismatches) |
| **Compatibility** | Social Homogeneity | High, based on mutual selection | High, based on mutual interest and shared esoterica | Low, sender-receiver interests unbalanced; social status diverse |
| | Component Match* | ? | ? | ? |

*Differentiating communication systems with respect to compatibility is difficult. Social homogeneity and component match are used as two illustrative dimensions. If the elements of the system (e.g., communicator and communicatee) are alike with respect to some social characteristic that enhances communication, they might be considered socially homogeneous. It is relatively easy to differentiate communication systems along these lines. The match among components is taken as a second indicator of compatibility. This refers to how well the parts of elements of the system "fit" together. A deaf person as a communicatee and a radio as an apparatus are incompatible elements. Question marks are entered because there are so many variable relationships in a communication system.

## Systems of Mass Communication

indicated the most important features that distinguish them. Whether all the components that comprise the model are necessary for these purposes is a question that may be answered only when these attributes of all major systems have been specified. In any event, if the model is to be useful, there is some benefit in making the component terms of system definitions comparable. It is to be hoped that this eventually will be possible, and that Carey (1988) referred only to the present, but not necessary, state of affairs in expressing the view that ". . . concepts and methods, which, if inadequate, are at least unembarrassing, when applied to interpersonal communication prove hapless and even a little silly when applied to the mass media" (69).

The material in Table 4.1 highlights a feature of mass communication systems that merits special emphasis. The identification of a portion of reality as a system inevitably requires working at a fairly high level of abstraction—a skill most of us think of as limited to theorists, unaware that we all do it routinely. We have no difficulty in shifting our thoughts between such specifics and generalities as particular persons, friends, people we know, neighbors, Americans, human beings. We know our car, that model car (e.g., Nova), that make car (e.g., Chevrolet), that corporation's cars (e.g., GM cars), domestic cars (as distinct from foreign cars), automobiles, and means of transportation. We move deftly between general and specific, narrow and broad classes, concrete and abstract—so long as we are not aware of having to do it. Similarly, we readily think about complex entities holistically—a meal, regardless of the number and type of courses, is a meal, not a snack—or we treat them as systems, complex entities of component elements linked by regularized rules and relationships (i.e., a meal as comprised of a fixed number of courses balanced for taste and nutritional value and served in a fixed sequence in an appropriate setting with appropriate utensils and service procedures). The point is that any element of a system itself may be treated as a system if looked at more closely and with little concern for the other elements — a work team building a car in a Volvo factory is both a single production unit within a factory system and a self-contained system in its own right.

In analogous fashion, it should be clear that a system of mass communication is a system of systems. We tend to think about and treat communicator and communicatee as unitary entities when analyzing the process of communication in a system. Nonetheless, they are collective terms whose referents are complex, organized systems, and any but the most simplistic analysis of differences among or changes in communication systems must deal with changes and differences in these component systems. The other two components—symbol systems and apparatus—also are systems. Indeed, in the first case the term designates them as systems, for they are varying collections of signs with symbolic value, the use of each being governed by its own set of rules. The apparatus, likewise, is a system. I have noted, for example, mechanisms of self-control (analogous to thermostats in climate control systems), or how the capacities of apparatus components match and affect their compatibility.

There should be no confusion. The principle applies to any system of communication, not just systems of mass communication. Even in dealing with conversations—one of the most elementary arrangements for interpersonal communication—the persons themselves can be considered systems, each sender utilizing and coordinating different skills and body parts to conceive and encode messages and each receiver doing the same to perceive and decode them. Analogies for apparatus are easily imagined and symbols are in systems by definition. The principle, then, governs the available spectrum—from person to person to group to group. Any communication system is a system of systems.

It may be possible and even useful to ignore this fact when trying to comprehend the minimal essentials for a communication act. However, the attention given certain variable features of systems—feedback, noise, compatibility—is explained, in part, by their pertinence to conditions that must be satisfied to keep a system of systems coherent and operating. Furthermore, it needs to be emphasized that, for questions concerning the ongoing operation of a system in which mixtures of acts of several types continually occur, it also is necessary to analyze in some detail features of the internal structure and workings of at least some, if not all, of the component systems. In analyzing mass communication, therefore, one must focus at least as much on components of the system as on the system as a whole.

## THE DISTINGUISHING FEATURES OF THE DIFFERENT MASS MEDIA

The need to focus on components of a system as well as on the system as a whole is even clearer when contrasting systems of the same type. Because systems of the same type (e.g., newspapers, magazines, television, radio, motion pictures) are much more similar than systems of different types (e.g., those in Table 4.1), both the dimensions and units of measurement for describing components must be more finely tuned. Here, it accounts for the differences in terminology in the comparable cells of Tables 4.1 and 4.2. In Table 4.1, for example, the terms represent an estimated average tendency for all media as contrasted with the two alternatives selected. In Table 4.2, the con-

**Table 4.2. Differentiation of Selected Media Systems**

| | | Print | | Electronic | | |
|---|---|---|---|---|---|---|
| | | Big City Newspaper | National Magazine | Local Radio Station | Television Network | Large Film Producer |
| **Communicator** | Size | Intermediate-stable | Intermediate-stable | Smallest-stable | Largest-variable | Large-variable |
| | Organization | Least complex-chain relationships | Least complex-corporate ties | Least complex-corporate ties | Highly complex-corporate ties | Highly complex-corporate ties |
| **Communicatee** | Size | Large-stable | Large-stable | Smallest-stable | Very large- varies with program | Varies widely with film |
| | Composition | Population cross-section, higher status bias | Homogeneous interest group, higher status bias | Homogeneous, status differentiated | Most heterogeneous and dispersed | Highly selective on age and interest clustered |
| **Apparatus** | | Simple-electronic composing and printing, human for communicatee | Simple-electronic composing and printing, human for communicatee | Simple-electronic transmitting and receiving, mobile | Complex-electronic transmitting and receiving, somewhat mobile | Complex, cumbersome |
| **Symbol System** | | Most generally esoteric | Most topically esoteric | Common, simple, esoteric for audience | Common, simple | Varies with film |
| **Feedback** | | Low- easily established if motivated, fast response possible | Low- easily established if motivated, fast response possible | Low- easily established if motivated, fast response possible | Low- somewhat difficult, response delayed | Low- most indirect and unusable |

**Systems of Mass Communication**

**Table 4.2. Differentiation of Selected Media Systems (cont.)**

| | | Print | | Electronic | | |
|---|---|---|---|---|---|---|
| | | Big City Newspaper | National Magazine | Local Radio Station | Television Network | Large Film Producer |
| *Message* | | Variable with items and proofing | Low, because of audience selectivity | Low | Variable with program | Low, because of audience selectivity |
| Noise | *Technical or transmitting* | Low | Lowest | Low | Infrequent, except for remote transmission | Low |
| | *Environment* | Variable | Low | Low | Variable | Lowest |
| Redundancy | | Low | Lowest | High | Highest | High |
| Capacity | | High | Highest | Lowest | Intermediate, because of symbol mix | High, because of symbol mix and audience selectivity |
| Compatibility | *Social Homogeneity* | Intermediate, depends on whether ownership is local | High, on basis of shared interests | Highest | Lowest | Lowest |
| | *Component Match* | High, on an item basis | Highest | Varies with quality of transmission | Lowest | Varies with film and exhibition locale |

trast is only among the five media, the reference points for the contrasts shift, and, hence, the descriptive terms are altered.

With respect to dimensions, using communicators as an example, number alone can not highlight differences. All the media employ relatively large, organized groups as communicators. Such other attributes as location and organizational structure also must be considered. The need to refine also applies to measurement. For example, adjectives are adequate to contrast the sizes of communicatee groups in conversations, seminars, and the media, but inadequate for the very large media communicatee groups. For them, number counts are necessary. In addition to more detailed specifications, interdependencies among components also must be examined in comparing systems of the same type. After all, they are what distinguish a system from a mere collection of elements. In many instances a component can only be assessed in terms of the quantity or quality of another (e.g., the dependency between sizes of communicator and communicatee groups, and between both of these and the costs of both production and distribution technology).

Three other matters also complicate comparisons of the media. First, characterizations vary with the inclusiveness or specificity of the unit and the aspect of the communication process being considered. Location provides a good case in point. Each medium, taken in totality, is a national industry. Daily newspapers, because they are published, circulated, and named locally, may seem to be exceptions, but they, too, are national inasmuch as they use nationally syndicated features and national wire services, hire professionals in national labor markets, and often are owned by national and even transnational corporations. Distribution (except for magazines, which arrive through the mail if not purchased at local outlets) and consumption, however, are local activities. These locale variations for different stages of the mass communication process have major direct consequences for system compatibility and efforts at control and indirect consequences for feedback and redundancy. Therefore, some aspects of media comparison must be tied to the stages of that process.

Second, the media change continually. As a consequence, popular conceptions of them usually mix features from several different periods. These conceptual lags earlier were alluded to as the legacy of mass communication. Examples abound. Laymen often are unaware of decentralization and still think of feature films as being made in Hollywood (Edgerton, 1986), or of the major newspaper chains as being owned by Scripps-Howard or Hearst. Indebtedness for outmoded technology impedes innovation. Perhaps the most important lag is the view that the media are "mass." Such persistent stereotypes, regardless of their accuracy, cannot be ignored in analyzing media differences because they shape significant behavior (e.g., communicatee and communicator actions toward each other, efforts to alter the process of control).

Third, with the passage of time our image of each medium and what it is like in reality diverge. Moreover, the differences among the media also change. At inception, each of the five media had major distinctive characteristics, for example, in the employment of print, sound, or both, in the time required to produce and transmit, and in areas and methods of distribution. As a consequence, they also differed in the immediacy of their material, in who could produce for or consume them, in conditions of consumption, and the like. In many respects, each responded to its predecessors' deficiencies. Since the introduction of television, however, the trend has reversed. Instead of perpetuating the differences that account for the characteristic advantages and disadvantages of each medium, new technologies are reducing them, for example, motion pictures can be viewed at home, newspapers and magazines layouts reflect television programming styles, and cable television prints the news. The combination of sound and illustration deemphasizes the importance of reading skill as a filter for media use. As a consequence, all the media are becoming both more immediate and simultaneously national and local. Multimedia ownership by corporate conglomerates fuels this trend. Thus, comparisons that emphasize the uniqueness of media systems may only be noting some transitory features.

A consideration of the circumstances at the time that the technology used by each medium was developed sheds light on the habit of associating print media with information and audiovisual media with entertainment. Print is an extension of writing. Writing surmounts the time and space limitations of oral communication; print increases the speed and quantity of production and standardizes the appearance of writing. In a sense, both developed in response to a need to preserve and distribute information. The Bible, poetry and drama, philosophy and theology, chronicles of warfare, and records of censuses, of tax rolls, and of legal codes preexisted print and were waiting to be recorded and distributed. As presses improved, political tracts and commercial information were printed. Each improvement in printing expanded capacity and eventually created excess capacity to produce and store information. This trend was accelerated by subsequent audiovisual innovations. By the time they appeared there was no backlog of material. Unlike print, the audiovisual media did not develop primarily in response to unmet needs for storing and sharing information. Rather, and particularly in the case of film, technology was the product, and material had to be found to generate a demand for it. Given those circumstances, audiovisual media have had a voracious appetite for material whose most crucial quality is the ability to attract consumers. In our parlance, entertainment value has taken priority over information value.

Despite the numerous reasons that summarized contrasts of the different media systems are very difficult to formulate and may be misleading, I offer an example of what they might look like in Table 4.2. It is modeled as closely as possible to match Table 4.1. As was the case with Table 4.1, the media units are not at the same level of generality. To have done that would have required much more elaborate and complex cell entries. The extended commentary on the similarities and differences among the five established media—chosen because they are the media that gave rise to and sustained the mass communication concept—that follows is meant to remedy that deficiency. It reviews the four system components and then offers several propositions that summarize relationships among the processes and conditions (e.g., feedback, noise, redundancy) and how each of the media perform. As appropriate, national and local cable and over-the-air television and radio stations and networks are distinguished. A discussion by category is only a matter of convenience, however, for, as Mowlana has observed (1990: 91), "[T]he operation of no one part of the mass media system and process can be fully understood without reference to the way in which the whole itself operates; or to put it more succinctly, no part of the mass media system stands alone...."

**Communicators.** With few exceptions, media communicators are corporate entities that employ anonymous personnel to perform a variety of specialized tasks. Radio and television personalities (e.g., news anchors, talk show hosts, featured players) appear to speak for themselves, but, if for no other reason than financial interest, with few exceptions they are agents of corporations. These visible agents require support from numerous unseen others who not only operate equipment, acquire revenue, distribute the product, and attend to organizational and legal matters, but very often also formulate the messages. All media organizations are staffed by nonvisible personnel, most of whose contributions to the transmitted material are not known to or understood by the receivers. In this respect most media communicators are drastically different. In most other communication systems, the identifiable source of a message usually is expressing him- or herself. Why this practice among the media? In view of the fact that the message is the product of an anonymous staff, why do they not simply print, appear, or speak without identification?

The traditional media are industries that wrestle continually with what they perceive to be a need to establish a personalized relationship with the individuals in their markets. They strive to seem to offer precisely the essence of personal social relationships: communication as exchange with no immediately apparent cost.[2] If successful, they involve people in what Horton and Wohl (1956) called parasocial interaction. To accomplish this, I have argued (1954), they must develop and rely on what I called personalizability, that is, a capacity to be treated as a person. The tactics used to implement this vary by medium,[3] but all employ appealing individuals as human faces to the public and, thereby, achieve a semblance of humanity. Two of several conditions that must be met to succeed may be noted: (a) the representation should be stable, that is, if many unknown people are used irregularly, the tactic is likely to fail; and (b) receivers should be able to feel that they know a lot about the representative. If representatives are never seen and/or never reveal anything personal, personification is not likely to succeed. The more that is revealed, the greater the success.

With respect to individual media, newspapers credit columnists and some reporters, although most readers are only familiar with the former.[4] Given the need to personalize, the longstanding practice of not crediting editorial writers—the very people who produce newspapers' most individualized and personal expressions—seems self-defeating. In contrast, magazines usually credit authors, but unless writers are already well known they, like editors and publishers, remain just names to readers. Major films, in contrast, do feature well known actors and actresses, but generally the smaller the budget and expectation of return, the more unknown the performers, directors, and producers.

Clearly, personal representation works differently at every level of each industry, but similar processes operate. Print media use pictures (i.e., represent more features of the person) when providing personal information. Radio and television stations develop local "personalities" by having their weather people, announcers, newscasters, and sportscasters participate in personal exchanges via call-in shows and attendance at local charitable and communal events. More generally, public relations people spread "information" about the private lives of the persons who personify the media industries to encourage members of the public to feel that they are interacting with people they know.

Corporate communicators usually are represented by persons when messages are ephemeral and nonmaterial (i.e., motion pictures, television, radio) and not represented by persons when messages are lasting and material (i.e., the print media). In the first case, personification may reduce the risk that the material, which may not be of deep interest and which disappears as soon as it is presented, will not hold receivers' attention. In addition, associating material with an apparent personal source may reward receivers for hard work or, if the material seems trivial or frivolous, may help them shift blame for wasting time from themselves to the sender.

Much of the personnel in communicator groups is hidden from audience members, most of whom are indifferent to, if not ignorant about, their existence, number, or roles. The numbers may be estimated from corporate information, but the task is fraught with ambiguity. Enumerations of media personnel vary markedly depending on assumptions about which personnel to include. Conglomerates present severe problems. How does one allocate the corporate executives of Gulf and Western, which includes Paramount Pictures among its diverse enterprises, or of Loews, which has a string of motion picture theaters among its investments. Even corporations that operate exclusively in the media pose problems because many subcontract work or do not maintain exclusive rights to the services of their specialists. Moreover, because organizational activity involves both people and equipment—and the equipment used by each medium is very different—numbers alone do not directly reflect the financial size or product volume of an organization. Numbers, however, are indicative of managerial and administrative requirements within an organization.

Despite these complications, several points may be made about the numbers of persons typically involved in each of the media. With few exceptions, local television stations that serve large populations, television and radio networks, the print media, and film employ large numbers of persons. Also, as noted, the numbers who operate newspapers, magazines, and television stations vary directly with audience size and the extent of direct competition. Beyond that, numerical regularities are obviated by inter- and intramedia variation in ownership patterns and in the organization of production and consumption. Radio, television, and motion pictures offer particularly complicated situations.

Low-powered nonnetwork radio stations usually have the least personnel. Automated stations offering syndicated programs may broadcast with only one engineer. Television stations and cable networks that do no live programming may not have much larger staffs. With so few employees, only their viewers may be aware of their frequent transmission problems. The fact that most nonnews television programs are produced independently adds to the ambiguity of the meaning of size for any unit at any level. Because independent production companies often operate in consultation with potential clients, it is reasonable to ask whether some of their personnel should be considered in estimates for large stations and networks.

Reliable industry-wide estimates of film production personnel also are difficult to make because of joint employment in other media and a very fluid corporate population. Production is financed and work contracted individually for each film. Each involves different numbers and types of roles and key production specialists (e.g., producers, directors, film editors, writers, cameramen, lighting specialists) with unique skills and strengths. Consequently, many organizations have small capital investments, few long term commitments, and large short term debts. Given these circumstances, theirs is a precarious existence that depends on the success of the last few ventures and the health of capital markets. Counts of personnel for individual films are tedious and ambiguous. Film production involves contributions from ongoing full-time corporate personnel, production specialists and performers on contract to produce a single film, and other specialists who work on only limited aspects of a single film's production. In view of these vagaries, the concept of the number of people responsible for a film as a finished product is, at best, extremely difficult or, at worst, impossible to specify and, therefore, to estimate. On average, however, the size of film production units tends to vary roughly with the level of financing.

Film industry employment, including production, distribution, and exhibition, is even more difficult to estimate. In Hollywood's heyday (1920-1950), eight companies that integrated all or two of the three functions of production, distribution, and exhibition monopolized the industry. Their total employment was reasonably close to that of the industry. Now, industry organization is much more complex. Producers usually do not distribute or exhibit, although some large exhibitors have ventured into production to assure themselves of a supply. Their annual output may be a single film or several, each with a different crew. Consequently, work forces fluctuate with volatility. Because specialists are simultaneously or sequentially employed on several projects, the sum of production units, difficult to specify in any case, does not estimate the production work force. Distribution and exhibition employment is more stable, but the production-side ambiguities make estimates of an industry total unreliable. Government reports of industry employment may be as good as can be gotten and, taken over time, should at least indicate trends if not amounts reliably.

With respect to the location of communicators vis-à-vis communicatees, newspapers are the most local medium. Local reporters cover local stories; smaller papers rarely cover nonlocal events with their own people. They rely on press services or on senior journalists employed by papers that syndicate their stories (e.g., *New York Times, Los Angeles Times*). Like consumption, printing and distribution remain primarily local, although the *New York Times* and *USA Today* have joined the *Wall Street Journal* and *Christian Science Monitor* as national newspapers. In a contrasting trend, daily newspapers are adding local editions geared to communities in their circulation zones. Except for avowedly national papers, and despite their use of standard services, dailies deemphasize their national links and may even go to some expense to continue as largely local operations. The population size of the community and area that a newspaper serves is extremely important in another respect. It sets a limit on circulation; circulation affects the amount of advertising revenue that can be generated, and the amount of advertising is related to the size of the newshole, which influences the amount and diversity of the news received (Bogart, 1980: 249-250).

Magazines are marketed nationally, but this masks a trend toward regional and local emphases. City (e.g., *New York, Philadelphia, Washingtonian, Manhattan, Inc.*) and regional (e.g., *Sunset, Southern Living*) publications are increasing in number, and many national magazines distribute regional editions that carry advertisements for businesses that operate only in the region in addition to their national advertisers. Catering to local areas, however, is not an exception to the generalization that magazine publishing is nationally organized. Rather, it fits the long-term industry trend of targeting homogeneous groups. The strategy of identifying strong interest groups that are willing to subscribe to a publication with a single focus simply is being applied on an areal as well as on social, demographic, and economic bases. Because almost all magazines are sold by subscription and delivered by mail, production, business, marketing, editorial, and production facilities all may be in different locales.

Commercial radio stations are community-based and identify themselves as such. Their assigned power and antenna orientation define their service areas. Most FM stations and low-power AM stations, many of which are restricted to daylight operation, serve relatively small areas. Clear-channel, 50,000-watt AM stations, in contrast, serve large areas during the day and can be received nationally after sundown. Signals originate locally, but material may come from any locale. Local news and talk shows are locally gathered, prepared, and presented. All but a few stations offer specialized programming. This approach and relaxed public service requirements encourage centrally produced automated programming (e.g., music, religious programs). Many stations try to build an identity by developing local personalities (e.g., disc jockeys, talk show hosts, early morning wake-up show announcers). Syndicated talk shows, network news and features, and automated music originate nonlocally.

Communicator locale varies considerably between over the

air and cable television. The latter transmit locally; the material is sent via satellite from a nonlocal source convenient to its producers (e.g., WTBS, ESPN). The insertion of local commercials by local cable systems, however, can create an impression that cable broadcasts originate locally. Over-the-air television stations also are heavy users of nonlocal material. All prime-time and much morning and afternoon programming of network affiliated stations originates nonlocally. However, network affiliates with large budgets also are likely to program local news, sporting events, talk, and community issue programs. The smaller the audience of an over the air station, the less likely it is to carry local material.

Film production and distribution is not local. Few films are tailored to the tastes of the communities in which they are produced. Distributors decide where, when, and for how long most films will show and use little local input. Most theaters are owned by national or regional firms. Exhibition, though, is always local. Consequently, moviegoers may think of theater operators as local business people who vie for the best films rather than as functionaries of national or regional chains that contract with distributors who determine which films can be shown, when, and for how long. Practices that give a local flavor to nonlocal media (e.g., having national television personalities mention local stations in promotional bits, originating programs from affiliates) are not acknowledgments of local support; the aim is to create the impression that they are local and personal.

The organization of communicator groups also varies among the media, but a detailed analysis requires delineating their boundaries. Because many are units in conglomerates or rely heavily on others for essential material or services, their production, distribution, and internal control processes cannot be specified accurately without considering these others. Financial decisions may be made by officers of a parent conglomerate (Bagdikian, 1987), or delivery times set by independent distributors. The complexity is especially clear in the film industry, which may avoid certain subjects or positions on social, political, economic, and religious issues out of deference to financiers or exhibitors (Dominick, 1987).

There is no one correct way to delineate a communicator group. Whether it should be treated as limited or extended depends on the issue. Decisions must rest on informed judgment, for each medium and individual enterprise uses auxiliaries to provide limited services, monitor performance, and establish and enforce standards. The organizational descriptions here deal with operating units (e.g., radio stations owned by conglomerates are treated as independent; contractors for programs, services, or resources are ignored). Organizations that produce and distribute media products encompass a division of labor and consist of tasks (process), positions (structure), and the relationships among them. Growth in the size and differentiation of organizations has necessitated the technological innovations that also are at the heart of media systems (Metcalfe, 1986: 40-41), although some of that organizational change also is in response to technological change. Organizations vary from simple to complex depending on how tasks and positions are structured, and the number, tightness, and formality of contacts and exchanges among tasks and positions. Among the key factors that shape organizational structure and complexity are production and distribution processes and the technology employed.

Organizational complexity is important for two reasons. For one, the more complex an organization, the more difficult it is for outsiders to understand and to influence it. Successful performance in a complex system enhances the status of its role incumbents with outsiders. Complexity, combined with public ignorance, contributes to media mystique and, thereby, to the power imbalance between senders and receivers. Second, the more complex an organization, the more vulnerable it is to disruption, and the greater the likelihood that the power to control the communication process will diffuse to people throughout the hierarchy who perform essential tasks, regardless of how high or low in the hierarchy their position might be. If their skills are scarce and difficult to develop, they may seem or be indispensable.

Complete media organizations produce, distribute, exhibit, finance, and manage. The components of their structures often are differentiated accordingly, each having one or several different positions with one or several persons serving in each. In small enterprises, several positions may be combined; in very small units, some of the five functions may be combined. The five media vary in their organization for several reasons; three are particularly important for the comments that follow: (a) the unique technology of each requires its own specialized skills, (b) income is acquired differently by each (e.g., sale of tickets and foreign and television rights for motion pictures, advertising revenues for commercial television), and (c) the media are subject to different legislative and regulatory constraints (e.g., antimonopoly agreements limit film companies' involvement in production, distribution, and exhibition; newspapers can own forests, produce newsprint, report, produce, print, and distribute).

Cable networks that do not produce programs, low-powered radio stations, and most over-the-air UHF television stations have the smallest staffs and simplest organizations. A few people handle program acquisition, advertising sales, financial management, and general supervision. Secretarial and clerical personnel, several engineers to monitor equipment and mount broadcast material, and maintenance personnel complete the roster. Local cable operations also must employ salespeople and installation and maintenance workers. People may do several jobs. If tasks are contracted out (e.g., janitorial, secretarial services), the organization can be minimal.

Large stations that produce their own news, talk, service, and sports shows are big businesses with much more complex organizations. They employ producers, directors, editors, reporters, meteorologists, publicists, camera people, lighting engineers, maintenance workers, personnel specialists, and various other functionaries. Making and maintaining schedules is crucial. Most are network affiliates, and several positions may be required to handle such matters as negotiating exceptions from agreements to carry specific amounts of network programs at certain times, payments for network services, and local feeds to the network. If a station is owned by a larger corporation, several people may be required to perform tasks involved in that relationship.

The networks, of course, are the largest and most complex organizations in television and radio. As producers of news, public affairs, sports shows, and some specials, they employ the specialists required to do the work, supervise it, schedule it, and pay for it. Almost all other programs and advertisements are produced outside. Experienced specialists conduct and monitor relations with suppliers. The networks operate several services—at least one radio network service, a television service, and several cable operations. Each network also owns and operates several television and radio stations. The networks, in turn, are units in conglomerates with interests in other media, media-related, and nonmedia activities. In short, the networks are large bureaucracies typical of modern Western business.

Both print media are organizationally complex but vary along lines that reflect major differences in their scheduling, distribution, and subject matter. Even if jointly owned, newspapers and magazines operate independently, so it is appropriate to discuss their organization without regard to intracorporate relationships. Newspapers specialize in information (i.e., news, weather forecasts, market summaries) and limited entertainment (e.g., crossword puzzles, comic strips, features) and service (e.g., recipes, television and movie schedules, medical and advice columns) features, produce several editions daily, and primarily distribute locally. Magazines offer specialized material (e.g., the news in review, business, photography, popular music, food, wine, architecture), publish periodically (e.g., weekly, monthly, quarterly; indeed, they are called periodicals), and distribute nationally.

Newspaper and magazine production, distribution, and advertising sales organization all differ. Differences in paper quality and in the dimensions, number, assembly, and binding of pages require different production methods. Most magazines contract printing; newspapers do their own printing. Editorially, newspapers collect, process, and write up large amounts of new, event-based material under severe time constraints; staffs are large and must gather and prepare information accurately. Magazines carry many fewer items, select them for reader interest, emphasize layout and writing qualities, and have somewhat looser schedules and smaller editorial staffs. Newspapers are distributed at newsstands and racks or by home delivery and depend on drivers for timely distribution. Magazines rely on the mails for distribution. Newspapers handle most of their own sales; cash must be processed daily for single-copy sales and monthly for subscriptions. Magazine circulation income is largely from long-term subscriptions, often sold by independent agents. Newspaper advertising revenue is largely from local merchants and from classified ads; magazine advertising revenue is from international, national, and regional corporations.

Clearly, although both newspaper and magazine production involve the same tasks, their importance and the work itself are quite different. Both depend on a variety of specialists—many people involved in complex relations create the product. However, even if Sunday editions of newspapers have separate staffs, print media organizations are not as complex as those of television networks. Neither print medium must monitor its performance for a federal regulatory commission. Nonetheless, both would be high on any scale of complexity.

Antitrust suits, in particular, have been responsible for major changes in film industry organization. In response to a federal suit, the fully integrated giants of the industry—Loews, Warner Brothers, RKO, 20th Century-Fox, Paramount—agreed to divest themselves of at least one of their three integrated operations—production, distribution, and exhibition. The new corporations diversified rapidly by entering mergers (e.g., ABC-Paramount). Although each new corporation rapidly grew larger than its original, the restrictions on film-related activities reversed 30-year industry trends from many to fewer firms and from fragmented to inclusive operations. The survivors are being acquired by highly diversified conglomerates that may use them to promote other corporate interests (e.g., Gulf + Western used Paramount and Coca Cola used Columbia productions to promote their other operations [Bagdikian, 1987]).

The dismantling of the integrated film giants (and the coincidental growth of television) led to the end of the studio contract system and the formation of many small firms engaged in limited parts of the business. Production, distribution, and exhibition links are more fluid, although some of the larger film operations have become involved again in all three activities. The corporate lists that introduce films and dot their credits are a startling contrast to credits in the 1930s and 1940s and testify to these changes. The emergence of complex interfirm relations also has created a need for brokering and coordinating. By and large, the industry has shifted from vertical to horizontal organization.

Feature film production is extremely complex. Consonant with the large numbers of people involved (cf. the proverbial "cast of thousands"), tasks are highly subdivided and specialized, mastery of much of the equipment requires experience and training, and schedules are involved and tight. What with reediting, recutting, rewriting, and reshooting, production is an open-ended process, especially if there is no firm schedule for exhibiting. The fact that films (like television productions) are not shot in sequence, but rather to accommodate the schedules of talent and facilities, suggests the complexities of the process. Business affairs and relations with investors who have deep and abiding interests in the outcome and are not shy about making them known also require attention. Task and, hence, organizational complexity are the hallmarks of filmmaking.

By contrast, the organization of film distribution and exhibition is simple. Aside from routine business management, the former entails scheduling films for theaters and delivering them at the right place and time; the latter entails selling admissions and showing films on schedule. The number of clients determines the number of workers and distribution of tasks. Storing and delivering films—the distributive tasks—require no special skills. As for exhibition, only projection requires any skill, and in theater complexes one person can handle several theaters without additional supervision. The same applies to cleaning, selling and taking tickets, and selling refreshments. Show times are set by management. In essence, the organization of exhibition and distribution is at least as simple as that of cable systems, small radio stations, and cable networks that show only reruns.

Organization affects performance. Although with many exceptions, the more complex an organization, the more prone it is to disruption. In the past, for example, newspapers suspended publication if linotypists or printers went on strike. However, automated electronic equipment requires less skill, and strikes by operators are no longer as disruptive. Work stoppages by drivers and loading dock workers, however, always disrupt operations because, absent distribution, papers clog the plant. In contrast, despite the romantic image of newspapers that puts reporters at center stage, their strikes have far less impact. Wire service and syndicated material is available, and editors can write essential local items.

It might seem that television networks would be more vulnerable than newspapers to interruptions. Television employs complex equipment and production processes; newspapers employ more generally available skills, less complex and time-sensitive production processes, and less esoteric equipment. Nonetheless, when television engineers and writers have struck, the networks have been able to continue to broadcast a backlog of films and tapes using experienced nonunion supervisors who have risen from the ranks to operate the equipment. Clearly, such factors as unionization, where in the process a task fits, timing, the number of people required for the task, interchangability and availability of skills, and the supply of replacement material all mediate the impact of organizational complexity on performance.[5]

**Communicatees.** Most media material and the purposes for which it is produced are so different from information that it is inappropriate even to attribute communicatee status to receivers. Moreover, even if each medium had communicatees exclusively, that group could not be described with precision for two reasons: (a) the voluntary and isolated quality of receivers makes it difficult to identify who is in the group, and (b) the composition of the group changes continually over time (i.e., different people receive and understand different parts of the full set of material). Nonetheless, although inappropriate for comparing media systems, the term *communicatee* is used here to be consistent with the model. Because people's engagement as receivers of a particular medium really depends on whether they are satisfied with the meanings they have negotiated from the text, and not on whether a meaning intended by the sender was received exactly as intended, it is much more appropriate to refer to receivers as audience members than as communicatees (Ang, 1989).

Although it is the more appropriate term for the collective targets of the media, the meaning of audience also is vague. It is used indiscriminately to refer to targeted receivers, actual receivers, or aspiring receivers—singly or in all possible combinations. Moreover, the criteria for defining intended audience membership may include any combination of socioeconomic attributes, media exposure, self-definition, or understanding of material. Furthermore, detailed knowledge of the specifications of an intended audience says little about a real audience. Ang (1991: 40) has noted that ". . . more often than not . . . programmes fail to attract the audiences they were intended to." Statements about audiences are rarely unambiguous or comparable because there is no consensus on criteria or measurement methods. The specific referent often cannot even be adduced from the context. The variety in audience measurement procedures (Beville, 1988; Wober, 1988: 6-8) reflects, among other things, the ambiguity of the concept. Indeed, the ambiguity is so great that Fiske (1989: 56) has remarked that:

> ... there is no such thing as "the television audience," defined as an empirically accessible object, for there can be no meaningful categories beyond its boundaries—what on earth is "not the television audience"? The "television audience" is not a social category like class, race, or gender—everyone slips in or out of it in a way that makes nonsense of any categorical boundaries: similarly when in "it" people constitute themselves quite differently as audience members at different times—I am a different television "audience" when watching my football team than when watching *The A Team* with my son or *Days of our Lives* with my wife. Categories focus our thinking on similarities: people watching television are best modeled on a multitude of differences.

Like many statements made to emphasize an important point, his remarks are somewhat exaggerated, even though they make several valid points. It still is the case that both in their compositional profiles and in the behavior required of their members, media audiences continue to vary among themselves as much as their individual members vary among themselves.

Given these several ambiguities, nothing said here should be taken to imply precise measurement. Rather, audience is used in a conventional sense, that is, the group exposed to a medium more or less regularly; for a specific unit (e.g., film, television program, magazine article), it is the group exposed to it regardless of regularity. Excluded from audiences are such people as newspaper or magazine subscribers who do not get around to reading them, moviegoers who sleep through the film, or cable television subscribers who do not watch it. References to audiences in this discussion indicate only people who attend to a media product, regardless of whether they like or understand what they read, hear, or see.

The behavior that makes one an audience member has a complex structure, occurs in settings that must meet several necessary conditions, and creates distinctive social collectivities. By and large, those behaviors, settings, and social distinctions differ for each medium. As a consequence, the consumption behavior of media audiences varies in terms of where, when, how, who, and how many. These aspects of consumption are particularly relevant to how systems work as well as for such issues as media "massness" and the mechanisms by which media may affect people. Both Heeter and Greenberg (1988) and Webster (1989) have found that a relatively minor technical innovation—cable—has reorganized television consumption behavior substantially (cf. also Becker, Creedon, Blood, and Fredin, 1989; Schoenbach and Becker, 1989; Sparkes and Delbel, 1989).[6]

It is easiest to begin with the conditions of consumption, for each medium requires a proper consuming environment. Poor conditions impede consumption and can be thought of as noise. Consumption of print media or television requires adequate light. All other things (i.e., conditions, opportunity, and personal ability) being equal, people tend to read less than they listen or view because they find it more difficult. Reading can be hard work, a matter of obvious pertinence to print media. People who find reading difficult often may be unaware that poor lighting rather than vocabulary and grammar deficiencies can be at the root of the problem.

All the media also require substantial quiet to permit concentration, minimize interference, and avoid annoying others. However, only radio and television have developed equipment (i.e., earphones) that minimizes noise for both the audience member and others nearby who do not wish to listen. The possibility of noise guides media consumers (except earphone users) in choosing locales in which to consume. By introducing considerations of time and place, conditions deter the potentially unlimited consumption of an otherwise seemingly free good.

With respect to the locus of consumption, because print material is portable, reading is possible wherever light and noise conditions and social conventions permit. Other media are limited in this regard, although miniaturization and the development of light, self-contained power sources have increased the portability of equipment. Earphone-equipped transistor radios, tape and compact disc players, and portable television sets can be operated anywhere. Small receivers generally perform poorly, however, so those who want high-quality reception may remain limited in where and when they can consume. Reflected sunlight on screens, in particular, can seriously hamper television viewing. The lack of a working technology for receiving portable cable or satellite television restricts those audiences to home sets. Theater relocation in response to suburbanization, automobile use, and the decline of city centers has altered traditional film accessibility drastically since the 1950s, although the combination of films being shown on television and the development of the VCR has drastically altered the locus of film viewing (Klopfenstein, 1989; Lindstrom, 1989).

Closely related to locus is the scheduling or timing of consumption. Except for live radio and television coverage of unscheduled news, there is a release schedule for all media material. Critics may preview programs, films, or news articles, but average audience members cannot access them until release. In most other respects, however, the print media differ significantly from the others. Because of the hard copy, print can be used whenever conditions are right—newspapers and magazines can be read at the consumer's convenience. In contrast, radio and television presentations are scheduled, and consumers must adjust their schedules accordingly or record them. Film exhibition in theaters offers consumers the least flexibility.

Scheduling is a constraint on audience participation with which the nonprint media must cope. Most radio programming is so similar, continuous, and noninformational, however, that, except for news and weather reports, which usually are repeated often, rebroadcasting is unnecessary and the impact of scheduling on listener behavior is minimal. Film and television adapt to schedule conflicts essentially by providing additional opportunities for viewing, each in its own way. However, weekday movie going is now restricted almost exclusively to evenings, daytime showings having been sharply curtailed in response to the competition of television and changing social, demographic, and economic conditions. Obviously, therefore, despite the very large audiences that these media attract, to various degrees they require prospective consumers to adjust their schedules. This excludes some heavily scheduled, busy people from their audiences and, thereby, gives print media a social and competitive advantage.

Each medium depends on different sensory receptors, and this affects both the nature of receivers' involvement and the way in which producers employ the symbol system (Ihde, 1982). The print media employ the eyes, radio the ears. Television and film employ both, although television sound may be received without the picture, an alternative that lends credence to the observation that television has yet to develop a style of its own that is not based on radio (i.e., that minimizes descriptions of the picture and, instead, uses sound in nonredundant ways) and film (i.e., that adjusts action and pictures to the capacity of television cameras, the quality and size of television screens, and the conditions of home viewing). Having not yet arrived at Huxley's brave new world, no medium employs the sense of touch or of smell, although some magazines print on paper selected for its tactile appeal or impregnate advertisements with scents being promoted by advertisers of cosmetics.[7]

Of the many ways in which audiences vary, the consuming unit is, perhaps, most significant. Reading is a private individual activity, so much so that the act of looking at another's reading material while that person is reading is considered an intrusion that is a common topic of humor. A particularly salient consequence of privacy—especially given the concurrent need for quiet, a combination that encourages reading in solitary—is that most readers must (at least temporarily) resolve uncertainty and react without being able to consult others. Isolated reception, interpretation, and response come as close as any audience situation to the conditions of true mass communication. However, any pressure for an immediate reaction is alleviated by the facts that (a) readers tend to have better education and critical skills, (b) informational texts tend to be clear, and (c) written material can be reread and reconsidered by readers who know that time is required to prepare, print, and distribute a text, and, therefore, an immediate response is unnecessary.

In contrast, all the nonprint media can be consumed alone or with others. Radio, however, adapted to television by tailoring material to the lifestyles of preselected homogeneous groups. Radio also encourages listening when other media cannot compete (e.g., while exercising, showering, driving to and from work). These are usually periods of solitary activity, many of which require earphones for listening (e.g., jogging). However, the social definition of appropriate behavior primarily determines whether listening is a solitary or group activity. Conventions as to whether the dominant activity (e.g., dressing, exercising, driving to work) can be solitary or collective set the conditions for listening. Situations, then, determine if listeners' understandings of and responses to radio can be mediated by others. Although television is subject to these same contingencies, most sets are relatively immobile and located where several people can watch. Even though portable sets encourage private viewing, cable tends to collect viewers around sets connected to the cable (Becker et al., 1989: 314-315). Indeed, unlike radio, for which equipment innovations now allow each person a choice, television program selection remains a significant point of family contention (Heeter and Greenberg, 1988: 295). Elliott (1986: 107), however, has predicted that technological innovations will privatize all media consumption and, by so doing, further separate and isolate audience members and increase their subordination to senders.

Moviegoing is particularly interesting from a sociological perspective. Although individual attendance is possible, in the United States most people attend film showings in small groups (e.g., families, dating couples, friends), despite the fact that the theater is dark during the showing and silence is the norm. The reactions of others cannot be seen or heard nor can the film be discussed as it is viewed. Presumably, then, the norms governing attendance are pertinent to the events around film going—entering and leaving theaters and pre- and postviewing discussions—rather than to viewing itself. The pattern may be an extension of young people's dating norms and behavior. Because dating indicates popularity, and a dark theater is a congenial environment for sexual play, moviegoing is attractive to the young, and solitary moviegoing an admission of insufficiency to be avoided.

Austin (1986), however, has suggested that recent technological innovations will end film going as we have known it. Sparkes and Delbel's (1989: 348) data confirmed that prediction with respect to television, and one can expect even more of a negative impact from the VCR.

In addition to attributes of the social units that constitute them, two aspects of audiences as collectivities deserve attention— their relative size and homogeneity. With respect to size, more than 50 years of continuous research is available to provide estimates covering a range from each medium as a whole to particular items within a medium. Precise statements about the size of the audience for each medium based on this research would be misleading, however, given the looseness of the audience concept and the fact that so much of all media research is client (e.g., media industries, interest groups, advertising agencies) sponsored and oriented (Halloran, 1986: 46).

Using an easily satisfied criterion—a simple claim of regular exposure that ignores the quantity, quality, subject matter, or conditions of the activity—at least three studies from approximately 40 to 45 years ago (Link and Hopf, 1946; Lazarsfeld and Kendall, 1948; Campbell and Metzner, 1950) that antedate the spread of national television showed newspapers and radio each including about 90%, magazines somewhere between 40% and 70%, and films about 60% of the American population in their audiences. Studies conducted during 1950-52 (Bogart, 1956), when the novelty effect of the wildfire-like spread of television on other media was at its greatest, showed no shift in the proportions regularly consuming other media but did report precipitous declines in movie attendance. A 1972 Educational Testing Service study was cited with only minor adjustments in both editions of Schramm's textbook (1973; Schramm and Porter, 1982). It reported regular newspaper reading declining slightly to 75%, the magazine proportion holding at 40% (the same as the Link and Hopf figure), and television viewing and radio listening as being almost universal among adults.

More recent figures from studies that tend to focus on regular media use primarily for news (Cutler, 1989; Dominick, 1990; Times Mirror Center for People and the Press, 1990) generally indicate lower proportions of regular use (e.g., the Times Mirror study of news suggests a television audience in the 70% range, a newspaper audience near 60%, and radio and news magazine audiences in the low 50% range; other recent studies report different levels but similar orders) with the order of size tending to remain the same. Recent studies of the impact of cable on other media use (Schoenbach and Becker, 1989; Wober, 1989) tend to confirm this pattern of stability in total media consumption and its distribution among the media but change in the distribution of time devoted to each and in the minutiae of planning and engaging in consumption. Finally, it should be noted with respect to newspapers that even though claims to readership may not have declined precipitously, such other measures as copies circulated per household and numbers of newspapers published have been declining so steadily since the end of World War II that it is a serious industry-wide concern (cf. Bogart, 1989, 1991). There could hardly be a better illustration of the implications of the differences in how audience membership is defined and measured.

Given the differences in populations sampled (e.g., the earliest studies employed national samples, the Times Mirror study used three samples from Lincoln, NE), focus (e.g., general exposure, use as a news source), methods of data collection (e.g., face-to-face interviews, telephone interviews, questionnaires), and criteria for audience membership (e.g., regularity of use, quantity of exposure, yesterday use), the variability in proportions is not surprising, but the stability in the ordering of media audiences by size may be. Finally, even accounting for the major differences in research methods, the decline in size of every media audience suggested by the studies is likely to be real, although not as great as the figures might suggest. This shift probably reflects the impact of major changes in work patterns and lifestyles as well as changes in the media themselves and the availability of new media (e.g., VCRs).

Most scholars attribute these differences in media audience size to a combination of differences in availability and skill requirements. Both apply to magazines. Initial costs are high—obtaining them requires subscribing or finding a sales outlet—and consumption requires reading skill and good eyesight. Film going requires an immediate substantial cash outlay, a suitable schedule, transportation, and eyes that are not strained by two hours of viewing. Basically, the easier it is to access a medium and defer actual consumption decisions, the larger its total audience. Thus, newspaper readers can structure their reading however and whenever they like, radio or television sets can be turned on and programs selected at will, but magazines and films have to be selected in advance and energy and planning invested in accessing them.

Obviously, audiences of individual items are substantially smaller than total media audiences. Even the most highly promoted television spectaculars rarely attract as much as half the sets in use, and that represents far less than half the population. Nonetheless, the audiences of network television programs tend to be largest, although a few magazines (e.g., *TV Guide*) sell as many as ten million copies. No daily newspaper comes close. Local radio, which offers more choice, has even smaller audiences. Some films attract tens of millions of viewers by accumulating audiences over a long period. Because they are promoted, audience size is positively related to production costs—producers do seek returns on investments. Film promotions usually equate production costs with quality and potential public interest.

A crucial datum for critics of the view that media audiences are masses is the homogeneity that results when material is targeted to specific groups. This is paradoxical, for if approximately 90% of the people are members of the cumulative audience of each medium—or, at least, of the three largest of them—how different can those audiences be? Obviously, not very. Clearly, the audience of a medium is an unusual construct implying either aggregation of individual unit audiences or a marginal criterion like medium preference. Only polemicists with little concern for precision and media trade groups out to raise income refer to the total audience of a medium with any frequency.

Even at the cumulative level, however, there are some fairly systematic differences in the composition of media audiences. Although the larger ones (i.e., radio, television, and newspapers) substantially penetrate all social groups, the newspaper audience tends to be somewhat older and better educated than all but the magazine audience, which has an even higher average socioeconomic status. The motion picture audience is unusually young compared to the others—moviegoing, at best, being sporadic after age 30. Members of minority groups are generally underrepresented in all audiences. Although no audience excludes any group, such systematic differences violate the model of random selection from a national population that underlies the concept of a mass.

Audience homogeneity for individual products is immediately apparent. Because most films are made for specific groups, their audiences are much more homogeneous than the moviegoing public as a whole. The concentration of theaters in higher socioeconomic areas is also a factor. Magazines also target specific interest groups and may attract large proportions of their members. Most items are read by even more homogeneous groups. Television programs rarely attract all segments of the population. Most cable networks and channels cater to very specific interest or population groups (e.g., evangelicals, sports fans, women). By comparison, newspapers have heterogeneous audiences, but, aside from compelling news and the weather, almost all the sections and items attract a very homogeneous readership. In contrast to the newspaper, individual radio programs, magazines, and films have by far the most homogeneous audiences. The seemingly heterogeneous audiences of over the air network and local television stations are cumulations of diverse homogeneous audiences drawn from targeted strata. Programs geared to the total population are rare.

**Apparatus.** Probably the one common element in anyone's

image of the mass media is a complex technology employed to produce, transmit, and receive material. Two important consequences of production and transmission equipment and how differently they impact on each medium already have been noted: (a) the media mystique that develops because technology isolates audiences from communicators, and (b) the diffusion of control within sending organizations that occurs when operatives acquire monopolies on expertise that can be converted into power over the creation and transmission of the product. Therefore, I discuss only three attributes of receiving apparatus that impinge differentially on the use of each medium—portability, skill requirements, and cost.

Receiving equipment may place significant constraints on consumption, not only by limiting its time and place but also by determining who may consume—to the extent that economic or social status limit access to equipment. Portability already has been noted as an equipment factor that impinges on consumption locales. The easier it is to move and access receiving equipment, the more numerous and diverse the places where consumption can occur.

Print media are hardly hampered in this respect. Almost anyone can carry a newspaper or magazine anywhere, and no equipment is required to access them; only poor lighting and norms that prohibit it in certain situations (e.g., while someone is speaking, while driving) limit reading. As a result of size and weight reductions in battery-operated sets, improvements in tuning and speaker mechanisms, and earphone miniaturization, radio has become almost location free. Sets can be as portable as magazines and newspapers and are unaffected by lighting conditions. Portable television sets are widely available, but do not receive as well or as readily as radio and require attention from eyes as well as ears. For these reasons, over-the-air network and local television is still, at best, low in portability. Cable television remains immobile; sets still must be wired into cable networks or connected to large dish antennas.

Film is unlike any other medium that requires equipment to access it. Viewers do not lay hands on projectors. Commercial films require large blocks of free time, and 35mm prints are expensive. These conditions, added to the expense, immobility, space requirements, and problems of installing a commercial quality projector and screen, discourage personal ownership of viewing equipment. For all practical purposes, it is inaccessible to most people. In a commercial economy, to view a film requires buying entry to a theater when and where it is being exhibited. As already noted, even before personal taste enters the equation that shapes attendance, this constraint seriously depletes the size of film audiences by excluding those who cannot afford the costs.

These observations pertain to viewing films in theaters and

ignore the wide deployment of videocassette recorders (VCRs) and cassette copies of many feature films. Watching a film cassette privately at home on a television screen is not the same experience as attending a movie. Most of the unique features of moviegoing—having a small choice further limited by show times and theater locations, traveling to and from a theater, being seated in the dark, not speaking aloud, arranging attendance as part of a larger event, entering and leaving the theater in a crowd—are missing. Except for sitting with companions, the theater is a more mass-like, impersonal environment. Home viewing is simply not the experience that moviegoing is (Marchetti, 1986). Morley (1989: 26) asserts that ". . . film . . . consumption either on television or on video in the home . . . provide(s) quite a different context of reception, and therefore quite a different set of subject positions for the viewer." Indeed, Webster (1989: 202) has suggested that the VCR be conceptualized as a "television channel" programmed by its owner.

The differences in the stimulus qualities of a cassette viewed at home on a television screen and a 35mm print of the same film viewed in the theater are another reason for distinguishing them. Every critical comment leveled at showing theater films on television also applies to home video. Charlton Heston, the famous actor, has been quoted (Associated Press, 1990a) as saying at a recent reopening of Ben Hur, one of his classic performances, that:

> Any film originally made for theaters suffers a great deal in the transfer to videotape. . . . When someone says "I just got a video of The Ten Commandments or Ben Hur, for my birthday," I have to tell them, "Sorry, but you haven't seem it.". . . Here (at a theater), the moving image arts are seen as they are meant to be seen, in all their glory.

Films made for projection by quality equipment on large screens lose sound quality, sweep, depth, and clarity at home. They are not experienced as intended. Films are to be viewed without distraction. The home is rife with distractions, and television material is produced accordingly (i.e., by not requiring much attention and by creating frequent points of tension, usually before commercial breaks). Serious filmmakers do not do this. They anticipate exhibition with a minimum of distractions.

For these reasons, all comments on film have been in terms of viewing in conventional movie theaters. This does not deny the growing popularity of home video viewing. Indeed, Klopfenstein's analyses (1989: 32-35) indicated that the growth and diffusion of VCRs has almost matched the explosive pattern of the first black and white television sets. Rather, the point is to emphasize that the VCR is a different genre of entertainment that may, perhaps, have more in common with books and book reading than with films and moviegoing. In fact, as home video becomes more firmly established, we might expect films to be made specifically for home viewing just as many films now are made primarily for television rather than for the movie theater. Austin (1986) even anticipated the end of the theatrical film that has been the hallmark of the industry.

Another aspect of receiving apparatus that shapes the systemic features of each medium is cost. Cost restricts access by imposing an ownership or rental fee and divides the public on the basis of ability to pay. Print materials require no apparatus; those costs are nil. Equipment costs for film also are nil, but, as just noted, for precisely opposite reasons. The absence of an initial equipment cost outlay to access these otherwise very different media helps explain why they share at least one feature in common—the product must be paid for directly, usually in advance.

In the United States, radio and television receivers are usually purchased. The cost may be considered a fee for private control of reception. A receiver is not a good that is used up in a relatively short time. Rather, it is available almost indefinitely to use on demand. Costs vary widely depending on construction quality, extra features, size, and fidelity in reception. Generally, radios cost less than television sets for comparable quality (if it could be measured). It is not surprising, therefore, that most households have more radios and that the quality of some radios may be considerably better than that of some television sets.

Because the quality of equipment varies in several respects, users are at a disadvantage if they do not know how to maximize its performance. The equipment-consumer interface requires knowledge of how well the equipment can perform, what its limits and shortcomings are, and how to compensate for these failings. Skill and knowledge are both involved in maximizing quality. Although conceptually independent—we may know how to do something but be unable to do it—in the case of media equipment the difference is largely irrelevant because receivers usually are so uninformed about receiving apparatus that they are in no position to improve their skills as users.

Equipment may distort signals so that they are not received as intended or may camouflage or hide signals that senders wish to have their targets receive (e.g., subliminal advertising) without impairing reception. Informed users know about both types of distortion. That may not make them skilled users, however. Knowing that a television screen distorts distances and perspective, for example, need not equip one to make the proper psychic adjustments.

Moreover, some adjustments require sensory acuity and practice. Thus, a listener with an untrained ear or hearing defect who knows that the receiver is excellent still may be unable to tell whether it is adjusted properly.

Equipment for each medium has its own knowledge-skill requirements. For print media, there being no equipment, only skill matters. Reading is a learned skill, and speed and comprehension can be improved by knowing how to do it, being able to apply that knowledge, and by practicing. Reading is considered hard work only because knowledge and training are limited. Knowing the source and structure of messages is also critical for media consumption. Advertising, for example, often employs otherwise unexceptional material but structures it in ways that are influential. Skill in deciphering message construction can be employed in all media consumption, but the same approach will not work for all because each medium has its own textual conventions and requirements. The structuring of material to produce an emotional response, change an opinion, or stimulate a purchase usually differs considerably for each. Consumers who want to be able to protect themselves against influence need that knowledge.

Each medium that requires receiving equipment is subject to an impact on its signals by the equipment. Ignorance of this fact and how it applies in each case deters the acquisition of otherwise easily acquired consumption skills. Among the many false impressions that can be given are distorted portrayals of events, inaccurate colors, sound distortion, tape splicing to create impressions not intended by the source, faked emotions, and persuasion masked as information. People can learn to be alert to these possibilities and to adjust for them.

Perhaps the most important comment that can be made about differences in the impact of apparatus on the various media systems is to note that the major innovations in telecommunication are likely both to change consumption habits and to alter or minimize current differences. In the former respect, it has been observed that the capacity of cable to provide many more specialized and general channels is altering viewers' choice patterns and, thus, producing entirely new audience configurations (Webster, 1989). New technologies that merge television, personal computers, cable, and satellites will result in tailored products that will totally change consumption patterns and replace audiences with individuals divided on the basis of economic resources and interests. Because the apparatus digitizes the material transmitted, it also alters general accessibility and the economic relationship between sender and receiver. Use of these media, moreover, will be affected by people's facility with computers (cf. Wilson, 1988; Wober, 1988). In line with Wober's (1988) interest in how new technology will require new sensitivities, Kubey and Csikszentmihalyi (1990: 136-137) noted that the introduction of high-definition television, an apparatus rather than a medium change, will require alterations in users' patterns of eye movement.

**Symbol systems.** Each medium employs the shared symbol system in somewhat different ways. Although all draw from the same array of meanings, expression varies. Gestures that fit television can only be rendered in words in print. The latter are word dependent. Nuances cannot be conveyed by enunciation or gesture, only by words. Radio has the advantage of speech. By using inflection, pronunciation, and voice modulation, fewer words can provide as much or more variety in meaning. Television and film not only can use the techniques of print and radio for meaning representation, but also can employ visual aids—gestures, spatial relation of objects and actors, color.

Although the symbols characteristic of the different media vary in many respects, two particularly matter for their impact on the size and homogeneity of audiences. One is whether symbols are known and used frequently by almost everyone in a group (i.e., common) or used so rarely that they are unfamiliar to most people (i.e., esoteric). Essentially this dimension reflects training and relates to education. The other aspect of symbol variation is their inclusiveness or exclusiveness. Some activities are open to almost everyone, and their relevant vocabularies are known by all (e.g. How much does that cost? What is tomorrow's weather forecast?). Other activities are limited to self-selected or qualified groups whose vocabularies only members are likely to know (e.g., stock market traders, stamp collectors, physicians). This dimension ranges, in the order of the examples, from general to specialized.

Newspapers, being addressed to an entire local population, employ a symbol system that is common and general. This is an obvious overgeneralization. Stories about special groups or events require special terms (e.g., as this is being written on an anniversary of the Three Mile Island nuclear accident, it is appropriate to note that accounts of the event required use of technical terms specific to nuclear power plants and reactions). However, in such cases there usually is an effort to educate readers in understanding the new symbols (e.g., by use of graphs and charts). Not only are items that may only interest certain groups placed in special sections, but items are brief and uninterested people need not search far for an item of greater interest. To the extent possible, editorial decisions are based on likely general interest. Newspaper emphasis on human interest exemplifies this attention to a common denominator for which common general symbols suffice. Finally, the priority of general symbols eases reading, an important plus for a medium that depends on the widest possible support in its competition with television.

In contrast to newspapers, radio stations try to reach as large a share as possible of a selected population segment and tend to rely on symbol systems that are common and specialized. Classical music stations or sports stations use the languages of those specialties, although they usually use more of the common than the esoteric terminology of the specialty. The same applies to cable channels and networks. Magazines, in contrast, often make a virtue of using the specialized language of the highly motivated, highly restricted special interest groups (e.g., automobile enthusiasts, photographers, body builders) they target, even at the risk of verging on the esoteric.

Over-the-air television networks and stations, because they try to capture as large a share of the total population as possible, select material that can be expressed in the most commonly and widely used symbols. Their target groups (e.g., youth, people interested in the next day's weather, the middle class) are much larger and more diverse than those targeted by cable systems or magazines. When material requires esoteric and specialized symbols, producers try to avoid them, even at the risk of oversimplification, distortion, and loss of authenticity. In reaction to the same predilection among filmmakers, motion pictures often have been described as being made for audiences with the average mentality of 12-year-olds. Movies, too, largely rely on material that can be expressed with a common and general symbol system.

**Processes.** The various processes and conditions to which communication systems are subject (e.g., noise, feedback, and compatibility) also vary among the media. Several more obvious differences were noted when these phenomena were introduced. Although these additional propositions may not have the same empirical support, they are, at the least, plausible hypotheses. Unlike system components, it is sometimes difficult and misleading to link them with individual media because they relate to qualities that change over time as technological innovations restructure communicator and communicatee groups and alter the relation of medium to symbol system. As appropriate, however, their relation to differences among media will be noted.

*Feedback.*

*The greater the distance in space and/or time between sender and receiver, the more difficult and limited the feedback.* Contact entails a cost of surmounting any impediments between actors; space and time always are impediments to contact. Technological innovations can reduce but, thus far, have never removed this cost. The impact of space can be viewed as cross-sectional; distance without regard to direction imposes a cost in terms of the time and energy needed to traverse it. Passage of time, because it is unidirectional, is a different order of impediment. Because people can change, as time passes, communicators to whom communicatees provide feedback are less and less likely to be the same actors, and the more time passes, the more likely is mortality to take its toll and make feedback impossible. The media, of course, vary in size of area served, time used to reach the consumer, and span of exposure. First-run films accumulate audiences for weeks; network television acquires an audience during the few minutes that a program is being aired. Moreover, when material is sent frequently, as is the case with newspapers and television news, feedback must be rapid and general to be useful because the product changes continuously. For such reasons, space and time should have their most detrimental impact on feedback for film, and, in decreasing order, for magazines, for network radio and television, and for local radio, television, and newspapers.

*The more expensive the technology, the more difficult and less useful is feedback.* Two factors are pertinent here. For one thing, expensive production technology automatically entails high production costs. This tends to restrict producers' options for altering their products and thus reduces the utility of feedback to them. On the receiver side, little if any media technology permits direct and rapid feedback. Adding feedback capability to equipment would increase its cost considerably. Assuming a ceiling on what receivers can and are willing to spend on equipment and given that most media consumers do not provide feedback now and never have done so, it is unlikely that persons who now pay close to the maximum they are willing to pay would be interested in spending even more for equipment with feedback capability. By such logic, generally, feedback would be most impaired for film (high cost of production and exhibition equipment) and television (high cost of monitors and receivers) and least impaired for newspapers and magazines.

*The more esoteric and complex the content of media material, the more difficult for the public at large and easier for the targeted audience to provide feedback.* The proposition employs an obvious argument. Feedback presumes interest. Specialized material is directed to homogeneous, interested groups. Members of general audiences do not select it should they come upon it or quickly drop such material. There is not enough interest to generate feedback. In contrast, the intended audience for specialized material presumably is interested in receiving it and better able to offer a critical response. Because all media now target special audiences to some degree, the proposition would seem to apply equally to them all.

*The greater the status difference between sender and receivers, the more limited the feedback.* This proposition, like the preceding one, applies to all media inasmuch as, on average, producers have higher status than consumers. The underlying mechanism is social distance. Persons of unequal status are less likely than persons of similar status to interact. Status difference creates social distance, and social distance impedes communication much as does spatial distance. Feedback is impeded partly because people of different statuses are less likely to frequent the same places and partly because people feel loathe to express themselves across status levels, even when they are accessible to one another.

*Noise.*

*All other things being equal, the main source of noise in print media tends to be internal and in audiovisual media external.* The key condition is "all others things being equal." Obviously, it is assumed that no background noise is loud enough to distract a reader. It also is assumed that the receiver does not have handicaps that impair reception. Given unimpaired conditions and an environment conducive to reading, the main sources of interference would tend to be ambiguities in messages, lack of background for understanding the message, and/or lack of concentration on the reader's part. Loss of light or interference by others are much less likely intrusions. Flaws in production that could distort printed material usually are caught and corrected at the source. In contrast, viewing and listening are much more subject to external impediments because audiovisual equipment fails relatively frequently and reception almost coincides with transmission (or exhibition in film). Moreover, a listener or viewer can easily be distracted by intrusions that an involved reader might not even notice. However, the audiovisual media—particularly television—do have the advantages of (a) being able to employ richer symbolism and thus reduce the chance of ambiguity of meaning, and (b) not requiring reading skill for easy reception and comprehension.

*The more costly the receiving apparatus, the more likely that the receiving environment will be designed to minimize noise and facilitate reception.* Indeed, more expensive receiving equipment is more likely to require a special operating environment. Reading requires no apparatus, only sufficient lighting and not too much noise. A large screen television set not only costs much more but requires a room large enough to permit proper viewing distance from the screen and lighting that does not glare or reflect off the screen. Proper film exhibition entails even more expense—projector, sound system, screen, a dark and quiet space of adequate size. Attention to noise reduction in designing settings for media reception, then, declines from film to television to radio to print.

*The more focused the targeted audience, the less the internal noise in a system.* This restates the mechanism behind internal noise. The more homogeneous a group, the more values, experience, and language the members share. Therefore, experienced communicators who know what is common to the group should find it easier to create interesting, understandable messages. This principle primarily applies to units within media, the range from more to less specialization being greater within each medium than among media.

*The more complex the message components, the greater the possibility of internal noise.* Although complexity can enhance meaning and, by reinforcement, increase the likelihood of a message being received as intended, it also can increase the risk of introducing confusing contradictions. For example, print and voice over can be inconsistent in film and television, as can repeated accounts of the same event in print. Because all media can produce and transmit simple and complex messages, the proposition applies to all of them. The proposition is superfluous for communication because repetitious complexity is redundant rather than informative. However, due to the facts that (a) communicators may consider their work to be artistic self-expression as well as an effort to transmit meaning, and (b) receivers may not understand the minimal information-laden message, complex message structure will continue to characterize media materials.

*Redundancy.*

*The more lasting the message format, the less the built-in redundancy.* This proposition underlies the observation that redundancy is less necessary in print than in audiovisual media. Print messages are relatively permanent, and readers can set their own pace and reread the same material as much as necessary; audiovisual messages are ephemeral and gone almost as soon as they are delivered. Among the audiovisual media, however, forms of built-in redundancy vary. In television and film, for example, material can be presented simultaneously in print and speech and repeated in either or both forms. Radio, in contrast, only permits repetition over time in the same or altered format.

*The greater the capacity of a medium to transmit and express various symbolic forms, the easier it is to disguise redundancy.* The trend has been to develop equipment that can capture, transmit, and receive material in various symbolic forms. Much of the appeal of film and television rests on their capacity to represent material in several forms simultaneously (e.g., picture, print, sound). Print media deliver pictures and words but not sound. Radio is most limited as it is restricted to only the various forms of sound.

*The easier it is to reverse sender and receiver roles and the higher the reversal rate, the less the redundancy.* Role reversal can be feedback, and feedback lessens the need for redundancy by indicating when messages fail. In those cases, repetitions technically are not redundant from the perspective of the receiver. To the extent, therefore, that a medium has attributes that impede feedback, it will rely on redundancy. Because all the media permit little role reversal, they do not vary much in this regard. Several innovations in audiovisual technology are geared in this direction, however, so some sorting out may be expected. Moreover, traditional technologies eventually will merge, and people will be able to get hard copies of what they see and hear immediately. As these changes cumulate, the mass media as we know them will be gone.

*Message.*

*The more exclusive and controlled access to reception is, the more can messages be targeted to specific groups.* Access to media material can be controlled in several ways, pricing being the most obvious. High cost cuts the number of people who can afford a medium and, thus, stratifies the potential receiving group economically. Two other widely used tactics are control by vendor and scheduling. Vendors can impose age, gender, or other requirements on potential consumers in order to create homogeneous audiences by excluding those for whom material is not intended. This obligation has been placed on purveyors of sexually oriented material and on theater managers who are expected to make audience composition conform with the film rating system by screening the ages of ticket purchasers. Late-night television scheduling restricts children's access to adult material. New technology denies access to cable television channels that show material intended only for limited groups. The goal in controlling access to a medium is to enable it to carry material that is acceptable only for some groups. Targeting by controlling access is a tactic of exclusion from rather than inclusion in an audience and, to the extent that implementation relies on human judgment and execution or behavior regularities rather than on technology, can be quite inefficient. However, inefficiency always has been a hallmark of voluntary systems of mass communication.

*The less the likelihood of noise, the more complex a message can be.* Complex messages are difficult to follow and understand and, therefore, demand concentration. External noise interrupts and distracts, so usually there is an effort to have a low-noise environment for such material. Internal noise is an entirely different matter, because complexity often is the noise that makes understanding such hard work.

*The greater the opportunity for redundancy, the more complex a message can be.* Redundancy for a sender can be an opportunity to correct failure for a receiver. Print's advantage in this regard is its potential for infinite redundancy. Moreover, print lasts, so readers can continue to refresh themselves as necessary.

Synoptic comparisons of media systems are gross generalizations. Statements that may fit *Popular Photography* may misrepresent *Time*. Statements about television series such as "Family Ties" may not apply to "Lonesome Dove," and those that apply to a commercial network may not apply to public television. The *New York Times* and *The Enquirer* obviously differ. Nonetheless, on average, media depictions provide a way to highlight some of their essential differences. The fact that media differ in both style and substance—and these are not just cosmetic differences—suggests that their survival reflects more than the ability of each to develop a niche not served by the others. It also reflects success in competition, for, in part, each provides similar substance to the same prospective audience, varying their presentation only enough to invite consumers to choose on the basis of taste.

Organizing the discussion around the components and processes of the communication system model unavoidably leads to redundancies. They reflect the fact that each medium is a system, for it is essential that viable systems have multiple strong ties among their components. Hence, it is almost impossible to consider one aspect of a system and not refer to the others. The redundancies also testify to how dynamic these systems are, for much of what differentiates them are their responses to their technological innovations and to each other.

## THE CONTEXT OF COMMUNICATION SYSTEMS

It is totally unrealistic to treat human systems of social communication as isolated self-contained units sealed off from outside forces. Figure 3.1 indicates this by arrows that cross system boundaries. At the most general level, at any given time all systems are shaped by the combination of social, political, and economic forces operating in the total national and international environment (Thorburn, 1988: 53). Mowlana (1990: 91) also affirmed this explicitly, but his statement that "[t]he boundaries of a mass communication system can be defined as all those actions more or less directly related to the formation and distribution of its messages in a society" does not help in distinguishing and identifying either the endogenous or exogenous factors important to the mass communication process. However, many exogenous factors already have been mentioned (e.g., the effect of sun spots on telecommunications), and many others still are to be discussed. In particular, social norms derive from, are shared by, and govern the behavior of all members of a social group, not just those directly engaged in a particular system of communication. Many norms (e.g. equity, justice) apply to all members of the larger social group in all circumstances. For certain sorts of questions (e.g., the perennial issue of controlling the media), it is absolutely essential to consider such factors as government agencies, financial institutions, and public pressure groups in order to understand the process that determines the characteristic message flow of the media.[8]

An infinite number of exogenous factors can have an impact on the structure and operation of communication systems. Some are considerably more important than others; which are more important depends on the particular system and the question. It would be useful to identify these factors for systems of mass communication because the view that mass media are the private preserves of their owners or those charged with operating them tends to neglect the roles of such pervasive and relevant factors as patent laws, the economics of technological innovation, standards and techniques of labor organization, public morality, the international economy, and the community of nations.

The role of the larger society in which communication systems operate has engaged the attention of many well-known social scientists (e.g., Margaret Mead, Edward Sapir, Daniel Lerner, Benjamin Whorf). Their path-breaking work suggests several prototypical propositions about the relationships of exogenous factors to system qualities. Among those that have had a major impact on scholarship in the social sciences are the following:

1. The direction of denotative elaboration of symbol systems reflects the cultural values and environment of a society.[9]
2. The smaller a society, the greater the probability that communication will occur in face-to-face systems and be characterized by expressive utterances.
3. The more complex the organization of the society, the greater both the segmentation among communication systems and the specialization of message content.
4. The more permissive are the social norms that govern individual participation in systems of communication, the more important are the factors that affect compatibility in the survival of communication systems.

Propositions such as these build on the implications of several empirical observations: (a) environment defines the conditions of contact, thus focusing group concerns and interests and shaping organization; (b) group size and heterogeneity are positively related to organization differentiation and specialization; (c) maintenance of organizations requires conforming role behavior; and, as a corollary, (d) in all systems of communication social norms prescribe who takes what roles under what circumstances and who may use what portions of the symbol system and apparatus to communicate what messages on what topics to whom. If this were a treatise on communication systems generally, these points would be developed extensively. For a consideration of media systems, however, only the general proposition that contexts shape and are shaped by systems is important, for the context in which the mass media developed has shaped them and our conceptions of them.

No discussion of the importance of context in shaping communication systems and how they operate can be adequate without mentioning the fact that scholars in every area of sociological inquiry are well aware that context influences the operation and structure of social phenomena. This accounts for both comparative analysis and multilocus studies of many phenomena (e.g., status attainment processes and occupational prestige, mate selection, extent and modes of political participation, different outcomes of social movements and efforts to accomplish change) including sociological studies of specific aspect(s) of the media. Park's (1955 [1923]) seminal studies of the role of the daily newspaper interpreted them from the specific context of a modern urban society and what such a system requires. Many years later, Janowitz (1952) took the same approach when he sought to understand the proliferation and popularity of weekly neighborhood papers in Chicago. Several years later, Riley and Riley (1954 [1951]) showed that various aspects of children's media behavior could be explained by taking account of their peer groups and families, and Smith (1954) reported high relationships between type of farm organization and farmers' use of media for market news. Throughout the 1970s, Tichenor, Donohue, and Olien (1980) studied 19 different communities in which they drew on the qualities of these places to explain differences in the role of newspapers in the resolution of common community conflicts, especially in terms of how local citizens thought about the issues.

All such studies implicitly reflect the principle with which the discussion in this chapter began, that the media are systems within systems. The problems in drawing generalizations from the many such studies are twofold: (a) the relevant context for particular studies varies enormously, and (b) studies that are properly designed to permit analysis of how context impinges on the matter under study are very expensive and time-consuming. Hence, although there are many studies that take account of context, most of them are at best only suggestive or illustrative of how context makes a difference. Studies of the media in a social context, be it a country, a community, a family, a peer group, a school, a church, a factory, or whatever, are a main part of the essential core of a sociology of mass communication. The other part is comprised of studies of communication as a social system and social behavior in its own right.

## NOTES

1. Long after this illustrative analysis was prepared, Ball-Rokeach and Reardon (1988) published a similar analysis in which they contrasted interpersonal, mass, and what they called telelogic communication. They coined the latter term to refer to dialogues mediated by equipment (e.g., e-mail exchanges, interactive television). Their cases not only differ from the examples used here but also vary by being at the same rather than at different levels of generality. In this respect they have an advantage. In addition, though, they employ many more dimensions for contrast, 43 to be exact. Although this strategy is very useful for identifying potentially important distinguishing features of the three types of systems, it employs far more concepts than are necessary for constructing a powerful concept of a communication system.
2. This is not to imply that any media material is free. It is the method of payment and its closeness to consumption that varies; hence, cost varies in saliency. Radio and television are the media with no apparent cost at the time of consumption, special pay-for-view telecasts are the exception. Cable television, in contrast, is more like home newspaper delivery and magazine subscriptions. All three are paid for periodically, independently of the place and time of receipt and consumption. Newspapers and magazines purchased at a newsstand and pay-for-view television are somewhat more like motion pictures seen at a theater. In these cases, payment usually is temporally close to consumption, although cost tends to disappear as a factor while the person is engrossed in the material.
3. The different apparatuses employed by the media constrain the ways in which their "personal" representatives can present themselves to the public. This is a major factor in the development of what have been called media styles (Cardiff, 1986).
4. The norms of thoroughness and objectivity that have been adopted as the hallmark of quality journalism militate against the development by print journalists of a personal style and, hence, a personal identity.
5. More detailed information on many attributes of communicator organization, particularly with regard to the markets with which they must deal and their financing, may be found in analyses of the economics of

media industries by Picard (1989), Owen and Wildman (1992), and Lacy and Simon (1993).
6. An extensive survey of recent studies of audience structure and of the consuming behavior of audience members can be found in the first two chapters of Comstock's (1991) book on television and children. Nelson (1989) argues that even the notion of consumption is a poorly constructed metaphor for the variety of experiences people have when the television set is on.
7. Wober (1988) has already begun to systematize all the sensitivities that may be employed in receiving potential new media.
8. Cogley's study (1956) of blacklisting in the movie, radio, and television industries is an excellent example of how exogenous factors interact with the mass communication process. Farace and Donohew (1965) studied the impact of numerous societal features on the mass media systems of more than 100 countries.
9. As an example of this effect in one of the media, after studying the wide divergence between how U.S. and Japanese newspapers use graphics, Beniger and Westney concluded (1981: 27) that ". . . cultural factors would seem to be most useful in accounting for the style of computer graphics. . . ."

# 5

# The Social Role of Mass Communication and the Media

The relationship of communication to the larger society is bidirectional. In some circumstances, to some extent, in some fashion, all communication systems are objects of pressures and subject to influence. Contrariwise, consideration of (a) why media processes are referred to as "mass," and (b) the aspects of modern life that are attributed to the media indicates that everything from the world system to single individuals may be influenced in some fashion to some degree by some facet of the media. These apparently contradictory contingencies are reflected in the study of mass communication. On the one hand, considerable research supports a picture of the media as the object and victim of societal pressures and conflicts. On the other hand, even more research treats the media as a dominant force that influences and shapes individuals and society, sometimes on their own—in which case senders as well as receivers may be influenced or constrained by them—but more often as a tool of rapacious owners or their confederates in a societal power elite. These several contingencies can be summarized in the following four models:

1. **Communicator ⟶ Media ⟶ Communicatee.**
   This is a simple model of media influence in which owners, managers, and/or operators of media systems use them to have some desired impact on those exposed to them. It is the classic picture of media advertising or campaigning.
2. **Communicatee ⟶ Communicator ⟶ Media.**
   This is a simple model of feedback. Receivers make their wishes and preferences known to senders, who, in turn, adjust their performance accordingly, or, in rarer cases, desist from media operation entirely.
3. **Media ⟷ Exogenous societal elements.** This model depicts an ongoing relationship between the media and society, in which, on the one hand, societal norms, practices, and interest groups constrain media performance (e.g., community norms on obscenity) and, on the other, the media change societal practices and expectations (e.g., changed scheduling of publicly attended sporting events to meet media schedules).
4. **Media ⟵ ⟶ Communicator**
        **⟶ Communicatee**

   This model depicts contingencies in any system in which the apparatus may be active and/or in which unaware or ignorant users are unable to control some of its capacities. It indicates both (a) that the performance of the media may be influenced by the limited capacities of those involved on either side of the communication process, and (b) that the performance of those involved may be influenced in ways they otherwise would not be by their inability to send and/or receive media material as they otherwise might.

The four models actually depict several relationships between two critical social processes—media effects or influence, and media control. In the former, interest is in the effects that the media may have on society, groups, and individuals through various mechanisms of influence; in the latter, interest is in whether and how the performance and operation of the media is influenced. Model 1 is a model of effects and model 2 a model of control. The essential difference is that when the arrowhead points away from the media it indicates a media impact, and when it points toward the media it indicates a controlling influence. Models 3 and 4 incorporate both processes. Model 3 depicts a continuous loop of impact between the media and societal elements not directly involved in the communication process as targeted or actual receivers or as senders. It reflects the view that the media are integral to rather then apart from society. Model 4 sketches a similar loop between those who are directly involved and emphasizes the systemic character of the media. The arrowheads toward the media represent control, those away from the media influence.

In this chapter I discuss in very broad terms more than a half century of research on media effects and influence. In the next I do the same for control. It must be emphasized, though, that the division is arbitrary and that the study of influence and the study of control both reflect the deep relationship between the two (i.e., control is sought by those who wish to influence and, in response, efforts are triggered to control those who are so motivated). Indeed, even if those in control make every effort to avoid this reaction, the occurrence of negative social or personal effects will often lead to efforts at further control.

## MASS AND MASS COMMUNICATION

Thus far, I have used the term *mass* without carefully specifying its meaning and what that implies for *mass communication*. Raymond Williams commented (Heath and Skirrow, 1986: 3) that, used as a modifying adjective, the term is particularly ambiguous. It would seem to attribute large size, bulk, or similar qualities to any phenomenon with which it is linked. Certainly one would not quibble with the notion that the mass media are large-scale enterprises. Typically, they involve large quantities of people as well as much money, time, and energy. NBC employed well over 1,000 people in Seoul, South Korea, to televise the 1988 Summer Olympic Games. Generally, this is the sense in which the term is used in everyday speech. In physics, however, mass refers to the quantity of material in a body, regardless of whether it is a small or large amount, that is, the mass of an object. The connotations it originally carried in the phrase *mass communication* probably did not derive from either of these usages, although the former probably has sustained it. More likely, it was adopted because its technical meaning in social science seemed to fit social conditions at the time that the media first commanded scholarly attention. I have been using it in that sense and will continue to do so.

In explicating the social scientific usage of the term, Blumer (1954) defined a *mass* as a large group of individuals whose interests are captured by a common stimulus and which, as a group: (a) has a membership that comes from all social strata; (b) is composed of anonymous individuals; (c) has little interaction or exchange of experience among the members, who are usually physically separated; and (d) is very loosely organized and unable to act concertedly. The stimulus to which the individuals are giving their attention is also special in that it comes from outside the local situation of those exposed to it and, hence, is not to be understood by their local rules, regulations, or expectations. In a sense, the definition specifies just the opposite of the minimal conditions for a social group to be one.

The mass is given special attention by sociologists because it is a limiting case that epitomizes the asocial. A person's attention—and it must be emphasized that it is a lone individual—is captured by a stimulus that is puzzling and confusing but, nonetheless, compelling. Because the stimulus is novel, it creates a sense of uneasiness and presses for a response. For the same reason (i.e., novelty), the individual is uncertain and without clues as to an appropriate action. By definition, the mass is an analytic and not a membership or a reference group at the time its members are exposed to the novel stimulus, that is, only an observer would know that they are experiencing the same stimulus. All that they have in common is the experience of perceiving the same stimulus at the same time, a sense that it calls for an urgent response, and no normatively supported idea as to what response is appropriate. The conditions of exposure prevent them from knowing that others are sharing the experience, checking on whether they are perceiving it correctly, and organizing to respond to it. When they do react they must do so as individuals without social support. The difficulty and frustration of being forced to act without knowing how others would judge one's actions creates severe stress. Unguided individual action is also socially threatening because unexpected and unconventional actions in response to a stimulus that others may not even perceive appears to be random, unpredictable behavior. Such behavior ordinarily is experienced as disconcerting and threatening. An acting mass would be disorganizing for a normal society.

More than 40 years ago Selznick (1951) analyzed how the threat of mass behavior has devastating consequences for society. He argued that, in order to alleviate the symptoms that lead to the potential for such individual behavior, the attention and activities of societal leadership and transcendent institutions—those whose social roles have gained them respect (e.g., higher education, religion)—are diverted from their traditional functions to ameliorative activities that address the immediate needs that vulnerable people express. This creates a major problem because there is nothing to fill the gap left by the diversion of these leaders and institutions from their traditional roles. Further, he noted that the individuals most prone to distraction by novel stimuli are also very susceptible to recruitment by demagogues who claim to know the causes of whatever is disturbing those individuals and offer attractive—although not rational—solutions. The theory of mass society predicts that, absent these adaptations in institutions and leadership or prevention of the occurrence of novel, compelling stimuli (e.g., censorship, media restrictions), outbreaks of mass behavior and the rise of demagogic social movements are always imminent in complex, rapidly changing societies. That is the connotation of "mass society"—a society in which demagogic social movements or episodes of mass behavior are always imminent.

Perhaps, the one clear American case of active mass behavior in this century was provided by responses to the 1938 Mercury Theater Sunday evening radio dramatization of H. G. Wells' "War of the Worlds" (Cantril, 1966). For people who tuned in too late to hear that it was a dramatization in news bulletin form and who also lacked the contacts to check out the "facts," the news that Martians had landed in New Jersey, were destroying anything in their path, and were impervious to the Army's best weapons, was indeed a novel and compelling stimulus. Their various responses—driving off at high speed, patrolling their front yards with guns, hysterical talk about Martians, and the like—were random, unusual for a normal Sunday evening, and disturbing to people who saw them and did not even know about the program. Novel stimuli, however, usually are not that novel, nor do they press so urgently for a response. More typical might be warnings that a country is on the brink of war or economic disaster. Most analysts suggest that, short of directly easing an otherwise threatening environment, participation in mass demagogic social movements that promise to provide easy solutions to such dire possibilities is the likelier outlet, unless the potential is defused by institutional cooptation of the sort described by Selznick.

Concerns about institutional cooptation and redirection and the rise of demagogic social movements reflect the tendency, when analyzing the social impact of "the mass," to focus on adaptive responses to its imminence rather than on outbreaks of random behavior. If this emphasis is realistic, the concept of the mass refers to a group in becoming rather than one in being—to a potential rather than a reality. In fact, episodes of mass behavior, in the literal sense, on any large scale have been rare. Episodes are fleeting and ephemeral; for an organized society they are intolerable threats. If the mass is imminent rather than real—it rarely is manifested in action and, if it is, the episodes occur unpredictably and are brief—mass communication cannot literally mean an effort to communicate to members of masses. In fact, in the true mass situation there could be no communication as it is defined here. Communicators would be unable to identify targeted recipients who comprised the mass. It is in this sense that mass communication is a contradiction in terms.

For similar reasons, the phrase *mass society* is a contradiction; the first word indicates randomness and individual isolation, the second, collective order. But the concept is useful in that it suggests that a society experiencing increasing complexity, size, secularity, and rapid change (among several well-recognized factors) can lead many people to become "mass-like," that is, prone to the reactions described. Accordingly, mass society conditions are reflected, at the level of individual behavior, in abnormal actions, frequent random occurrence of such actions, or affiliation with mass social movements. At the societal level it is expressed in such developments as the preemption of the major culture-bearing institutions and their adoption of demagogic techniques, the creation of large organizations to serve special interest groups (e.g., unions, political parties), and the growth in size (massification) of institutional units (e.g., the trend from small business to large business, conglomerates, and cartels).

Historically, societies that developed these characteristics also were societies in which the mass media developed. Social scientists long have recognized that large, complex, rapidly changing societies could not maintain their integration without the technical capacities of such systems. To survive, such societies require reliable and effective means of receiving and disseminating information and beliefs rapidly and widely. Systems that employ media technology enable them to monitor their larger environments, make coordinated rapid responses as threats arise, and create and sustain effective organization. Consequently, large, complex, rapidly changing societies and fast, widely available, technically mediated communication systems have tended to develop in conjunction.

Confusions about the relation of mass society to mass communication have tended to occur because, in the effort to understand these developments, co-development and correlation based on common antecedents can be confused with causation. Just as there is no evidence that media systems ever have been used expressly to reach those individuals most likely to participate in outbreaks of mass behavior or to join in mass social movements, there also is no evidence that they have been used intentionally to create or facilitate the type of institutional adaptations that Selznick identified. Moreover, even if there had been such efforts, they would not have been instances of communication because they would have been conceived predominantly as programs to influence rather than to share meanings. Nonetheless, the growth of large, populous countries with heterogeneous, dispersed populations isolated from traditional communities and activities creates needs that encourage and hasten the development of technologies essential to the growth and expansion of the communication systems that we now call the media.

## Social Role of Mass Communication

Figure 5.1 summarizes the main features of these relationships among the mass society, the mass, and the mass media. Mass societal qualities developed, and the mass media came to prominence in their early modern forms (i.e., not the first, but the first *mass circulation* magazines and newspapers), at approximately the same time in the same social conditions. The mass society designates the social conditions in which the potential for the mass to become an acting group is high. The mass, in rare instances, may become active through the agency of an inadvertent stimulus carried by the media or, more commonly, may become passive or have its energies diverted into other activities through the agency of other characteristic types of media material. In either case, the media are only one of several agents that contribute to these outcomes. Finally, when there are causal relationships, the most common one may be ameliorative—the media may help to avert the more destructive varieties of mass behavior.

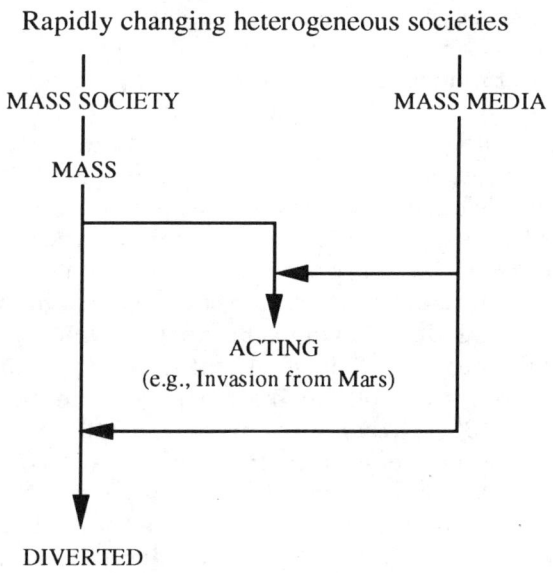

**Figure 5.1. Relations among mass society, mass media, and the mass**

Friedson (1954), in a particularly insightful analysis, assessed a number of other senses in which these systems of communication have been characterized as mass-like and concluded in each instance that they are not. The mass image, for example, would suggest that the typical consuming person is engaged in an isolated experience. In reality, this is not the case. People attend the movies in small groups, watch television with others, and so on. These groupings may, indeed, be isolated but, nonetheless, they are groups that offer opportunities to check one's responses. Lazarsfeld's (Katz and Lazarsfeld, 1955; Katz, 1957) conception of the "two-step flow of influence" accords with these observations. It describes the typical consumption of mass media materials as a social rather than an isolated process. Sindlinger polls repeatedly show that people use the media to provide something to talk about with others, behavior that would be impossible if media users were not embedded in social networks.

Friedson also pointed to a number of characteristics of media systems and the process of mass communication that contradict the mass image: No audience is all-inclusive, membership tends to be selective on socially meaningful criteria; media managers target intended audiences which, despite their large size, are almost never intended to be all-inclusive; and, in the vast majority of cases, audience reactions to mass media materials are predictable rather than random and inexplicable. Had he written 30 years later he could have emphasized these points even more, particularly the targeting of intended audiences, a practice that has helped older media survive the pressure of television and that now characterizes all media production.

If a discussion of the mass and its implications for the phrase *mass media* seems inappropriate today, it probably is because the "mass society" construct that relates the mass to the media is time-bound and value-laden. It was a product of wistful romanticizing about an idyllic past and fear of the future in the rapidly changing, disorganized conditions of the West between the two World Wars (Shils, 1951, 1963; Parsons and White, 1960; Wilensky, 1966). Because its substance reflects the instability of the period in which it developed and because instability continues to characterize our times, the mass society concept may capture the contemporary mood. However, it does not capture contemporary structural conditions. Many of what had been reasons for individual unease earlier have been accommodated by changes in societal structures. Save for random violence, other destabilizing threats have been "normalized" by the way in which the media treat them. Understanding of the media is hindered by linking them to such time-bound concepts as the mass and mass society.[1]

This is not to claim that modern media have nothing to do

with mass society. The point is only that they are not *primary causes* of whatever is perceived to be threatening or dysfunctional in mass-like situations. In truth, several features of the media have considerable potential for prompting mass behavior or for generating mass movements. They do distract the attention of large numbers of persons at the same time. They do emphasize easier-to-transmit, emotionally laden, provocative symbols and contribute to the development and dissemination of mass culture more than do most other systems of communication (Heath and Skirrow, 1986). They are likely to attract the attention of individuals who have the greatest potential for mass behavior. This is significant even if those persons constitute only a small proportion of the population. The threat of a mass society expressed in mass behavior, after all, is in the disorganizing consequences rather than the quantity of random, unpredictable behavior. To grasp the point one need only imagine how disruptive a small number of drivers suddenly and randomly driving on the left or ignoring traffic signals would be. In view of the potential affinities of the mass media to the mass society, the appropriate question is not "Is the society a mass society and to what extent does mass communication contribute to this situation?", but, rather, "What is the potential for 'massness' in the society and how do the media affect that potential?"[2]

It is too late to establish more appropriate terminology. However, if we accept mass communication and mass media as firmly established terms, at least we may enhance understanding of the structural features and internal organization of the media by looking into how and why they came into use. Understanding this can sensitize scholars to some broad social functions of the media that otherwise might not be apparent. The possibility of such consequences does not preclude the possibility of others (Lazarsfeld and Merton, 1948). And Phillips' (1982) claim that his data showed that media reports stimulate the imitation of aberrant behavior and Singer's (1970) evidence that media coverage stimulated participation in an urban riot suggest that contemporary social conditions may not be so different from those of mass society.

The practice of associating the media with mass society conditioned the study of mass media in the period between World Wars I and II. European scholars focused on mass society in response to the social climate and political events of the period—the rise to power of the Nazis in Germany, Fascists in Italy and Spain, and Communists in Russia and the relative disinterest of people in the Western democracies in these developments; the rabid antisemitism in Germany and its somewhat less violent manifestations in other countries; the repression and execution of Kulaks in the U.S.S.R.; the proliferation of demagogic sociopolitical movements such as Social Credit, the Townsend movement, and Huey Longism; the apathy of the unemployed during the Great Depression—rather than in response to concentrated, overt manifestations of random, bizarre, mass-like behavior (cf. Ward, 1989: 10-11). In their view, economic turmoil, warfare, and major social changes (e.g., loss of local community with urbanization, loss of worker skills with the growth of mass production industry) increased the vulnerability of people to the rhetoric of demagogues who promised to identify their enemies, redress their grievances, and lead the nation from a deprived existence in a vale of frustration and incipient doom to a better life in a restructured world.

These scholars were well aware of the promotion of demagogic movements through the new media (e.g., the Nazis' use of radio and film, Father Coughlin's radio talks) and came to view the media as integral to the mass society. Their primary interest was in whether and how the media furthered the most negative manifestations of mass society and in the underutilized constructive potential of the media. They focused on the chronic rather than the acute (i.e., such rare events as "The Invasion from Mars" reaction) consequences of mass communication. It was not that the latter were of no concern—this was a period in which it was thought that the media had what is now called a "hypodermic" (Bineham, 1988) effect (e.g., viewing a crime film would by itself lead some adolescents to commit crimes)—but that the former was more pressing. After all, their lives were threatened by these developments.

The intellectual approach to mass communication that developed in that social climate continues to influence scholarly interest in the media. Because of their use by totalitarians in bringing about a democratic collapse, most intellectuals of that period considered the media to be tools for organizing mob-like mass behavior and, therefore, enemies of free intellectual activity. It colored their scholarship. Their acceptance of Lasswell's proposal to organize the available research and the further study of mass communication around the paradigmatic question, "Who Says What In Which Channel To Whom With What Effect?," is not surprising. It is a formulation that reflects a view of the media as an institution of great potential effectiveness that can be used intentionally by powerful groups for (good or) evil social ends.

## THE SOCIAL ROLE OF THE MASS MEDIA

The question of whether the media are "mass" directs attention to their most distinctive features and the broad issue of their role in modern societies. It would be fair to say that the explosion in media studies over the last 25 years is a response to renewed concern about those roles, one that has waxed and waned at least since William Randolph Hearst was accused of using his newspapers to instigate the Spanish-American War as a way of promoting his personal political ambitions (see, e.g., Winkler, 1928: 143-63; Lundberg, 1936: 66-82). The heightened recent interest is based on concern and not curiosity, for on balance the social role of the media still is viewed as negative rather than positive, destructive rather than constructive, and socially dysfunctional rather than functional. Such disparate matters as the refusal until 1976 of the Union of South Africa to allow domestic television broadcasting (cf. Harrison and Ekman, 1977; Hachten, 1979), concerns that young children are unable to distinguish fact from fiction in the media, claims that the media convert people in modern industrial societies from participants to observers, and charges that media coverage rather than citizens' informed rational choices decides elections express this concern. Continuing surveillance of and demand for new controls on the media by a broad spectrum of groups are direct consequences.

Public and scholarly interest in the media's social role are premised on the conviction that the media are effective. Gitlin's (1978) analysis of early media sociology, its sponsorship, and its substance, advanced the thesis that Rockefeller Foundation officials decided to fund radio research on the belief that support for administrative research (Lazarsfeld, 1941) would provide knowledge that could be used to direct the development of radio along lines that would serve their patron's socioeconomic interests (cf. Rowland, 1983: 53-86; Carey, 1988: 69-88).[3] Perhaps the classic example of such administrative research is a study done in the late 1940s, the primary purpose of which was to help develop a replacement for radio soap operas, then under attack as socially undesirable polluters of the air waves.[4] Soap opera fans were interviewed in depth to identify exactly what it was in the stories, their presentation, and dramatic devices that made them devotees. The goal was to reproduce these features in a new format not as easy to label as "escapist fantasy." The product—the audience participation quiz show—had the virtue of disguising escape as education while retaining the basic appeal of the serials, that is, a string of suspenseful events culminating in a positive outcome for ordinary, good people like the audience members. Both types of programs, although manifestly different, could divert people from critically examining to uncritically accepting the status quo in society by fostering confidence in the belief that playing by the rules produces valued rewards. In this manner, they served the interests of dominant groups by averting demands for basic changes to assure that the practice of socially approved means would lead to the attainment of socially desirable ends.

Media research during that period was largely funded by foundations and corporations and emphasized identification of specific effects and the mechanisms through which they were produced (e.g., the Payne Fund studies[5] on whether gangster movies caused juvenile delinquency; Merton's [1946] study of Kate Smith's marathon radio war bond drive to identify the factors that motivated people to buy; and Katz and Lazarsfeld's [1955] study of the chains of interpersonal relations through which media impacted on women's decisions on which movies to attend, positions to take on public issues, fashions to wear, and where to shop). It was oriented by the aforementioned "hypodermic" view of media effects, that is, the media are likened to a hypodermic needle that inserts a causative agent (media messages) into passive recipients (audience members) who react as the content of the message suggests (e.g., DeFleur and Ball-Rokeach, 1982: 160-64; Bineham, 1988; Tuchman, 1988: 603; on the similar notion of "bullet theory," cf. Schramm, 1971: 7-11; Severin and Tankard, 1979: 125-26).[6] The mechanism presumed to link media and effects seemed analogous to a stimulus-response model (Berlo, 1960: 73-104).

Well into the 1950s, such studies were cited by media executives and business leaders resisting efforts to control their industries. With a few notable exceptions, most publicized research purported to demonstrate either beneficial, limited, or no effects of media (e.g., Sears and Freedman, 1967; Sears, 1968; for a review and evaluation of such research, see Comstock, Chaffee, Katzman, McCombs, and Roberts, 1978: chap. 7). The latter was the usual conclusion of studies to evaluate claims of specific negative media effects. One set of elegantly designed studies, for example, evaluated the charge that, either directly through the distribution of coverage and editorial support or indirectly by creating bandwagon effects with reports of how the electorate was leaning, the media were determining the results of elections. Their general conclusion was that there were no significant media effects on voting.[7] Skeptical critics were not surprised; research that routinely showed that the media primarily did only good things or nothing helped media interests avoid more stringent regulation.[8] Tuchman (1988: 605) has suggested that the "no effects" position also explains the slackened sociological interest in media research from the mid-1950s to the early 1970s (cf. Wright, 1986b).

Ironically, the claim of limited or no effects as a defense against regulation was self-defeating for the industry. Given the costs to produce and consume media material, why waste money and time on something with so little impact? Moreover, there were serious problems with the methods available to explore links between media exposure as a cause and reinforcement of or changes in specific beliefs and behavior as effects. In addition, the notion of no or limited effects stretched credulity, particularly so soon after the Nazis' innovative use of radio, print, and motion pictures for propaganda, their even more grandiose plans for using television after World War II (cf. Thorburn, 1988: 53), and Franklin D. Roosevelt's effective "fireside chats" on radio. It did not seem possible that steady exposure to large quantities of materials that portrayed a distorted world could have no individual or social consequences. It was and is an unconvincing position, but it has never died and is reexamined repeatedly (cf. McGuire, 1986). Indeed, one of the most striking things about the specific issues studied is the recurrent focus on negative consequences—the media and children, . . . and pornography, . . . and violence, . . . and the depoliticization of society, . . . and passivity, . . . and consumerism, . . . and the hegemony of capital.

Increasingly, the weight of scholarly opinion is that there are media effects, but the hypodermic analogy no longer is used as a model of how they occur. The declining dominance of the hypodermic model of effects has had two consequences. First, it has refocused ideas on what it is about the media that might have an effect from an almost exclusive emphasis on content to a much wider range of attributes of the media as a social institution and process. Second, and relatedly, it has opened conceptions of the mechanism of effect to a broad spectrum of complex possibilities that go far beyond simple stimulus-effect models. Perhaps most noteworthy is the range of ideas about the consequences of attributes of the media as such. These include a range of media properties from size and structure to personnel to the topics treated to textual organization and style. Selected results of studies premised on a belief in real effects can support any position on effects. In no particular order, the media have been identified as agenda setters; they tell us what to think and talk about (Thayer, 1988: 4-65), but not what positions to take (McCombs and Shaw, 1972; Shaw and McCombs, 1977; Weaver, Graber, McCombs, and Eyal, 1981; Wilhoit and deBock, 1981; Becker, 1982a). They are said to reenforce; they stabilize knowledge, attitudes, and behavior, whatever they may be, rather than introduce new ones (Comstock et al., 1978: 337-341; Parenti, 1986: 20-22). Thereby, they also inhibit change. It is claimed that they divert people from reality (Lazarsfeld and Merton, 1948; Klapper, 1960: 166-

205), but neither the reality nor the individual or social consequences of diversion are specified. Some scholars (McLeod and Reeves, 1980; McLeod, Kosicki, and Pan, 1991) have tried to categorize the various aspects of the media and their processes that are emphasized in studies of media effects, but, like any such effort, helpful as the results are, they tend to reflect the positions from which they begin.

The ten consecutive annual Videotown studies (Cunningham and Walsh, 1958) that traced the impact of the introduction of commercial television in New Brunswick, NJ, almost 40 years ago, and Williams' (1986) more recent studies of three British Columbia towns—one with no television, one with newly introduced television, one with long-established television—both document in detail the consequences of the introduction of television for community participation, family life, other media consumption, and the like. Even more sweeping have been sophisticated analyses by such scholars as Innis (e.g., 1951),[9] McLuhan (1962, 1964, 1967),[10] Meyrowitz (1985), and Postman (1985) that suggest that the character of the technology of each medium and the physical form of the messages they produce, rather than any specific message content, profoundly alter general patterns of behavior and the fundamental structure of social relations (see also Brenkman, 1979). Other analysts (e.g., Hallin, 1987; Bennett, 1988) suggest that reliance on entertaining material to promote sales of the first radio and television sets and the subsequent practice of selling audiences to advertisers, contingent on the audiences satisfying specific size and quality criteria, has cultivated their image as entertainment media, and that this, in turn, has eroded the potential of serious informational material to serve that function. They argue that because people have been so conditioned to expect entertainment from the media, informational material must be treated as stories and organized to fit entertainment formulae. Consequently, it is no longer veridical. In contrast to these broad analyses, Phillips continues to study very specific effects, for example, he has concluded that three days after the appearance of media items (e.g., news items, soap opera events) detailing suicides, violent crimes, accidents, and other deviant behavior, real events of the same type increase for about a week (Phillips, 1977, 1979, 1982; Bollen and Phillips, 1981).[11]

Almost as diverse is the variety of media sources of these possible effects. They vary from the media as a whole to a specific medium (e.g., newspapers, television, motion pictures) to particular operating units (e.g., the *New York Times, National Geographic*) to specific media products (e.g., Orson Welles' "War of the Worlds" broadcast, "Dallas," a set of stories in the newspaper) to aspects of presentation (e.g., color vs. black and white, broad vs. narrow columns). In this regard, a particularly important difference is the focus on messages or texts, on the one hand, and on technology and the related act of consumption, on the other. Attention to texts or messages reflects an interest in the impact of ideational material on those exposed to it. Focus on how technology shapes consumption reflects an interest in how the behavior that a technology calls for impacts on users irrespective of the messages conveyed.

Message and technology are particular manifestations of two broader, more inclusive classes of media attributes that may be the sources of effects—content and structure. Questions about the effects of messages, by virtue of either their interpretation by receivers and/or the intentions of their senders (i.e., aspects of meaning) or their style (i.e., aspects of form), concern consequences of media content. Questions about the effects of the format, organization, technology, availability, control arrangements, and/or patterns and conditions of consumption of the media without regard to or independently of content, address consequences of media structure. The distinction implies that they may be independent—that each can have an effect independent of that of the other—but they need not be. Even Meyrowitz (1985: 19), a strong proponent of focusing on the effects of media structure in order to redress their undeserved neglect, has noted that "... medium theorists are arguing that the form in which people communicate has an impact beyond the choice of specific messages. [Nevertheless, t]hey do not deny the significance of message choice *within* a cultural milieu" (emphasis in original).[12] Indeed, content and structure often operate jointly to produce the same effect, for example, monopolizing the media with propaganda increases the likelihood that people will accept it.

The difference between the impact of content and structural aspects of communication is illustrated by some widely voiced claims about the impact of media on children. On the one hand, the heavily publicized and long studied claim that media violence cultivates aggressive behavior in children illustrates how effects may be tied to media content. Tying the media to violence in children is not an isolated instance. Michael Jacobson, Director of the Center for Science in the Public Interest, is described in a newspaper feature (Pratt, 1991) as having said that "[c]hildren today may be more knowledgeable about nutrition than children of the 1970s, but they also are fatter and more sedentary, probably because of television. . . ." His comment employed similar reasoning. Jacobson suggested that fast food ads and seeing characters eating fast food and junk food on television inculcate children with bad nutritional habits. Presumably, children would not be as aggressive if they were not exposed to aggressive media characters. Likewise, their dietary habits might be better if they did not see ads for food products that are not good for them or bad food habits being practiced by television characters with whom they identify.

In contrast to assertions of this sort is a statement explaining the low average scores of North Carolina high school students on national college examinations. Suzanne Triplett, state Assistant Superintendent for Research and Development, was quoted as attributing the poor results to "... a lack of advanced courses, a lack of rigor in courses, a lack of homework and too much TV watching" (Associated Press, 1991). She did not claim that the scores were low because television programs empty students' heads of skills and knowledge or give students the message that it is to their advantage to score poorly. Rather, she claimed that the amount of time students devote to watching easily available television detracts from homework, hence, learning and, ultimately, test scores. Her concern was structural—time spent before the screen that is unavailable for other activities—not content related. Concern with what students watch clearly is secondary to concern that watching takes time from homework.

Structural aspects of the mass communication-mass media complex are so numerous that they defy easy classification. They range from highly specific aspects of the circumstances of consumption and production to the relationship between the two to much broader, inclusive aspects of the context of the activity and institution. Although, as indicated, they address such issues as how the inclusion of media consumption activities impacts on other facets of life, they also extend to such broad issues as the impact of new communication technologies on the underlying bases of social stratification systems, for example, the role of print in undermining the privileged status of those who produced and administered rare, hand produced copies of texts. Luhmann (1990c: 100) has suggested the possible breadth of the impact of communication systems by asserting that:

> ... [S]ociety ... is simply a network of communication. Therefore, if media and techniques of communication change, if the facilities and sensitivities of expression change, if codes change from oral to written communication, and, above all, if the capacities of reproduction and storage increase, new structures become possible, and eventually necessary, to cope with the new complexities.

A recent manifestation of this contingency is the attribution to new media technologies of what many observers feel is a new societal form—the information society (Higman, 1979; van Cuilenburg, 1987; Brooks, 1990).

With respect to content, a distinction between two types of content derived from a comparison of George Orwell's and Aldous

Huxley's negative depictions of modern media in their respective "dystopias"—*1984* and *Brave New World*—can be quite useful. In *1984*, Orwell depicts a world in which the media are used for constant surveillance of every person. Depending on what they observe, the authorities deliver explicit, pointed orders for what to do or not do to which people acquiesce out of fear. In Huxley's world, enjoyable, relaxing, distracting materials cause people to lose interest in anything beyond the satisfactions provided by the sensations they experience. This renders them unable to respond to the machinations of those who control society. The content addicts them to media consumption to a degree that they ignore the real world. The contrast sharply depicts direct and indirect messages with the same intentions. Even more than it captures two very different aspects of content that may have similar effects, the comparison captures essential differences in techniques which those who control media systems may employ to reach their goals.

The locus of effects that are studied is also highly varied. They may be in social structure, all members of a society, specific cultural elements (e.g., home furnishings, how families dine), small groups or sectors of society, or in individuals and their habits of thought and behavior. Moreover, they may be evaluated as positive, neutral, or negative for the unit on which they impact, as intentional or unintentional, or as being or not being at a level of public or individual consciousness and awareness.

The evaluation of effects warrants special comment. Judgments are relative to values, so they often arouse sharp disagreement. Evaluations of effects can vary without disputing their reality or causes. Positions on logging certain areas, for example, reflect relative values placed on preserving the spotted owl or the economic base. Furthermore, a media event may have both negative and positive consequences in two different ways: (a) it can be positive in some respects and negative in others (e.g., watching a film relaxes the student but takes time away from studies), and (b) it can be positive for some people and negative for others (e.g., a candidate's speech cheers supporters and angers opponents). This relativity makes it difficult to resolve controversies because partisans of each option on a media issue find it easy to defend and promote their view by claiming that the net value is on their side. Thus, even when scholars agree on a broad media function such as societal integration, they may disagree on whether it is a benefit (Allen, 1977) or a detriment (Cardiff and Scannell, 1987).

Claims about the roles of the media are so diverse that they can only be summarized succinctly at a very high level of abstraction (cf. Klapper, 1960; Blumler and Katz, 1974; McQuail, 1977, 1985:

104-107; Rosengren, Wenner, and Palmgreen, 1985; Tuchman, 1988).[13] It is important to understand that this is because each analysis or study is based on very different underlying models of the character of media consumption and assumptions as to whether the significant locus of their impact is individuals or collectivities (e.g., families, peer groups, industries, communities, society).[14] With regard to consumption models, the mass society approach implies passive consumers who accept uncritically and unselectively whatever happens to come. The image of audience members is that of fans—heavy and indiscriminate consumers of similar material from all media. It treats consumption like addiction—an uncontrollable, self-perpetuating end in itself—and is colored by the view that the media massify and dehumanize their audiences and society as a whole. A contrasting view of consumption is that audience members participate actively in the process by deciding in a selective and discriminating manner whether and what to consume and how to interpret it (cf. Cantor and Cantor, 1986a; Bryant and Street, 1988; Newcomb, 1988). This model has been more appropriate for studying change—the creation and loss of audiences—and resonates with a "uses and gratifications" explanation of media consumption. That approach suggests that audience members actively select materials that satisfy their individual needs and interests and then interpret them from their own personal perspective (cf. Liebes and Katz, 1988).

With regard to the consequences of placing a priority on individuals or collectivities in addressing the question of the social role of the media, there is a poorly delineated, subtle distinction between effects (i.e., the roles of the media for individuals) and consequences or functions (i.e., their roles for collectivities). The term *effects* tends to be applied to changes in or reinforcement of the beliefs, attitudes, knowledge, or behavior of individuals by various psychological and/or ecological processes. It implies identifiable linkages between specific influences and particular consequences. The connection tends to be treated as invariant, and contextual factors tend to be ignored as if they do not matter. Individual effects may have no net collective consequence, such as, for example, if equal numbers of people, influenced by the media, switch their support for two candidates, the use of two products, support for positions on an issue, or whatever. The similarity of this view of effects to learning and attitude change, for which there are well-established theories in psychology, has led some scholars to believe that an understanding of how media affect individuals is well in hand (except, of course, for startling instances of imitation of reported incidents of pathological behavior of the sort Phillips has been studying). Concepts used in studying effects have been applied in advertising, propaganda, and audience building.

How individual effects relate to social consequences is a major interest. It is arguable that almost every positive personal experience attributable to media exposure is of one or both of two types—informational or recreational. Each term describes experiencing one or both of two associated processes—learning or reinforcement in the first instance, and substitute gratification or escape in the second. Among synonyms for informational and recreational, educational is the most obvious for the former and entertaining for the latter. The mechanisms, in turn, refer to sensations audience members may experience and attribute to direct or indirect exposure to media. Learning is a term used broadly to refer to increments in knowledge and information and to changed or added values, opinions, attitudes, and tastes. Reinforcement implies strengthening commitment to knowledge, information, beliefs, values, opinions, attitudes, or preferences already held. Escape involves temporarily leaving a stressful reality either physically or through the imagination and can occur whenever a person is caught up in a motion picture, news item, magazine article, or other media product. Substitute gratification is the experience of the satisfaction of achieving otherwise unattained goals or rewards by identifying with real or fictional persons who do attain them, thereby affirming that the possibility of attaining them is real.

If the usual media fare reflects the hegemony of those in power, these experiences have the social function of maintaining the status quo (cf. Gandy's [1982: 3-5] comments on Marxist scholars) because none of them gives people cause to doubt the rightness and value of how things are. *Information* tends to justify and reenforce the status quo (cf. Tuchman's [1983: 330] comment on studies of the news in that respect), *recreation* to defuse dissatisfaction and frustration. Becker and Schoenbach (1989: 15) summarized the position of members of the Frankfurt school on this distinction in a similar manner:

> Mass media are supposed to keep the populations quiet—even apathetic. For this purpose media entertainment is a major vehicle. Entertainment has the task of maintaining the stability of unjust social conditions and emphasizing their unalterable nature. Entertainment offers escape and distraction. It thus keeps people from becoming aware of their class interests.

People do not examine the social order critically if they are led to attribute failure to their own weakness or the malevolence of others rather than to fundamental problems in social structure. The net result is little different than what Gerbner and his associates postulated as cultivation effects, that is, the fictional images presented on television, because they are repeated so frequently, are absorbed incidentally, and lead to a shift in perceptions of reality.[15] Figure 5.2 depicts how individual effects and societal functions may relate.

The variety in how views on consequences of specific aspects of the media or the media as a whole are expressed, and the range from individual effects to social functions, is illustrated by four contrasting studies: *News: The Politics of Illusion* (Bennett, 1988), *The Early Window* (Liebert and Sprafkin, 1988), *Amusing Ourselves to Death* (Postman, 1985), and *No Sense of Place* (Meyrowitz, 1985). Bennett analyzes the impact of news on individuals even though his thesis is that news has taken on the role of maintaining the status quo. He argues that the demands of a regular schedule on media professionals and of maintaining a bridge to the public on politicians leads to the episodic, nonanalytic product that shapes people's conception of what news is. Liebert and Sprafkin, in contrast, address the consequences for children of numerous features of television (e.g., commercials, character depiction in sitcoms, cartoons) and, hence, consider a wide range of possible roles (e.g., from stimulating aggressive behavior in play groups [individual] to undermining the nation's future health [social]).

Postman argues that, unlike reading, which is a rational activity, television viewing is incompatible with learning because entertainment is intrinsic to the sort of attention rapidly changing pictures stimulate. Therefore, because people rely heavily on television news, they become inattentive to important issues, and this diminishes prospects for effective democracy. Meyrowitz, arguing that the capacity of television to cross traditional barriers creates

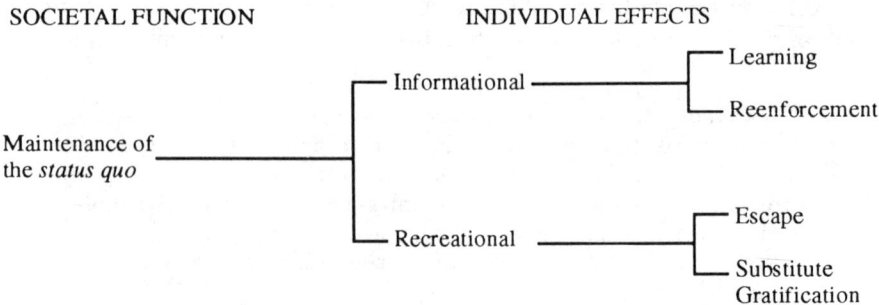

**Figure 5.2. An example of the relation between social functions and individual effects of the media**

new concepts of what one can know and where one can be, credits it with eroding traditional economic, age, and gender distinctions as well as with increasing the vulnerability of public leaders to criticism—obviously major social impacts.

The differences among the four works should not be taken to suggest a fixed relation between the media qualities and whether their impact is primarily at the individual or social level. Society may be an expression of the patterns of belief and behavior of individuals, but it is a distillation of those patterns that, once expressed, can exist independently of them. Hence, any of four contingencies between individual effects and social consequences are possible:

1. Changes in individuals may have no impact at the social level. This is the case when changes balance and produce no net effect.
2. Changes in individuals are felt as social change, for example, the electorate becomes more conservative.
3. Changes at the societal level may stimulate individual changes, for example, an F.C.C. ruling that local cable systems need not carry every television station within a certain radius enabled systems to change their offerings and subscribers had to alter their viewing.
4. Changes at the societal level may not involve individuals, for example, a technological innovation leads to corporate reorganization.

A critical aspect of societal consequences or functions is that they need not be intended. This may reinforce the tendency in policymaking to promote schemes that focus on the individual rather than the collectivity, a practice also related to the greater public acceptance of psychology and its emphasis on the person and personal responsibility than of sociology and its emphasis on structure and groups. For example, the claim that the extensive coverage of sports on television has made people more sedentary carries no implication that this was intended or that learning had to occur. The consequence simply follows from the fact that only a limited number of hours are available after sleep, work, meals, and household tasks.

Because collective consequences often are unavoidable outcomes shaped by contingencies of social organization, they also are more likely to be undesirable or dysfunctional (Lazarsfeld and Merton, 1943; Adorno and Horkheimer, 1972; Kellner, 1981). If they often occur unawares and are inevitable outcomes of physical and structural constraints on how groups may organize, and if, in addition, we are inattentive to those matters, know little about them, and think about them even less, then inevitably we will be surprised by these consequences and the outcome of policies meant to deal with them. Perhaps the most consequential aspect of whether an approach to the role of the media has an individual or social focus, however, is that even when obvious to others, scholars and practitioners often are unaware of their own predilections and, therefore, also are unaware of how they affect their understanding of the social role of the media and their role in the determination of policy.

Not surprisingly, many roles or effects of mass media have nothing at all to do with communication (cf. Serfaty, 1990; Schlesinger, 1991: 17-28). Two points should be repeated in this regard. First, media systems have impacts regardless of their messages or even whether messages are sent, for example, the development of radio and television accounts for the occupation of repairman. As another example, the dominance of certain types of Western logical thought has been attributed to the habits of horizontal linearity encouraged by the way in which printing places lines on a page (McLuhan, 1964; Meyrowitz, 1985).[16] Daniel Schorr's poignant commentary on the irony of television coverage of the Chinese students' demonstrations in Tianenmen Square provides a telling final example. He noted that a classic case of what often is claimed to be a major social role of mass media—weakening tyranny by exposing it to a broad public (Keane, 1991)—actually enabled a tyrannical government to identify and punish dissidents. Communication—intentional sending of information to targeted receivers—has no direct role in any of these cases, but the media do. Despite the extensive literature on the consequences of the existence and distinctive features of the media,[17] except for recondite scholarly works, such effects rarely are considered even as possibilities.

Second, as already discussed at length, because very little of the material conveyed by the media constitutes information in the formal sense, sending is rarely communication. Rather, material is created and transmitted to hold and otherwise influence audiences. In this way, the media are just one of many institutions through which the dominant culture is expressed. In terms of media studies, Tuchman (1983) has suggested that "... U.S. researchers began to recognize the study of media as the study of consciousness and formations of consciousness. . . ." (330) and that ". . . one can do theoretically informed and empirically rich studies without accepting a narrow, linear, sequential model. . . ." (340) of media effects. Hers is just another way to state the independence of media and communication effects.

In the light of this stringent definition of communication, communication through the media can occur only when preannounced informative materials are provided. Even then, it would be communication only for the targeted persons who seek it. In that light, the regular scheduling and placement of weather reports, news, and sports results can be understood as implementing the implications of these conditions, for they are tactics that increase the chances that material that can reduce uncertainty will be received by those who want their uncertainty reduced. That dissemination process is communication. This is not to say that people do not learn from the media or secure material from the media that turns out to constitute information for them. Rather, it is to say that offering and receiving media material by themselves may not constitute communication. The difference is that the usual media fare—music, drama, cartoons, and the like—is there to be experienced just as is the rest of nature, and like all experience can become a basis of knowledge. The fact that those materials become available through the agency of the media does not alter the fact that they are not intentionally produced and disseminated to inform. If the media are not intentionally sending information to targeted recipients, then they are involved in a sort of pseudo-communication—disseminating noninformational material through a potential channel of communication.

The principle is that both the elements of communication and an entire system or institution can serve noncommunication purposes (Thayer, 1988: 69). Placing a bowl of pretzels on a television set neither makes the pretzels a message nor the television set a table. A sender who emits and transmits "significant symbols" with no primary intent to have the symbols received as information is not a communicator, just as a consumer who receives but does not understand a message as it was intended is not a communicatee. The sender may enjoy the activity and the receiver may feel informed by it, but the minimum conditions for communication have not been satisfied.

## *ADVERTISING AS INFLUENCE*

In view of the ubiquitousness and centrality of advertising in the media and its relevance to effects, its neglect in the discussion might seem an oversight. Though successful advertising usually is equated with effective communication, my approach requires treating it as successful influence rather than as communication. Admittedly, every aspect of communication is employed in creating and disseminating advertisements, but the process is not communication for two reasons.

First, in advertising, with few exceptions, the primary purpose is to influence beliefs and/or behavior, not to transmit information successfully. It is hard to believe that an advertiser whose campaign doubles sales would be disappointed to learn that new buyers had seen but not understood the ads. It is even more difficult to imagine that an advertiser would be happy that an ad reached and was understood by everyone targeted if sales fell. Advertising's primary purpose is to shape actions or beliefs in a desired way; its primary goal is successful manipulation. Communication, if a goal at all, is secondary. Second, with few exceptions, advertisements carry no information despite being made to appear informational. Except for material such as prices or schedules, ads rarely contain information. They rarely provide all the material needed to compare competing products that would constitute information by reducing uncertainty for users and purchasers. Rational, skilled consumers would know this and not seek information from ads. Instead, they would use a reliable source that assembles such material. Because ads are not primarily intended to convey information, the use of significant symbols in advertising is a counterfeit for communication.

Although advertising and communication are distinctly different phenomena, the affinity of the two is real and intentional. In the absence of direct financing by the state and/or consumers, both the media and the advertising industries derive major benefits from associating. Advertising professionals know that they need camouflage—the appearance of altruistically disseminating information. They use what seems to be a strategy of "innocence by association." Some such appearance is needed because efforts to persuade and influence, particularly if intended to promote unnecessary consumption, are socially disapproved for both their manipulative methods and the waste they may encourage. Communication, in contrast, is socially valued. The closer the resemblance and affinity of advertising to communication; the less recognizable it is, the easier it is to mix advertisements and other media materials, the more the industry and its practices are out of public scrutiny, and the less likely advertising is to be criticized or disparaged.

The media not only facilitate advertising's acceptance by capitalizing on public confusion of the media and the advertising they carry with communication, they also create the most important product required for successful advertising—large regular audiences with known characteristics (Freiman, 1984).[18] Because ads are meant to stimulate the actions or beliefs of the members of targeted groups, they must be received by them to have any value. Mass media, on their part, need large regular audiences to cover the cost of producing and disseminating their materials. When media sell their audiences and distribution capability to help advertisers reach their targets, both their interests are served. What has come to be called demographics is the exercise of matching specific media audiences to targeted markets. The ability of the media to produce and sell audiences is the second basic consideration in the very close association between advertising and commercial media. The dependence of the media on advertisers for income helps advertisers who feel that their interests are being harmed to influence editorial or programming practices and decisions (Curran, 1986)—although direct pressure on media by advertisers is rarely necessary.

The symbiotic relationship between commercial media and advertising affects the public by shaping the material. To get advertising revenues, a medium must produce desired audiences reliably and provide opportunities to deliver advertisers' messages in conjunction with the material that creates the audience. These advertising-based requirements are among several factors that contribute to the development of what may be called media genres, that is, distinctive forms that reflect the stereotyping of topics and conventions of presentation associated with production in each medium.

The costs of professionally produced and operated media encourage genres, even in state- or user-funded systems, for in the long run there is no way to pay for systems that disseminate material in which no one is interested. The pressure to secure a reliable audience encourages the emulation of material that does generate and hold an audience. More than 50 years ago Lowenthal (1944) studied the content of popular magazines and noted that they (a) regularly included biographies of public figures, and (b) used a fixed formula to present their lives and the factors that affected them. Other studies of popular culture revealed patterns in song lyrics (MacDougald, 1941; Peatman, 1944) and regular event and character progressions in radio soap operas (Arnheim, 1944). The need for advertisers' support reenforces this tendency because it makes the loss of an audience even more threatening. It also requires material to be organized so that advertisements can be presented without losing audiences. Two examples of how dependence on advertising revenue shapes media material will suffice.

The practice of inserting commercials in broadcasts shapes comedies, drama, and films made for television and radio in several ways. First, breaks for commercials interrupt dramatic flow and, thus, force writers into story lines and dramatic devices that provide natural-seeming breaks every so many minutes. Second, lest some of the audience be lost at each commercial, the main plot must remain unresolved. Relatedly, and third, if possible the break must come at a point of great tension whose resolution is imminent so that audience members will not want to miss the resumption of the show. This helps hold them through the commercial instead of allowing them to leave or change channels. A longer term effect is to condition viewers to semi-episodic story lines whose regularly recurring peaks of tension are resolved along the way. Fourth, because programs are fitted to multiples of 30-minute time slots, in contrast to the variable timing and fluid pace of films, stage plays, and print material, television audiences become conditioned to standard length material. The recent practice of showing identifiable products and services in films is also pertinent in this regard. It permits a medium that derived income only from box office and television rights sales to use the equivalent of advertising sales to finance production. Ironically, this practice is inappropriate for anything to be shown on commercial television, for identifying recognizable products and services limits the pool of potential sponsors for reruns.

The case also has been made that sponsorship of nightly television network news programs by advertisers affects the selection and presentation of stories and, thus, shapes the public's concept of news (Bennett, 1988; Hallin, 1987). Among the reasons this may happen is that items must be presented in a way that keeps an abrupt switch to a commercial from being inappropriate and discordant. Therefore, it is argued, techniques of presentation are developed that condition audience members to judge news more in terms of its entertainment than its information value—although that quality of television news also has been attributed to the association of the medium with entertainment rather than information as a consequence of the affinity between advertising and media.

Among the conventions of television news presentation that have developed, in part, to accommodate commercials in news broadcasts, are minimization of the time allotted and details given for the events covered, and depiction of their course as somehow being normal, that is, whatever the event, it is under control by the proper authorities, will follow a predictable course, and negative consequences will be minimal. Interviews with specialists and experts that help convey normality and predictability rather than uncertainty are typical. How much such formulas facilitate the intermingling of mundane commercials with otherwise upsetting and disturbing news becomes dramatically clear in live coverage of unexpected catastrophes, such as the killing of Israeli athletes during the 1972 Munich Olympics and the occurrence of an earthquake in San Francisco just before the start of a 1990 World Series baseball game. In these dramatic cases, the inexperience of professional news people in handling newsworthy events, the desperate resort to practices that normalize, and the inappropriateness of commercials are very apparent.

In keeping with the entertainment motif of televised news, given that most items report unresolved situations, material is presented as a narrative with little attention to context or analysis of causes or significance. It is fitting for newsworthy items to be called "stories." In the case of both drama and news, then, what the public is given and comes to expect as appropriate is shaped, in part, to accommodate advertising throughout the broadcast. This sort of effect of advertising differs basically from the more common concern with outright audience manipulation. The possibility that what popularly passes as news or entertainment may be only a limited and distorted version of what those terms embrace is rarely raised as an issue. Alternatives are being lost and devalued as they become less accessible and familiar. Formulaic media products inundate them, and the implications of their absence become a nonissue.

## MEDIA EFFECTS REVISITED

This discussion of the social roles of the media may give the impression that the issue of media effects has been resolved once and for all. Although the large majority of analysts now accept the position that the media do have substantial and significant social and individual effects, skeptics remain. McGuire (1986), a distinguished social psychologist, not so long ago examined the evidence for 12 frequently mentioned intended and unintended media effects and found it lacking. He wrote ". . . that the demonstrated impacts are surprisingly slight. Even in the areas with the most impressive results, including frequent statistically significant effects in methodologically adequate studies, the size of the impacts are so small as to raise questions about their practical significance and cost effectiveness" (233). He reported that even his salvaging efforts to find conditions under which there might be evidence to support the claimed effects failed, and he suggested, as I have, that the "no effects" position may have lost its support because the absence of evidence of sizable impacts of the media on the public is embarrassing to both their friends, who must claim there are effects to gain the financial support of advertisers, and foes, who claim there are effects to justify proposed media control policies. However, in the same volume, McGuire's article is preceded by a report of a metaanalysis of 1,043 studies that examined media effects on social behavior (Hearold, 1986) and is followed by a synthesis of 11 "found experiments" that explored links between media violence and real-world aggressive behavior (Phillips, 1986). Neither of these two authors doubted that the media have a significant social role.

The entire situation regarding what may be said about media effects begs to be clarified. The wild swings between claims of no effects and jeremiads about catastrophic effects, and the current wide diversity of viewpoints is no accident. To a considerable extent it reflects fundamental differences in concepts of what an effect is. They range from very narrow cause-effect connections between media and subsequent events—conceptions of the sort captured by the "hypodermic" concept—to very broad contingencies that depend on networks of connections—very much like saying the effect of dropping a pebble in a pond is to make a leaf wobble because ripples eventually spread to where the leaf is floating. Causal assertions are always questionable because of the tendency to consider cause and effect as directly and inexorably related, that is, whenever the cause occurs, the effect may be observed. Thus, the tendency to say, for example, that a television program or film caused adolescents to imitate a crime always can be countered by the claim that all adolescents who saw those programs or films did not commit that crime. On the other hand, claims about broad effects usually seem so obvious as to be trivial and hardly worth noting, for example, the use of television for political campaigning affects campaign style. The first conclusion with regard to these differences, then, is that claims about effects will continue to be in conflict unless the sort of effect and the process that supposedly connects it to media and their qualities to it are specified clearly.

A second point about these differences in views on the effects of media relates to evaluations of the presumed effects—whether they are so disturbing that they must be avoided—and ideas as to whether interventions can prevent them—a policy issue that will be explored more thoroughly. The view that negative effects must and can be prevented usually is related to a concept of the media as some alien pathological agent from outside the bounds of normal everyday life. The analogy is that of a germ causing a disease, an accident causing an injury, a crime causing a death. The implication seems to be that if we could sustain normal conditions, those causes would not arise and/or could be avoided. That, however, is a totally unrealistic view of the mass media in modern societies. One of the main points of the analysis of the term *mass* and its implications vis-à-vis the media was to make it clear that the media are simply one of a complex of phenomena that constitute contemporary society and enable it to exist as we know it. To treat them as somehow alien or exterior, as removable or drastically alterable, does violence to social reality. Views of effects based on unrealistic conceptions of the relation of media to modern society are bound to produce differences of opinion that can only be resolved arbitrarily.[19]

Finally, I must admit that I prefer the term *social role* to *effects* even though I have used the latter term repeatedly. It is almost unavoidable given the motivations behind so much public attention to the media and media research. Effects are the concerns of practical people, of movers and shakers; most of the literature uses this terminology. Social roles interest only iconoclastic scholars. However, the decision to speak of social roles whenever possible is more than a reflection of professional bias. It is influenced by the facts that the idea of social role carries no prejudicial implications—it may be positive, negative, or neutral—and that it carries no implication that the referent of the phrase—the thing that has a role—is somehow alien. Indeed, it is more likely to be an intrinsic element. A final virtue is that an enumeration of such roles requires recognizing as many as can be identified without any implication that any of them are trivial simply because it is patently obvious or generally unrecognized or covert. Bearing this in mind may be of some help in assessing the welter of counterclaims. It certainly should be relevant to the sorts of important media roles and concerns considered in Chapters 8 and 9. Many of them are covert, unintended, or patently obvious (but only when brought to our attention). They are not trivial for most of the world.

## *NOTES*

1. Given these considerations, it is surprising that such an eminent media scholar as McQuail (1987a: 30-31) continues this practice.
2. Baudrillard (1988 [1985]) makes a very different argument, treating the mass as real and as inextricably intertwined with the mass media. The latter may be either an instrument that subjugates them or through which they destroy reality by expressing the meaninglessness of existence.
3. A more sanguine view of later foundation involvement based on the same premise of media effectiveness is presented in Engelman's (1987) analysis of the roles of the Ford Foundation and the Carnegie Corporation in promoting national public television in the United States.
4. The original study was conducted in 1944. A summary of pertinent findings appears in Lazarsfeld and Schneider (1949). Other examples in which the media are involved, but which examine the effectiveness of propaganda rather than the employment of administrative research, may be found in Jowett and O'Donnell (1986: chap. 7).
5. The series included 13 studies conducted by leading scholars between 1929 and 1932 (Blumer and Hauser, 1933; Dale, 1935: 30-73; Dysinger and Ruckmick, 1933: 110-119; Peters, 1933; Peterson and Thurstone, 1933; Shuttlesworth and May, 1933; Forman, 1935: 12-27). They are discussed by Lowery and DeFleur (1988: 31-57). For a broader historical overview of such research, see Wartella and Reeves (1985).

6. Ward (1989: 11) has attributed this model of the effect process by this name to the analyses of the members of the Frankfurt school.
7. Two of these studies dealt with presidential voters in Erie County, OH, during the 1940 election campaign and presidential voters in Elmira, NY, in the 1948 campaign. The results are detailed, respectively, in Lazarsfeld, Berelson, and Gaudet (1944) and Berelson, Lazarsfeld, and McPhee (1954).
8. Chaffee (1988: 247) explicitly claims that the ideological premise behind his analysis with Hochheimer (1985) and Gitlin's study (1978) is that the limited effects model was promoted to deflect regulatory efforts.
9. For a thorough discussion of Innis's work, see Melody, Salter, and Heyer (1981) and Carey (1988: 142-172). Carey has asserted that, "During the third quarter of this century, North American communications theory . . . could have been described by an arc running from Harold Innis to Marshall McLuhan. . . . Innis's work . . . is the great achievement in communications on this continent" (142). That both Innis and McLuhan were Canadian and that modern communication technology and media are deemed crucial for Canada's survival may be more than coincidence.
10. For an incisive critique of McLuhan's ideas, see Fekete (1973).
11. For additional citations and an important methodological debate, see Baron and Reiss (1985) and the following exchange with Bollen and Phillips.
12. For Meyrowitz's term *form*, read *structure*.
13. More than 40 years ago, Lazarsfeld (1948) sought to categorize the approaches to these issues at that time. The task proved virtually unmanageable even then. Thirty years later and more than 15 years ago (Chaffee, 1977), the task required even more elaborate and complex schema.
14. Lull (1990 [1980]: 28-48) differentiated what McQuail, Blumler, and Brown each identified as personal uses of the media from what he called social uses. His examples lead me to conclude that both are primarily what I refer to here as individual.
15. The essence of the argument is presented in an early form by Gerbner (1972: 30), who, in reporting on a content analysis of television violence, wrote that ". . . the almost ritualistically regular and repetitive symbolic structures of television drama cultivate certain premises about the rules of the game of life." A volume (Melischek, Rosengren, and Stappers, 1984) that appeared 12 years later, in which Gerbner (1984: 329-343) reported a study of political content on television, contains a full set of citations to the various papers from 1972 to 1984 in which the thesis was developed. A good synthesis is available in Wober and Gunter (1988: 1-19). Cultivation as a process is somewhat different from the postmodernist assertion that media reports and imagery simply have become reality because people accept and respond to them. Rarely, if ever, do postmodernists specify how this replacement happens.
16. Current technological changes, their impact on the newsroom, and

their social implications are discussed in a similar manner in Smith (1980b). It is important to realize that these examples of the impact of technology are chosen for their illustrative value. Otherwise, it is easy to slip into the trap of media technology determinism (Levinson, 1984).
17. A volume edited by Allen (1987) contains illustrations of eight different theoretical positions from which to analyze television as a process and its consequences.
18. Ang (1991: 53) says that ". . . what advertisers buy from the networks is not time but audience: commercial television is based on the principle that the networks 'deliver audiences to advertisers'. . . ." This applies to any medium that depends on income from advertising to meet costs and provide profits.
19. For a similar perspective, cf. Jensen (1990).

# 6

# Control of the Mass Media

The possibility that the media have deleterious effects is linked inextricably to processes of control in media systems. The issue of control—in everyday usage it often comes down to "who runs the show and how"—probably would not be of much interest were it not for the widespread conviction that the media have socially undesirable effects that could be avoided if something about the system could be changed. The existence of valid evidence to substantiate that belief is irrelevant. What is pertinent is that people believe that the media will or already do have undesirable consequences and that policies and actions are needed (Starker, 1989). In these situations, typically only two modes of control are considered—self-control or control by delegated institutions (Wober and Gunter, 1988: 223-233). The delegated institution is almost always a state agency, and the pressure for this approach builds when it is generally believed that self-control will fail and that it is too costly or risky not to make changes.

Underlying the belief that effective policies can be formulated, adopted, and implemented is (a) a commitment to the concept that specific factors in a situation, under identifiable circumstances, have a known, unacceptably high likelihood of producing undesirable consequences (i.e., simple causality), and (b) faith and confidence that those causal factors can be identified and counteracted. This style of thinking also helps explain the stimulus-response-like character of much media effects research.[1] The appeal of the policy approach to deal with problems rests on an assumption that the causal nexus can be altered and the undesired outcome avoided (or, as in the case of the invention of the quiz show, that a desired outcome can be accomplished). Even more fundamental and usually taken for granted is an assumed consensus that the condition at issue is indeed bad, is a result of mass communication, and should be ended.

In addition to these implicit assumptions in policy responses to problematic situations considered media related, a flawed conception of a presumed chain of relationships often is involved. For example, pornography is attacked as bad not only in and of itself and because it is believed to promote violence and sexual aberrations, but also because its producers—the Mafia and other such people—are bad and profit from it. Such convoluted arguments suggest that proponents of controls may sometimes base their proposals on conceptions of cause that do not always proceed in the usual causal direction. In the case of pornography, the judgment about the material spills over to judgments in two directions—both to its producers and to its effects on its consumers. Moreover, the emphasis on policy to solve problems involves a potentially contradictory two-sided orientation to control. On the one hand there is the view that negative media effects are the intentional products of those who control the media and can be alleviated by doing something about control on the inside. On the other hand, proponents of policy promote the view that some superordinate control agent—the state, an industry-monitoring group, an angry public—can be invoked to produce the desired effect. In short, control serves as both culprit and savior in diagnosing and remedying the media-related problems of everyday life.

## THE NATURE OF THE CONTROL PROCESS

Control as a process and its policy implications clearly generate public concern, but control would be of scholarly interest even without it. For scholars the concept refers to the process that determines how media systems work. Unlike the view of control that directs approaches to policy, this process of control operates at all levels, from a system as a whole to its smallest constituents.[2] Indeed, it is so diffuse that there is no consensus on whether society or the media is the user or the used (McQuail, 1986a: 4). The study of control focuses on the field of forces that shapes every facet of mass communication (e.g., how much and what kind of material is produced; who is and who may be involved in production, technology operation, innovation, and the determination of who may participate in these activities; the distribution and targeted destination and consumption of the products; the role of extramedia system factors in how the media operate). New telecommunications technologies that link media and nonmedia apparatus (e.g., television and home computer networks) promise to extend and reshape the field of forces.

The idea of a field of forces that controls how media systems perform has evolved over a long period.[3] Concepts of control have become more complex as societies have grown in size and heterogeneity, technologies have become more expensive, both have become more complex, and state authority over private matters has continued to expand.[4] The process of control is more complex in the United States than elsewhere because historically the state has permitted private entrepreneurs to fill the role of developing and operating media systems. In most other countries the development and operation of audio and audiovisual media had been assigned to the post office or to a state corporation. In many, the government and the dominant political party publish their own official or semi-official newspapers and magazines. These have been considered activities of states that fulfill a basic obligation to maintain social order and sovereignty. If this approach was standard, the analysis of control probably would be quite different, emphasizing comparisons of administrative structures and the relations of those structures to organizational behavior. Even in our unique American system, however, control probably never has been as simple as depicted in most models of the process, which tend to view it primarily as top down.

Control processes, then, vary with time and place. The identity and weight of the forces in the field vary with social conditions and norms. Some unique features of the American case already have been noted. In addition, the United States constitution provides for freedom of speech to a degree unparalleled in most other countries. Some countries permit private ownership of radio and television receivers, others require government licenses, and still others do not permit individuals to have equipment. Countries vary with regard to censorship. Some societies ignore private behavior that affects only the actor; in others all behavior is a public concern. Some countries, for all practical purposes, lack media whose existence we take for granted; certainly prevalence of the different media varies by country. Variety is the rule, for ". . . all . . . systems of communication and technology are controlled by the . . . forces governing the cultures in which they appear" (Thorburn, 1988: 53). The discussion in this chapter focuses on control in the United States; control elsewhere differs. Comparative analyses would reveal that it is highly varied, rarely simple, and that the trend has been for the field of forces to expand in number and complexity (Martin and Chaudhary, 1983; Gerbner and Siefert, 1984; Howell, 1986).

## THE STRUCTURE OF CONTROL OF AMERICAN MEDIA

In private enterprise economies, owners of media businesses have a major role in control (e.g., Liebert and Sprafkin, 1988: 81-85, 107-108; Bagdikian, 1987). Prior to the development of radio and of government regulation to avoid band interference and assure access to frequencies for military and maritime uses, the American view was that owners decided what was in the media. That view still prevails, and on particular issues (e.g., denying media access to labor unions that wish to present their case to the public) their exercise of power has been well documented (Douglas, 1986: 134-178). However, because owners rely on financial institutions for the capital to buy equipment and pay expenses, representatives of those institutions also may play a major part in decisions on production and distribution (Compaine, Sterling, Guback, and Noble, 1982; see also Guback, 1969; Murdock and Golding, 1977; Wasko, 1981, 1982, 1985; Audley, 1983; Dominick, 1987). Owners' obligations to pay off equipment loans before the approval of new loans can be a major factor delaying early adoption of new communication technologies (e.g., television, sound motion pictures).

Proposals to extend government control of media always have produced counterproposals, usually in the form of industry self-regulation. Industry associations promulgate codes of conduct that all members pledge to follow (Liebert and Sprafkin, 1988: 54-58). The codes are self-enforced by employing such techniques as licensing and threats to withhold cooperation and services. Despite periodic challenges on grounds of restraint of trade, such codes operate with varying degrees of stringency for all American media. In terms of our model of a communication system, these actors in the process represent the communicator system (i.e., industry associations, owners) and outside or exogenous factors (i.e., lending institutions, the government).

With the increasing absorption of media organizations by conglomerates, the communicator system continues to be of special interest to students of control, particularly in light of disagreements as to whether concentration of ownership in large corporate entities affects content. Bagdikian (1987), for example, cited several cases of conglomerate corporate executives who, feeling that the interests of other units in the corporation might be harmed by certain manuscripts, countermanded publication decisions by units acquired by the conglomerate. Coulson (1988) argued strongly that the acquisition of independent newspapers by corporate chains decreases diversity and increases conflicts of interest, and Litman (1979: 139) concluded that vertical integration in television broadcasting (i.e., networks) ". . . has created the power of self-preference." In contrast, Simonet (1987) reported that film companies diversified their productions after being acquired by conglomerates, and Hale (1988) concluded that his data showed no changes in the editorial pages of formerly independent newspapers acquired by chains. The impact of changing ownership patterns on control clearly is complex and, if past experience applies, probably does not go in any single direction.

These developments occur in the context of community control, that is, a set of widely shared social norms as to what is acceptable in communication and media performance. Although usually taken for granted, most members of a group have been effectively socialized into accepting them, feel they are right and good, and, ordinarily, conform to them voluntarily. If the operators of local media are members of the same communities as everyone else, and many of them are, they, too, are likely to share these norms, deviations from acceptable media standards will be minimal, and the constraining force of the norms is not a burden. Serious violations of the norms are offensive. They mobilize public opinion, which serves an overt constraining control function and supports efforts to punish any immediate transgressors (cf. Jarvie, 1985). The strength of these norms is dramatized by McCombs' (1988: 136) unexpected conclusion, after studying the impact of the end of competition on newspaper quality, that the idea:

> . . . that the demise of a competitor will be followed by diminished quality in the survivor is totally rebutted by the evidence of these content analyses. Only a few changes from before until after the end of competition were found, and all of these were positive changes in the quality of editorial product.
>
> In short these data support a sociology of news perspective that newspapers competing for the same geographic and demographic market will produce highly similar products due to the similarity of their professional values, beliefs and practices. The increasing professionalization of journalism during this century has resulted in a convergence of views among journalists about what is the news of the day.

The development of control in the motion picture industry provides a good example of this process. Increasingly, during the 1920s, films were being criticized because religious and moral standards were being violated by the scandalous behavior of prominent film personalities (Anger, 1975). Public demand for government control of the industry and the boycotting of films grew (Carmen, 1966). Fearful of the consequences, corporate heads, through their association—the Motion Picture Producers and Distributors of America (MPPDA)—created a mechanism, informally called the Hays Office, to clear and license films for exhibition (Moley, 1945; Hays, 1955; Ward, 1989: 129-130). The Motion Picture Production Code enunciated standards for what could be said and shown and who might be employed in films. It centralized power within the industry and shaped the character and quality of American films for almost 35 years.[5] If control is a process of interaction in a field of forces, though, then the Hays Office, despite its dominance, must be considered only one of many interacting agents of control for a communication system. Its opportunity to amass power resulted from public pressure, an exogenous force.

Had it been left to ownership and had there been no public pressure, owners would have been the only significant factor in control and there would have been no creation or eventual dismantling of the Hays Office. What did happen, though, after some years, was that changing public standards and tastes created new, unsatisfied market demands and motivated producers to try to serve these markets. This stimulated several successful challenges to the rigorous procedures by which the Office had monopolized control (Haralovich, 1985). The Hays Office, by then an overly rigid entrenched bureaucracy, eventually was terminated. Instead, in many communities the functions of the Hays Office were assumed by local government or voluntary censorship boards that had been operating and continued to operate to assess whether media materials met local standards. These boards operated like the Hays Office. Many reviewed publications, radio and television programs, and artistic performances and exhibitions, as well as films. Most have gone the way of the Hays Office, although media entrepreneurs still may regret having lost the national marketing advantages of being able to advertise that one's film or book had been "banned in Boston." Film scholars have noted the emergence of functionally equivalent local censorship methods (Trauth and Huffman, 1985).

The role of consumer demand illustrates how audience members (or receivers) can play a determinative role in shaping media materials. Clearly, enterprises can be made or broken by how the public receives them. This force has been described as consumer sovereignty and, as shown in Chapter 9, it can create problems when it conflicts with societal interests or, as it is called, national sovereignty (Freiman, 1984). Producers try to defuse consumer sovereignty because they must make all their production decisions before getting a consumer response, and they usually are unable to remedy what turn out to be problems. Film reediting, for example, is a limited possibility and may not be sufficient to save a big ticket item that fails to appeal to an audience. Producers strive to forestall the impact of consumer sovereignty by various advertising and public relations ploys intended to entice members of the public into joining audiences, but the failure of well-established programs, newspapers, and magazines owing to the loss of audiences indicates how consequential the impact of people acting on their own or in concert can be.

A dramatic illustration of audience control is provided by a major magazine publisher that would not print any item without pretesting it on a reader panel. Editorial revisions were required until panel members were completely satisfied. Pretesting of films and of radio and television programs also has been a long-established practice (Jowett, 1985), although rarely is it given the priority accorded it by the publisher, who, for all practical purposes, had relinquished editorial control of the creative process to the intended audience, as represented by the panels. The six-year long Newspaper Readership Project of the American Newspaper Publishers Association and National Advertising Bureau provides a final example. The study was designed to be used to stem and, perhaps, recoup the loss of newspaper readers. It not only probed the preferences of and dissatisfactions with newspapers held by members of the public, but also scrutinized all facets of newspapers as organizations to learn how to apply the results of the study of the public effectively (Bogart, 1991).

A more subtle process of consumer control over the meaning and impact of media material is suggested by Newcomb's comments (1988: 104-106) on Hartley and Fiske's idea of "semiotic excess." Their idea, put simply, is that media texts are so rich in meaning that, even though they have been produced with a specific intention (i.e., the "preferred" reading), the otherwise subordinate consumer may still derive other meanings from aspects of the text that have escaped the producer's control. Fiske (1989: 67) is so taken with the possibility that he refers to it as "semiotic democracy" in discussing the same phenomenon in television. He described it as television's ". . . lack of authority over its viewers, its democratic delegation of the meaning-making functions. . . ." This seems to be a rediscovery of the fact that the connotative richness of symbols always endows messages with more potential meaning than producers may wish. Therefore, consumers always can infuse them with meanings and consequences that were not intended. Of course, in this conceptual framework only intended meanings bear on communication. Any other consequences relate to influence. However, because communicating is rarely unmotivated, and because outcomes with respect to these motivations—that is, whether communicators get what they want from their efforts—affect whether communicating continues, the impact of semiotic excess, or any similar phenomenon, on performance is relevant to the consumer's role in control. Interpretation being a consumer activity, Newcomb's point is that the extent of consumer participation in control is to a significant degree a function of how active consumers are as consumers.[6]

Technology, because it shapes and limits the character and quality of what can be produced, transmitted, and received, also plays a role in control. Its impact is more by way of setting limits—what can and cannot be represented and transmitted with accuracy—than by determining content. Sometimes, however, as with radio static or distortions in recording or playback, material is changed independently of senders' or receivers' actions. Generally, technology is more limiting when it is new than when it has been perfected. Although some control is imposed by a technology's intrinsic qualities—the fact that sound motion pictures and color television could be imagined but not achieved until the equipment was developed illustrates how critical a role technology has in shaping the qualities of media materials—by and large, much of its impact is in concert with human operation. Indeed, the aspect of technology that usually impinges on the control process is the interaction between equipment and its operators.

Ignorance or errors on the part of users of both sending and receiving equipment can significantly affect message construction and reception. The importance of the unique perspective of the television camera in both production and consumption has been recognized ever since Lang and Lang's (1953) path breaking study of General Douglas MacArthur's Chicago homecoming parade revealed that the impression that he was very popular and had widespread support was a by-product of camera placement. At the time, only one camera was used, and it was focused on the General and the few scattered groups of enthusiastic supporters in the stands. It could not pan the otherwise empty areas immediately beyond them. Thus, camera use can deceive receivers who, more often than not, accept what is on the screen as an accurate depiction. Television receivers also distort theatrical films. The distortion of perspective and cramping of scenes that can occur exemplifies how the interaction of equipment and symbols, executed by senders and receivers, alters messages. Consumers, especially, are at the mercy of technology because they have little or no training in how to receive and, thus, are unaware of what they themselves are doing as receivers and how the equipment they are using affects their performance. They are further handicapped by knowing even less about how production and transmission equipment already has shaped the stimuli coming to them (cf. Delia and O'Keefe, 1979; Wober, 1988: 161-200, on training).

Production and transmission workers are often neglected in analyzing control. Training and experience gives them an expert understanding of their equipment and, in many cases, of every aspect of production, transmission, and exhibition (McQuail, 1984: 101-120; Turow, 1984a). Moreover, if expensive, complex, new equipment is not automated, their skill and experience enhances their importance and indispensability. If they develop strong craft unions, as they did in the Hollywood film industry from the 1920s to the late 1950s, they may become as major a force as highly placed executives. In general, so long as there also is no deskilling through task fragmentation or equipment automation, occupational differentiation tends to increase the role of craft workers in control.

Finally, as indicated, a wide array of exogenous factors are also part of the dynamic field of forces that control American media systems. Individuals who may become the subjects of media items can exercise a modicum of indirect influence by using libel laws to protect themselves from unflattering, inaccurate treatments. However, the potential protective value of libel suits depends on how public a figure the person affected is. It also varies greatly over time depending on judicial interpretations and on the sorts of penalties deemed appropriate for media defendants who lose suits. In addition, it varies even more among countries, in some of which the notion of media responsibility for accuracy and the subject's right to protection through civil suit do not even exist in a form that Americans would recognize. Much more direct and effective measures for subject control have developed as the media have come to rely increasingly on extended personal interviews with "newsworthy" persons as a way to generate news. Interviewees have come to recognize that the interviews are essentially conversations in which each participant can draw on all the normal tactics they have learned for controlling and directing any conversation in everyday life (Heritage, Clayman, and Zimmerman, 1988).

Several other important participants in the control process that are not intrinsically involved in the communication process per se also should be noted. Community public interest groups and special interest pressure groups (Montgomery, 1982, 1989; Starker, 1989), large corporations (Dreier, 1987 [1983]), and conservative groups and representatives generally (Lazere, 1987) are among the exogenous forces that maintain surveillance and generate demands.

High-status elites, operating through foundations, think tanks, and what Brown (1986) has referred to as the policy-planning network, are active in questioning current practices and situations or proposing solutions to chronic concerns. Government participates not only as an arbiter, monitor, and enforcer through regulatory agencies, but also tries to influence content by many of the same means used by interest groups and the public generally. Spiro Agnew's claim that media coverage misrepresented and thereby undermined the Nixon administration's efforts to implement its campaign platform, and charges by Reagan administration officials that the press threatened national security by injudiciously publishing sensitive material, exemplify the efforts of state agents to shape what becomes available through "free" media. That is one outcome of control. These cases differ from administrative agency or court rulings in that the latter are legitimately empowered and obligated to exercise control. In these cases, however, government officials tried to use celebrity status and the prestige and power of office to exercise influence.

## CONTROL AND MEDIA HEGEMONY

If control over the media at any time reflects the balance at the time in a dynamic field of complex interactions, then such seemingly straightforward questions as "Who runs the show?" or "In whose interests are the media being operated?" are not easily answered. The pertinent facts will vary over time and among media, so the questions, as phrased, may be meaningless. Rather, as the discussion of effects has suggested, operation of the media may be akin to a hegemonic process in which, by implicit common consent, the disseminated material controls by shaping and reenforcing beliefs, attitudes, and knowledge on such key matters as people's place in society, what they have a right to expect, how society is organized, whether it is just, what is the appropriate way to redress grievances and achieve change, and how one's own society relates to other societies.

Modern complex societies include a wide variety of groups—social classes, ethnic groups, religious groups, races—with very different positions on these matters. If, as is widely believed, the media are effective in disseminating and implanting uniform ideas on these issues, interest groups must compete intensely for control, for it would follow that those who determine what the media provide can shape a country to their own ends. The competition of such groups as the Moral Majority's Coalition for Better Television and Norman Lear's People for the American Way (Montgomery, 1989: 166-167), and efforts to avoid single ownership of a community's major newspaper, television station, and radio station are consistent with that scenario. The ambiguous equal-time doctrine for radio and television is a response to that concern, as is the counterclaim that a free market will have the same effect.

These examples suggest that conflicts over control will occur often given the frequent differences that arise in complex modern countries fraught with social and economic inequalities and cleavages. It would be reasonable to expect a well-endowed contestant to exert power, consolidate it, and dominate control. However, if Smythe (1986) is correct and the continuous quiet contests over control produce only shifts in emphasis, those conflicts may be more apparent than real. They may concern who personally is in charge and profits, but not which group's interests and concepts of an proper society are being promoted.

Perhaps the more appropriate question may be "Why hasn't there been more rancorous conflict over control of the media?" There are several possible reasons. For one, numerous potential competitors may lack the numbers and/or resources to compete. For another, conflicts can be avoided or managed by various techniques of accommodation. For still another, even though the idea of conflict among powerful opponents may convey an image of violent warfare, much of a period of conflict is devoted to building the resources to fight successfully (e.g., amassing economic resources by earning large profits, creating an image of concern for public welfare by behaving in a socially responsible manner, converting that image to one of moral rectitude that sanctions invoking social norms in one's behalf and against a competitor). Commendable, socially acceptable activities can disguise covert or imminent contests for media control. Furthermore, when there are conflicts, only some of the tactics may be overt—strikes, outspending a competitor, legal action, claims of violations of such norms as free speech. Others, and perhaps the more effective, are covert—demonstrating moral superiority by conforming to norms, exerting informal influence through social networks, acquiring public support by exercising self-restraint. For these reasons, even much real conflict escapes public notice. These possibilities by themselves, however, may not account for the relatively low level of public conflict over media control.

A possibly more plausible explanation is suggested by studies of disagreements, such as those between newspaper publishers and advertisers, or between owners, publishers, editors, and reporters (cf. Hart, 1980). Aside from case studies of particular conflicts, studies uniformly report less conflict than might have been expected (Breed, 1955b). The reason becomes obvious from the comments of those likely to become involved. Within the business, people are trained to compete for advancement, so they tend to share the same standards of performance (see, e.g., McLeod and Hawley, 1964; Tuchman, 1972; Johnstone, Slawiski, and Bowman, 1973; Janowitz, 1975; Golding, 1977; Becker, 1982b) and have the same ideas about appropriate responses to various situations that may arise (Tuchman, 1978; Gans, 1979; see also Fishman, 1982, and Schudson, 1988). As Bogart (1980: 254) stated in discussing the results of a survey of newspaper editors, ". . . editing appears to be a profession whose members really have common values. There is a surprising degree of consensus as to what makes a newspaper good and what makes it attractive." Rachlin (1988: 12) has clarified how this conformity is largely a response to broader societal forces rather than to intraorganizational pressures on personnel:

> Journalists have been socialized, like most of us, in our culture. They have been exposed to the same constellation of understandings and values as most of us. That exposure has, for the most part, been exclusive of other constellations of world understandings and values. Like the journalists themselves, journalistic institutions are integrated within society. Their societal integration requires them to be responsive to the same social forces that press on all institutions. The press then is unavoidably of reality, of our social context, not removed or detached from it.
> [Although] . . . [j]ournalistic convention frequently is explained in terms of demands required by organizational . . . and professional . . . interest[,] . . . [t]he recognition that the work of journalists is part of, rather than simply a representation of reality, belies this notion of organizational determinism.

His statement is a strong version of my observation in Chapter 1 that too much commentary and research tends to treat the media as acting on rather than in society.

Rachlin's remarks are also pertinent to understanding what happens in communities, the level at which conflicts between churches or businesses and the media might be expected. Here, the same mechanisms are at work. The media units themselves are businesses. Their owners and personnel are socialized into the same standards and goals as are local ministers and businessmen. Not surprisingly, their values, goals, and judgments usually agree and occasions for major conflicts are relatively rare. Perhaps most important is that the persons and groups that have the resources to enter a conflict with a reasonable chance of prevailing usually share a common interest in maintaining a system that has helped them achieve their positions.

As a result, it rarely is necessary to use power in conflicts; rather, conflicts arise much less frequently than might be expected. A hegemonic process obviates conditions that might occasion them. The media participate in—indeed, may dominate—that process (Gitlin, 1977, 1979a, 1979b, 1980; Hall, 1977; Williams, 1977; Bennett, 1982; Haralovich, 1985). So long as there is a status difference that favors senders over receivers (but see Kellner, 1979; Turow, 1984a)—and there will be so long as technology separates them and insulates an exclusive and glamorous sender group—and so long as the message supply is selective—and it must be because capacity is finite rather than infinite—the media will be major players in the hegemonic process by which certain advantaged groups dominate society (Westergaard, 1977).

## CONTROL AND THE MEANING OF MEDIA MATERIAL

The involvement of the media in hegemonic processes suggests that any group able to exercise effective control in production could use the media purposefully to manipulate society if it wished to do so. That possibility keeps questions about the "real" meaning of media material alive. Because sheer quantity requires the adornment of messages to make each product (e.g., television series, film) distinctive, many media scholars believe that details rarely carry essential meaning, but, rather, that it inheres in the patterns of themes and modes of presentation and in the different quantities of various types of items. To identify essential meaning, semiotic analysis—a process of identifying the deeper meanings thought to underlie manifest messages (Barthes, 1968; Eco, 1976; Hall, 1980; Baudrillard, 1981; Berger 1987 [1982]; Gottdiener, 1985; for examples of applications see Fiske and Hartley, 1978; Williamson, 1978; Goldman, 1982)—and various similar techniques (e.g., discourse analysis; Connell and Mills, 1985; Gerbner, 1985; van Dijk, 1985) are applied to media texts. All these analyses—and their quantitative variant, content analysis—require inferences about something not overt in a message that are consistent with what is there. For example, the theme that the "good" guy always wins may not be stated in single shows but emerges from a study of similar shows with similar plots. The less apparent the deeper meanings, the more the inferences depend on auxiliary information and assumptions, for example, what usually influences decisions on content, or what will it mean to receivers? However, if one accepts this model of control as a changing field of forces, then there are no uniform rules for choosing assumptions.

Accordingly, semiotic and related analyses yield plausible hypotheses rather than reliable propositions.

Regardless of whether producers are free to produce as they wish and regardless of whether receivers must supply their own idiosyncratic meanings because they are unable to verify their understandings with producers, the meaning of media material may be a peripheral concern if the possibilities in any "reading" are narrowly constrained by the social context of production and consumption. The critical question about the hegemonic process is whether the ruling class is able to set the terms of debate on the media by determining what becomes an issue and what are the feasible, acceptable alternatives for resolving it. They may be able to do this because they supply the members, executives, and managing personnel of the government commissions and boards, private foundations, and think tanks whose reports and press releases heralding imminent crises shape policy planning in Western democracies. In the case of the media, this would mean that they determine which fundamental issues (e.g., financing, monopoly ownership, technology development) warrant attention and what the options for dealing with them are. Specific content may be a minor concern if such matters as whether the media are to be commercially or publicly financed, whether their primary function is informational or recreational, what role, if any, government may have in regulation and surveillance, and what topics are outside the realm of propriety are not also issues. The inattention to the issue of U.S. withdrawal from UNESCO after international communication became a policy issue in that organization and the absence of any attention to media issues that are major concerns in almost every other country illustrate how the media participate in hegemonic issues by structuring public reality and, thereby, limiting the ability of people to interpret the meaning of events for themselves. It is for this reason that the issues discussed in Chapter 9 are nonissues for most Americans rather than issues on which there is no consensus.

Gandy (1982) is so convinced that societal elites control the media through agenda setting that he argued that scholars should move beyond the study of the agendas that the media set to the study of the process by which agenda setting is accomplished. Mowlana (1990: 91) agrees, writing that what is needed is:

> ... a shift in emphasis in the analysis of communication systems, from an exclusive concern with the source and content of the messages toward analysis of the message distribution process. Control of the distribution process is the most important index of the way in which power and values are distributed in a communication system. ...

Berkowitz (1992) considers agenda setting to be the outcome of a shifting, ongoing interaction between policymakers and media professionals, suggesting a model much like this model of control. Gross (1988) accepted such knowledge as already established and went on to propose an ethical code for constraining the biased agenda setting of the elites that control the media. I would argue that there is no one way to accomplish this, even though certain methods may be more frequently employed than others. It is for this reason that control is postulated as being the product of a changing field of forces.

Irrespective of how one weighs the relative importance of structure and content in explaining effects, control clearly impacts on both. The weight of each element in the field of forces that constitutes control, however, varies with the issue. To explain why any particular policy, practice, or product is as it is requires examining in greater detail and specificity the actions and interactions of the elements involved. With respect to media structure and operation and such general matters as ownership, the role of government, and mission, the evidence, on balance, suggests the preeminence of communicators loosely defined—owners, top-level executives and managers—and a small number of key actors outside the system—financiers and lenders, corporations and other prospective owners, political groups and office holders, and unions. The reasons for each to maintain and exercise property rights and to determine the parameters of media activity are obvious, as are the major economic, social, and political resources that each is able to bring to bear when conflicts over or threats to control arise. Technology can significantly limit or otherwise affect their options, though for several reasons—owners are likely to still be carrying large debts, it is more likely to have bugs and low capacity, users have yet to develop the expertise to exploit its potential—this is more likely to be the case with new technology than with equipment that has been available for quite a while.

In contrast, explanations for the content of media products may require consideration of all the elements that comprise the active components of the communication system: communicators, communicatees, apparatus, and context. As for communicators, every part of the sending organization is included: ownership, management at all levels, creative professionals, production and distribution workers, and advertisers. Several cases (Bagdikian, 1988) indicate that sometimes it may be necessary to deal with two levels of ownership—parent conglomerates (e.g., Gulf and Western) and operating firms (e.g., Paramount Pictures)—as groups and interests represented in a decision. Sending, conveying, and receiving equipment may have to be treated separately. In mass communication, inasmuch as communication rarely is occurring, the communicatee is usually an audience. It may have to be treated collectively or individually—collectively for questions concerning how decisions on content are influenced by such tactics as group pressure or withdrawal from the role, and individually for such questions as the meaning or interpretation of material. Although contextual factors are numerous, only a few are likely to be significant in accounting for particular products. Among the likeliest to matter are investors and lenders; stockholders; larger units with which the operating unit is affiliated (e.g., networks, industry-wide trade associations that enforce codes and rate products); independent producers (e.g., production companies, syndicates, press services); sponsors; public interest groups, especially those composed of relatives of audience members (e.g., PTA); national, state, and local governments; censors, regulatory agencies, and courts; and social norms that become focal points of public opinion.

## THE VARYING DYNAMICS AND TACTICS OF CONTROL

The relative importance of all the elements in the field of forces that constitute the control process varies among the media and through time. Examples of media variation are obvious—the absence of government regulation of print media, the much greater public concern over what is depicted on television than what is depicted in films. Changes over time in the structure of the field of forces involved in media control usually reflect broader secular trends in society, the swing toward deregulation and privatization being a recent example. Sometimes these changes affect only a single medium (e.g., the declining impact of technicians and performers in television production as the potentialities of tape are mastered), and sometimes they affect all of them.

Despite the fact that patterns of control vary over time and among media as the roles and importance of the active components (i.e., everything but the symbol system) change, several examples of general propositions about control may be suggested. In each case, the assumption is that all other things are equal. First, the power of consumers is a function of how many approximately equivalent systems are available to them. Second, power varies directly with economic resources. This implies both that (a) the power of communicators is a direct function of their economic resources; the weaker that owners are, the greater the power of audiences, investors, and lenders; and (b) that the larger the organizational span of ownership (e.g., conglomerates vs. single operating unit corporations), the more is production control held by executive officers and their representatives. Third, the power of media owners varies with their economic strength and their independence of production and transmission personnel, thus: (a) the more complex the production process, the more diffused control is throughout the organization; (b) the less standardized the apparatus, the more the weight of technology in control; and (c) the scarcer and more esoteric production techniques and skills are, the more control production workers have. Fourth, the state's ability to act informally is a function of the level of popular support for the incumbent regime (e.g., the Nixon regime's pressure on media was more effective pre- than post-Watergate). Fifth, the more damaging the consequences of media are thought to be, the greater the efforts at control by exogenous interest groups. Sixth, the more ignorant about system structure and operation any group in a system is, the more will control be with those components about which the group is ignorant.[7] Finally, seventh, the norms pertinent to mass media operation need not be consistent or complete and may even be in conflict, for example, freedom of speech and national security, communal moral standards and individual rights (Bassiouni, 1982, and references therein; Weimann, 1983).

These illustrative propositions pertain to imaginary quantities of control—more precisely, relative weight in a field of forces—and the factors that may affect their balance. They say nothing about how that weight is exercised. Any student of power, however, is aware that how power is exercised is among the most important factors in maintaining it. The ideal, if power is to be retained, is to be able to have others comply with one's wishes without having to use one's resources and, relatedly, to be able to avoid the use of force when resources must be used. Compliance without invoking authority is preferable to compliance to authority; covert use of power is better than overt use; coercion is better than brute force (cf. Wrong, 1979). From this perspective, what are the more typical tactics by which the players seek to exercise their roles in media control?

Technology, or apparatus, is by far the least overt or forceful element. It basically limits the quantity, quality, and, much more rarely, nature of messages. Active interference is rare and usually results from breakdowns and accidents. Except, perhaps, for possible developments in artificial intelligence, apparatus does not control by freely initiating interaction with or responding optionally to the actions of others. Equipment is manipulated by people within the limits of its capacity, their knowledge of those limits, and their skill at operating it.

In contrast, the tactics that communicators, communicatees, and exogenous groups use on each other run the gamut of all those available for human interaction. However, the social units to which these terms refer differ in important basic ways. Audiences essentially are comprised of dispersed individuals and exist only as analytic categories (Ang, 1989; Seiter, Borchers, Kreutzner, and Warth, 1989), communicators are social categories that have real social standing as corporate persons, and exogenous actors run the range from real to corporate persons and also include formally and informally organized groups that lack status as corporate persons. There is an asymmetry in the tactics that such diverse units can use on one another (cf. Coleman, 1974) in the competition to have their way on media issues. Audiences typically are reactive. Only if asked on terms set by others are they likely to express a desire for particular material in advance of its preparation. Individuals support or reject material by consuming or not consuming, at least that is the view of one network official who has been quoted as saying, "'I don't give a damn what people say. I care what they do. . . . If they watch it, they are satisfied'" (Wober, 1988: 8). If they feel very strongly, they may write a letter expressing their dissatisfaction, join an organized boycott of a sponsor or a media product (e.g., film, theater, publication), or lobby for restrictive legislation. They can, however weakly or ineffectively, exercise pressure on communicators or exogenous groups to cease or begin some activity. Others may prevent them from doing certain things by cutting off the supply, but they cannot make them do things by direct pressure. They can only encourage or entice or seduce them into doing things.

Communicators depend on audiences and must attract and hold people without using patently coercive tactics. Accordingly, they advertise and try to get favorable reviews of their products in the media. They also use the difficult and unreliable tactic of trying to ascertain what people will choose to consume and then try to provide it. To disarm the public, public relations efforts are mounted to create a favorable corporate image by depicting the corporation as public spirited and its products as public services. Claims are made that the country could not have become what it is without the corporation, medium, or product. Government is communicators' other constant concern. Communicators target the same population whose welfare the state is obligated to protect, and the state can employ very effective and punitive tactics against anyone who compromises that welfare. Accordingly, corporate media actors often seek to curry favor with candidates, public officials, and administrators by supporting their endeavors (e.g., campaign contributions, gifts, space, public support). Only when attacks on their status are considered critical do the media undertake legal action in response to state actions, although they may promote legislation that they feel will improve their position.

Perhaps the most interesting control activities of the communicator group are internal, the actions taken to assure that the material disseminated is what ownership wants it to be. In this regard, the key interaction is between those at the top of the hierarchy—owners, executives and managers—and employees in lower positions. Here all the classic tactics that employers have developed to manipulate the labor process come into play—replacing workers with machinery, breaking down and rationalizing activities so as to deskill the work force, combining with other producers to set wages and working conditions, speedups, and the like. Employees, who in our conception are included in the communicator component of the system, adopt complementary tactics for maintaining or improving their position vis-à-vis ownership—strikes, union organization, slow downs, and the like. Although many of these tactics come close to the use of raw force, relations usually are relatively smooth and workers, managers, and owners accommodate to each other with more covert tactics such as high-quality production and pay raises.

Because exogenous groups are not intrinsically part of the system, in a sense they must intrude in order to have a role. In our society, the most extreme overt form of such intrusion is censorship. Although we tend to think of it as a measure so stringent that it is necessary and adopted only in wartime, Jansen's (1988: 131-246) study of censorship in the United States indicates that it always has been common but disguised. Only general social norms that carry moral sanctions and with which we are indoctrinated as children are not experienced as onerous or oppressive, and even they may cause a sense of conflict. Even when state actions are meant to be facilitative (e.g., grants for research and development), the rationale is that benefits will be in the collective interest; performance is supposed to be monitored to assure that the benefits do not go to the grantees. Surveillance is intrusive and coercive in its nature. It destroys privacy and, thus, limits alternatives for action. More stringent acts (e.g., not renewing licenses, levying fines, taking rule violators to court) are overt demonstrations of the power of the state.

Although manifestly different, the actions of other key exogenous actors are no less coercive, intrusive uses of power. When citizen groups are upset by something attributed to the media (e.g., child violence as a result of television cartoons) or by material they deem unacceptable (e.g., records with obscene lyrics), their initial requests for change always carry a threat of more drastic steps (e.g., court suits, boycotts, legislation, campaigns to get advertisers to withdraw support) to follow if the media do not comply. In one case, conservative groups tried to change news policy at CBS by buying a controlling stock interest, a tactic that clearly reflects the popular belief that lenders and investors hold a heavy hand over those who produce media material and apply pressure on a wide variety of decisions ranging from who to hire to what themes can be treated. Clearly that potential is there.

The exogenous factors that help shape the media and their content are not limited to people and groups and the norms and values they promote and accept. I have already mentioned the effect of sunspots on radio transmission, although that obviously is unusual. Much more important and telling is the environmental context—both physical and cultural—within which the media operate. Thus, for example, low-power, daytime-only radio stations in cities of equal size are better able to reach the entire population in densely settled cities than in cities spread over much larger, more sparsely settled areas.

Perhaps the most important instance of a media system being affected by an environmental factor is the afternoon newspaper. Since the 1950s, almost all the afternoon newspapers in the United States have stopped publishing. In addition to the competition of national network news on television, perhaps the single most important factor contributing to their demise has been the suburbanization of America's cities and the transition from mass transit to the private automobile. As the downtowns of American cities have ceased to be centers of employment and shopping and these activities have moved toward the peripheries, distribution of afternoon papers by truck through street and highway systems beset with traffic jams has become increasingly expensive and unreliable. To be sure that the papers were distributed on time required pushing press runs back earlier and earlier in the day. This made it impossible to produce an afternoon paper significantly different from the morning paper and printed late enough to cover most of the items likely to be featured on early evening television and radio news (Kamiss, 1991: 13-41). Control, then, is not a static outcome of the differential distribution of power across the units that comprise and impinge on a system, but a pattern of forces in interaction that changes as the system and its social setting changes.

## CONTROL AND PUBLIC POLICY

Any critical analysis of control eventually requires a comment on policy because efforts to change the media's role or effects require a commitment to intervene in the processes that shape current media practices and products. Any such policy requires an understanding of whose behavior should be guided in what directions. That is not a simple, clear-cut issue. A model of control as the outcome of interaction among many diverse forces implies that interventions, rather than being directed to a single source of control, requires mapping the relations among controlling elements inside and outside the system and identifying what they control and how they exercise it.[8] Moreover, the prognosis for such efforts is not good, not only because of the uncertainties about both media effects and control processes, but also because of several matters that impinge on policymaking. In a democratic country that professes to subscribe to freedom of speech, proposals for control policies are likely to be contested.[9] Indeed, the recent resurgence of political conservatism has been manifested, among other ways, in deregulation. Control policies requiring regulation conflict with this trend. Furthermore, public pressure, which always is a major factor in control, is not unidirectional in a pluralistic society. The strength of the many various views on an issue continually waxes and wanes. This, in itself, calls into question the urgency of any current demand for a particular type of regulation.

There is perhaps an even more compelling reason for caution in the area of control policies. In characterizing public and scholarly approaches to the media, I stressed the continuing importance of the legacy of early concepts of the media that do not fit the current situation. This is particularly relevant for new control proposals because, regardless of the character of a specific media product, the usual approach has been and continues to be to view mass communication as largely an unselective public process in which communicators disseminate materials very widely with little control over who receives them. It implies that these materials can and may reach individuals and groups for whom they were not intended, who can be harmed by them, and who are unable to regulate their flow. It assumes, in short, inability to control consumption and inequality in resources for initiating messages.

That view of mass communication is captured by the broadcast metaphor. The term *broadcasting* antedates radio and television, literally describing an act of casting something about broadly. Farmers use the term, for example, to describe planting by tossing seeds widely rather than by inserting them in the soil individually at selected spots. However, the emphasis here has been on how technological innovations have facilitated the targeting of materials to preselected groups and otherwise altered the mass communication process. Equipment being developed, for example, will permit programming the times at which and channels on which children will be permitted to view television when there is no immediate parental supervision, or the transmission of the entire range of viewer responses to material as it is being watched rather than the mere recording of stations to which sets in use are tuned. Any broad gauged effort at media control, then, needs to take account of these trends toward (a) privatizing the media and (b) enhancing the capacity to utilize communication equipment, and its attendant potential for equalizing the role of consumers in the process.

These trends suggest that concerns about the media and attendant control needs will shift. For example, because technically mediated communication and its consequences will not be as public, different approaches to monitoring will be required. Even more important is the likelihood that the apparent growth of equality between senders and receivers, which might suggest that even less public control is needed, will be spurious. The initiator will still "know" much more about the receivers and the reasons for initiating the process than the receivers will "know" about the initiators. In that sense, the communicator will remain anonymous to the communicatee, whereas the latter will not be anonymous to the former. The very nature of the role differentiation indicates that the power imbalance in the situation will continue. Communicators still will initiate the process, and receivers largely still will react.

Wilson (1988) has put the new telecommunications technology in a very negative light in assessing the implications of its potential for ending uncontrolled, wide access to the media. He foresees that information and news will no longer be a widely shared public good, that digitizing permits senders to charge receivers for each bit received and thus to make the material a valued commodity, that the poor will be cut off from information if they cannot be free riders, that information as a commodity can be restricted both in terms of its variety and its potential recipients and, therefore, that there will no longer be a "free market place of ideas" (cf. Murdock and Golding, 1989). Thus, he argues, eventually the possibility of a public being an effective presence in the control process will be destroyed. Wilson's horrifying vision of a media system in which the public will be a completely dependent element and a nonparticipant in the control process is one extreme possibility. Kellner, in contrast, a few years earlier (1987 [1983]), urged disadvantaged groups to use newly available public-access television to promote their views and provided a primer on how to do so by recounting his own group's successes in that medium. It would be foolish and unrealistic, however, to believe that the requirement that a public-access television channel be available can be counted on to counterbalance the possibility of merchandised information available only by paying for access to a high-tech system controlled by private interests.

The implication of technology-driven change, then, is not that we are entering an era when control need no longer be an issue, but rather that the problems that will evoke efforts at external control and the measures that will be considered are likely to be very different from those associated with the media as we long have conceived them. Probably, though, it would be a mistake to rely on countervailing power to stabilize the field of forces contesting for control. The evidence is that the involved units are rarely equal, some actors lose interest and drop out (e.g., the Capitol Club's loss of interest in taking over CBS), and others lose their independent source of power (e.g., capital).

In light of these considerations, are no standards in order and is there no need for control policies? Not quite. Experience with freedom of speech suggests that general values are serviceable over the long haul, despite the exigencies of circumstances and variations in how they are interpreted and applied in the short run. The meaning of such standards inevitably will change. Given advances in knowledge and understanding, it would be catastrophic if they did not. If a democratic society has such standards, policies that protect them, even if they cannot promote them, are very much in order. Experience and an evolving understanding of media effects and control suggest, however, that the more specific policies are, the likelier they are to be ineffective and counterproductive.

It should be sobering to realize that Tunstall (1986) not only credited communication deregulation with undermining the broadcast networks and further weakening Hollywood's position in the feature film industry, a truly unexpected result given the absence of government regulation of that industry, but also went on to suggest that the net effect will be ". . . the partial merging of the mass media into, and takeover by, telecommunications" (19). For Wilson (1988: 132), the prospects for effective regulatory policies in this era of new technology are very dim:

> In the case of telecommunications, deregulation is taking place against a background of a regulatory crisis which has called into question the very legitimacy of traditional regulation itself. Because frameworks for regulation have been designed according to an earlier "transportation" model of communication proper to the regulation of land transport, they do not apply to new telecommunication services which typically must integrate data processing and communication as a condition for introducing them.

If so, it would seem that reregulation must involve a great deal more than simply reinstating or revising old arrangements.

## NOTES

1. Ward (1989: 77-80), discussing the development of the media in the period between the two World Wars, has characterized thinking about

the social role of the media and how it might be managed in just this way. He identified Walter Lippman and Harold Lasswell as two influential thinkers who were concerned that the press would misinform and stir up the mass of the citizenry, which would then mount strong demands for government action. They argued, in response, that governments should create alternative sources of informational inputs so as to have bases for action other than the claims of a misinformed public.
2. Hill's (1979) review of control and regulation in American broadcasting is unusual in that it avoids a static, hierarchical perspective by considering a wide variety of actors in the field.
3. Shortly after the conceptual analysis that underlies this discussion had been formulated, an analysis of control that employed less systematically a somewhat similar notion of forces interacting was published (Shoemaker and Reese, 1991).
4. Guback (1987) has suggested that there even is state participation in film and television production by means of subsidization via tax benefits, even though there are no accompanying *overt* efforts at state control.
5. An entertaining account of the Office, the factors that led to its establishment, its tactics, and the pressures that led to change and its eventual demise as a force shaping film content is provided by Leff and Simmons (1990).
6. For a thorough review and analysis of the evolution of the idea of the active consumer, the ways in which the active consumer may influence the communication process, and the important differences between the impact of consumer activity in interpersonal and mass communication situations, see the article by Bryant and Street (1988). Morley (1989: 29), however, cited Modleski to the effect that ". . . stress on the 'active' role of the audience/consumer has been carried too far."
7. This is what underlies Postman's (1985) despair for the future of democracy. He has advanced the thesis that television's emphasis on entertainment misleads people into believing that entertainment values are the proper standard for judging news and that this misunderstanding prevents them from acquiring the critical skill needed to understand what is disseminated under the guise of news.
8. Brown (1986) pointed out that this may bear no rational relation to what is happening. Cf. Liebert and Sprafkin (1988: 38-108) for a review of the formal mechanisms that apply to television and the process by which change was accomplished to deal with the issue of the impact of televised violence on young children and adolescents.
9. Anyone skeptical of a state policy approach to media regulation will find ammunition in Brown's (1986) discussion of the role of what he called the policy-planning network in that process, and of how a "national communication culture" (273) generates a strain toward consistency among individual media policies. Brown claimed that these factors result in some proposals being quite irrational remedies for the situations they were intended to address.

# 7

# Public Policy and Control of the Media

No comprehensive discussion of mass communication can ignore media policy. In the United States, media policy setting and its results are unique because of the complex process that leads to the setting and enforcement of policies and because of differences over interpretations of the meaning of long-standing historical commitments to free speech, a free press, and freedom of information. Some of the complexities of the issues raised when policies are contemplated to deal with public concerns about media abuses or problems are exemplified by the most recent legislation to improve television for children. In response to charges by child advocacy groups (e.g., Action for Children's Television) that children's programming is primarily a vehicle for marketing to children and, consequently, that children's television fails to reach its educational potential, Congress passed the Children's Television Act of 1990. The legislation limits commercials to $10\frac{1}{2}$ to 12 minutes per hour on weekdays and weekends respectively, and requires stations to provide educational programming for children as well.

Because it was supported by parents but opposed by the

Justice Department as a violation of the First Amendment, the Act created a dilemma for then President Bush. He was quoted as saying that "The First Amendment . . . does not contemplate that government will dictate the quality or quantity of what Americans will hear—rather it leaves this to be decided by free media responding to the free choices of individual consumers" (Associated Press, 1990b). Having campaigned for office on a commitment to be an Education President, Bush resolved his dilemma by allowing the legislation to become law without signing the bill. The incident involves almost every issue that arises in considering media policies in this country—government policy versus self-regulation, consumer sovereignty in a market economy versus national sovereignty in a regulated market, specific policies for particular problems versus overriding norms and values, who makes policy and how, and who enforces policy and how. These are the matters to be discussed in this chapter.

Because public policy is a function of the state, its formulation and implementation involve government. Most countries have explicit, proactive, inclusive media policies. In the United States, in contrast, only when the public becomes concerned with an issue, as has been the case of heavily commercialized children's television, or when an industry itself cannot resolve its problems independently is there pressure for government involvement.[1] Issues are legion. Government is asked, among other things, to forbid pornography, assure fairness in broadcasting, and regulate advertising to children. As protector of society and the only legitimate monopolist of the use of force, government is petitioned to protect, redress grievances, improve performance, or whatever. Each demand generates a counter demand. Branches of government also promote their own interests when officials believe that an action is necessary in the national interest, as in the barring of direct reporting of Operation Desert Storm. If government acts to alleviate these pressures without intending to set general policy, the action usually becomes policy anyway. Such policies are understood to be commitments to maintain certain standards and goals for both governmental and nongovernmental actors.

It is largely because government is the arena in which policies are instituted and executed that it is included as a major player in elaborating the control process. Although clearly exogenous to media systems in the United States, it helps shape their structure and operation by exercising policymaking, rule making, surveillance, and enforcement functions. In fact, it is tempting to revise the model of control as an interacting field of forces to indicate that, at any time, control operates within constraints set by government policy, for, in a sense, by setting limits media policy dictates what control processes can determine. However, governments—more so than the state—are subject to constituency pressure and, so, themselves are vulnerable to efforts at control. If it is useful to consider them to be the preeminent rule setters for the interplay of other forces, these rules can only apply for finite time periods.

Regardless of whether priority should be accorded to government policymaking as the process of media control actually unfolds, states claim it by virtue of their rights and responsibilities as guardian of the public and of the national interest. In some countries, those functions are acquired and legitimated by collective symbolic acts (e.g., the American Declaration of Independence and subsequent adoption of a constitution). In others (e.g., Great Britain) they accrete informally and are sustained by tradition and common law. In still others, the style is authoritarian and they simply are arrogated. Regardless of how modern states have attained and legitimized these rights and responsibilities, perhaps their key activity in the collective life is the determination of national policy. From a rational perspective, once policies are set, rule making, surveillance, and enforcement presumably are all simply means to assure their implementation (though they also are covert techniques for making policy).

Policymaking, however, often is not of interest to the public for several reasons. For one thing, when it is undertaken it is legitimated by the claim that the policies being considered are necessary to achieve or protect more encompassing rules and norms—fundamental social values and constitutional commitments and guarantees—that are not at issue. Moreover, citizens are usually unaware of the issues and options that policy debates deal with because overriding values remove options from consideration that otherwise might be rational alternatives. In the United States, so many fundamental rights are entrenched in the Constitution—freedom of speech, limits on government—or enshrined as basic values—free enterprise, sanctity of the family, private property rights—that the options being debated often may seem secondary and derivative. The situation becomes quite vague, and it is unclear whether policies themselves or only their implementation are at issue.

Policymaking may not generate wide interest not only because the policy arena is not a forum in which all possible goals and all options for reaching them are weighed rationally, but also because it is not a well-defined process. Often it is not even clear when it is under way. Therefore, the public is not alerted. Furthermore, during the infrequent debates over new policies, the attractive contenders are promoted and legitimated as the only way to achieve or defend basic societal values and goals. Consequently, policies usually survive for long periods and are only considered periodically. Once adopted, the manifest role of the state is not to reassess policies but to execute them routinely.

Government, however, often does not work that way. Rather, policies deemed necessary but likely to be unpopular may be executed covertly in legislation whose policy significance is hidden. That, for example, is how Leff (1984) analyzed New Deal income tax policies. He claimed that although high rates for the rich were proposed as necessary for income redistribution, in fact, this was done only to protect a capitalist economy. The high rates on high incomes reduced criticism of the income inequality that capitalism produces without threatening the property ownership system or the basic wealth of the capitalist class. Lundstedt and Spicer (1990) have suggested the concept of latent policy to cover such strategies and illustrated it by examining the patterned discrepancy between stated policies on local broadcasting station ownership and the actual decisions and actions of the FCC. Similarly, Horwitz (1989) interpreted steps taken by the government to deregulate telecommunications from this same perspective. Although they are justified as needed to improve the array and quality of material and services available to the public, Horwitz concluded that they actually have triggered a process that is so economically inefficient that it runs counter to the public service responsibilities of the industry.

Because they can be disassociated from the policies they are intended to implement, it can be very risky to infer unstated policies from actions. Even a correct inference may appear unwarranted if action and policy are poorly articulated. Because actions to implement policies may fail if they are inappropriate, employ false assumptions, are poorly executed, or do not anticipate relevant contingencies, when policies are unstated there are no safeguards against mistaken inferences as to their nature.

Various combinations of these conditions contribute to the neglect of policies and the policymaking process in other ways. If policymaking is infrequent, if most policies are in place for long periods, and if most public debate deals with implementation rather than substance, then most people, including government officials, are likely to ignore policies and goals. Administrative agencies and their implementation routines become ritualized and maintained as ends in themselves. The policies they were meant to implement are forgotten—this, of course, is one of the cardinal sins ascribed to bureaucracy. Despite the growing scholarly interest in public policy and the policymaking process, public interest in and scholarly understanding of these matters is low for several reasons: many important alternatives on the matters at issue are not considered, and those alternatives that are considered may be in unresolvable basic conflicts; the evidentiary base to support alternative proposals is often weak, inconsistent, or biased (Meyer and Hexamer, 1982); the process is spasmodic and often covert; programs become valued in their own right and eclipse the policies they are meant to implement; and program and policy decisions may be confused. Although these points are not elaborated on here—they are well illustrated in Rowland's (1982) analysis of the effort to reshape public broadcasting policy in the United States in the late 1970s—they frame this discussion of public policy and the media. The aim is not to suggest or evaluate specific policies, but to clarify how the policy process does and might impact on mass communication.

## LOCUS OF CONTROL AND PUBLIC POLICY

The fundamental point made in discussing control is that it is a process of constant interplay among forces. The endogenous forces include the activities of communicators, apparatus, and communicatees, each responding to and evoking responses from the others. If that were all, however, the main value of the concept would be its emphasis on the role of all active elements of a communication system in control. But the concept also emphasizes the influential role of a large group of exogenous factors. In the short run, like endogenous factors, many exogenous factors—although not all (e.g., social norms, atmospheric conditions)—also respond to one another and to the actors in the system. The first point to be made about policy is that it sets the limits within which all other forces in the control process—both endogenous and exogenous—operate.

There is a question, however, as to whether public policy is an exogenous or endogenous element in control. The answer depends on whether policy is treated as static—a set of publicly legitimized goals and means for reaching them—or as dynamic—a process in which goals and means evolve over time with periodic public discussion and legitimation. From a static perspective, public policy is located within the state and is expressed as government action. The state has a monopoly on the legitimate use of force and, thus, controls the only sure means of implementing its will. It acts through the various arms of government. From that perspective, media policy is exogenous to communication systems. At least that is so with respect to where standards are set and how they are implemented. But if one asks why actors in a system of communication conform to policy, often the reason is that they know what is expected of them and fear sanctions if they do not fulfill expectations. In that case, which is quite normal, the locus of influence is exogenous, but short term implementation is endogenous—no one external to the system maintains surveillance or directly guides the behavior of the actors.

From a dynamic perspective, the role of the actors is enhanced even more because the existence and content of policy as well as its execution are at issue. The key questions about policy in understanding control include not just what the policies are and how they are executed, but also why certain matters and not others enter the policy arena and why adopted policies no longer are as clear as they once may have been or no longer are interpreted, implemented, and enforced as they once were. Viewed dynamically, every exogenous and endogenous factor that has a role in control also is implicated in policy.

As for its target, by definition, a communication policy is directed to the operation of a communication system—some or all aspects of the performance of communicators, communicatees, and/or apparatus. It also may be directed at exogenous elements that can affect how systems operate. It is produced and implemented in a political process in which participants compete or cooperate to determine an outcome. The outcome of a public policy debate is legitimated by governmental action. If government is at all representative, then all groups with interests in the outcome also can try to influence governmental actions. Being directly affected by policy, communicators and communicatees are deeply interested in shaping the policy agenda, the outcomes of the debates, and the implementation of decisions—sometimes ignoring each other in self-interest, sometimes contesting with each other, and sometimes cooperating to oppose third-party interests. The government may also be a party to the process when its functionaries feel that current policies are unworkable or in conflict with other policies, needs, or goals.

Typically, proposed or established policies are found in public documents, for example, party platforms, commission reports, statements by government leaders, and justificatory preambles to legislative or administrative acts. Implementation is assigned to new or preexisting structures and may be the only act of legitimation. Thus, for example, the 1927 legislation that created the Federal Radio Commission, the predecessor of the Federal Communication Commission (FCC), both expressed and implemented a policy to make radio signals available without interference. Interested parties, often through professional lobbyists, try to influence both the policy proposals considered in the process (i.e., become part of the agenda) and its outcome.

Legislative and administrative actions do not end the policy process. Those responsible for implementing policies need guidelines, and interested groups often try to influence their formulation and monitor implementation, seeking opportunities to alter or terminate a policy. Even without external pressure, agency personnel may intentionally or unintentionally alter their performance over time in ways that effectively change policy. Foley (1990), for example, examined how the policy being administered by the FCC had been transformed by introducing and then reinterpreting ambiguous language. He noted that the goal of broadcast regulation stated in legislation—to take actions that will most benefit the "public interest, convenience, and necessity"—had come to be referred to as *value* because it is a social value, and that over the years the goal of maximizing the value of broadcasting had been transformed to maximizing its economic value. This raises the question as to whether actions taken to maximize economic value are compatible with maximizing social value. Policy, then, is a *dynamic* body of commitments to goals, means, and conditions. How it impacts on its targets, therefore, varies over time. Consequently, its locus is in the political and economic matrix that affects its evolving implementation. In communication, the concerned actors who are part of that process are also part of the control process. Thus, although policy, viewed as a static entity, may only be exogenous to communication systems, viewed as a dynamic process it is both endogenous and exogenous.

## LOCI OF COMMUNICATION POLICY

One consequence of the vague line between programs and policy is that it may not be clear where in government the locus of communication policy is. Often the loci for setting and implementing policy differ. Executives may propose policies or even order them by administrative action (e.g., ending segregation on railroads by executive order under the authority to regulate interstate commerce), but not enforce them. Although legislatures also may set but not enforce policies by stating the purposes of legislation, they also may renew the force of lapsed policies by investigating their nonenforcement or violation (e.g., congressional hearings on university expenditures of overhead funds received with federal grants).

Government agencies with administrative and enforcement responsibilities usually implement policies—the police as enforcers of criminal law provide a clear example. In telecommunications, the prototypical example is provided by the FCC and its responsibility to regulate those industries.[2] The absence of any comparable organization for newspapers, magazines, and films exemplifies how the priority of overarching value commitments—freedom of speech and a free press—

cuts off debate on what might otherwise be public concerns about policy. Those media, of course, also are subject to control, but the interactive field of forces in their case excludes an explicit role for government policy. The state can only pursue its interests in them indirectly.

The FCC merits attention because it provides good examples of the indirect means by which executives and legislators play policy-making roles, even when that function has been delegated by law to an administrative agency. The FCC is responsible for assigning and renewing a limited number of licenses to broadcast. To help sort out applicants, the FCC evaluates them in terms specified in the legislation—for awarding a license, personal qualities, for renewal, operating in the public interest. Because the legislation is no more specific than this, the commissioners either overtly or covertly must specify what does and does not meet those standards. In doing this, they set policy. A president who wishes to change those policies cannot do so directly for the FCC is an independent public agency subject only to control by the courts. However, presidents are responsible for appointing commissioners, and the power to determine the makeup of the Commission does provide a mechanism, albeit not a completely reliable or direct one, to accomplish such policy changes.

Enforcement of the Children's Television Act provides a concrete example of how execution of a legislative mandate by a government agency defines a policy that shapes control. Administration officials at the time of enactment, despite having received large campaign contributions from broadcasters who had opposed the Act, had had to accept unwanted legislation requiring licensees to provide evidence of their commitment to the educational needs of children when applying to the FCC for renewals. However, the Chair of the FCC was an administration appointee, and during his term agency officials argued that the law was written so vaguely that cartoons and reruns of sitcoms like "Leave It to Beaver" could qualify as educational. Within weeks of his resignation to make way for the new administration, the Commission was holding up relicensing applications for evidence of more substantial conformity with the law's requirements. Although the Commission had been given authority from the Act's passage to write rules as to what would and would not qualify as proper children's broadcasting, it had not done so. Only after the new administration took office did it note that there had been little change in programming since the Act had been passed and that "We do not believe that this level of performance is, in the long term, consistent with (its) objectives" (Andrews, 1993).

Although new rules have yet to be set, the case dramatizes how policies underlying legislation can be defined through interpretation by administrative agencies. Moreover, it demonstrates how much it distorts the process of policymaking as an aspect of control to conceive of predominant power as being concentrated at any one place. Congress has power to legislate a policy, an administration has power (up to a point) to approve or veto its actions, an administrative agency has power to interpret and enforce the law, and political activists who contribute to campaigns have power to influence all three. Despite these contingencies, however, it is clear that, within limits, administrative agencies can make an independent contribution to the process because their experienced personnel—"the entrenched bureaucracy"—have some autonomy from the elected officials and political appointees who would be handicapped in implementing promised programs without their cooperation.

Although it can initiate the process of establishing policy by legislating, Congress also is constrained in changing broadcast policy. Once it has created an independent agency, it can only change its mission by legislation. Legislating is not easy, however, especially if it affects an agency with a decent reputation as a guardian of the public interest. Indeed, despite the changes in technology and public expectations during the period, 42 years passed before there was an effort to rewrite the Communications Act of 1934 that created the FCC. The difficult and unreliable legislative process helps explain the persistence of originating legislation. Congress, though, like the President, also has indirect means for making policy. One is its appropriation function. Congress has been notorious for keeping the FCC on a very tight budget. It is claimed that the industry lobbies Congress to do this in order to restrain the Commission (cf. Krasnow, Longley, and Terry, 1982) from acting on complaints by various groups that many stations do the minimum or less to serve the public interest. Tight budgets keep the FCC staff too small to conduct the thorough investigations required to provide evidence for nonrenewal decisions. Consequently, the Commission's actions imply an unstated lenient licensing policy—although, if anything, that is Congress's choice—despite the fact that it expresses and even may wish to enforce a strong one.

As for the unregulated media, the record suggests that they are subject to unstated federal policies implemented at national, local, or even private levels. The practice of film and magazine censorship by local boards—the famed "banned in Boston" type of case—has been mentioned. The long period during which the Justice Department has not brought suit and Congress has not legislated suggests that those bodies were quite satisfied with the results of local censorship. More directly, the Post Office's authority over special low mailing rates for printed material sometimes has been used to deny them to periodicals with which the government has been displeased.

The most important factor that encourages covert policy processes may be public opinion on whether there should even be media policy. Those opinions reflect widespread commitment to two pervasive values: (a) the traditional view that the press is the watchdog over government and the belief that it could not do this effectively if it was part of government or subject to regulation, and (b) the superiority of a market economy and the derivative belief that government should not own or operate any business enterprise or regulate a market. Indeed, Horwitz (1989) dramatized what he felt to be the "real" thrust of government regulation of broadcasting from the inception of the FCC to the present by entitling his chapter on the events of the period with a comment in a 1939 Supreme Court decision to the effect that "Congress intended to leave competition in the business of broadcasting where it found it" (155, 332[fn. 48]). These values help explain why the United States has less direct government involvement in the media than almost any other country. Hall (1979) cited Branscomb to the effect that ". . . the USA seems unable to cope with any rational and/or centralized look at communication policy!" in speculating that "[p]erhaps it is the policy of those that make communications policy that a (publicly open and publicly based) rational and/or centralized look at communications policy is not to be desired" (172). There is no public ownership, no formal government control, no formal censorship (but cf. Jansen, 1988: 131-247).

Even broadcast policy is minimal and sketchy, largely being directed at technical matters. The overriding values of free speech and a free press have become an ostensible broad media policy that limits any more specific actions or policies that seem to violate them. This particularly involves actions that affect content—as is the case with the Children's Television Act. They rationalize recent deregulatory policy expressed in the loosening rules that limit the number of stations a network can own, the total minutes of commercials that can be broadcast each hour, and the like. Such regulations are said to be unnecessary because technical advances have enlarged the supply of broadcast frequencies, and market mechanisms will provide an optimum broadcast system (see Spitzer, 1986). Nonetheless, reflecting the inconsistencies that always characterize basic values, the FCC recently has restricted broadcasting of "adult" materials to the hours between midnight and the very early morning.

The consequences of these overarching values for media policy are paradoxical. Thus, even though explicit general policy is minimal and what there is constantly is under attack, government creates ad hoc, limited policies whenever they seem necessary. Contradictions among them are obscured by the lack of a broad media policy. Furthermore, the absence of general policy encourages a vigorous market for policies expressed in a constant public clamor for actions that would automatically become policies if they were to be implemented. These inconsistencies cause fewer problems than they might, however, because covert policy processes usually afford ways to defuse them. In that respect, the United States differs considerably from many other countries that also do not consider broad media policies openly. In those countries, public discussion of policy usually is muted by government ownership or censorship. It is a moot question as to whether constraining values or restrictive systems are more damaging than explicit broad policies. The two may be equal handicaps.

## PUBLIC POLICY AND SELF-CONTROL

The minimalist stance of the American state on media policy has important implications. Handicapped in initiating policies, the state, instead, uses its extensive resources (e.g., tax policy, purchasing power, operation of the postal service, responsibility for the environment and work place standards) to shift the burden of setting and enforcing policies to the media themselves. Hall's (1979: 172) comment that ". . . the giant telecommunicators have done pretty well by keeping policy making to themselves" suggests that this has not been a burden, indeed, that it may be desired. Even if industry policies are not exactly what the state might implement if it could, it seems reasonable to assume that they are quite close. Although self-regulation may serve the industry by averting state action, it is analytically confusing, for it is not clear whether it is simply a surrogate for government policy or an independent force in the control process.

Regardless of whether industry and government policymaking produce the same results, self-regulation has several deficiencies that can be clarified by reviewing how it developed. Long before any of the media became major industries, governmental passivity seemed to suggest that entrepreneurs were free to develop and promote communication technologies for private profit-making purposes so long as government could access them to meet its responsibilities (e.g., protecting the public health and safety, national defense). Except for times of crisis, national interest would be served by pursuing private business interests. Owners and entrepreneurs could develop and use the media, presumably in accord with their main goals, earning a profit. Even if profit was not the first priority, the cost of development capital soon made it that.

The history of each medium can be read as a process in which capital needs eventually forced the replacement of pioneering entrepreneurs by large corporate entities for which profits were paramount. Ward (1989: 80-109) has described the inter-World War period as one in which the media were transformed by extensive consolidation. The primacy of profit in this process is captured in the view attributed to members of the Frankfurt School that "[t]he basic purpose of the media is not as most Western social ideologies demand, to inform, educate, and enlighten their audiences, but rather simply to make profits" (Becker and Schoenbach, 1989: 15), and in Ang's (1991: 53) blunt statement that ". . . production for profit is the sole objective of the commercial broadcasting industry. . . ." From the corporate viewpoint, the ideal role of government is to enhance conditions for profitable operations by decreasing uncertainty and insuring against risk, in other words, to provide a good investment climate. Other than that, industry prefers no policies, for policies can hamper corporate actions that might be necessary in the unforeseeable future. Therefore, as media corporations developed, in order to justify and legitimate that preference, they worked to create an image as good corporate citizens that could be counted on to do the right thing. They promoted a doctrine of corporate responsibility.

The priority of profit has important implications for government policy when seen in the larger picture of media development. Early media technology was not developed to satisfy already existing public demand. Rather, it evolved in response to dreams of profit combined with the pleasure of the intellectual challenge or curiosity, the need to solve commercial or military problems, or the opportunity to test new principles of fundamental science by developing their spin-off implications.[3] Neither current media systems, the materials they offer, nor the technology they employ were anticipated. The public responded to the early products as novelties and curiosities. Our present systems developed in response to unanticipated, though desired, public demand (e.g., television, film) or to lures developed to stimulate sales of receiving equipment that, by itself, had offered little to the average consumer (e.g., radio).

Except for television, direct sales were the main—and sometimes only—source of income in the earliest days of each medium. The idea of generating income from advertising came later. The small enterprises of the past were not created to be vehicles for advertising. They expected their income to come from direct consumer payments for use of what was offered. Dependence on income from advertising came later. Film is a unique relic in relying so heavily on admissions for income. The legitimacy of using films to advertise is still questioned—the industry still is criticized for allowing product promotion. Regardless of their early differences, all the media now are owned in great part by large private corporations that must make a profit. Profits, in turn, depend on attracting and holding audiences, primarily for their market potential to advertisers and only secondarily for their direct support.

In the United States, the course of media development also was influenced by the lack of interest in using them to further national interests. There were such options. The state could have claimed for itself an interest in educating the populace, building national support, controlling information and public opinion, or furthering other goals with the new media. Most other governments pursued one or more such goals by retaining ownership, using public funds and license fees to produce material, financing production and distribution facilities, establishing publishing houses, monitoring the material offered, and the like. Decisions on such matters are basic to policymaking for the media. The American government passed on the chance to be involved. This is not surprising, given that "[t]he extent to which a government avails itself of such powers, and the interpretation it gives to such responsibilities, are directly related to the political and social principles upon which it has been founded and continues to exist. The state . . . in democratic societies . . . would rarely intervene directly" (Ward, 1989: 14). Development of new communication technologies was left to private enterprises, for which profits are paramount. Because profits depend on audiences, audiences become indirect arbiters of media decisions by expressing their tastes.

In this situation, the wisest course for a profit-oriented business is to provide members of the public with what they want. But this creates problems if, as happens, what is wanted conflicts with the government's obligation to preserve the nation and guard the public's health and safety. If that happens, the government may threaten to reenter the scene, as it also may do if public tastes or media professionals' judgments about those tastes lead to widespread opposition and complaints. However, because media executives know they must attract and satisfy large audiences, major public complaints about media performance ought to be rare. But that would be so only if the population is homogeneous, and, as has often been noted, it is not. Accordingly, the media find it most profitable to tailor materials to various population sectors. Because the materials are public, however, others can monitor them—parents can see children's programs, Christians can see pornography, Republicans and Democrats can see one another's campaign material—so frequent, widespread complaints with the media, sometimes in conflicting directions, are always possible.

As a consequence of population heterogeneity and the public character of media material, demands for government action to control the media are frequent. Hence, media enterprises operate under a constant threat that the government will activate control policies. The industries have learned that self- regulation can be effective for warding off government action. "The result is a form of self-censorship within media organisations, attempting to define the shifting limits of public taste and political acceptability without incurring the interest and intervention of the government" (Ward, 1989:14).[4] Self-regulation may take the form of industry codes of conduct drawn up by trade associations and supported by the major players in them, auxiliary rules such as the agreement among television broadcasters to allow only "family" programming until 10 P.M., formal organizations set up for restricted purposes such as the film rating operation of the MPAA, or tacit agreements among the media such as the unwritten rule not to name rape victims. The key to understanding the effectiveness of self-regulation as a foil to media policy is the larger national commitment to minimum interference with a free market and avoidance of any restraint of media industries. As long as they constitute policy, it seems reasonable to expect no other broad, explicit, public media policies.

It might not seem to matter how media policy is made or enforced so long as it is desirable and works. However, the case can be made that it does matter, for self-regulation has several deficiencies. First, its primary purpose is to quiet complaints against industries that thrive on "giving them what they want." Therefore, the only reasons to change policy are reactive. Policies become an issue only if there are threats. Second, policies adopted to quiet complaints and protect profits are not positive in the sense of being geared to achieve other goals. Moreover, because those policies usually are presented as valuable public services, there are few occasions for considering what else the media might be doing for public service. Third, there are few, if any, reliable mechanisms for public input. The media claim that the market is that mechanism—that they drop practices and material that the public will not support—but, even if true, there still is no input on choices. The media always determine the alternatives. Moreover, market-based decisions on what to drop can deprive smaller groups of materials important only to them.

To sum up, the essential concerns are that self-regulation hinders the development of expertise in media policymaking and, thus, hampers any effort to consider what might be accomplished with the media and how. In addition, it buttresses norms that minimize state participation in media policymaking, entrenching even more firmly the expectation that there will be no public involvement in that process. In short, media development in the United States has subordinated any public interest in the media to private interests.

## PUBLIC POLICY AND INDIVIDUAL RIGHTS

Contemporary aversion to interference with communication media derives from long-established norms of freedom of speech and the press. Whatever was intended by protecting the press and speech from restrictive legislation when the members of the Congress and of state bodies drafted and adopted the First Amendment to the Constitution, clearly they acted in the sociopolitical climate of England and America more than 200 years ago. Their passion on the issue indicates that they must have known how important the writings of Tom Paine and speeches of Patrick Henry were in promoting the revolutionary cause. However, Paine and Henry's words were not disseminated in anything like our media. The euphoria of that time is gone, the political and social environment has changed, the media have emerged, and Americans are left with the unexpected dilemmas to which these prohibitions contribute.

The comment by Supreme Court Justice Holmes that no one has the right to yell "Fire!" in a crowded theater (Kerner, 1979: 198-200; Hixson, 1989: 289) captures the nature of the unanticipated problems that can arise. The commitment to unfettered communication has been a frequent source of value conflicts. One of the more recent dramatic instances was Mario Savio's highly publicized Free Speech Movement at the University of California in Berkeley during the student upheavals of the 1960s. Savio used a strategy of publicly uttering socially unacceptable language to dramatize how the enforcement of traditional social norms limits individual freedom. Movement leaders had the perspicacity to promote their cause by using a constitutionally protected right rather than an illegal act such as narcotics use. By staying within the law while intentionally violating a social norm, they forced anyone who was offended to realize that they would have to jeopardize their own right of self-expression if they wished to prevent others from communicating offensively.

The Movement's strategy also highlighted the constant tension between the individual and society. In communication that tension is particularly acute. On the one hand, communication requires individual production. The media make concerted efforts to enhance interest in and acceptance of their material by associating it with individuals. Even though the product is collective, it emerges from interaction over the productions of individuals. On the other hand, true communication is quintessentially social and requires consensual acceptance of the rules of usage. It cannot work unless its components and conventions are shared. That is why so much of the social investment in education is devoted to reading and writing.

Although basically comprised of acts of individual production, communication can only be a vehicle for personal creativity within carefully defined limits. To create by completely violating or destroying its basic rules or components minimizes the ability of others to understand and respond to one's production and, thus, defeats its purpose. In most societies language—vocabulary and grammar—is sacrosanct. To gauge how deeply this feeling runs, consider the jokes about how the French react to mispronunciations or grammatical errors, the sentiment in Quebec to leave Canada in order to protect French, or the fervor to make English the official language of the United States. Even so, communication also is an acceptable means of creative self-expression and, accordingly, a major medium for displaying individuality. Indeed, people who violate laws while using other forms of expression—art, dance, attire—usually base their defense on freedom of speech—speech being a code word for any mode of expressing one's thoughts and urges (Hixson, 1989: 126, 303).

The paradox of pairing protective orthodoxy and creative innovation in communication mirrors the tension between the collectivity and the individual. How can languages be protected—or, indeed, should they be protected—if they are basically pragmatic, that is, means to accomplish something? Usefulness requires that they be dynamic—always open to adjustment to the requirements of situations. That quality is most crucial when individuals need to express immediate, urgent needs and feelings in the absence of authorities to maintain proper usage or approve innovations.

Despite protective efforts, however, languages do change by informal and unstructured processes. Legislation cannot preserve a language by enforcing proper usage. Vocabulary and grammar are protected only by authorities who produce dictionaries, grammars, style manuals, and judgments that legitimize current usage, but who lack legal status, have no way to enforce their rulings, and, at best, derive their authority from their association with legitimating organizations like universities and professional associations. However, they do perform an essential societal service by retarding rapid, ungoverned change in the shared means essential for communication. In doing that, however, they also restrict the opportunities to create and to innovate that languages afford so well.

The conflict between individual impulse and social conformity is especially acute in communicating despite—perhaps also because of—the intensive effort put into training. The key factor is variation in what people learn and their use of it. It is reflected in marked differences in their skill as communicators. Because proper communication is highly valued and all adults are expected to perform well, people who fail to meet standards are often sanctioned by being shamed.

Consequently, many people who are less skilled than others or lack confidence in their skills avoid communicating for fear of embarrassment. This impedes social interaction and organization by preventing relationships from developing or by misleading others in ongoing relationships. Poor communicators also are frustrated by being unable to express themselves and by losing social status—social rank being based, in part, on skill in communicating.

The burden of expectations for performance as a communicator comes, in part, from indoctrinating people in a tradition that emphasizes the importance and responsibilities of the individual. The French Revolution marked the ascendance of a philosophy that raised the status of the individual to at least that of the collectivity. Combined with a faith in rationality, it supports a belief that people should make, be responsible for, and be able to express their own choices, and breeds disinterest in and opposition to a policy role for the state. Resistance to stronger and broader national media policy, then, not only reflects norms of free communication and the organized resistance of the media, but also is reenforced by a doctrine of individualism magnified by concern that communication policy implies categorical rules—prescriptions and prohibitions that apply to the media-related behavior of everyone without regard to whether they suit the individual. In societies that value the individual and individual rights, this is an anathema. It makes the goal of avoiding the unwanted effects of the media even more difficult to achieve.

In part, the resistance to media policy in the United States also can be traced to an early theme of this analysis—the close affinity and resulting confusions among influence, aesthetic expression, and communication. I would argue that the norm of freedom of speech refers largely to activities that I have defined as communication and only secondarily to influence or aesthetic expression. Indeed, the rationalistic philosophy of the French Revolution suggested great faith in people's ability to draw the proper conclusions from information. In assessing proposals for national media policy, it must be emphasized that the concerns that motivate them usually are raised by efforts to influence and by entertainment materials that are not the stuff of communication. Complaints concern violence, sex, and language in films, advertising that children cannot identify as such, news selected for its entertainment rather than for its information value, an overabundance of misleading advertising, and so on. The speech and press that the First Amendment addressed were far different from today's media.

When resistance to government policy is breached, the products, positive and negative, largely reflect a transmission perspective in the terms in which transmission and cultural production views of the media were distinguished in Chapter 1. Public television, low postal rates, broadcast frequency allocations, equipment standards, and cable requirements to carry local broadcasters all emphasize transmission. Although it might be argued that the founding fathers were primarily concerned with production if one views the press at the time as largely an enhancement of personal speech rather than as a transmitting channel for a wide variety of information, the First Amendment would seem to refer to both. Regardless of whether the intent was to protect production, transmission, or both, current public concerns tend to focus on production—pornography, violence, children's television. When faced with such issues, public officials usually do not mandate controls, but, rather, try to place the responsibility for regulating production and consumption in the private sphere. The difference in the substance of government policies and the issues that are referred to private control and resolution suggests that the government orientation to policy is informed, if it is informed at all, by the production-transmission distinction. My view is that, if anything is relevant, it is the communication-entertainment-influence distinction because the concerns at the time the First Amendment was adopted had to do with communication, that is, information sharing. In any case, simply putting aside the status of entertainment and influence, if the First Amendment was and is intended to maximize the availability of material intended to be and felt to be informative, then it should be understood the both production and transmission are to be protected and insured.

Even if a successful case were made that the First Amendment was never intended to protect current media practices, it would be extremely difficult to establish public policies for the media because individualism and the rights and responsibilities of the person are so firmly established.[5] The irony is that the prospective target—the media—exist and prosper by producing and responding to people categorically. Media industries resist policies that would control them and protect the public by asserting the sanctity of individual tastes and arguing that people can be relied on to choose what is good and useful for them and to avoid what might not be. The tactic is particularly ironic inasmuch as the media prosper by ignoring and demeaning individualism and base decisions on a categorical approach to audiences.

## *TARGETS OF POLICY*

Industry self-regulation limits the scope of public sector policy, but it still is important to identify the primary targets of those policies. Are public policies largely directed toward apparatus, communicators, or communicatees? The compatibility proposition (see Chapter 3) implies that, because each medium is a system and a system's survival requires compatibility among its components, regulation should focus on all components and their relationships. However, because policy-making and implementation are political processes, differences in the power of components are relevant to whether they are likely to be targets. Assuming some correlation between the power of a component and its impact on system performance, with respect to restrictive or coercive policies one would expect that the greater the power of a component, the more likely it is that policies to change system performance will be directed to it. On the other hand, because governments rely on the support of constituencies, one also might expect that the more powerful a component, the less likely it is to be a target of government policy. With respect to policies that reward or encourage certain actions, the expectations would be just the reverse. These contradictory expectations provide the backdrop for this discussion of targets.

The potential to influence how media systems operate not only is diffused through the systems, but also extends to elements in the larger environment. The balance among endogenous and exogenous factors shifts over time and among places as conditions vary. The success of recent efforts by several interest group organizations to keep a program on homosexual black males from being shown on public television stations and of local groups to ban retail store sales of a magazine with a cover photograph of a nude pregnant actress, on the one hand, and the fact that the program and magazine were produced and distributed, on the other, exemplify both points. Although so many factors do affect mass communication systems and might be targets of media policy, public policies are directed largely to system components, perhaps because it is so difficult to address all the exogenous elements that may try to exert influence.

Just as the Constitution prohibits congressional abridgment of free speech and a free press, legislation could prohibit abridgments by noncongressional groups and persons that attempt to interfere with the media. The problem, though, is that abridgments often involve informal processes that are difficult to prevent because they cannot be detected. Consumers change stores, potential viewers choose not to watch offending stations, community residents shun local media personnel and officials, and communicators avoid certain actions simply because they value and want to be accepted by those who might sanction them informally were they not to do so. Influence operates at different levels in different ways and is a natural and normal part of social life (e.g., education, peer emulation, socialization). Consequently, often it is neither visible to nor recognized by those involved. The nebulous character and social acceptability of implicit, covert influence places it beyond the reach of effective policy.

In accord with the expectation that the objects of coercive policies would be ordered inversely to their power as constituencies, the few overt public policies seem to be directed first at apparatus and second at communicators. The principle would imply that communicatees might fall between the two, but (a) the private character of most consumption, (b) the relative effectiveness of self-selection as a principle of audience membership, and (c) the efforts of communicators to control public consumption and their claimed success in doing so may combine to discourage further attempts to influence consumer behavior directly. There can be some doubt about the relative positions of the targets of policy for several reasons. Although the government can set standards for equipment in development or production, or performance standards for broadcast stations, apparatus is developed, produced, and operated by people. In that sense, much like the symbol system, technology is passive. However, incompetent operation of receiving equipment is seldom a target of policy both because reception is so difficult to monitor and because manufacturers compete by claiming to make receiving equipment "user friendly."

Extant policies for apparatus tend to set minimum standards for assembly, components, and performance. Because usually only broadcasting equipment can be monitored, these policies are legitimated as a government obligation to see to it that private use of public resources serves the public's best interests. Policies have governed such matters as the choice of a principle for color television tubes, tube clarity standards, set wiring standards, technology for high definition television (HDTV), and, especially, transmitting equipment configuration. Policies may be implemented indirectly, for example, recently, while agreements were worked out with domestic firms that produce and market analog audio recordings, import licenses were denied to domestic marketers so as to delay foreign development and manufacturing of digital tape machines capable of copying analog recordings. Conceptually, although most technology policies regulate manufacturers, they also indirectly regulate senders and receivers.

The question of where policies targeted to apparatus really are directed is further complicated by the fact that, in the formal view of communication, equipment manufacturers are exogenous to systems. However, television and radio broadcasting are systems that were developed to spur receiver sales. Sometimes the broadcasting-manufacturing connection was maintained, and sometimes it was broken. Therefore, it is conceptually ambiguous as to whether equipment manufacturers are endogenous or exogenous to the systems. This is not an issue for print media and film. The absence of explicit public policies that pertain to them means that no justifying rationales are required.

State policy targeted toward communicators primarily exists in television and radio where it can be implemented through the licensing and relicensing function of the FCC. Most licensees tend to be politically conservative, although whether this reflects the conservatism of commissioners, the political leanings of business people with access to the substantial capital that licensees require, or both, is not clear. Recently the government has applied a broader media policy indirectly by acknowledging public concerns about the growing number of large cross-media conglomerates. It has ordered enterprises with properties in other media to relinquish some of those properties or surrender their licenses when they acquire firms with broadcasting licenses.

The proposition that the targets of restrictive policies inversely reflect the power of system components seems to apply more clearly to self-regulation. The fact that communicators in all media have been able to preempt so many of the issues with which public policy might deal and to forestall government action by doing so indicates the extent of their power. So does their ability to gain fairly dependable compliance to their self-set standards. However, self-regulation should not be taken to mean that they have made themselves the chief targets of their policies, even though they are the objects of the codes their associations promulgate. The appearance is deceiving for several reasons.

Industry codes are rather weak and ambiguous and largely countenance the established practices of media firms. Because codes usually are adopted only after violations of social standards begin to accumulate and stimulate threats of action, the targeted violators are usually in a small minority. However, even in those cases, the newly prohibited activities usually are not what we have been defining as communication. The material usually is meant to entertain or influence and, moreover, creativity is a relatively minor concern for the targets of the codes—if it is a concern at all. The primary goal and measure of success is profit. In that sense, compliance to industry codes promulgated in response to threatened action does not bear on communication. It does not require a change in goal, only a change in the means of achieving it. Because there is no intent to mean or it is secondary to the intents to transmit and to influence, and because even the latter two are subsidiary to the profit motive, the appearance that self-regulation constrains communicators is misleading. Self-regulation is intended and designed to permit firms to continue pursuing their basic business interests by making some minor adjustments to forestall state interference.

If we consider the codes and actions that constitute self-regulation to be public policy, where is their impact primarily felt? I have suggested that communicators do not feel it because the codes countenance most of what they do and any changes they require are largely cosmetic. Protests by the media against proposed or actual changes in industry codes or government rules are primarily obligatory reflexes, occasioned largely by the need to maintain the pose of real communicators in order to pursue their activities. There is little in the codes that bears on apparatus, although the adoption of industry standards for equipment in most media might be taken to be policy. Equipment standards, although usually justified as benefiting consumers, also can be interpreted as standardization to cut costs, to allow competing firms to help one another meet emergencies, to minimize destructive competition, and to save on R&D costs. I would argue, therefore, that of the endogenous elements, the prime target of any policies implicit in self-regulation is the communicatee.

Despite restricting production so as not to offend public sensitivities, media industries tend to put the burden of implementing their policies on consumers by asserting that, because of variations in individual tastes and standards, people have to monitor their own behavior and that of those for whom they are responsible. Examples are common. Movie ratings are necessary because film makers reserve the right to make a range of films. They put the burden on the public to restrict viewing to its categories of choice. The same applies to television. Network censors remove material they think may offend, and "adult" materials are scheduled for late evening hours, but it is still left to parents to control what their children watch. Magazine publishers print what they want and tell parents and newsstand managers to control what is bought and read. In short, media self-regulation requires little self-restraint but much consumer responsibility. Even the burden of decisions not to produce is on consumers, for it keeps the material from those who might have wanted it. Taking public and industry policy together, appearances to the contrary notwithstanding, the burden of self-regulation falls largely on the communicatee.

I am not suggesting that self-regulation should be a draconian program that whips communicators into shape and does not address other sources of control. If anything, I would opt for minimal controls. However, even minimal policies imply some controls, and it is only fair to distribute them equitably. Government policies and industry efforts at self-regulation give the impression of careful surveillance of communicators, many restrictions on what they might do, and a choice between producing materials that conform to others' expectations or severe sanctions. I suggest that this is spurious—that the appearance of constraints on communicators is deceiving—and that, because the media are only incidentally involved in communication, the imposed constraints do not interfere with either communication or their main activity, earning a profit. Rather, the burden of any constraints required by whatever constitutes media policy falls largely on consumers, who are both limited in the choices the market provides and made responsible for monitoring their own consumption and that of others.

## THE RANGE OF MEDIA POLICIES

This discussion has addressed the targets of policies, but not their range of prescriptions and proscriptions or how they are conveyed to their targets. The source and targets of policy are particularly relevant in this regard. The source of a policy shapes how it can be conveyed and enforced, and targets are only capable of certain activities and not others. In addition to sources and targets, a third relevant aspect of policies is whether they are positive—in the sense of calling for new goals or new means to achieve existing goals—or negative—in the sense of proscribing actions. A policy that promotes new means or goals is positive; it enables people and, thus, can build their sense of accomplishment. Proscriptions are negative in that they restrict or disbar activity and are likely to be experienced as repressive and constraining rather than expansive. I first consider government-based and then industry-based policies.

The source and implementation of public policy is located with government—the manifestation of the state. The unit of government that enacts policy is usually a legislature, or, less often, an executive, administrative agency, or court. The parallel processes of adoption are legislation, executive order, issuance and enforcement of rules, and judicial review. Policies and their requirements are disseminated by an appropriate administrative unit, or the media themselves if the information must be widely distributed. A staff of inspectors usually monitors compliance. Policies that call for licensing or for granting privileges may require expert technical staffs to assess whether requirements are met. Enforcement rests on the threatened or actual use of the police power of the state.

With few if any exceptions, public policies for mass communication are negative. Because our norms and political culture discourage public goals for the media, policies usually are justified as necessary responses to specific problems that require intervention and control (e.g., limiting broadcasting station transmission, prohibiting seditious material). They almost always are proscriptive and experienced as repressive and negative by their targets. There can, however, be positive policies, for example, countries have decided that media should be educational or further national consensus or development (Siebert, Peterson, and Schramm, 1956; Howell, 1986; Hachten, 1987: 14-34; Meyer, 1988; Stevenson, 1988; Browne, 1989; McNulty, 1989; McPhail and McPhail, 1990: 19-53). In such cases governments may provide facilities, training, or both. There have been two major positive policies in the United States—provision of public broadcasting, and low postal rates for publications. Having both been in place for many years, they may no longer be perceived as positive policies.

The statute that created public television was enacted to assure access for educational programs, to provide an outlet for viewpoints and materials that do not appeal to a broad public, and for other public purposes. Channels were reserved for state governments or educational institutions, and programming consisted largely of informational materials or regular credit and noncredit courses for people who could not attend state institutions. Over the years the stations have increased news and cultural programming (e.g., classical music, panel discussions of public issues, operas and dramas) and decreased course offerings. The change can be attributed primarily to the inhibiting impact of the normative opposition to state operated media. The legislation authorizing public broadcasting had to avoid antagonizing private broadcasters, many of whom felt that it might divert potential audiences and valuable channels. Consequently, it only reserves channels for nonprofit groups and does not provide startup or operating funds for stations, or, except for radio news, for programming. The shift in programming is a consequence. The stations soon found it necessary to carry programs that could draw larger audiences so that they might seek support from individuals, foundations, and corporations. Thus, public broadcasting has evolved from an educational system to a service for special interest audiences. Most of the public is ignorant of or indifferent, if not hostile, to it, and commercial broadcasters often look on it as an unfairly privileged competitor. No effective effort at positive action ever really got off the ground.

Low postal rates for publications were instituted on the grounds that they would expedite the distribution of information in a country with a political system based on informed citizen participation. At best, that purpose is only served in part. Although all publishing is not informational, almost every publication profits from inexpensive distribution. Indeed, since the privilege has been in place, political participation and the proportion of the public that is well informed and interested has declined. What began as a positive effort at improving citizen involvement has become a business right of which few people are aware. In the course of time, its rationale has been lost. It is only publicized when publishers object to rate increases or applicants are denied the privilege. This places it in a negative rather than the positive light that was intended.

In the United States, and perhaps only in the United States, government communication policies not only are at a minimum but, except for public television and low postal rates, seem largely to be restrictive. Policies that seem negative because they constrain an action (e.g., awarding licenses, allocating frequencies, setting standards for equipment), however, may be positive for operators (e.g., by reducing unfair competition they give the stability needed to sell air time to advertisers) and manufacturers (e.g., by making their products more attractive to customers and controlling foreign competition). Although there also may be, as already noted, informal policies intended to reward political supporters or to discourage dissemination of certain materials, they are unstated and lack legitimacy. The large number of possible positive and negative policies pursued in other countries are left to private enterprise to be implemented, if at all, under the guise of self-regulation.

Because it is in the form of codes and standards of practice to be monitored and enforced by industry functionaries, self-regulation —indeed, the very term—appears to restrict the activities of communicators. However, basically the codes and conformity to them protect the opportunity to profit. Moreover, because that, and not communication or aesthetic expression, is the primary goal for most mass communicators, they do not experience the codes as restraints on communication or creativity. Operators might profit more in the short run without codes. However, because self-regulation mitigates the threat of loss of public support and consequent government action and the media assert that the public is the best judge of what is proper, the pursuit of profit is best served in the long run by codes that respond to public sensitivities.

The absence of sanctions to buttress enforcement is another indication of how little codes constrain communicators. Codes are sustained primarily by consensus. When the film producers found it more profitable to ignore the code, the Hays Office could not enforce its standards. When several newspapers and television stations recently named a rape victim whose case was still in jurisdiction, the transgression only evoked criticism. The only way to penalize sensational tabloids for serious offenses and breaches of honesty is to sue for libel, a course of action that usually only the wealthy can afford to pursue. Print media in the United States have not even been willing to participate in the press councils that minimally enforce standards in other countries.

In effect, self-regulation constrains and makes responsible those members of the public who are the potential audiences of the various media. The constraints result from the willingness of the media to restrict production whenever pressures seem very threatening. Consequently, usually only small minorities or nonvocal groups are affected. Given the variety of production and changes in the even wider variety of public tastes and interests, however, there are always complaints about the media. Until the dissatisfaction becomes strong enough to cause withdrawal or a change, however, the media resort to a free market response—all people need to do is select what they want and like and ignore what they do not. It is a response that obligates the receiver. This has been especially clear when parents have complained about children's media or adult material to which they do not want their children exposed. When the pressure is not too intense, the industry position is to assign parents responsibility for monitoring and training their children. Self-imposed limits on production have not impeded the media's main interests. Rather, they have made receivers responsible for restricting their behavior and that of those for whom they are concerned.

## *PROSPECTS FOR POLICY*

If the vision of mass communication as the medium for maintaining a well-informed citizenry in a democratic polity is ever to be realized, public media policy will be needed. The industry-structured market, though accepted by the public, has not produced media that serve this function. However, devotees of public solutions to the problem cannot be overly optimistic. There is scant, if any, evidence that, short of a totalitarian approach, positive media policies can achieve that goal.[6] After several decades of broadcasting during which the BBC was built into a world-renowned system, the British were unable to maintain its monopoly. Strong market forces, including entrepreneurs wanting to profit from broadcasting and large sections of the public wanting more programming at lower cultural levels, eventually forced the system to open to private competition. In Canada, the highly subsidized CBC has never succeeded in building the national identity and support that is its mission because it never has had public support for the monopoly on programming that would be necessary (Collins, 1990). Other examples abound.

In addition to the scant evidence that positive media policies can produce the results intended even with the most desirable of goals, the point has been made that in the United States entrenched norms impede positive polices. To override those norms would require a strong national consensus or a recognized dire threat, unusual conditions for representative democracy in a diverse society. Thus, whatever policy innovations may be desired must be crafted carefully and, probably, promoted in other terms. Although they might not have to be as fully disguised as was the policy to promote the home building and mortgage banking industries by providing personal income tax deductions for mortgage interest rather than by direct subsidies or tax remissions for the industries, media policy could not achieve collective national goals by explicitly requiring changes in media. That would only mobilize strong ideological opposition. How to make and implement policy is a matter for political expertise. Here I only consider some potential policies that have a reasonable prospect of success in the kind of society that the United States is.

One recurrent theme with policy implications bears repeating —the absence of training in media consumption. The fact that consumers do not know how media technology and production techniques misrepresent reality and, thus, can mislead them, is a frequent theme in the study of effects. More than 40 years have passed since the Langs' pioneering paper on the unique perspective of television and its capacity to misrepresent reality and, thus, to divert the course of future events. Yet, nothing has been done to equip people to compensate for these qualities of the medium. Similarly, although it is more than 20 years since young children's inability to distinguish television cartoons and advertising from reality was first noted, the response is to demand changes in the material rather than to train children to deal with the media. This is a task that must be undertaken early, for as Giroux and MacLaren (1992: xviii, xxiii) have pointed out, children's very identities and understanding of the culture are being shaped by the media as soon as they become exposed to them, so their critical facilities are already somewhat impaired by the time they begin attending school. Children also could be prepared to handle the difference between regular language and media language (Bell, 1991). It seems reasonable, then, to suggest a policy of media consumption training to help make people more sophisticated consumers.

This suggestion antedates Kubey and Csikszentmihalyi's proposal (1990: 214- 216) to train school children in how to view television and films. Television and film may be current concerns, but, had Kubey and Csikszentmihalyi done their research earlier, they would have found themselves dealing with analogous problems with the other media. Children would profit by training in the consumption of all media. Such a policy, if properly justified, ought to have a reasonable chance of success, although it would first require selective research on how children learn to deal with technologically mediated communication. Haslett and Alexander's (1988) review of how children acquire both interpersonal and mediated communication skills identified similarities, differences, and relationships between the two processes, but it also identified several lacunae in our understanding of them that need to be resolved before fully effective training programs can be put in place. Their review indicates that training should be started well before the age of ten. Masterman (1987 [1980]), evaluating his disastrous experience trying to teach film studies to high school students, concluded that students' sense of familiarity with the media is so well established by the time they reach secondary school that they feel very experienced and are turned off by the idea of being taught about something they already feel they know so well.[7]

Whether such a policy can be implemented successfully given the necessary knowledge is less of a question than whether there is the will to implement it. It would not be the sort of undertaking for which there is no previous experience. Three decades ago, Omar K. Moore demonstrated that three-year-olds could be taught successfully to use typewriters. Schools already train youngsters in technology use. Driver education is well established and justified on grounds of safety. Computer training is increasingly available, being justified as both a study aid and a business necessity. Moreover, television, VCRs, film, and printed material long have been used for instruction. In this light, the failure to take the necessary steps for establishing training in media use is surprising. In part, it may reflect the lesser emphasis on consumption than on production in communication skill training. I have noted how we train people to write and speak but not to listen or view, and how little training is offered to develop reading skills. We hardly touch on differences in the effects of various types of reading materials. We do not provide the skills needed to distinguish accurate and reliable sources from their opposites. A skeptic might infer that communicators realize their advantage and block efforts to train in consumption skills. In any case, there are no obvious reasons other than tradition for not providing such training.

The exogenous factors that intrude on communication systems also merit some innovative policy initiatives. Physical intrusions are not a problem because the media themselves work to eliminate interference with transmission. Rather, the concern is with groups and persons that try to influence how media systems perform, even though they themselves are neither producers nor consumers. They are the interested groups and individuals that apply pressure to senders and receivers with boycotts, blacklists, and other such forceful tactics, or with moral and social sanctions. They work at forcing senders to alter material or face economic pressure, or receivers to reject material or be ostracized or shamed. The obvious longer term effect of their interference is to head off behavior or attitudes that might have been stimulated by the aborted material. The goal of policy would be to end such disruptive intrusions into media systems.

There would be several obvious difficulties in implementing such a policy. For one, because the media are so widely accessible, the line between receiver and exogenous groups is always vague. If the media claim they are involved in communication, however, then any group or person not intentionally targeted or active in creating material may be considered exogenous. A more basic difficulty arises from the democratic principle that people have the right to have opinions and act on matters in which they are not involved because, ultimately, those matters may affect them. People vote for judges even though they never have been or will be in court. Certainly the role of men in the anti-abortion movement would be difficult to understand were it not for such a principle. Indeed, the concept of the press as a watchdog is premised on an external element entering situations in which it is not directly involved. Certainly, press surveillance is proper and respected—if it can be managed effectively, a possibility that Rachlin's earlier quoted statement (174) calls into question.

An antidote to the problem of intrusions by exogenous elements in a democratic society is to create countervailing power. Those involved always feel strongly about their positions. In contrast, their targets, be they sender or receiver, often lack the resources to make a contrary case. Receivers are especially disadvantaged in mass communication because they lack organization. If this is at the heart of the problem, the most effective remedy would seem to be an ombudsman system. In such a system, the only sanction that could be invoked by exogenous groups would be to appeal to an impartial refereeing system operating in accord with long-established, uniform standards and rules. In such a system even unorganized individual receivers could defend their tastes against exogenous elements.

Practitioners, critics, and teachers of the various media often evaluate the current situation and propose policy remedies. Proposals to disperse ownership have been frequent since the 1930s. They assume that more producers will diversify the supply and that this will obviate the threat of undue power in a monopoly. Such policies do not seem promising, for media developments have run counter to their assumptions. There has been antitrust legislation to maintain consumer equity in the market for almost 100 years, but it has failed to counter deeper economic forces. Weak legislation by legislators who must compromise to legislate and politically influenced court decisions to resolve the resulting ambiguities undercut it.

The tactics of monopolistic corporations may have changed in response to antitrust legislation, but the trend toward monopoly has hardly slowed. There are fewer and fewer, larger and larger corporations in every industry as a result of consolidations, and there is little to stop the trend. This applies to the media as well. When criticism of the monopolization of daytime network radio by soap operas mounted, some were replaced with audience participation contests. Now we have both, both night and day. There are fewer large newspaper chains but more common corporate ownership and fewer newspapers. Large broadcasting networks have merged into even stronger conglomerates and are permitted to own more stations. Large conglomerates have become multimedia owners. New technology encourages new startup companies at first, but with failures and mergers, the numbers decline. Given the absence of public concern and visible negative effects, it is difficult to oppose the constant consolidations.

In light of this, it would be foolhardy to propose or expect a dramatic shift to more restrictive media policies in a democratic society. The two proposals offered here empower participants without taking rights and privileges from others. Although senders may think themselves hurt by equalizing the power of receivers, they would not be deprived of any rights. Media producers could still do as they like. Exogenous groups could still register their dissatisfactions. They simply would not be dealing with others who are unequipped to respond. Removing a disadvantage does not take away another's resources.

It may be that in the long run less expensive new technologies will enable more producers to serve markets for smaller audiences profitably. This could obviate the appeal of the ombudsman-type suggestion by providing the countervailing influences to balance intrusive exogenous elements. It would not, however, redress the imbalance between senders and receivers endemic to a mediated communication system in which only senders can initiate action and maintain the system. Even the ability to respond that two-way technology could provide will not redress this situation because the established hegemonic processes have already shaped the tastes, expectations, and attitudes of receivers, and, thus, have also shaped the likely responses of consumers. Skill training in reception may be the most desirable and potentially effective antidote. At least it has the merit of requiring activities that schoolchildren already enjoy.

## NOTES

1. Horwitz (1989) summarized a widely held view in stating that government ". . . regulation of broadcasting came about as a way to alleviate technical chaos and market instability" (154).
2. Useful reviews of the FCC's structure and mode of operation, as well as the ways in which its decisions and rules impact on the broadcasting industry can be found in Crotts and Mead (1979) and Horwitz (1989).
3. Gitlin (1987 [1982]: 261) noted that each new technological innovation in the media is ". . . imprinted by the structures and strategies of the political-economic system at the moment." It is not clear whether he meant that they are developed for that purpose or that elites quickly take them over to promote their interests. Because the comment appears in a discussion of why hegemony operates only in a situation of absolute power (240-241), he probably meant the latter.
4. Serfaty's (1990) discussion of the media and foreign policy and Schlesinger's (1991: 17-28) analysis of the media and terrorism are instructive cases of how media coverage creates problems that governments of states that adhere to Western ideas of press freedom are unable to handle with direct restrictions Both authors suggested that the media response, based on concern that government will intervene despite the general norms, is self-regulation. Self-regulation in the arena of public affairs weakens trust in the media because, regardless of whether the choice is to release or not release an item, the media can be accused of improperly influencing the course of events. For example, in the 1992 U.S. presidential election, release of a story of a grand jury indictment that might involve the President four days before the election was claimed by his supporters to have been politically motivated and a contributing factor in his loss. In contrast, a story that ten women were charging an incumbent senator running for reelection with sexual harassment was available before the election but not released until two weeks later. The newspaper with the story said that it was delayed because they had not been able to confirm the charges. The incumbent, who won by a small margin, well might have lost had the story appeared earlier.
5. Kerner (1979) showed that the values of the individual's rights to privacy and to freedom of speech have come into conflict more and more as technological innovations in information storage and processing have made it possible to amass and integrate personal information to a degree never before possible and then to disseminate such material in the public media. The issue dramatizes how major normative values with no apparent inconsistencies can be in basic conflict.
6. Mosco (1988) has offered a potentially optimistic proposal for more effective media policies that depends on state actions which take account of the politics of the media and media regulation.
7. Schwoch, Reilly, and White (1992) also support training on the basis of their experience with what seem to have been older students. The con-

text of the experiment was a university. At that level, the sorts of people Masterman described as having been turned off would have left the student population, and more intellectually inquisitive individuals would have predominated.

# 8

# Development of the State and Public Communication

In the model of mass communication, government is treated as one of the elements outside the system that participates in the struggle to influence the system and its operations. The specification reflects an American bias noted in discussing policy. In most other countries, governments are partly or wholly identified with the communicator role for some or all their media. Mowlana (1990: 94), discussing the media in every country, stated that ". . . central to the . . . theory of the mass media and culture is the role of the state, with its own special and unique image of itself and the role it perceives it should play." The ways in which governments are involved in their media vary with their country's experience in becoming a sovereign state and with the medium. Different types of states with different histories hold different concepts of the role of their media and how they should operate. Those concepts apply differently to the various media. Moreover, as new technology destabilizes traditional media and involves them in processes that go well beyond the provision of entertainment and information, the public communication process intrudes even more on critical state interests. Because these new technologies also enable instant worldwide transmission and reception of any material that can be expressed in digital form, other countries also are becoming important players in the field of forces that impinge on and shape each national communication system.

The development of the United States as a sovereign state and its relation to the development of its domestic communication systems is quite different from the experiences of most countries. Consequently, most Americans are not familiar with the issues that recent and impending developments raise for other countries. This and the next chapter are devoted to these matters. In this chapter I consider the course of development of the state and its relation to the interests of states in communication generally, their problems with contemporary media and impending innovations, and their different philosophies with respect to the state's role in communication. In Chapter 9 I examine several issues that have arisen because the diverse developmental backgrounds of states shape their present concerns with the media. Their different positions on these matters generate major international debates and disagreements that receive little public attention but will have significant implications for this country.

## *WHY LOOK ELSEWHERE?*

The emphasis thus far on material and issues that refer almost exclusively to the United States may obscure the fact that contemporary media are a worldwide phenomenon. Each country has a system that is unique in at least some, and often in many, respects—density, mix, pattern of availability of media material, social roles of the media, control patterns, policies. Moreover, because American media control patterns and policies have been atypical, one cannot fully appreciate mass media issues by considering only this country (cf. Morgan, 1989: 135). Events since World War II also provide compelling reasons for looking at other countries. They dramatize the degree to which the United States exists in a global economic system in which each nation has a niche and from which none can isolate itself. A review of the media policies and concerns of other countries provides perspective on how events and actions in any country can have significant consequences beyond its borders.

Because American media have dominated their sector of the global economy, the measures foreign governments take with respect to their own media often have a substantial impact on our media industries. Several matters are pertinent to understanding how and why this happens and the likely consequences.

## Development of the State

1. World economic developments have eroded American economic dominance by creating a negative balance of trade. This has led to both a substantial flow of capital to other countries and the sale of domestic assets to foreign interests. One of the few surpluses has been produced by American film and television exports. The policies and actions of foreign governments and entrepreneurs, as well as changes in foreign consumers' tastes, directly affect that trade.
2. Many foreign government officials and elites believe that media imports from the United States undermine their efforts to build national identity and reenforce societal integration. This can lead to the erection of trade barriers against American media.
3. Deregulation, which has been at the heart of recent American economic policy, also is being practiced in other countries and has weakened state media monopolies. This has encouraged their domestic producers to expand production and has effected the demand for imports.
4. American production of consumer audiovisual equipment has largely ended. Foreign factories and firms dominate manufacturing. To assure that material is available for their new products (e.g., high-definition television, VCRs, CD and digital tape players), they have acquired control of many of the largest U.S. media firms.
5. The trend toward regional free trade areas creates larger markets in which it is economically feasible for foreign entrepreneurs to produce media material for their own domestic consumption. This exacerbates the decline in foreign demand for American products.
6. Development programs of poorer countries are thwarted by their inferior position in a global economy in which communication and communication-related service industries are becoming central. They have responded by pooling their political strength and, with UNESCO as a forum, have promulgated a New World Information Order (NWIO) that they consider necessary in a broader program to end Western economic domination. Western media and governments interpret these tactics as an attack on freedom of the press.
7. New digital and satellite technology makes national boundaries increasingly permeable and, by doing so, increases states' concerns that their national sovereignty is at risk.

In almost every country but the United States, media policy is being shaped to take account of the anticipated consequences of these developments.[1]

An examination of foreign media situations also can help in dealing with what Americans consider domestic problems, for their problems often parallel ours (cf. Dutton and Blumler, 1989).[2] They, too, face and deal with such issues as the place and effects of pornography in popular media (cf. Einsiedel, 1988), the impact of television and film on children, the effect of free speech on the ability to govern (cf. Serfaty, 1990; Schlesinger, 1991: 17-28), the role of public broadcasting and the place of the government in that enterprise, the necessity of government secrecy, and the protection of domestic media software production. Only the last is not an American problem—as yet[3]—and it could be an unrecognized one if the increased reliance on foreign markets for profit has made it necessary to homogenize our products so that they will be accepted widely in foreign markets (J. D. Phillips, 1982: 325). There are, in addition, two other, perhaps even more fundamental, reasons for considering mass media in other countries.

1. Comparison can provide perspective on the relativity of our perceptions and understandings. The media are intrinsic to all modern societies and the structure and operation of each country's system is shaped by the features of that society. People in each country are habituated to their system and take its version of social reality for granted. They are handicapped in appreciating the extent to which this affects their understanding if they examine only their own case. The tendency is to consider it "natural" and "normal," the *only* way that things might be. Throughout this discussion I have tried to counteract this tendency by focusing on principles of communication as a process and system that apply universally and by deemphasizing specific examples. I try to avoid giving the impression that the media are the most important factor in any explanation by emphasizing the reciprocal relations among them, other institutions, and personal behavior. However, our limited perspective can be expanded even more by looking at other countries as well.[4]
2. Looking elsewhere provides perspective on domestic policies and actions. The following two cases provide examples of these contingencies:
   a. The American negotiating position on free trade with Canada had to be revised to accommodate Canada's insistence on excluding media products in line with their long-established policy of protecting domestic cultural indus-

tries. That policy has been in place and implemented in various ways since Canadians became aware that their media were being deluged by American imports and that young Canadians knew much more about the United States than about their own country.

b. The United States delayed issuing import licenses for Japanese and European digital tape players that can copy analog tapes. The machines are on the market because other countries' industrial policies call for subsidizing the basic research and manufacturing techniques required by new products. American policies do not authorize a similar role for government and domestic producers lagged in producing a competitive machine. When they pressed for extra time to produce one, government officials felt that they had to acquiesce.

Both cases illustrate the need to look elsewhere to obtain a richer picture of the interacting effects of states' domestic and foreign policies and actions (cf. Barton, 1990; Koizumi, 1990; Crane, 1992). Examination of the policy process in other countries also can be instructive for understanding and improving the domestic process (cf. Dutton, 1992).

Finally, consideration of other media systems helps clarify the reasons for international concerns about (a) the control of many media software and hardware developers, producers, and distributors by transnational conglomerates (cf. Locksley, 1987: 197-198), and (b) the commercial and industrial impact of the new technologies that are revolutionizing information and communication and drastically altering traditional media. These issues make American priorities for media policy—their deleterious effects on values and behavior and their monopolistic character—seem misplaced and trivial. They suggest a failure to see the larger picture. Indeed, Americans' sense of the priorities may testify to the success of the big players on the world scene in distracting attention from these developments.[5] It also suggests that there are structural deficiencies in the apparatus for American government media policymaking that enable corporate interests to have a major impact without there ever being an opportunity for the public to become aware of what is happening (cf. Mosco, 1979). Regardless of whether these things are so, we can avoid a limited and narrow perspective on the media by understanding other countries' concerns and why they have them.

# Chapter Eight

## THE NATURE OF THE STATE

A recent radio newscast and newspaper article (Associated Press, 1992) reported that supporters of a dissident preacher in the Malagasy Republic had seized the state-run radio station for three hours. He used it to criticize the incumbent government and declare himself the country's new leader. The facility then was retaken by government troops and the restoration of peace and tranquility announced. Most Americans probably were not aware of the event. Had they been, it probably would have had comic opera overtones for them. Not only might they not have been sure that there is a Malagasy Republic or where it is, but that the first act in overturning a regime would be to occupy a radio station might seem a ludicrous and incongruous touch.

Madagascar (the Malagasy Republic) is real and, so far as I know, the abortive rebellion and occupation of the central broadcasting station did occur. Reports of such events in developing countries are not uncommon. Broadcasting facilities are primary targets in insurrections for good reason. In order to rule, a centralized regime must have the support and compliance of all its citizens and must be able to disseminate its requests and edicts and silence the opposition. That is why rebels so often target central communication agencies. Control of communication is critical for a new regime to demonstrate its authority. It is not by itself sufficient, however. Legitimacy and monopoly control of the means of violence are other necessary conditions for orderly and effective rule.

On the same day that the radio report of the Madagascar insurrection was broadcast, I also happened to read a review of a recent history of the portable radio (Wise, 1992: 1037) in which the author was quoted as having written that:

> Some historians believe that the Civil War would have ended in six months with much less bloodshed had the location of opposing troops been known in a timely manner. It should come as no surprise, then, that even before the turn of the century, wireless would be drafted by the military.... In the first years of the new century ... the [U.S.] military provided a sizable market for wireless apparatus ... and helped to sustain the efforts of the independent inventors.

Both the Madagascar insurrection and the historic support of the U.S. military for the development of wireless communication technology exemplify the deep functional relationship between states and communication. That connection reflects a concern with sustaining the state itself rather than an incumbent regime. The central radio station in Madagascar was there to be used for the prematurely optimistic announcement because it was needed by previous regimes for the same purpose. Ever since the island received its freedom from France, the Malagasy state as an independent entity has survived coups, rebellions, and more legitimate regime changes. The same applies to the United States. The state's interest, expressed through its military, in developing wireless communication continued regardless of incumbent administration, party in power, peace or war.

The concept of the state[6] refers to this transcendent aspect of a centralized, orderly, structured governing process. The state is the fictitious entity to which everything in the country is subject and whose interests are represented overtly by the current form of government and incumbent regime. Although it is tempting to equate state with government, that would be a mistake. Government forms can be as transitory as regimes. The French state, for example, has survived the Revolution and the several Republics. Every country that was ruled by a dictator in the 20th century also experienced major changes in government form in their transitions into and out of dictatorship. The United States has existed as a continuous state since its founding despite numerous major changes in its borders, the status of territories, the number and boundaries of its component states, the method of electing Presidents, and the responsibilities of government departments. In addition, court decisions and legislation have instigated change by clarifying, defining, and redefining the rights and prerogatives of the federal government. Despite these changes in form over time, the state is the continuing entity in whose interests federal prosecutors and attorneys in the United States and their counterparts elsewhere say that they are acting in courts of law. It is the locus of sovereignty over territory.

The importance of communication to the state is reflected in the pattern of state ownership of media and the elaborate communication policies to be found in most countries, the United States being a notable exception. State interest in communication reflects a concern for the process of rule as such as much as for maintaining the capacity of a particular governmental form or regime to operate effectively and successfully, for the role of communication in rule and governance antedates states. The modern Western state—the form that is now dominant regardless of what preceded it—and its precursors followed non-state forms of rule that relied heavily on communication. The classic empires of antiquity and prefeudal Europe—Assyrian, Persian, Macedonian, Egyptian, Roman, Frankish—were all relatively short-lived arrangements held together by military force. Seton-Watson (1977: 15) underlined the difference by entitling an early section of his treatise on nations and states "From empire to sovereign state." The effective use of force by the rulers of empires required means of communication superior to those of their enemies. They held position by virtue of possessing an unusual amount of some quality (e.g., charisma, strength, wealth, knowledge, divine status) accorded very high value at the time. Rarely did they accede to office by an orderly, legitimized process. They relied on their control of superior means of communication to apply their superordinate qualities once their authority had been established. At a more general level, referring to the entire period from the empires of antiquity to the present, Mann (1988: 9) specifies ". . . rapidity of communication of messages . . ." as one of four logistical techniques that states have employed effectively to penetrate social life and establish their autonomous power. The state, as an arrangement for orderly, continuous, consensually supported, centralized rule, is a comparatively recent invention. Although scholars are deeply divided over whether states have interests and can act independently of incumbent regimes or of interest groups that vie to influence government (cf. Miliband, 1969; Skocpol, 1985), my premise is that states as such have interests in communication media that may be separate and different from those of their regimes and of private interest groups.

The role of communication in the centralized rule of an area and its peoples, however, is only one contemporary media policy issue. In addition to a universal concern with defense, state debates on media policies also focus on many other seemingly unrelated matters. An understanding of these other concerns can be aided by a sense of how the modern Western state has developed (cf. Thomas and Meyer, 1984; Barkey and Parikh, 1991), for that experience defines the domestic concerns of most modern countries as much as a precarious position in a hostile world defines their external interests.[7]

## THE DEVELOPMENT OF THE MODERN STATE

Despite the facts that every bit of space other than Antarctica is now under the rule of a country and that every country is an independent state, the position of states is always precarious. This is not to be confused with the instability of regimes. Regimes are even more precarious, as the dramatic changes throughout Eastern Europe and the frequent rebellions in Asia, Africa, Latin America, and the Caribbean attest. In contrast to nonorderly regime changes, which often are routine "palace revolutions," the demise of the U.S.S.R., Czechoslovakia, and East Germany and the violent dismemberment of Yugoslavia testify to the strong centrifugal forces that subject modern states to great stress. Great Britain, France, Belgium, Spain, and Canada are other countries experiencing these pressures to a lesser degree.

The state form itself, however, is not under threat. Marx's scenario for the withering away of the state under socialism notwithstanding, the state form has thrived even in socialist countries. Moreover, the scope of the state expands, with the public arena continually intruding on the private. Dismembered states spawn smaller states that exercise sovereignty over part of their former land. Most separatist movements want to create new states with sovereignty over a portion of an existing country. Even if all should fail, there is no reason to expect the present array of states to remain constant, for the virility of the state form as such is not reflected in the viability of individual states. A glance at world maps or at the membership rosters of international organizations over time dramatizes the vulnerability of individual states.

If the state is an invented form that has become universal because it has been so successful for centralized rule and for the conduct of relations among countries, how is it that individual states can be so unstable? The answer would seem to lie in the forces that gave rise to early feudal states and to their transformation through *Ständestaat*, absolutist and constitutional phases to their current form.[8] It is a story of the extension of centralized rule over widely disparate areas lacking a common culture. Consequently, conflicting interests have been the rule rather than the exception. The maintenance of an uncoerced widely shared sense of identity and purpose has been an elusive state goal. Pursuit of the goal in specific historical circumstances has required major changes in ideas of what people are and ought to be as social persons and individuals. Those ideas, in turn, largely set the parameters for strategies thought likely to produce adequate, uncoerced integration within the state's territory.

Although circumstances at the time that the state form appeared—or, later, was imposed—differed in each area, they all had one thing in common. The state form developed to solve problems inherent in personal rule—generally some combination of ensuring the continuity of the realm and of its rule by the family after the ruler's death, legitimizing the ruler's control over any means of violence necessary for holding the realm together, and providing a mechanism for independent action in disputes with or violations of church edicts (cf. Coleman, 1974: 13-31, esp. 19-21). Rule usually was not established as a choice of a common cultural community but was forcibly imposed by some local leader. Although their original domain may have been a small, ethnically homogeneous area, successful rulers who initiated the transition to a state form usually expanded their realm quickly, thus creating an ethnic patchwork. On occasion, particularly when rule was established by marriage, the domain may not even have been the ruler's native area. To lighten the expense of royal courts and reliance on the force of arms to retain power and expand the realm, rulers forged hierarchical agreements with subordinate lords, granting them rights of local rule in return for support, loyalty, and a share of the spoils of rule. These contractual arrangements were the essence of feudalism; their rationale and bases for legitimacy are what constituted the early feudal state.

Even with the emergence of the state form as a fictional justification for rule over a domain, however, the domains of these rulers were not nations as we understand them today. They were not the equivalent of single societies or entire groups with common cultures. Even in those few instances when the original domain over which the ruler had sovereignty might have been the equivalent of a nation, given the continuous process of expansion and decay of the domain through conflict, marriage, agreements, and the like, they soon ceased to be. They were areas over which and people over whom rulers ruled.

Before the emergence of the constitutional state, rule was largely predatory and personal. Actions and decisions were particularistic. Many rulers ruled only for the spoils of rule, taking what they could for their own use from those too weak to protect themselves. The state form was simple and largely authoritarian, serving rulers' goals of coordinating the realm, defending it against outside enemies, and expanding it. Domestically, the state produced military forces, rooted out treachery, and secured resources that the ruler needed or desired. The preferred state was a minimal state because its primary function was to expedite the rule of the ruler, not replace it. It was structured to meet a sovereign's needs. Self-interested sovereigns were heads of state rather than rulers of the people and could escape responsibility for arbitrary and abhorrent actions by claiming that they were unavoidable or necessary in the state's behalf.

Because a malleable state of convenience requires transcendent legitimacy, it usually was claimed to have a mythic or supernatural, often religious, basis. Such rationales, though, were of questionable value because they could constrain rulers by obliging them to act in accord with some doctrine or ethical standards. Rulers, therefore, preferred to rule personally rather than through the state, invoking the state only when it was needed as an instrument of convenience—a fiction for defying the church, continuing family rule, or making agreements with other states while plotting against their rulers. It was not an instrument of fairness, order, or due process within the realm. Law was canon law, natural law, or common law, not state law. Order normally came in response to God's, nature's, or the community's dictates, not the state's authority. The state did little, if anything, for the populace; it served the ruler. Louis XIV's famous aphorism, "*L'état, c'est moi,*" captured this aspect of the state well into the 18th century.

During the feudal period towns were at the margins of a largely rural society with a land-based economy. They were the centers of what foreign trade there was, the processing of raw materials, and, with monasteries, were the locales of the literacy and higher learning of the period. The combination of these resources and the blindness of the traditional established land-oriented nobility to their value enabled towns to accumulate the wealth that helped many of them acquire autonomy and power. By learning how to improve and rationalize processing, town entrepreneurs were able to employ people to produce goods rather than to depend largely on their household labor. They prospered by increasing production, decreasing costs, and maintaining prices. The system was nascent capitalism. The workers became the core of a working class or proletariat, a group whose labor value was being alienated, at least partially, by being sold for a wage considerably less than the return for their product to those who paid them. Their employers, the eventual bourgeoisie, retained as profit the difference less the costs of raw materials and of selling and delivering the product. Marxist scholars consider the alienation of the surplus value of labor to be the basis for conflicting class relations, and capitalism, with its requirement of ever-expanding markets to consume increasing productivity, to be an inherently unstable system embodying severe contradictions.

The developing classes and class relations of town residents were different from that of the manor and those who lived on the land. They did not fit the hierarchical feudal form, particularly because wealth was produced by control of surplus labor value rather than by control of the produce of land and the people living on it. Feudalism was adapted to a largely land-based economy. It gave those toward the bottom protection, access to land, and the resources to produce from it, and those toward the top assured labor on the land and a share of what was produced. It was not an adequate system of rule for towns, for, in contrast to rural areas, they depended as much on trade outside the realm for income as they did on the ruler for protection. With the profits derived from trade and manufacturing, town residents could buy protection by hiring mercenaries rather than depend on the ruler. Rulers had little to offer these subjects.

Feudal rule was ill-fitted for these emerging, complex social relationships. They required rulers to acquire staffs of technical experts and put more men under arms. The minimal feudal state was insufficient. As personnel expanded, the state as a bureaucratic structure began to develop. Obviously, developments were not uniform. Nonetheless, as wealth came to be based more on commerce than on extraction and a capital-based economy began to dominate a resource-based one, the ties binding subjects and rulers changed. The costs of royal courts and the state rose precipitously with the increasing complexity of governance; courts, state functionaries, and armed forces all required more money. Rulers' dependence on economic support from town dwellers increased as their control over them decreased.

Because the feudal system did not easily accommodate the new town-country and bourgeoisie-worker relationships, and because towns and their residents were achieving more autonomy than rulers wanted to permit,[9] the state gradually evolved into a form that has been called the *Ständestaat* (Poggi, 1978: 36-69). It was a dual system of rule that, without disturbing existing feudal arrangements, allowed townspeople and others outside the feudal hierarchy to organize in estate-like corporate groups and share some aspects of rule with the sovereign. *The Ständestaat* was significant for innovating a state-building process that was driven by multiple societal interests rather than only those of a sovereign. Like feudalism, however, it did not last, eventually giving way to absolutism for reasons related to commercial expansion (Poggi, 1978: 60-67). And absolutism, in turn, being incompatible with rapidly growing entrepreneurial capitalism, gave way to constitutional forms of the early modern state.

The growth of towns and the bourgeoisie not only destabilized feudalism but also expanded membership in society, a process that has reverberated in various ways through the centuries. During the long period when the modern state form was emerging, nothing approximating modern care, concern, and respect for people as human beings existed. Most people in the countryside were bound to the land through the manorial system. They owned neither the land on which they labored nor the buildings in which they lived. Their status in the manor was that of real property. Society included the nobility, church officials, and categories of people whose rare and critical skills and talents merited special status.[10] Town residents, because they did not earn their livelihood by labor on the land, had the advantage of being outside the feudal pattern of relations. This provided the opportunity to acquire the knowledge and material resources for the entrepreneurial activities that eventually enabled them to be accepted in society.

Society did not expand in a series of magnanimous gestures. The nobility, faced with sharply escalating costs of rule, needed access to the growing wealth of the bourgeoisie but could not simply confiscate it. The bourgeoisie knew how to use their wealth and foreign trading partners to protect themselves. Moreover, rulers could not eradicate them without disrupting the vital services that towns provided. However, the nobility could acquire income by taxing the bourgeoisie. Improved status was the price that rulers paid for exercising the privilege of taxing the bourgeoisie to pay for their extravagances of rule. Because a group with improved status and growing wealth always was perceived as a threat to the regime, rulers linked improved status to new reciprocal arrangements.

As with traditional feudal relations with subsidiary nobles, the new rights of the town bourgeoisie came at the cost of new obligations to the ruler. These new relationships, because they were outside the established manorial system based on labor on the land and the provision of manpower, were central to the destabilization of feudalism and the emergence of the *Ständestaat*. In addition to the importance of this new system of rule in its own right, the process of change itself impressed more sagacious rulers with the considerable potential that the tactic of altering established status relations could have for solidifying the position of a regime. It demonstrated that managed social change could be an effective way to meet exigencies. Once this was understood and adopted as a normal tactic of rule, over time a class system began to evolve that granted recognition and rights even to some members of even lower classes.

An intrinsic feature of capitalism also contributed to some slight long term improvement in working class conditions. Ongoing capital accumulation—the core of a capitalist economic system—by selling goods produced by other people's labor at prices higher than cost and the merchants' own personal needs required growing markets. Increased consumption by the workers who produced the goods was one avenue to growth, but tapping it without wage increases required cutting production costs so that prices could be lowered. Factory systems for volume production provided a way to achieve this, but also required that at least some workers understand the logic behind the rationalization of production and know how to operate and repair the machinery employed. Consequently, some workers had to be trained to be able to read, keep records, and understand plans. By the end of the 17th century, some members of the working class were receiving the basic education that provided these requisite work-related skills.

The hierarchical system of rule of feudalism, the horizontal system of the *Ständestaat*, and absolutism all required state control of effective systems of communication. It was not unusual for realms built by conquest and marriage to include noncontiguous areas inhabited by very different cultural groups divided by language and, even before the Reformation, often by religion.[11] Medieval history is, in part, a history of dynastic wars among families seeking to extend their territorial control, regardless of whether they had any historic ties to the areas coveted. Hapsburg rule at times extended from Spain to Italy through central Europe to much of what is now Germany. England had a Norman king and, centuries later, imported a German royal family. For a time, the Catholic church, through the Vatican, ruled large areas in central Europe. Such conditions made reliable communication a sine qua non for monitoring events and disseminating orders to subordinates throughout the realm. The complex relations in which states were engaged required detailed, reliable record keeping.

When the so-called Dark Ages were ending and the state was an emerging adjunct of rule, literacy was rare. Priests and scribes had a central social role, their ability to read and write being essential for recording edicts and messages and producing copies of important works.[12] The general illiteracy, however, was more of a boon than a problem, for it enabled rulers to keep their subjects in ignorance and control what they might know. Media historians credit the invention of movable type and the printing press with breaking this monopolistic control of communication and, eventually, opening the political, religious, and other processes. Zaret (1980: 85; 1985: 19-40, 53-60; 1992) has reported that, as early as the late 16th century, the nascent popular religious press in England played an important role in forming the religious concepts of Puritan laymen and fomenting dissent from the preaching of their clergy. This was a radical shift in the relations of religious functionaries to laymen. To satisfy the needs of developing industries for skilled, literate workers, other people from the lower social strata also were trained to read. This equipped them with the ability to access directly the growing variety of material that printers were making available. Such changes altered the character of rule and the state forever; they sowed the seeds of popular democracy.

In concert with the end of the narrow monopoly on the ability to read, write, and reproduce texts, there were people who understood that freedom of the press would allow a young print medium to play a key role in advancing personal liberty. By the late 17th century, John Milton and others were espousing arguments for press freedom that culminated in the writings of Tom Paine and the enshrinement of press freedom in the First Amendment of the American Constitution. Keane (1991: 1-50) attributes the connection among printing, a free press, and democracy to the role of press freedom in providing diverse opinions on important issues. The availability of alternative views on issues, in turn, provides a basis for forming public opinion. So long as there is a free press to stimulate its formation, he argues, the existence of public opinion changes the fundamental character of rule by making long term totalitarianism impossible. (See Neuman, Just, and Crigler [1992] for a model of the current relationship between the media and public opinion.)

In England and France, the countries on which this account primarily rests, the number of people whose views on public affairs constituted public opinion initially was quite small. The audiences for printed materials grew, however, with the wider provision of the basic education required by expanding modern industries and militaries. Although a growing informed and opinionated citizenry drawn from groups that often were in conflict with one another and with the regime was risky for an absolutist state, capitalism's growth requirements left no other course. The constant pressures of their economies on absolutist regimes necessitated societal expansion, even at the risk of destabilizing the political order. Powerful entrepreneurs lobbied for more services to subsidize domestic labor and production and, to secure foreign markets and sources of supply, promoted aggressions that often led to expensive military adventures. Initiatives on this scale required heavy borrowing and taxation as well as extensive conscription.

These fiscal and manpower needs forced rulers to raise their demands on subjects who increasingly were less inclined to accept them passively. Owing to the impact of printing, more people were literate, informed, had reasoning skills, and expected state responsiveness to their concerns and a voice in governance. To legitimate the increasing burdens of taxation and conscription and not alienate the diverse classes and ethnic groups being brought into the orbit of the state, and to respond to a growing restiveness that had been apparent long before the American and French Revolutions, rights to citizenship and services to the population gradually and grudgingly were being extended. The Revolutions only increased the urgency to do so. Both the portion of the population with which state functionaries had to communicate and the portion whose communication practices might concern the state have continued to expand and in most countries include almost everyone.

By the mid-19th century, give or take some years depending on the country, most groups had been recognized, and societal inclusion no longer could serve to repay the spiralling burdens that states were imposing. Consequently, modern states have had to create and promise new rewards for acquiescence and support. In the 19th and 20th centuries, these have run the gamut from satisfying collective nationalist goals (e.g., territorial expansion, subjugating enemies) to extending individual services and welfare (e.g., social security, health care, unemployment insurance) to providing highly valued intangibles (e.g., a clean environment, a happier life). This is not a reliable way to generate support, however. There is no room for failure when promises cannot be fulfilled either because they are beyond the regime's power to determine (e.g., vanquishing enemies) or because the state cannot afford them. Hence, states continually need ways to motivate people to comply voluntarily as a proper duty that does not require a return.

When states promote their economies by pursuing aggressive external and exploitative internal projects, cultural and social diversity and, consequently, internal conflict and instability usually increase. If this happens, there is a concomitant increasing need to integrate the population and assure its loyalty by cultivating a positive national identity that everyone shares.[13] Schlesinger (1991: 139-151) has questioned whether there is evidence that links identity generated through media-delivered cultural products and the integrative condition of a country, but he does believe that in many countries state policy is based on an assumption that there is a link. The state's disparate interests in supporting military activities, monitoring developments both inside and outside the realm, and creating an informed citizenry with a common sense of identity, all contribute to a long-term need to develop and maintain an efficient communication system. To the degree that these are contradictory imperatives, states have had to fashion delicately balanced communication policies. Their experiences over the last 100 or so years reflect the variety and inconsistencies that such a dynamic can create.

## NATION, STATE, AND COUNTRY

Given their aforementioned lack of common cultures and national identities, the early European states that developed more or less along these lines were not nations in any usual sense (cf. Seton-Watson, 1977: 1-13). They were political contrivances for ruling the population of an area (in the case of the church, a nonterritorial group). The people were subjects of the ruler, not citizens. Realms were not countries as we know them today—continuous areas ruled by single central governments with inhabitants holding citizenship. Even that simple concept is contaminated by our practice of using it interchangeably with nation, despite the fact that few, if any, contemporary countries are nations. Indeed, the United Nations is an association of countries, not nations, and has as a major mission the resolution and accommodation of the difference. Its predecessor, the League of Nations, was similarly constituted and charged. Both were created after world wars were fought to achieve nationalistic goals (i.e., national sovereignty) or to realign borders with ethnically homogeneous areas (e.g., Italy fought Austria-Hungary in World War I in part to acquire control of the Italian part of the Tyrol, Germany used this rationale to justify its annexation of Austria and Sudeten Czechoslovakia prior to World War II).

If most countries are not nations but strive to become nations, what is a nation? There is no universally accepted definition for this relatively modern concept.[14] Most uses imply that a nation is an ethnic group (i.e., a social group with its own distinct culture) that has taken on a political identity in the sense that it strives for self-governance and self-determination. Deutsch (1966: 86-106) indicated that communication is central to this process when he suggested that a people become a nationality by sharing information and that ". . . nationalities turn into nations when they acquire power to back up their aspirations" (105). If we accept the Gypsies' claim to being a nation, then the concept need not be tied to territory, but it almost always is (cf. Smith, 1983: 122-135). If nationhood becomes an ideology, as it did for the Nazis and similar groups in Europe, it may assert a primordial tie between the group and a territory that is, a homeland. However, a key factor driving the communication policies of many countries is that nation and country rarely are synonymous in geopolitical reality, even though they are in rhetoric.

There are two major reasons for the disjuncture. One is that countries are political contrivances whose borders are defined in diplomatic negotiations that, as part of an imperialistic process, are conducted in hostile circumstances for purposes of avoiding or ending warfare. In almost every case, because of the great strength of some of the negotiators and the considerable weakness of others, the negotiations have produced agreements to divide and/or merge ethnic groups with either disparate interests and/or long and deep antagonisms. The other is migration. For a wide variety of reasons and with greater or lesser ease, people often have moved voluntarily or forcibly from traditional areas to new areas that already are occupied by an indigenous population. When groups become mixed they may or may not assimilate and may or may not accept one another as equals. Recent events in many apparently stable countries and the study of social inequality within countries both reveal that assimilation and acceptance often are only apparent, and that ethnic identities and animosities may run deep and resist resolution. For these reasons, although some nations may be reasonably well integrated and cohesive, many countries are not.

The boundaries of most countries that existed prior to World War I or that were created in its immediate aftermath, therefore, contain several ethnic—and, hence, potentially national—groups, one of which dominates regardless of whether it is a numerical majority. The location of any ethnic group within a country is simply a matter of its degree of segregation, the pattern of segregation, and the location of segregated areas vis-à-vis the borders. With respect to country of rule, members of a group may dwell in a single segregated area that spans or falls wholly within a country's borders, in two or more segregated areas in one or more countries, or, if they are not segregated, in homes scattered among those of members of other ethnic groups in one or more countries. Segregation of some members of a group and scattering of others is not unusual, particularly if the group has been in exile or there has been extensive migration. Often, the several groups contained within a single country have different languages, religions, and customs, and views about the proprietorship of the land and self-determination that are at odds with one another.

The situation is somewhat similar in countries that became independent after the World War I period. Almost all of them were colonies that, after securing independence piecemeal in the face of considerable resistance, had to accept their colonial boundaries. Rarely did these boundaries coincide with traditional ethnic areas. Rather, they had been drawn intentionally to include many groups that long had been enemies and to divide others in different jurisdictions. The tactic was intended to weaken the resistance of indigenous groups to colonial rule. Moreover, because the countries were liberated piecemeal rather than simultaneously, they did not have an opportunity to negotiate with one another for boundaries that might produce more cultural homogeneity. A colony securing independence, bordered on all sides by other colonies, could not negotiate boundaries that would approximate those of a nation. Much, if not all, of the instability of Third World countries can be attributed to the unresolved ethnic disagreements that are the heritage of this process. Ogunade (1982: 23) noted this with regard to Africa and the media, when he observed that "[m]ost African states are yet consciously to employ mass media to create symbols which bind people as a nation not as disparate ethnic groups." Something analogous underlies the conflicts in sections of the former U.S.S.R. and in former sections of Yugoslavia. The discontinuity between country—the emergent form of the state—and nation—an emergent form of ethnicity—is key to understanding the state interest in communication policy everywhere but in the United States.[15]

The tie of communication policy to the state-nation discrepancy is particularly well illustrated by Canada. Canada is among the newest of the pre-World War I countries, having been created by the British parliament in 1867, just 47 years before the outbreak of that war. The new country initially consisted of three British colonies (New Brunswick, Nova Scotia, Canada [which became Ontario and Quebec]), and they were joined very shortly by Prince Edward Island and British Columbia. Within four years the infant country stretched from the Atlantic to the Pacific Ocean and from the United States border into the Arctic Ocean. The entering colonies differed from one another in interests, area and population, culture and language, and topography. They were thinly settled, and the eastern provinces were separated from British Columbia by a vast unorganized and sparsely inhabited area. Although some of the leaders of some of the entering colonies supported the idea of an independent country that would be part of the Empire, many others they did not. It required considerable British pressure as well as very hard bargaining among the leaders on their conditions for participating before an agreement could be reached. One such condition required building a railroad to traverse predominantly French-speaking, largely Roman Catholic Lower Canada (Quebec) and link the English-speaking colonies on the Atlantic with Montreal and Upper Canada (Ontario), and another to link British Columbia with the east. Why was Canada—basically a group of settlement colonies located in a very sparsely populated region rather than a colony imposed on a thickly settled indigenous society—so late to reach independence, and why was independence not eagerly sought by its people? Several factors were at work.

The three founding English-speaking Atlantic colonies contained sizable groups of United Empire Loyalists, descendants of colonists who had opposed the American Revolution and chosen exile to Canada. Regardless of the fact that 90 years had passed, these Canadians felt a deep loyalty to the British crown and a deep sense of rejection by and distrust of the United States. English Canadians, who also had been loyal to the Crown during the Revolution or who had arrived in Canada afterward, tended to share their sentiments. At the time of American independence, these people felt they were being cast adrift without protection next to a neighbor they feared and held in contempt.

In addition to concern about being left at the mercy of the United States without British protection, a new Canada would have to come to terms with the large French population that had been surrendered to the English approximately 100 years earlier as part of the settlement of the Seven Years War. One of the larger colonies, Lower Canada (now Quebec), was predominantly French. Significant portions of the populations of Nova Scotia, New Brunswick, and Prince Edward Island also were French, and numerous French settlements were scattered through the unorganized, undeveloped areas in the west and north that were expected to provide the base for the new country's prosperous economic future. The English and French had a healthy dislike and disrespect for one another. Except in Lower Canada, where the English essentially had agreed to let the Church run all but the formal aspects of public life, the English were dominant, held the French in contempt, and treated them accordingly. Many English Canadian leaders were not anxious to become part of an independent state in which the French might hold equal legal status.

Perhaps most important was the timing. The United States had just gone through its Civil War, was heavily armed, and had developed a powerful military infrastructure. It was opening its territories to settlement and was on a path to developing and integrating its entire area. During its short history it had proven itself to be aggressive and expansionist. Although most of its territory beyond the 13 original colonies had been purchased, it had used military force to make Mexico sell land, and had had several brief conflicts with Britain involving Canada subsequent to the War of 1812. The British colonies and unorganized territories shared a long, transcontinental border, some parts of which were still under dispute, with this aggressive, military giant. Their total population was less than 10% of that of the United States. The British government had been pursuing military and economic interests elsewhere that seemed much more economically promising than Canada. During the Civil War, Britain had supported the Confederacy by buying its products and allowing Confederate blockade runners and warships to use its ports. During the war, Confederate agents had raided St. Albans, VT, from Canada. With the Union victory, the British foresaw possible hostilities over Canada and did not want the burdens of a defense. Their solution was a largely autonomous Canada, responsible for its own defense but still tied to and loyal to the Empire.

At its birth, then, Canada was a new country bordering a potentially hostile, heavily armed neighbor with at least ten times more population. Canadians were thinly spread from coast to coast, mostly within 100 miles of the American border. Even now approximately 90% of them live in that long narrow belt. The colonies had separate histories and identities, and several had no means of transportation connecting them, no history of working together, and vastly different economic levels and bases. The English and French had only formal relations, and this distanced the area that became Quebec from the others. The Canadian future required the development of the resources of the large unsettled middle of the country and the inhospitable North. There were no roads or railroads connecting the colonies from east to west. A 700-mile-long sector of the Laurentian Shield, a sheet of pre-Cambrian rock covered only by a very thin layer of soil, separated the then-settled part of Ontario from what was to become Manitoba. The area lacks any of the resources that attract settlement, and the Shield is an extremely difficult environment for building highways or railroads. Norton (1988) observed that even now the country does not make economic sense, and many Canadians think that being in the shadow of a major world power has given the country a national sense of inferiority (Pendakur, 1988).

Given the circumstances that made autonomy from Britain less than a long-sought, desired goal, it is no surprise that from the passage of the British North American Act in 1867—indeed, even earlier—the country has been preoccupied with communication. Canadians have been fascinated with the potential of every new communication technology for furthering the country's development and integration. The extent of this fascination is mirrored in the work of Babe (1990), who, in reviewing what he considers the mythologies that have influenced Canadian telecommunications policy, refers to three of the first four in a much longer list as technological nationalism, technological dependence, and the efficacy of regulation (cf. McNulty, 1989). Canada's experience dramatizes the contingencies between the conditions of national birth, internal and external insecurities, and reliance on the technical infrastructure and content of communication to address these matters. Canada has not had the colorful history of most former European African, Asian, or Latin American colonies, but has experienced the whole range of problems involved in transforming a country into a nation. It has the ethnic heterogeneity of an old European country, the dependence of a new, ex-colonial country, and must deal with the problems that attend both. The pivotal role given transportation and communication in Canada typifies how most states with these problems try to resolve them. Consequently, much of the discussion in the remainder of this chapter and the next chapter is illustrated by Canadian material.

## STATES AND COMMUNICATION POLICIES

Several major themes in this synopsis bear directly on the structure of the mass media systems of many countries and on the policies that govern them. They include the following.

1. There is a conception of the state that makes defense of the realm from hostile competing states its primary legitimate responsibility. Accordingly, the chief functions of the state are seen as maintaining a capacity to conduct warfare, pro-

vide defenses, and, if those costs become exorbitant, negotiate international agreements. It sees the state as survival oriented, outward looking, and, except for dealing with internal subversion and selected matters that may threaten society (e.g., declining public health), inactive in the domestic society, economy, and polity. Its internal activities are only those essential to its external responsibilities. It grants the state preeminent authority and the right to use such draconian methods as martial law, conscription, condemnation, invasion of privacy, censorship, and suspension of due process to accomplish its tasks.

2. There is a conception of the state as obligated to respond to the possibility of societal deterioration. It complements the above conception by adding to the state's functions an internal allocative or distributive role, that is, the allocation and reallocation among residents of rights, privileges, and resources for the purpose of maintaining an essential level of domestic welfare and harmony. The legitimating assumption for this extension is that the state must rely on its population and could not survive if society were not viable. In this view, the state not only must comply with demands of the market, but also may participate in and control the market when necessary. Thus, the state also is a participatory entity that must attend to due process, morality, and ethics.

3. There is a polity—people who have the right to participate in decisions about the state and government, and to whom the state is accountable. As society expands by the extension of participatory rights, the polity grows. The rights of the polity constrain the power of state functionaries to do as they wish. The rights are the price regimes pay for support and control. Members of the polity need information, access to one another, and access to state functionaries if they are to participate rationally and effectively.

4. Because countries vary in social and cultural heterogeneity, consensus on common goals and values grows and ebbs and state actions rarely receive universal approval. Consequently, support for the state, the form of government, or the incumbent regime cannot be taken for granted. Similarly, compliance with its edicts and directives cannot be assumed. Groups that are not sufficiently satisfied may attempt to control the state or try to separate. These factors contribute to a continuous, varying level of tension between state functionaries and the populace.

5. There is a world system of states that operates on a myth of universal state equality in formal international relations. However, in trade relations and nonpublic negotiations there is a hierarchy that reflects each state's advantages and disadvantages in resources and circumstances of origin. Most states seek to rise in the hierarchy, to avoid falling, or to escape it completely (cf. Gibbs, 1986).

All five aspects of the modern state come into play when policies are set on any matter, communication included. The first two are particularly important. Poggi (1978) organized his entire analysis around this distinction, as did Service (1978). The first accounts for the emphasis on defense and military expenditures and the size and use of armed forces. It also may justify states' long-claimed right to control and monitor communication (Blatherwick, 1987: 10). The second accounts for welfare and educational programs, state regulation of domestic activities such as markets and consumer product quality, and the operation of state-owned enterprises. Katz (1979) suggested that it also can account for the efforts of some developing countries to use their mass media to promote continuity in their changing traditional cultures rather than to permit them to be submerged by media-carried international popular culture. Both of these two conceptions may account for the state's interests in developing, maintaining, and regulating transportation and communication systems in the interests of integrating the country as a nation. The other three bear on such varied matters as the direction of foreign policy, maintenance of the political process and protection of citizen rights, cultural policy, and science support and policy. The substance of any national policy reflects the balance among the five at the time the policy was formulated.[16]

Even in relatively short time periods, the policies of individual countries may vary wildly as regimes change, different interest groups or sectors of the polity gain ascendancy, and world conditions and the positions of individual countries in the world system change. As a dramatic example, with the implementation of a Europe without trade barriers at the end of 1992, long-established policies intended to protect and promote national cultures and improve cultural tastes are officially at an end, and all members of the Community are open to materials from any other member of the Community.[17] For such reasons, brief reviews of current media policy in various countries to highlight issues that are unfamiliar to Americans necessarily misrepresent the details of their situations and may be misleading. Moreover, until the appearance of the politics of the NWIO and the concept of development journalism, almost all non-European countries were appendages of colonial powers, even if they were nominally independent. Only the systems of European countries reflect their environments directly enough to provide useful contrasts with American systems.

A basic fact that shapes any comparison of media systems is that, due to the circumstances in which the state developed, most European countries have much stronger states than does the United States. The preceding sketch chronicles a process in which European rulers gradually surrendered power and prerogatives to the functionaries of a fictional entity—the state—which the rulers themselves had created for their own benefit. In Europe, the contests for power between expansive and aggressive rulers and the groups that dominated the economies from which they had to draw financial support for their agendas eventually strengthened autonomous state structures to such an extent that they have been able to survive major changes in regimes and governmental form.

The European revolutions between the late 17th century and World War I led to constitutional innovations that weakened rulers and strengthened the political role of the public. They also gave control over many aspects of everyday life to the state because of uncertainty about the loyalty of conquered peoples and of groups that still did not have, or had had to wait much too long to acquire, full citizenship rights. The maintenance of surveillance and censorship, reliance on the police and military to sustain regimes, and continuing deep animosities for neighbors and competing colonial powers contributed to the growth of extensive state apparatuses considered essential to maintain order and guard against enemies. France, in particular, has been singled out as a strong state expressed in a state bureaucracy that has continued intact through the Revolution, Empires, various Republics, and the German occupation during World War II.

Great Britain, with its strong tradition of personal rights and common law, and its relative isolation from mainland Europe, is usually considered the weakest of the European states. The securing of the Magna Carta, the early establishment and resilience of Parliament as an institution for sharing rule, the break with the Church of Rome, the Cromwellian Revolution, and a tradition of religious dissent all underlie this characterization. The success of the Thatcher government in converting broadcasting to a market economy at the same time that it obligated the state to continue subsidizing innovation and development for the information society (Collins, 1986a: 301-303)—in essence, making it a "cash cow" for the market—is indicative of the British state's relative weakness. The legendary civil service was staunchly behind public service broadcasting but unable to ward off the actions of an ideological regime. The American state is subordinated to personal independence even more. Constitutional specifications as to what the federal government can and cannot do reflect the revolutionaries' sensitivity to the English state's disregard of norms of representation in governing its colony. The force of the desire to restrict state power and to participate in its necessary activities is not surprising in view of the fact that so many of the colonials had left England to assert their personal choice in religion or escape autocracy.

Variations in state strength underlie important differences in policy processes and in the span and techniques of control to which citizens are subject. The range and variety of activities the state controls is a particularly important indicator of its strength. Acceptance of state intrusion usually indicates that the activity or behavior affected falls in the public rather than the private sphere. The typical legitimating argument for such intrusions is that the activity so significantly affects the welfare of the collectivity that the state, being responsible for the collectivity's interests, has a right and obligation to intervene. The distinction between areas in which the state has and has not exercised this prerogative usually is taken as the line between the public and the private, and, analogously, between the state and civil society. The state is expected to monitor and manage the public and to refrain from participating in the private sphere, where such informal processes as socialization, competition, reinforcement, and avoidance are expected to enforce social standards. Ever since the appearance of the state, the public sphere has expanded at the expense of the private.

Strong states tend more than weak states to increase the public sphere at the expense of the private. Generally, their techniques are more forceful or draconian than those of weaker states. Functionaries of strong states are more likely to intrude on the private sphere without consultation, to provide fewer and less accessible channels of redress to aggrieved citizens, and generally to behave in ways that portend the imminent erasure of the line and the loss of the private. People come to feel that government intrudes on their freedom of action and claim either that their actions neither inconvenience nor harm others or that, if they do, it is not their responsibility. The distinction between the public and private bears centrally on the state's role in communication, and, specifically, on what is considered discretionary for the state and for individuals. The former is exemplified by a debate over whether a government should prepare news items containing information about itself or leave it to the media to formulate such items (Nillesen and Stappers, 1987). With respect to individuals, it is a key factor in what is available to whom through what medium. I would argue that communication is focal to the politics of the public versus the private because, regardless of the type of system under consideration or whether the issue is raised at the state or the individual level, the term *communication* usually conjures up an image of private interpersonal conversation.

## RULE AND COMMUNICATION

Every social relationship requires communication. Rule is a structure of relationships of superordination and subordination that requires reliable communication to be stable. Types of rule vary, however, and shape the kind of communication that is required. Rule before the emergence of the state often employed overt coercion. That form of rule required orders from rulers to reach subordinates and eventually subjects, but did not always require reciprocal communication from the ruled to the ruler. The subsequent emergence of the state slowly changed the character of the communication required for effective rule. The state, because it developed to provide regimes with a legitimate basis for continuity and for priority over or equality with other authoritative competitors for people's loyalty, needed a transcendent basis of legitimate authority in addition to or instead of force to generate compliance. With the decline of coercion and the growth of voluntary action for assuring compliance with their dictates, regimes urgently needed access to communication systems that permitted broader, multiway contacts with their subjects.

As indicated, the forces that eroded feudalism and started the evolution toward the modern state also led to the inclusion of more and more of the state's subjects in society. At the same time, communication systems with the essential capacities of mass media—rapidity of sending and receiving, span of contact, public availability—were developed and played critical roles. The inclusion of ever more sectors of populations in civil society and the rising demand for workers who could follow and give instructions without needing face-to-face contact with superiors fed the spread of literacy. When the introduction of printing facilitated widespread public distribution of political ideas, it enabled the development of public opinion as a political force and the expansion of participatory democracy.

At the international level, Western states with capitalist economies required geographic expansion to sustain economic growth. When they met this need by annexing new territory or establishing colonies, they also created discontinuities between country and nation. Consequently, public communication media became critical not only for circulating information, but also for disseminating material that might integrate disparate ethnic groups into sharers of a common national culture. During the last two centuries, all countries increasingly have had to deal with these problems in a global environment shared with other states pursuing aggressive, expansionist projects. For these reasons, they have had to give full attention to both their international and their domestic communication.

The circumstances of state development and the political culture of each country are unique. Consequently, the structures of, social roles imputed to, and official policies toward their national media systems vary considerably. There is no clear and direct relation between these system qualities and the nature of the political system. Great Britain, long a stronghold of democratic rule, exercised total control of its radio and television systems until recently and still places limits on print media (cf. Evans, 1990). Canadian media law differs from both that of the United States and Great Britain (Beckton, 1982). After passage of Law 103 in 1975, Italy moved quickly from exclusively public broadcasting to a very mixed system. National variety characterizes every aspect of the media. Early on, for example, many European governments heavily subsidized the development of radio and television technology; the American government, in contrast, did not. The British government launched the BBC in part because private interests only envisioned being involved in receiver sales and had not thought about why people might want receivers; the American government did not involve itself in the provision of programs for broadcasting. Only recently have European governments permitted private ownership of broadcasting facilities. The American government always permitted it. Canada did not create the CBC until 1932 when it became clear that the country was being inundated with American broadcasts and that the programming of the private stations operating for profit like their American counterparts and of the public system operated by the Canadian National Railroad was not counteracting their impact. Subsequently, it has experimented with various protective policies including state ownership, subsidization of private initiatives, and control of imports. Until recent steps to privatize and to implement their commitments to an integrated regional economy, European governments, wanting to develop and protect their national cultures, enhance their people's intellectual skills and knowledge, and integrate their nations, stringently controlled their systems. The United States did not; it invested in its education system.

## STATES, MEDIA SYSTEMS, AND POLICY

Differences among states in their goals for and involvement in developing and operating their media affect both the capacity (e.g., number of stations, volume of transmission, quantity of material produced) and the qualities (e.g., type and balance of programming, types of films and programs produced) of systems. By and large, the United States has more stations broadcasting more material than do most countries.[18] With respect to material, most countries other than the United States encourage and even participate in the production of informational (e.g., news, documentaries, instructional films) and cultural (e.g., lectures and discussions, classical musical performances, dance) materials. In Canada, for example, the National Film Board produces documentary films, Telefilm Canada finances commercial film production, and the CBC produces many of its own programs. All are public organizations. This is not simply state socialism; Canada, like the United States, has a capitalist economy. However, as discussed earlier, the Canadian concept of the role of the state is quite different. In sum, national systems vary in magnitude, patterns of ownership, mode of finance, and quality of materials made available, and this applies to all the media. Barring official censorship, however, the range of state roles tends to be greatest for television and radio, in contrast to the state's minimal role in the production of feature films and publication of newspapers and magazines.

The connection between state development and political traditions, on the one hand, and media systems, on the other, is not as strong as it might be if economic conditions were not also a factor. Wealthier countries tend to have more media outlets and a greater quantity and variety of material. Economic conditions by themselves, however, cannot completely account for the variation, for there are other ways to invest both public and private economic resources. Most theories, however, suggest links between economic development, the character of the political system, literacy, and media availability. Lipset (1959) and Cutright (1963), for example, have shown, although perhaps not explained adequately, linkages among level of economic development, type of political system, and mass media. Schramm (1964, 1967; Schramm and Ruggels, 1967) documented linkages among social change (e.g., industrialization, urbanization), literacy, and mass media. Weaver, Buddenbaum, and Fair (1985) have provided evidence of a relationship between economic development, urbanization, and press freedom. Even the spread of VCRs in a world already saturated with media has been found (Straubhaar and Lin, 1989) to be related to urbanization and the presence of other media (which already reflects the influence of many of the above mentioned factors).

Clearly, there is reason to expect such linkages, but not a simple causal chain. Surely there are feedbacks. The history just synthesized sketched one such set of relationships. Early industrialization did spark economic development and increased leisure and purchasing power. Informed people with resources are more capable of and interested in political participation. Industrial development did require worker literacy, and literacy did provide access to other material. Capitalist development promoted national expansion, which required a media-like infrastructure to integrate and coordinate the large, diverse subject populations. The relationships are all reasonable and observable, but the particular structure of each country's media system—what is available to whom and how—still tends to reflect the historical circumstances in which the state developed, concepts of what is politically feasible and a proper role for the state, resources available for the media, and events elsewhere in the world system.

Abundant, specific information on the quantity and variety of media available in all the countries of the world is provided by the United Nations and its UNESCO affiliate.[19] They periodically inventory the numbers of newspapers, magazines, and books published; the number of films produced and theaters showing films; and the number of AM, FM, and television stations and hours of broadcasting. With the occasional expected exceptions (e.g., large numbers of films produced in Hong Kong and India, coverage of Radio Luxembourg), generally there are high associations between population size, GNP per capita, and media availability. More detailed studies (e.g., Dyson and Humphreys [1986], Howell [1986], and Dunnett [1990] on the structures of broadcasting systems; Blumler and Nossiter [1991] on financing of broadcasting; Martin and Chaudhury [1983] on all media) add rich detail on ownership, concepts of media responsibility, press freedom, international flow of materials (Nordenstreng and Varis, 1974; Guback and Varis, 1982; Varis, 1984a, 1984b, 1985; Mowlana, 1985; Wildman and Siwek, 1988), and the positions of various countries on such controversial issues as access to satellites, access to satellite information, radio channel assignments, and the NWIO. The extent and origins of this diversity, however, have not been discussed simply as a prologue to a description. Descriptions are available from many sources, cited and not cited. Rather, the diversity demonstrates the deep ties between the larger social order and the type of media systems to be found and, relatedly, the relative narrowness and provincialism of American concerns with the media.

It is difficult to specify the nature of the real variation in national media policies because of the loose link between asserted policies and actual programs or actions. One cannot always be sure what a country's policies are. Policies are abstract commitments to goals and means that are usually congruent with some deeply held and widely shared values; they are not the organizations, procedures, and operations that implement them. When the policymaking process itself is ambiguous (Seymour-Ure, 1987), or the policies that result have not been stated explicitly, one recourse is to infer them from what seem to be the consequences of state activities in that area.[20] However, experience even in countries where the practice is to declare the underlying goals of and rationale for state actions—and that includes most countries that follow democratic legislative and administrative procedures—indicates that policies and operations may change independently. However, there are enough cases of countries with long records of trying to guide actions with goals and of countries staking out positions on issues that require international negotiation to inform a discussion.

Many of the media policies of other countries address concerns about which most Americans are uninformed but that are pertinent to the United States. Indeed, on these and most issues of international significance, the United States does take positions and act. Issues that concern and shape both the international and domestic media policies of most of the world's countries but that do not concern most Americans include the New International Information Order and the withdrawal of the United States from UNESCO (in considerable part because of its adoption), a proposed international code for responsible journalism (Fisher, 1982) that also was a factor in American withdrawal from UNESCO, the allocation of satellite orbits and the rules for allocating transponders on satellites that have been the subject of rancorous debates in the WARC conferences (Gunter, 1978; Clippinger, 1979), revisions of the numerous technical regulations to which International Telecommunication Union (ITU) members must conform (Codding, 1979), and negotiations to standardize the conflicting rules that countries have adopted to control access to information stored on satellites (Wigand, Shipley, and Shipley, 1984). The future role of the ITU is a particularly important matter because, as Renaud (1990) noted in reviewing that body's involvement in recent agreements on international telecommunications, the technical issues that fall in its jurisdiction dramatize both the ambiguity of telecommunications (45) and the inadequacy of individual states and negotiations between them to meet either the domestic or international communication needs that are emerging (43-52).

In most of the world's countries there are lively debates about appropriate responses to technological developments that in a few years will merge the media and their conventional functions with shopping, household management, word processing, and similar tasks. Eventually, media behavior as we know it will be transformed totally. The changes will be far more extreme than such a change as the switch from passively viewing films in theaters, where operations are controlled by others, to viewing film cassettes at home on self operated and controlled VCRs. They will be much more profound in their extent and impact and are likely not just to reshape the technology and mode of consumption of single media but to erase or reposition the lines that now distinguish them. Even more important from the perspective of states, they also threaten to erase the line between the public and private and to minimize the significance of national borders. From this perspective, many of the hotly debated policy issues in the United States seem trivial.

As an aftermath of the French Revolution, with varying levels of concern, European countries have monitored peasant and worker restiveness. The spread of the factory system created massive social dislocations, and peasants and workers alike organized and protested the rapid changes that were reducing their control over their lives and resources. Periodic worker insurrections, eventually culminating in the Russian Revolution, and the overthrow of royal families in other countries at the end of World War I fueled domestic insecurity. The extension of citizenship rights, curtailment of arbitrary rule, and introduction of the precursor programs to the welfare state were all being tried as remedies for these concerns, and the climate of incipient radical change left rulers feeling threatened and insecure. In addition, through much of the pre-World War I period, some major European powers (e.g., Germany, Italy) were engaged in contentious unification processes, and even more were involved in other nationalistic projects aimed at insulating and solidifying their national cores. Finally, many major European powers had embarked on imperialistic ventures intended to buttress their regimes by expanding the realm and shoring up and enriching the domestic economy.

The hostile, threatening environment engendered by the combination of aggressive international expansion and competition, on the one hand, and an impending major domestic political upheaval, on the other, accentuated awareness of the state's responsibility to preserve society. By comparison, the allocative function basic to social satisfaction, though necessary, was, at most, only an emerging role. However, by monitoring overt and covert foreign aggression and domestic disloyalty and sedition, states were able to balance off both roles. Consequently, it was a period in which almost every continental European state monitored and censored the foreign and domestic press (Ruud, 1979)[21], in the first instance to detect signs of imminent foreign aggression or domestic unrest and in the second to conceal or prevent the spread of ideas and information that might incite the populace.

Faster communication also was important to states, and they invested in the development of electrically based technologies—the telegraph, telephone, radio—and in schemes to frustrate other countries' similar efforts. Regardless of treaties, all countries were potential enemies, and communication policy was shaped, in part, by the imperative of knowing and foiling any schemes they might be hatching. In complementary fashion, internal policy was shaped by the need to monitor disloyalty and thwart rebellion. Throughout most of the period, what we now call the media were print-based—newspapers, magazines, books, and pamphlets. Although the distinction between information and entertainment had not been well articulated, both types of material had wide currency. News was evolving into its modern form, and novels and short stories intended for reader enjoyment were being produced for every segment of the population. Political material appeared in every print form, and activists wrote for both the intelligentsia and the masses. State monitoring generally tended to be directed more to nonentertainment than entertainment materials, although incidents of banning the printing or importation of novels and other such material considered damaging to public morals and standards also were not unusual.

The situations in England and the United States differed considerably from this scenario. Like the continental European powers, both had their imperialist projects; unlike them, both had relatively weak states and were not primarily concerned with the state's preeminence. Thus, although neither practiced overt censorship nor closely monitored the importation of foreign printed material in peace time, both were deeply interested in the development of radio telephony. The financing of the development of the technology and the various corporate entities that were involved reads like a network of early 20th-century intrigue. The web of patents and corporations involved in the commercial development of the radio, the phonograph, phonographic recording, and film reflects extensive English and American, as well as deep French, Italian, and German involvement, in what might have seemed to be a private sector activity.[22]

The utility of the basic technology on which these media depend (e.g., vacuum tubes, amplifiers) was apparent to state functionaries. The miliary potential for rapid transmission of information about the enemy already has been noted. The capacity radio could provide for the metropole to coordinate colonial adventures and to monitor and respond quickly to events in the colonies also was tremendously attractive. In addition, given the reliance of the colonial powers on navies and merchant marines to link their far-flung possessions, the value of radio for providing almost instant contact with ships at sea was well understood. Although all countries left manufacturing to their private sectors, they guided technology development and kept a wary eye on its control, sale, and use.

Governments foresaw the immense potential of radio and, somewhat earlier, the telephone. On the one hand, they could facilitate the conduct of the state's business and enable large numbers of people to be reached quickly with the same material. On the other hand, they could harm the state by bringing material that could provoke domestic unrest to wide public attention. Consequently, all the major European countries, including Great Britain, kept the provision of those services to the public in the hands of the state. Either because private entrepreneurs lacked the means for or interest in such an undertaking[23] or because the function was deemed too vital to be left where decisions about service might turn primarily on considerations of profit, state-provided postal service already was universal. This is an indication that states already were sensitive to the potential unreliability of a private, market-based economy for providing essential services. Generally, therefore, as telephone, broadcasting, and, much later, television services developed and their strategic importance was understood, they, too, were assigned to PTTs—postal, telegraph, and telephone agencies.

A somewhat similar course of events occurred in every core country but the United States.[24] Since the 1920s, except for the United States, all the major countries have had mixed public and private media systems. Film and print media tend to be more privately than publicly owned and operated, although more authoritarian states took stringent measures to assure that nothing was produced or disseminated in print or film that might contradict or conflict with regime positions. In contrast, until the end of World War II, radio, and later television, was almost exclusively publicly owned and operated.[25] Even production may have been done by state agencies, although the more democratic the state, the more likely were private producers to have provided the nonnews broadcast material.

## STATE "THEORIES" OF THE MEDIA

Acknowledgment of the forces that drove and still drive communication policies would place states in a very self-serving light, one that hardly could be admitted by those states that proclaim to be democratic or, at least, committed to advancing their people's interests. Not surprisingly, therefore, state functionaries and bureaucrats in every country developed more publicly acceptable rationales for their policies and actions. In the mid-1950s, Siebert and his associates (1956) referred to these as "theories of the press" and suggested that all national media systems could be characterized as one of four types—authoritarian, libertarian, social responsibility, or Soviet Communist. Despite dramatic changes in many regimes and a proliferation of independent states, later analyses also conclude that four or five very similar categories are adequate to encompass the claims, structures, and performance of national media systems. Both Hachten (1987: 14-34) and McPhail and McPhail (1990: 29-53) have subsequently identified five "concepts of the press"—the authoritarian, western, Communist, revolutionary, and developmental (or Third World) by Hachten, and the authoritarian, libertarian, social responsibility, Soviet totalitarian, and development journalism by McPhail and McPhail. Presumably, future schema will drop a "Soviet Communist" category. Ignoring the differences in detail, all these categorizations reflect several similar aspects of media systems—their perceived purpose, features of the material they provide, ownership patterns, and the state's position in the system of control.

A table (Table 8.1) constructed by McPhail and McPhail (1990: 51) summarized the distinguishing features of each of their concepts. Although, like all typologies, it oversimplifies complex features and suggests that countries fall into one and only one category,[26] their summary highlights aspects of the different types of national media systems that are most relevant here. The concepts differ in their prime beneficiary—the state (authoritarian), the people (social responsibility, libertarian), society as a system of structured relationships (Soviet totalitarian), and sectors of society (libertarian, development journalism). The presumption of each is that attention to that particular aspect of social reality will enhance the good of the entire collectivity. Clearly, though, these rationales do not obviate the possibility that there also is an underlying concern with promoting the state and its dominance. This is particularly clear with the authoritarian and Soviet categories, for there is little evidence that party functionaries and government bureaucrats in Soviet-type states ever worked toward the ostensible Marxist goal of the withering away of the state or that the preexisting traditional state apparatus ever lost power or was expendable when a European country was taken over by a restrictive, authoritarian regime. The social responsibility approach characterizes most of the OECD countries, several of which, as already noted, have strong states that have demonstrated their capacity to survive dramatic changes in regime and form of government. Development journalism, however, applies only to the policies of several Third World countries with authoritari-

**Table 8.1. Five Concepts of Mass Communication**

| | Authoritarian | Libertarian | Social responsibility | Soviet totalitarian | Development journalism |
|---|---|---|---|---|---|
| Purpose | to support government | to provide information and entertainment and support the economic system | to enhance the general welfare | to serve the interests of the social system | to contribute to national development |
| Content | no criticism of government policy or dominant values | broadest possible range of views | full, balanced and accurate accounts | complete view of the world from a Soviet perspective | pro-development information, no criticism of development policy, reduced foreign content |
| Ownership | private | private | public or private | public | public or private |
| Control system | state-controlled negative mechanisms | the self-righting process | self-regulation preferred; state control if necessary | state-controlled positive and negative mechanisms | state-controlled positive and negative mechanisms |

From *Communication: The Canadian Experience* (p. 51), by T.L. McPhail and B.M. McPhail, 1990, Toronto: Copp Clark Pittman, © 1990 by Copp Clark Pittman, Ltd. Reprinted with permission of the publisher.

an "great leader single party rule" and state forms as unstable as those of feudal Europe that were contrived largely by their rulers for their own purposes. Nonetheless, nothing in the concept or the countries' circumstances would prevent the development of a strong state. Indeed, long-term successful implementation of this concept would seem to require a strong state. Only the libertarian concept implies a commitment to a weak, limited state form, but the concept only applies domestically. Moreover, it is held by private media practitioners and is not a principle that states apply to their own role.

It must be emphasized that as the number and variety indicate, these are descriptive categories created by scholars to bring order to chaos. The titles simply convey a sense of the content and the cases from which they are derived and to which they are referred. These are not formal categories derived from a theory or accepted by state functionaries or media practitioners as the finite set of alternative ways in which media systems might operate. Consequently, it should not be surprising if there is little evidence that states referred to as fitting one or another of the concepts actually are committed to them. It should be even less surprising if responsible public officials disagree with this specification of the alternatives for characterizing their country's media system.

The distinctive contents attributed to the libertarian and social responsibility concepts really describe ideals that are supposed to guide those responsible for media systems modeled on these concepts. Performance, though, obviously falls short, as indicated by the growth of virtual industries of media criticism where those concepts are professed. In addition to the possibility of poor performance, the structure of systems modeled after either of these two concepts also discourages efforts to satisfy the ideal because the combination of owner autonomy and consumer sovereignty is antithetical to provision of the ideal content.

Most owners have vested interests that might suffer if all alternative viewpoints were widely promoted. Even if they were disinterested or so altruistic as to suppress their own interests, the goals imply either that they can behave routinely in ways that meet these standards or, even more unlikely, that even though most of them cannot do this, the material produced by the system as a whole somehow will meet the standard. Moreover, even if this last unlikely condition were to be achieved, to satisfy the intent of the concept in any meaningful way, individual consumers would have to choose from the available material so as to have a proper diet. Finally, in addition to the fact that normal production and consumption practices deflect reality from the ideal, the subjects of press coverage usually also try to promote their interests by applying their understanding of how the press operates to shape coverage in their favor. These concepts of what media content should be are advanced because it is believed that the media are important—that the media, in fact, have the role in the public affairs of democracies that is claimed for them—but this belief alone cannot produce breadth, fullness, balance, or accuracy. Ironically, the claim to pursue these goals in a system that supports private, independent action creates a felt need for state intervention that eventually receives public support.

The standards for content that are associated with the three other concepts come closer to referring to performance rather than ideals. Nonetheless, they are flawed descriptions of a complex reality. One weakness is that the terminology is shaped by Western liberal perspectives. Media professionals in systems guided by any one of the three concepts probably would not characterize the content in that way. Thus, for example, even if *Pravda, Izvestia*, and Moscow television had been providing a world view from a Soviet perspective, Soviet press professionals were likely to have viewed their perspective on events and their newsworthiness as the proper and reasonable one, not the Soviet one (cf. Gaunt, 1987; Afanasiev, 1990 [1982]; McNair, 1991: 23). Certainly Gerbner and Márványi's (1984) "Many Worlds of the World's Press," by demonstrating pictorially the sharp differences in area coverage of leading newspapers' reporting of foreign affairs, shows that the relativity of judgments as to newsworthiness is not simply a product of blind ideology (cf. Atwood and Bullion, 1982). In any case, granted the approximate precision of these content descriptions, by and large, the extent to which they are achieved is a function of the extent and effectiveness of state control. The weaker a state, the more difficult it is for its officials to produce conformity to goals. In a sense, then, a serious commitment to a press that provides such content is also a commitment to a state form that is sufficiently strong to do whatever is necessary to assure that that will happen.

A second inadequacy of these three descriptions of content is that they are sometimes significantly incomplete. For example, the content attributed to the authoritarian concept is specified only minimally. In most modern virulent authoritarian states, the state not only monitors criticism but also, to the extent possible, employs all the media in a continuous and intense propaganda campaign to aggrandize the regime, its goals, and ideology, and to denigrate its enemies. Marxist theorists understood this to be an implication of Marx's comments on the power of those who controlled the production of ideas and information and employed the media accordingly (McNair, 1991: 9-51). Goebbels not only implemented censorship of the German media, but used them to promote Nazi ideology and mythology (Ward, 1989: 111-118).

Finally, the concepts describe ideals rather than reality. This is particularly true of the development journalism concept of press content. In part, this is because current world news gathering and distribution practices make it almost impossible for media in developing countries to produce and emphasize this material, a situation that led directly to promotion of an NWIO. In part, it is because many countries that embrace this concept nevertheless permit private ownership. Being ex-colonies, much of the private ownership is foreign and the need for substantial foreign investment deters the state from doing anything about this. Foreign interests rarely are served by development journalism, and weak states cannot make programs that lack public support work. The frustrations of proclaiming programs that cannot be implemented or that inevitably fail can tempt leaders into the arbitrary exercise of authority that leads to authoritarianism and their eventual downfall. Although these descriptions of content come closer to describing how systems in countries that subscribe to the three concepts actually perform, they, too, tend to misrepresent the complexities of reality.

The two remaining dimensions both involve aspects of control. Because ownership eases access to managerial decisions on a day-to-day basis, the notations of private ownership can give a misleading impression that control by capitalists is prevalent and state involvement rare. As already noted, however, in countries that take either a social responsibility or a development journalism stance on their media, the electronic media usually are publicly owned and a sector of the film industry may be. In addition, there may be state- or party-owned newspapers and magazines with substantial circulations. In the single-party states typical of many Third World countries, party and state ownership are equivalent. Thus, in most mixed cases, private ownership is limited largely to film and the print media. More representative in this regard are the comments on control systems. In all but the libertarian case, states are heavily involved in control. The emphasis on self-regulation in the social responsibility concept does not mean that it is a reliable means of control. It is not surprising, therefore, that countries with policies based on this model eventually assign responsibility at least to monitor and regulate media performance to a state agency.

Many countries, particularly those in Western Europe, North America, and the former British Dominions, would claim to have media systems that reflect the social responsibility concept. Only in Western Hemisphere countries, however, is public ownership relatively negligible and, in truth, only in the United States is direct state participation in the media almost nil. In Canada, for example, even if television and radio were not modeled on the British system, the subsidization of film production by government agencies and the imposition of Canadian content standards for print and broadcasting media reflect much greater state involvement than in the United States. The variety in the extent and modes of public involvement in media systems modeled on a social responsibility concept is a product of defects in the Libertarian concept. In some countries that initially tried that concept, it failed because the self-righting processes that are expected to operate never did produce or maintain the broad and balanced representations that are desired. In other countries (e.g., Great Britain, France, Germany), views of the mission of the state and its importance were such that the libertarian approach was never tried and social responsibility always has been the prevailing concept. In the United States, the libertarian view has held sway and, even though its weaknesses have become apparent, increased state involvement still is resisted on the basis of its free press heritage and because the libertarian position still serves the interests of several very powerful groups.[27]

## THE GLOBAL ECONOMY AND NATIONAL MEDIA POLICIES

The globalization of the world economy in the latter half of the 20th century has had paradoxical consequences for state policy on media systems. With the growth of transnational corporations (TNCs) and the free flow of capital throughout the world, peripheral countries experience an influx not only of foreign capital and businesses, but also of people, a few of whom come as upper level managers, considerably more of whom come as tourists, but most of whom come as legal or illegal workers. In contrast, the core countries from which capital, business, and people are drawn tend to be hurt economically. Although their weakened currencies attract tourism, usually they lose capital, incomes and standards of living fall, and underemployment in service industries and unemployment rise. Regardless of whether they gain or lose, countries tend to become dependent and to lose control of their economies, in part because involvement in a global network of commercial relations renders them always vulnerable to economic events in other countries and in part because attempts to control domestic business practices and decisions can lead firms to move, leaving their workers unemployed and without income (cf. Schiller, 1979). Growing realization of the erosion of effective control can prompt regime leaders to feel that they must show their continued independence in order to retain popular support. The result can be resurgent nationalism and protectionism.

Globalization also is manifested by the introduction into most countries of a wide variety of foreign commercial products, foods, dress styles, and nonmaterial cultural elements. Given the global nature of the economy, countries are restrained in complaining about this very vigorously because they also depend on exports to foreign markets to maintain their own economies. Consequently, citizens are relatively free to consume and to develop tastes for foreign cultural materials. The consequences of these two aspects of globalization are manifested in domestically oriented protectionism, on the one hand, and open market, consumer taste driven demands, on the other. Both are reflected in what might be characterized as schizophrenic media policy.

Regimes and state functionaries have a vested interest in maintaining their states as independent entities. Without the state there is no need for their special skills and services, nor would they be in a position to govern and exercise the power that the state monopolizes. The state, in turn, requires that people acquiesce in its right to monopolize power and rule them. That means that a sufficient majority of a country's population and leadership must share a set of beliefs that supports and legitimizes the extant political arrangement, that is, that the political system is superior and proper. For this reason, state leaders are interested in building and promoting a national culture that justifies the political system. The media, it is believed, can play a key role in this project in several ways. They can introduce distinctive cultural elements by conveying them to the entire population. They can promote and reenforce such materials by presenting them in a very positive light and repeating them as much as necessary (cf. Cardiff and Scannell, 1987). At the same time, they can explicitly or by implicit contrast denigrate cultural alternatives. Finally, they can help develop a cultural elite by supporting and providing employment for talented producers and performers of domestic cultural materials for media presentation. It is no surprise, then, that policies that in one way or another control the supply of materials that do not serve these purposes—chief among which would be imports from potential foreign competitors—and policies that encourage the domestic production of materials likely to enhance support for the state directly or indirectly are particularly attractive.

Despite these reasonable responses to globalization, involvement in a world economy lessens countries' freedom to foster their autonomy.[28] Market pressures keep them from stringently regulating imports of foreign materials, including media material. The importation of foreign standards and materials not only can create tastes that inspire insistent public demands for more,[29] but also, if imports include the idea of state responsiveness to public opinion, can lead to consumer sovereignty, that is, the legitimate priority of market demand as the determinant of supply (cf. Freiman, 1984). Acceptance of consumer sovereignty tends to limit policy options to those that minimize government interference in the media marketplace, and, when interference is wanted, puts it on the side of influencing producers to meet consumer demand.

The infrastructural requirements of the global economy also militate against protectionist policies. Global economic activities require storage and almost instantaneous access to or transfer of vast amounts of information. Satellite technology is being utilized and refined at least as much for these purposes as for military and entertainment uses. Satellite data storage and transborder information flow has become a major service industry. Governments have not tried to restrain the TNCs that require and utilize these services lest they move their operations elsewhere. Within their home countries, these industries lobby for technology development and against protectionist actions that might lead other countries to respond in kind. Thus, conditions in the growing world economy simultaneously encourage the tightening and loosening of domestic controls over all aspects of the media. The impact of the interplay between rapidly changing telecommunications technology and the international economic system is reflected in the high priority being given by every modern industrial country to developing and refining a total communication policy.

## NOTES

1. Cf. Humphreys (1986) for a graphic account of the extent of government involvement in media in several western European countries.
2. Although they are difficult to obtain in English, a sampling of research reports conducted by the national broadcasting services in several European countries showed that they dealt with such topics as young children's learning from Sesame Street, the impact of television on children, television programming for foreign guest workers and how well it meets their needs, the meaning of television serials to viewers, and the like. In addition, there were the usual studies of audience size and composition in total and for specific materials.
3. The motion picture industry, however, provides examples of what could happen in the way of lost production. In addition to the rash of so-called "spaghetti Westerns" produced in Italy and Spain in the 1960s and the long-standing participation in co-productions for which work is dispersed widely, producers of B and lower level films for theaters and television have been cutting costs by moving production elsewhere for at least ten years (cf. Pendakur, 1988: 165-166).

4. A good example is provided by Evans' (1990) analysis of differences in how freedom of the press is understood and implemented in Great Britain and the United States.
5. The concept of an "information society" is an apt example of such possible distraction. When first broached, it suggested that new electronic communication technology would maximize democracy by facilitating citizen rationality and participation. People could obtain information from reliable sources and register their feelings on issues whenever they wanted. Critics, however, point to the potential for authoritarian control by the providers of the information and/or technology (cf. Schiller, 1981; Lyon, 1988: 86-105). They fear that people's ability to act wisely will be eroded—that passive participation and acceptance of information deadens understanding of the nature of inquiry and the provisional nature of information. This, in turn, lessens the capacity to pursue one's interests actively. Thus, rather than being an active, rational society, the information society will be a passive, controlled society whose citizens will have been deluded into believing that they are their own masters when, in fact, nothing could be further from the truth.
6. For the sake of simplicity, I am writing this as if there were consensus among state theorists. Even a cursory review of the literature would show that this is not so. Among some of the more important statements from which this discussion derives are those of Cohen, 1978; Durkheim, 1986; and Mann, 1988 [1984].
7. As noted earlier, though, the domestic-external distinction is eroding as very large corporations develop widespread transnational operations.
8. These terms are adopted from Poggi (1978, 1990), on whose work and that of Badie and Birnbaum (1983), King (1986: 31-85), and Mann (1988 [1984]) much of the synthesis that follows is based. The *Ständestaat* evolved from feudalism with the growth of towns and the pressure of their citizens for collective representation in the process of rule. Poggi (1978: 36) referred to it as "the polity of Estates." The French system of an assembly of Estates lingered almost to the Revolution and probably is most familiar (see King, 1986: 38-39).
9. In fact, several cities did achieve special status during medieval times. Some, like Genoa and Venice, became independent city-states.
10. The practice of excluding ordinary people from society was normal. A major goal of the French Revolution was to extend status as members of society to all people. It was reflected in the practice of addressing everyone as "citizen." The American Revolution, in contrast, focused on sovereignty, procedures of rule, and securing rights for people who already were members of society. It did not basically restructure social relations. For this reason many scholars consider the French Revolution, though the later of the two, to be the first true social revolution. The concept of "high society" that was popular until the 1950s in Western countries also reflects the possibility of restricted membership in society. A popular pastime was to speculate about who was "in" and who was "not in" high society. It implied a basic distinction between special and ordinary persons.

11. The areas that are now considered Eastern and Western Europe practiced different versions of Christianity from the division of the declining Roman Empire. In addition, the spread of Christianity throughout Europe was not complete. Somewhat later, invading Turks brought Islam to the Balkans and southern Russia.
12. Later, their importance was reflected in their special status in the French system of estates. In discussing much earlier states, Smith (1986: 236) noted that effective communication in the service of rulers of limited literacy who governed even less literate people involved much more than mastery of and control over the technology of communication and transportation. In listing the functions of the very early empires that some scholars would not consider states, he included "... that of information control and transmission. Here . . .the state usually has to fall back upon specialist literate classes, which . . .were usually priests and scribes . . . and were even trained by special government educational establishments."
13. The premise of Cardiff and Scannell's (1987) analysis of early BBC radio programming is that it was geared to the generation and reenforcement of national unity. (Also, cf. the material on the development of Canadian broadcasting in Chapter 9 in this regard.)
14. Cf. Seton-Watson (1977: 463-483), Breuilly (1985 [1982]: 1-41). Almost all discussions of the phenomenon refer largely to 19th- and 20th-century events. Seton-Watson, though, distinguishes the two periods, writing that "[t]he nationalism of the twentieth century has usually been more bitter than the nationalism of the nineteenth" (465).
15. The rescue of Catalan culture from destruction by international popular culture provides an arresting case of a spatially and politically fragmented population segment of a modern state (Spain) attempting to reestablish and protect its cultural integrity. Groups of people who share Catalan culture are located not only in Spanish Catalonia, but also in Valencia and the Balearic Islands in Spain, in an area north of Catalonia in France, and in independent Andorra (Gifreu, 1986). The case is particularly interesting because the Catalan agenda seeks complete separation from Spain or autonomy within it.
16. Ward (1989) provided several very clear examples of these contingencies in his discussion of "The Media and the State in the 1930s" (110-132). Also see Wigand, Shipley, and Shipley (1984).
17. However, several factors may impede achievement of the goal (cf. Le Duc, 1979; Locksley, 1987; Shorrock, 1989; Negrine, 1990). The question is whether impediments are being actively erected or supported by states that talk one way but act another, or whether they simply are unavoidable circumstances that the member states will overcome as quickly as possible. In any case, like me, Schlesinger (1991) was struck by the inconsistency. He wrote that "[w]hile working in a 'European' academic institution, I was struck by the disjuncture between the official ideology of the common culture and the persistence of national diversity amongst my colleagues and friends" (137).

18. Because national differences in the organization of media systems make them noncomparable, these statements are difficult to document with the statistics provided by international organizations and the research services of domestic media. For example, countries in which state-owned corporations—usually PTTs—operate the broadcasting services may have only a national service with a limited number of radio and television broadcast channels In countries like the United States, stations are all local, so there are many more. In 1988, *Electronic Media* reported that France had six television stations and Italy 1,394, suggesting that the numbers say more about organization than availability. They also hide the fact that almost all of the Italian stations are very low powered and that each of the six French stations are available throughout the country. Moreover, for international comparisons of supply, hours of broadcasting are at least as important as numbers of outlets.In some countries, a few national newspapers provide all the supply. In the United States, with the exception of the *Wall Street Journal* and *Christian Science Monitor*, until recently all newspapers have been local. In film, because dubbing and subtitling permit films made anywhere in the world to be exhibited and coproductions are common, the number and sizes of exhibition facilities and the number of showings per week are more indicative of supply than is the number of domestic productions. Furthermore, long term trends also vary among countries. For example, in the United States and Canada, the numbers of newspapers have been declining and the numbers of radio and television stations and, in the United States, screens for film exhibitions recently have been increasing. The same trends do not apply to countries with primarily national rather than local media services. Countries in which these trends apply may be experiencing them at different rates or at different stages of the process. Consequently, comparisons of numbers in any given year do not mean much, and the generalizations offered here should be considered only informed impressions.
19. UNESCO maintains a Division of Statistics on Culture and Communication within its Office of Statistics. Data collected by that division provided much of the empirical justification for the proposals for the NWIO.
20. Cf. the discussion in Chapter 7. Contact with persons involved in deciding on policy is, of course, an alternative. Given the numerous political reasons why their reports might not reflect intentions when the matter was under consideration, individual differences in perceptions of the situation, and other sources of inaccuracy in personal reports, this approach to identifying unstated policies is no more likely to be useful, valid, or reliable than is direct inference. Inference is suggested, however, primarily because participants in events in the distant past may be unavailable and may not have left any reliable records. For matters on which contact with key actors is possible, a process of checking inferences against reports from all or most of them is the best approach, assuming, of course, that the matter at issue does not involve state secrecy.

# Development of the State 263

21. This also applied to Japan from 1868 on as the Meiji embarked on a campaign of national modernization (cf. Kasza, 1988: 3-118).
22. Ward (1989: 80-81) offered the following brief summary of some of the details:

> Wartime experience had confirmed many government officials in Europe and the United States in the belief that wireless, as a form of communication, was an important national resource, and the ownership of technical facilities should not lie outside national boundaries. The preponderant position of Britain in wired telegraph communication before the First World War had alerted governments to the possibility of wireless as a way of bypassing British control, but the monopolistic tendencies of the Marconi Company led many to fear a similar development in wireless telegraphy and telephony, particularly in the United States.
> 
> The US Department of Commerce had taken responsibility for licensing of wireless transmission facilities under the Radio Act of 1912, but many of them were owned by the American Marconi Company, which was a subsidiary of the main British company. During the war they had been taken over by the government, and in 1919 the Naval Department argued that they should not be returned. While anxious not to intervene directly in the commercial organisation of the industry the government approached the problem of control by suggesting the creation of a new company, the Radio Corporation of America (RCA), which was established in October 1919. Initially, American Marconi was asked to transfer stock and assets to the new company, and recognised that there really was no alternative. The government had set the direction for the future in the creation of a private monopoly of which the stockholders were the major wireless equipment manufacturers and cable-owners in the US: General Electric, American Telephone and Telegraph Company, United Fruit and Westinghouse. They held between them, the majority of US patents for the development of radio. . . .
> 
> In 1919 . . . [t]he main centres of interest in industrialised countries were in the armed services, particularly the naval personnel, and the government agencies concerned with internal communication, although as we have noted, responsibility in the US lay in the Department of Commerce.

23. Hearst (1992) has asserted that the early developers of radio did not foresee the public demand for broadcasting: ". . . the manufacturers of broadcasting equipment, who were shareholders in the British Broadcasting Company, expected their profits to come from the sale of receivers, not in any shape or form from the programmes" (62-63).
24. Schiller (1989a) has made this the basis of his analysis of how he

believes American business interests use privatization and transnationalization to commodify and make profits from culture.

25. The time at which countries with state monopolies on broadcasting began to open in a variety of ways to private sector participation varied considerably. The process began in the early 1950s in Britain, Canada ended its public television monopoly in 1959, precipitous action was taken in Italy in the 1970s, change was introduced in France in the early 1980s, and the situation is still developing in Germany. These variations reflect the influence of local conditions that are too specific to pursue here. By now, however, most of the initial monopolies are mixed systems (cf. Howell, 1986: 45-46; Blumler, 1992c: 24).

26. Robinson's (1981) brief discussion of media in the People's Republic of China illustrates how unrealistic it is to treat these models as categories that reflect with any accuracy all the details of any country's system. Her analysis can be read equally as an instance of the Soviet totalitarian or development journalism models. Furthermore, it is clear that without relinquishing dominant control, depending on its reading of what the country's situation requires, the Chinese state changes policy and, consequently, how the system operates.

27. This characterization of the situation in the United States is based on the facts that: (a) the media industries always vigorously defend themselves against any efforts at regulation by claiming that they self-regulate effectively because they share common values with all Americans and because they must respond to market pressures; (b) governments have been committed to and practicing deregulation for approximately 15 years; and (c) public complaints with the media usually are premised on the assertion that they answer to no one but themselves. At a more covert level, however, it could be argued that even the United States intervenes in the market by pursuing protectionist policies for its media and, hence, that it is libertarian only in the breach. The protectionism is most graphically revealed in its opposition to efforts in UNESCO to establish a NWIO and a new code of practice for journalists (cf. Schiller, 1989b). However, even if those issues had not arisen, it would be reflected in the government's willingness to accept monopolistic practices in restraint of trade designed to give market advantages to domestic producers (cf. Pendakur, 1986) and to exclude foreign materials whenever they disagree with American policies or practices (cf. Waldman 1988).

28. Keane (1992) sees this process as a "crisis" that is undermining the ability of states to use their media systems to promote domestic democracy.

29. Guback (1977; 1982: 346-349) also pointed out that domestic material can have the same effects as imports through the vehicle of funding. He identified a variety of mechanisms including direct investment and indirect investment through subsidiaries through which Americans have had roles in financing important European films. The assumption is that investors always, as some argue, or sometimes, as others argue, have a major influence on films.

# 9

# Contemporary Media Policy Issues in Comparative Perspective

The complex forces discussed in the preceding chapter are manifested in contests over international and domestic communication policies being played out in almost every country of the world. It is as though they not only are taking seriously Deutsch's (1966) concept of a country and Luhmann's (1990c) concept of a society as a network of communication, but have extended it to the entire world as well. Those contests are being pursued largely under one or more of three rubrics—privatization and the demise of public broadcasting, cultural imperialism and the NWIO, and the "Information Society" and "Wired Cities." All have been alluded to already. Although each country experiences and responds differently to the realities that give rise to these issues, most countries define their concerns similarly (though not in the same terms) and shape their responses from the same limited set of alternatives. Indeed, the last two are common currency because they have been defined and discussed in international organizations. I consider each of the three from the perspectives on mass media and the state discussed in the previous chapter.

## PUBLIC BROADCASTING AND PRIVATIZATION

Most analyses of public communication since the advent of the printing press treat the media as causes and social conditions or individual behavior, knowledge, and opinions as effects. However, proponents of public broadcasting usually view the media either as (affected) objects of the (causal) pressures of a public that is deficient in the requisites of good citizenship (e.g., knowledge, good taste, understanding) or as passive objects that unscrupulous manipulators employ to exploit and organize a naive public. Generally, public broadcasting proponents believe that the better informed, educated, and skilled the public is, the better the quality of people's lives and of society as a whole. Even if there were no other reasons for a state to be interested in controlling the media, they argue that the state is obligated to assure that a technology that depends on access to the public air waves serves socially constructive ends. In their view, public broadcasting is essential because, even if media operators and entrepreneurs were altruists who wished to provide only educational and informational materials, an uneducated, ill-informed, boorish public would not be interested. It would prefer to patronize and support outlets that pandered to their basest interests and desires.[1]

The belief that the media fail in a serious social mission when they distract the public from important matters is an aspect of a social conservatism that, prior to the French Revolution, promoted absolute monarchies as the way to assure social order and that, during the Revolution, was affronted by the spectacle of Parisian mobs. It assumes that ordinary people are motivated only by self-interest and likely to form an unorganized mob or rabble behaving in pathological and destructive ways if left without stringent social control. Most collective action is considered antithetical to social order because it can destabilize traditional authority as well as distort market relations among equally able, rational actors.

The state, in this view, must restrain mass action and, if possible, without costly state intervention, raise people's cultural level and understanding so that they will practice voluntarily the restraint necessary for social order. Private media in a competitive market are considered an impediment to this goal because they must rely on such an undependable public for support. Properly protected, however, the media can be used effectively in the ongoing struggle for order. Other supporters of public television attribute public disorder to poverty and deprivation produced by the excesses of capitalism and claim that ordinary people want and need the sort of materials that only publicly supported, nonprofit systems provide. Murdock and Golding (1989), for example, assert that public communication assures that poor people will have access to the information that they need to practice full citizenship. They argue that because private communicators will make their decisions in market terms rather than on the basis of an obligation to provide a public service, privatization will saddle poor people with information poverty as well as economic poverty, and this will increase political inequality.[2] Beyond supporting the concept of public control, then, the two positions disagree on every aspect of public service broadcasting (cf. Rowland and Tracey, 1990: 12-13).[3]

The public-private debate is a 20th-century issue primarily involving the electronic media. In the 19th century, the precursors of today's media were print based. In most countries, publication of newspapers, periodicals, and books was mainly a private activity. Early in the century, literacy was concentrated in the more well-to-do, politically conservative groups, and printed matter offensive or threatening to the state had a small audience and was more readily controlled. Presses and paper supplies were difficult to move and hard copy difficult to disguise, so surveillance and censorship was relatively easy. Late in the century, immobile production and exhibition facilities and the hard form of the film itself facilitated the monitoring and censoring of the infant motion picture industry.[4]

When radio and later television came on the scene, public officials were quick to understand that their novel features of production and consumption, ephemeral and intangible form, and universal appeal made surveillance and censorship of private media more urgent but less feasible than ever before. In the context of their potential for informing and raising the cultural level of the population, on the one hand, and their equally great potential for diverting or arousing and inflaming it, on the other hand, this circumstance led strong states to retain control of the development of radio and television services. Although measures varied, generally they included required licensing to operate a receiver, publicly owned transmission facilities, an independent authority and/or advisory board, broadcasting hours stipulated by state officials, programs produced by public employees or by contractors approved and selected by public officials or system managers, and, often, state ownership of receivers requiring license fees paid like rental charges. With respect to material, programs included talks and discussions on public affairs, classical music, theatrical drama, straight education, and news. Regardless of whether officials and societal elites had Machiavellian motives for prohibiting private broadcasting, the creation and operation of public systems was justified by some form of an argument that the state is obligated to improve both the quality of life and the capacity of people to understand, enjoy the higher products of human creativity, and participate as rational voters and citizens.[5]

In democracies, state control or support of broadcasting raises concerns about reliability and integrity because such systems can be subject to uncertainties that arise from budgetary shortfalls and to political pressures from within and outside of government. Consequently, some countries (e.g., Great Britain) mandated governing boards that were insulated against political pressure and guaranteed some minimum amount of funds for an extended or indefinite period. Some gave public broadcasting a monopoly. Others permitted private ventures but asserted the priority of the public system by giving it regulatory responsibility for the private system or limiting the private broadcasters' hours and type and source of programming. Except for the United States, then, in these countries broadcasting has been dominated by autonomous public systems somewhat insulated from both public and private pressure. Control as a field of interacting forces in flux was somewhat simpler for those systems than for the American system. In countries that have been or are becoming duopolies—the situation in most public broadcasting countries—the full picture of media system control is particularly complex because both the public and private systems have their own formal structures, in addition to which interested nonstate actors must mount more complicated, subtly balanced campaigns to influence them (cf. Flichy, 1984).

The discussion is intentionally phrased to modulate the picture of dominance of public broadcasting because public monopolies have been eroding for at least 15 years. The decline is manifested in several ways that Hoffman-Riem (1986: 126-134) summarized as a variety of shifts from a trustee to a market model, from cultural toward economic legitimation of the broadcasting system, from freedom of communication to freedom of broadcasting entrepreneurship, from freedom of communication to freedom to supply services and establish businesses, from primacy of the communicator and recipient of information to primacy of the entrepreneur, and from culturally based to economically based legal regulation. His intent was to capture a movement away from the primacy of public service as defined by the state's interest in promoting the national culture to the primacy of market demand in shaping broadcasting systems.

Accounts of how and why this has been happening reflect the arguments on the pros and cons of public broadcasting more generally. Proponents see the change as a triumph of the "yahoos" and part of a general decline in the state's ability to play its essential roles (Murdock, 1984). Some add that foreign imperialists—usually the United States—subvert public broadcasting purposely in order to reestablish hegemonic control by swamping local culture and replacing it with a dependent, cosmopolitan one rather than by employing overt aggression. Opponents see it as part of the inevitable triumph of democracy over state authority. They propound some pure or mixed versions of the libertarian or social responsibility concepts, argue that a state-funded system can only promote the interests of the state bureaucracy and/or incumbent regime, and champion market mechanisms as the only reliable way to provide the public with what it most needs and wants. Both accounts cannot be correct and, possibly, both may be wrong, but each may be correct for some countries and neither for others. Regardless of the merits of these arguments and of one's position in the debate, several facts that relate to the decline of monopolistic or quasi-monopolistic public broadcasting systems are pertinent and merit brief comment. They include the following:

1. The public broadcasting model was never exclusive; successful alternatives were always available.
2. Broadcasting knows no boundaries; most people have had access to programming that their own country did not provide.
3. Whatever models of man and of collectivities supplied the rationale for public broadcasting service programming, educational and uplifting materials have lacked broad appeal and have failed to attract wide interest and support. This has been the case particularly in countries with mixed systems or in which substantial portions of the population were able to receive and understand foreign popular entertainment.
4. Ordinary citizens who were not members of the cultural elites always have pressed for more popular materials in the public systems.
5. The economic problems of advanced industrial economies in the 1970s made it increasingly difficult to give public systems the funds they needed to satisfy at a high level of quality all the demands on them.
6. States that have economized by "privatizing," that is, selling off state-owned properties and decontrolling other economic activities, have lost their rationale for maintaining state control of broadcasting.
7. The formation of regional blocs to meet economic competition has required states to open themselves to trade with their neighbors.

**Alternative models to public broadcasting.** Public radio and television systems have not dominated because there were no alternative models. As noted, the United States did not adopt such a system and the first Canadian stations also were licensed to private interests. Moreover, except for the U.S.S.R., all the European countries had a form of capitalist economy during the period when radio broadcasting was developing. In addition, many of them allowed private corporations to launch overseas wireless businesses using the same technology, and American and European corporations formed subsidiaries to develop private broadcasting in several Latin American countries (Schwoch, 1990: chap. 1). Finally, as it has become increasingly difficult to fund systems that satisfy mounting public demands for more and different programming, a typical response has been to permit private interests to invest by advertising and/or by financing production. Because these alternatives always have been available but arouse great resistance whenever they are proposed as economizing measures during fiscal crises, it may be inferred that the view in most countries is that the broadcast media require extensive state control.

**Availability of alternative programming from external sources.** Early in the development of European public broadcasting, Luxembourg made a niche for itself by providing commercial broadcasting to people in Great Britain, Belgium, Germany, and France (Dyson, 1990). In Canada, where most of the population lives within 100 miles of the United States border, in the early days of the two media, all radio and television broadcasting emanated from the United States. Great Britain has long been bombarded by pirate radio stations broadcasting alternative programs from ships offshore. All countries receive foreign short-wave broadcasts and some, like the former Soviet bloc countries, were targeted by regular foreign broadcasts in medium-wave frequencies. The use of dish antennas for international satellite pirating is now so widespread that it contributes significantly to diversity of experience (cf. Ogan, 1989a). Regardless of the source, significant portions of the populations of almost every country, regardless of how satisfied they are with their domestic systems, have been aware of and had access to alternative programming.

**Programming on public broadcasting has not been widely popular.** The BBC initially began service with a single national radio network carrying the type of programming that constitutes much of what is now available on its Third Programme and on its BBC 1 television network. Its programming consisted largely of news, lectures on abstruse topics, discussions and analyses of domestic and foreign policy issues, concerts, serious dramas, and the like.

Everything was at a high cultural level. Such programming tends to lose its audience over time and rarely attracts a majority of the total audience when alternatives are available. Given this exclusivity, most national public monopolies have had to provide more diverse programming and open the airwaves to other broadcasters. Their publics have not been satisfied with an exclusive diet of culturally and educationally uplifting material.

**The public prefers light entertainment to cultural and educational programming.** The limited popularity of so many public broadcasting programs does not mean that people are not interested in receiving media material. To the contrary, people simply want other choices—light entertainment for most of them and specialized programming for particular interest groups, for example, ethnic and racial minorities, youth (cf. Saxer, 1992: 144-145). Only after World War II ended did BBC radio respond to the diverse tastes of the British public by dividing its offerings into the Light, Home, and Third Programmes. Since the BBC began its national television operations, it has added a second channel, ITV has been chartered to operate a third channel, a Welsh channel has been added, and a considerable number of regional stations have been encouraged to begin operations, all in an effort to respond to the fact that in Britain and in all other contemporary societies, members of different social groups and strata want different programs. By and large, CBC only attracts the largest share of the Canadian audience from CTV, independent stations, and American stations when it carries American or American-style programming.[6] In the past, several countries that used their media to promote national identity and integration jammed transmissions from the Voice of America and Radio Free Europe not just to block material that might promote domestic dissension, but also to attract listeners and viewers back to their national systems. Owing to audience pressures, the overall cultural level of broadcasting in countries dominated by public systems has declined because of changes in programming and/or startups of private systems.

**Recessions contribute to the decline of public broadcasting.** Since the oil embargo of the 1970s triggered severe economic problems, national budgets in the Western industrial nations have been under strong pressure. Support for workers whose jobs either have been lost to other countries or have become subject to frequent, long stoppages requires larger shares of their national budgets. The same forces responsible for under- and unemployment restrict state revenues. Eventually, these pressures have taken their toll on public broadcasting. If earlier appropriations had been lavish, current economies might not be damaging. However, partisans of public broadcasting long have argued that the systems never have been funded sufficiently. Radio music and talk shows, and television news, panels, and documentaries are common fare because they are far less expensive to produce than are dramatic presentations or entertainment reviews. Public systems' budgets cannot provide for more, some (e.g., CBC, BBC) because of substantial budget cuts and others because their budgets have lagged behind inflation and rising costs.

**Privatization and the rationale for state control.** The economic crises experienced by Western industrial nations in the mid-1970s led many of them to begin to deregulate their economies in hopes of stimulating competition and increasing business activity and employment.[7] Deregulation can have the symbolic impact of an admission that it was wrong for governments to impinge in any way on a market economy. Not surprisingly, therefore, just a few years later several regimes committed to minimizing the state's role in the economy by deregulating it and privatizing some or all of the state's enterprises were swept into office (e.g., Sweden, Britain, Canada, United States). Privatization has ranged from sell-offs, at one extreme, to greater reliance on private vendors to supply materials and services to state enterprises at the other. In broadcasting, the measures taken to privatize have varied. No state systems have been sold as yet, but many are being severely retrenched. Funding cuts have required them to cut their broadcasting hours and/or to go to less costly productions (Murdock, 1984). To fill the supply gap, for the first time governments are permitting private broadcasters to compete with state systems. In addition, many state systems have been ordered to curtail production and contract with private sources instead. Although the states themselves have not altered their ostensible goals as to the sort of society they would want for their country, the philosophy sparking deregulation and privatization (i.e., uncontrolled markets optimize welfare) suggests that the state should have a minimal role, if any, in reaching that goal.[8] In broadcasting, however, privatization and deregulation provide opponents of these larger state goals with means to oppose them. Moreover, ironically, permitting private operations has required an increase in state regulation and surveillance of broadcasting both for licensing purposes and to assure a spread or balance in the views made available. Thus, economic policies that suggest that states have no right to intervene in markets are contributing indirectly to a developing regulated market for broadcasting.[9]

**Integrated regional economies and public media.** Commitments to unregulated markets are not just domestic but extend to participation in large regional "common markets" within which there are to be no trade barriers. Europe '92 (Ungerer, 1989), the U.S.-Canada free-trade agreement, and the North American Free

Trade Agreement are all examples. However, only some products that will flow freely in a region fill national needs. Others duplicate domestic products that are already available or in development. Moreover, there are exclusions by one or another member to protect products considered crucial for making the society and national culture unique (e.g., foods, popular culture). Although this is not a major consideration in formulating media policies in the United States, it is in most other countries. McPhail (1987a: 262), for example, in suggesting future Canadian policies on satellites, transborder data flow, and related technological matters, began by observing that:

> A major underlying theme in the range of Canadian communications issues has always been that of Canadian identity. Both communications structures and content play an organic role in defining Canadian society. Few Western countries have struggled to the extent Canada has to define, study, protect, and encourage its own national identity. The questions, "What is Canadian culture?" and "How do we preserve it and promote it?" are at the core of Canada's past, present, and future approach to communications issues.

States strongly committed to developing a national culture and identity through the media typically have encouraged production and consumption of domestic materials and discouraged imports (cf. Wildman and Siwek, 1988: 99-116; Noam, 1991: 21-25). Such protectionism has been a characteristic strategy of neighbors that traditionally have used each other as threats in order to reenforce their national identities and unity (Barton, 1990: 125). When these countries join regional trading blocs, however, they come under pressure to discard a traditional cornerstone of policy—controlling imports and using the media to present traditional enemies in a poor light—and accept the principle that all goods can enter the country freely. They must act as if their new partners, even if they once were their worst enemies, are their best friends. Such radical changes are not made easily. Indeed, to make such changes as if they were of no special significance might even suggest that states and their borders really are not necessary and should not be taken too seriously. It is not surprising, then, that in negotiating regional markets there is extended bargaining to exempt several practices and items, and that media materials often are among the exemptions (cf. Locksley, 1987: 200-202; Garnham, 1990 [1979]: 208).[10]

The convergence of these circumstances has been forcing advanced industrial democracies to reconsider traditional media policies, but not along the same lines as Keane's (1991: xi-xii) project to create a new model of public service communication (cf. Burgelman, 1986, for several alternatives). Their citizens and trading partners are pressuring them to accept new products, and their responses to now chronic economic problems imply that they are unable to respond as strong states have in the past. Claiming to act in the best interests of the nation and its citizens, strong states usually have managed their media with one or both of two approaches. One is protectionist and involves stringent control of imports. The other is manipulative and controls the supply of domestic material.[11] Generally, public systems have broadcast much more domestic than foreign and serious than light material. Audiences were provided by restricting competition and choice. Banning private broadcasting buttressed state control of consumption. However, recent state actions—bowing to consumer demand for popular materials, privatizing broadcasting, dropping barriers to trade in cultural materials—lead in another direction. Every advanced industrial state is in the throes of a conflict between the policy needs of an old nationalism and a new world economy.[12] In McQuail's (1986b) terms, they must consider relocating their policies along two axes, that between public and private and that between cultural and industrial. In his view and that of Hoffman-Riem (1986), state actions indicate that most countries are moving away from the first and toward the second pole in both cases. After discussing France's problems in developing policy for new media that would not undermine long-standing cultural policies—and France is a country that McQuail considers to be moving toward the private industrial quadrant of policy—Miller (1990: 339) concluded by observing that "[t]he ultimate effectiveness of any state's communication and cultural policy actions will increasingly be decided by the vagaries of global-trade politics—and by the sheer might of transnational corporations." If free trade must be the cornerstone of future economic policy despite its erosion of protectionism and other established cultural policies, and if foreign cultures can subvert significant sectors of their population easily, then many states face major nonmilitary threats to their survival.

## CULTURAL IMPERIALISM AND THE NEW WORLD INFORMATION ORDER

*Cultural imperialism* refers to a calculated effort by a country to seduce other countries into dependency on its cultural products in order to establish control over them. The idea that colonial powers might retain or reestablish control in this subtle fashion emerged as colonies attained political independence. Mowlana's analysis (1990: 51-79) suggests that the dependent relationships that facilitate the process formed as the colonial powers involved themselves in the development activities of the new countries. The concept has generalized and now seems to be used to apply to any such effort by any country to establish its hegemony regardless of prior colonial relations with the targets.[13] The charge of cultural imperialism clearly is a complaint that countries lodge when they feel that they are losing their freedom of action. To apply with any accuracy, not only must the country be dominated and controlled by another, but also the agency of control must be dependence on the other country's cultural products. Finally, the intentional cultivation of cultural dependence requires satisfying several conditions involving cultural and economic inequality, the intentions of the other country, and the nature of cross-national contact. They underlie the possibility of cultural imperialism and must be considered in evaluating any such charge. However, before examining the reality and impact of the phenomenon, it is helpful to elaborate on imperialism and colonialism.

Unmodified, imperialism refers to aggressive action to establish control over an area, usually in the form of political rule (cf. Smith, 1983: 18-36). Ostensible reasons for aggressively establishing one's rule in an area have included bringing peace and order to an unruly area, removal of a threat, overpopulation, aggrandizing a realm by extending it, and spreading religion or civilization. Nonetheless, many scholars now argue that most colonial ventures were undertaken for economic reasons such as securing a source of critical raw materials and/or a population to provide cheap labor and a captive market for goods.[14] Because military incursions now are more temporary and, when they are undertaken, formal political independence is preserved, there are fewer cases of the sort of imperialism that was practiced until World War II. However, given the association of imperialism and economic exploitation, perceptions of diminishing economic autonomy usually are attributed to the imperialistic schemes of the economic powers.[15]

Ex-colonies consider themselves exploited for many reasons. Unless they have nationalized foreign-owned property, significant portions of their economies still are being operated with little regard to domestic interests. Regardless of ownership, infrastructures and living and working conditions generally are poor. As colonies, their capital was drained. Consequently, at independence they were very poor. Even if they rid themselves of foreign ownership, lacking capital, they have been unable to improve their situation by educating and providing health care for their people. Because they are peripheral in the world economy, their workers remain unskilled, their GNPs and wages remain low, and they are at the mercy of the foreign markets in which they must sell their products. Most of them have been unable to accumulate the capital needed to attend to their deficiencies and improve their position in the world system.

Historically, it was typical for colonial powers to develop one urban center as an entrepôt[16] for the hinterland and as an administrative center from which to govern. The geographer Mark Jefferson (1939), noting that these places were much larger than other cities in the colonies, referred to them as primate cities. Other scholars noted a considerable gap between the size of the primate and the next largest city. This is reflected in a city size distribution that deviates from that of developed countries in a consistent pattern that characterizes colonially based economic underdevelopment. In the urban centers that are now the primate cities, many Western amenities were introduced to make colonial posting healthier and more amenable for the colonists. To a somewhat lesser extent, these changes also were shared by portions of the cities' native populations, who also "benefitted" from the metropole's civilization by being educated to serve in the homes of the colonists and to fill lower administrative positions in the colonial enterprises. To encourage a sense of identification with the colonial power, some native families also were granted citizenship privileges and encouraged to send their sons to the mother country to be educated. The rest of the colony, however, received little attention. Its resources were extracted and little was returned. Often tribal, clan, or other traditional conflicts were exploited as a divide-and-rule tactic and to provide the justification of peacekeeping as an excuse for continuing colonial occupation. The combination of amenities, better economic conditions, and law and order in the primate cities attracted migrants to them and sparked excessive growth.

This pattern of colonial development has produced two totally different sectors in most of the ex-colonial countries. There is a large Westernized urban area with more amenities and modern goods, including the media, than can be had in other areas. Most of the rest of the country is a less developed and poorer rural hinterland. Life is harsher, illness more frequent, and medical care and education less available. Hence, the primate cities are a strong magnet for migrants, even if only as temporary residents trying to accumulate capital to start an independent life in their home communities. Because the large urban centers are no longer isolated from the rest of the country, many people who never have left the hinterland as well as the return migrants want the same goods and amenities that some city dwellers have. However, because of the rural poverty and the growth of poverty in cities that are attracting more migrants than their economies can accommodate, most of the people in these former colonies, rural and urban alike, are aware of and want but are unable to secure modern goods, cultural products, and services.

The countries are politically volatile because large numbers of their people are disenchanted and easily destabilized. People have an intense desire for foreign goods. Not realizing that the little they can purchase drains the country's meager funds, they become angry with regimes that can do little to alleviate their frustrations. If the regime is corrupt and wastes wealth ostentatiously, as is often the case, political volatility increases. From the perspective of the regime, foreign media materials exacerbate the situation by distracting people and making it difficult to mobilize them to address national problems. Given their feeble economies, poverty, and continued dependence on their former rulers for markets, goods, and services, it is not surprising that rulers of many new states perceive a new imperialism. Their independence becomes a bitter burden and not a boon when they no longer receive free technical and military assistance from the former ruler. Whether this new dependency is a product of cultural imperialism depends on the intentions of the dominant core country.[17]

After years of failed economic development plans drawn up in collaboration with lending agents and international organizations dominated by the former colonial powers (e.g., World Bank, United Nations development organizations), most leaders of Third World countries have come to realize that their financiers either do not know how to encourage development or do not have their interests at heart. The long-term strategy of Western powers to develop Third World countries by providing information and technical assistance was not working (McAnany, 1978; Rogers, 1978). Third World leaders now understand that they have to rely on themselves and their peers to improve their countries' economic position and quality of life. Successful development involves building on local advantages, deferring unnecessary expenditures, and sacrificing all but the bare necessities. It has two basic requirements:

1. Citizens must know where the country stands, the goals of the regime, and the nature of the strategy. They must accept these and be willing to do what is required. In most cases this includes hard work, deprivation, and deferred gratification, perhaps for several generations.
2. The country must preserve its rights to future use of international resources, even if it cannot use them now but other countries can. These resources include radio frequencies, satellite orbits, and the like.[18]

In short, it requires doing whatever is necessary to catch up and preserve the control of resources to use competitively when the economic base improves.

Viewing development as a long-term self-help project that mobilizes everyone to contribute and sacrifice helps clarify why poor countries struggle to maintain their freedom to determine how they will allocate whatever scarce resources they are able to devote to communications (Samarajiva and Shields, 1990). They want to retain control of their media despite the limits on what they can provide and the quality of the competition. It is true that, lacking cutting-edge technology and the money to put into their media, their productions often are unpolished and that they lose many of their most talented people to much better financed foreign centers of production. However, their concern is not to provide entertainment. Rather, they want to inform and remind people about what their development goals are, what is required of each person, and what has been accomplished.

Television and radio are relied on to get out these messages because many people are unable or lack the time to read. Most of the material is not well suited to these media, though, and is unlikely to hold an audience if more distracting, entertaining material is available—and it is, in tape or satellite transmissions of Western programs and advertising. If that material creates demand for unavailable goods and activities and calls attention to the deprivation, it can weaken people's resolve to persist at seemingly endless tasks that repay hard work with minimal essentials. Eventually they may become disillusioned with a regime that demands these sacrifices. Not surprisingly, therefore, many poor countries committed to developing and solving severe economic problems by means that require widespread interest and acceptance, unwavering support, and chronic deprivation would prefer that such programming not be available.

In addition to considering Western entertainment a destabilizing threat, officials in developing countries also are concerned that the five international news services do not carry the information they want their people to have about themselves and their plans. It is not considered news. They can distribute their material domestically, but they also want comparable information from similar countries to measure their progress and to let their people know that they are not alone—that others have the same problems and are making similar sacrifices. They argue that their plans and accomplishments are news, and good news at that (cf. Machado, 1982; Meyer, 1988: 17-39; Stevenson, 1988: 141-145), but that the services report only their failures, problems, and catastrophes. They fear that the negative imagery will lead their people to lose confidence in their ability to succeed and the rest of the world to look on them as inept and as unreliable failures, incapable of caring for themselves and, therefore, not deserving of independence or help. They believe that an emphasis on negative news influences developed countries not to treat developing countries as equals.

They are concerned, furthermore, that the problem with the news services requires more than simply gaining access to additional stories of a different sort. They see themselves and their media as complicit in the failure of the traditional international news services to provide them with what they now believe they need. Local reporters have been filing the sorts of stories they think are wanted, and the agencies have been transmitting back what has been used in the past, assuming that that is what is wanted. The local media continue to use the material because they assume that professionals in the newsgathering centers transmit only what is important and because their own users, conditioned by years of exposure to such material, have come to expect it and consider it important. Professional participants and consumers of the products of the international newsgathering agencies in Third World countries, then, unwittingly join in affirming their relative unimportance in global matters, their problems and insufficiencies, and their deprived position in the world order. Consequently, many representatives of the poorer countries believe that they need not only services that have not been associated with the established system, but also domestic media that will gear their editorial activities toward promoting their countries' plans and fulfilling their aspirations (cf. Matta, 1979).

An even more subtle aspect of the influence of Western media on developing countries is deplored by critics as cultural imperialism. Their concern is that journalists in Third World countries, either directly because they have been trained in developed countries or indirectly because they are attracted by the esteem accorded journalists in those countries, are adopting a professional stance toward their roles. It is argued that this leads Third World journalists to place a high priority on professional norms of objectivity and impartiality with the result that they become primarily peer-oriented and operate with a narrow, highly focused concept of what should be reported and how (cf. McCombs, 1988: 136). As a consequence, they ignore material that promotes development goals and report on social and economic problems without holding anyone or anything accountable.[19] The complaint is that the insistence of developed countries on promoting their version of press freedom and norms for journalistic practice internationally subverts Third World countries' efforts to create media that can expedite their development. The promotion of and insistence on those views by developed countries, then, also leads Third World countries to charge them with practicing cultural imperialism (cf. Katz, 1978; Golding 1979).

The emphasis on entertainment rather than on development news, the negative depictions of their countries by the international news services, and the implantation of professional journalistic norms are not the only disservices that developing countries feel that Western countries do to them in communications. Since the first space probes, core countries have been developing communication technology and applying telecommunications in worldwide commerce; peripheral countries, in contrast, largely have been excluded from participating because they lack equipment. Moreover, their hand-me-down communication equipment does not meet their needs very well. In addition, when peripheral countries must use telecommunications to participate in international business (e.g., monetary markets, transfers of funds among financial agents), they find that they cannot control the process and that their private information is accessible to others.[20] In short, they must participate in a world of media and telecommunications that permeates their economies and everyday lives with technology that does not serve them well and that they do not control. Every aspect of modern media, from the technology to the content that invades their countries, they experience as part of a diabolical effort to keep them in their dependent position forever.[21] These concerns led them, as the majority of member states in UNESCO, to request the organization to examine their claims that the gross deficits in their economic status and conditions of life were the result of colonialism and imperialism, and to support their proposals to redress and correct these inequalities.

One aspect of their efforts to redress North-South economic disparities was a proposal for a New World (or International) Information Order that would affirm each country's interest in what is available to it, right to determine what may circulate in it, and legitimacy of its measures against detrimental competition.[22] Essentially they proposed support for and protection of "development journalism",[23] the underlying philosophy of which is that ". . . media autonomy is not absolute; journalism simply cannot function as a totally independent and neutral factor in any society; it is always bound to certain values. . . . [T]he media should be committed to the overall social orientation of the country" (Nordenstreng, 1986: 185). Proposals for the operation of the media that were in line with that philosophy appealed to poor countries that felt that they would aid their development efforts and to semi-peripheral and core countries (cf. Melody and Samarajiva, 1986) that felt that their national cultures were being undermined or that their media industries were being swamped by imports. Indeed, Renaud (1990: 33), discussing conflict within the ITU, observed that differences among the economies and communication rules of developed countries now produce as much antagonism and disagreement among them as between first and Third World countries. Although such terms as *censorship* and *propaganda* were not used during the debates in UNESCO, in which the specifics were settled during the more than ten years that it took to adopt the program, the United States, Great Britain, and a few other countries based their vigorous opposition on claims that the program would sanction their use.

The background documents were being assembled long before any actions were taken (Eek, 1979) and their implications, absent significant intervention, were sufficiently well known that in 1975 Lent wrote that "[i]t would seem that developing nations . . . really only have two options concerning their mass media: foreign owned and influenced media, at the risk of extinction of the national culture; government owned and controlled media, at the risk of loss of freedom of expression" (135). The UNESCO documents included both claims as to what national media could do for developing countries and their people and compendia of information on bias in international media markets (MacBride et al., 1980). Data on trade in film, books, and television programs showed that most trade flowed from rather than to the United States (Nordenstreng and Varis, 1974; Guback and Varis, 1982; Varis, 1984a, 1984b, 1985; Mowlana, 1985). The imbalance was attributed, in part, to pricing far below what costs should have required. It was implied that exports were being subsidized and dumped in order to drive local producers and foreign competitors out of targeted markets. Data showing that foreign-owned theaters gave preferential dates to films from their own countries and that most of the receipts went back to those countries also were cited as supporting evidence that the media giants were engaged in imperialism. In addition, control of world news services by core powers—two American, one British, one French, and one Soviet—was emphasized. Finally, it was charged that media giants, blessed with large, profitable domestic markets, overproduced, exported the surplus, and used domestic profits to hire foreign talent.[24] In short, complaining countries charged that they were being inundated by foreign media materials that were undermining their programs and, because the market favored imports, domestic media. Talent was being drained off, and they could not afford to finance productions of comparable quality to imports. Hence, they increasingly were unable to attract their people to their own materials.

There is little evidence that the New World Information Order has done more than give moral sanction for measures that several countries seeking to reclaim their media and audiences already had tried unsuccessfully. It has, however, led the United States, Great Britain, and several other countries to drop their memberships in UNESCO.²⁵ Its rationale suggests that core countries have been morally wrong in exporting media materials and should cease, that they should divest their overseas properties and activities when asked to do so, and that they ought to provide funds, more or less as reparations, to countries requiring financial help to establish viable media industries. To understand how little really has changed and to make sense of the few things that are happening as a result of the NWIO, it may help to see many aspects of the program as a product of a Cold War skirmish between Soviet and Western views of the causes of and remedies for underdevelopment (cf. *Journal of Communication*, 1979). Each bloc sought the support of developing and nonaligned countries by offering aid on its terms. The NWIO, promoted as essential to Third World countries and appealing to them, was strongly supported by the Soviet bloc. Its scholarly support was strongest among Marxists, who attribute underdevelopment to the imperialistic efforts of advanced capitalist countries to extract capital and labor value from the rest of the world.²⁶

The NWIO, indeed, is a slap in the face to advanced capitalist countries. It lays responsibility for underdevelopment and its problems on them and warrants a charge that their commitment to press freedom is a sanctimonious justification for an inequitable system that permits them to practice cultural imperialism by controlling the information available to the rest of the world.²⁷ Its adoption was a symbolic defeat for the West. Regardless of their validity, these claims help explain the support of some Second and First World countries for measures the NWIO promotes. Among those already tried by some countries to control their media supply are bans on foreign ownership of media properties, requirements to purchase media material from domestic producers, and bans on imports. Although the NWIO, development journalism, and the measures taken in their behalf seem largely directed at content, they also respond to form, for exclusion of foreign material that profits from superior production facilities and equipment protects poorer quality domestic material from invidious comparisons.²⁸ Most poor countries no longer routinely acquiesce to international agreements on broadcast band allocations, equipment standards, and the allocation of satellite positions, but take stands in terms of perceived national interest. Several countries also have joined in international wire services to provide the sort of material they claim that the established services fail to provide. An evaluation of material carried by an 85-country pool established in response to a Non-Aligned Countries summit meeting in 1976 supported their claims of not having their interests met; only 22% of the items were of high interest to the major services. Nonetheless, it was still difficult to get the range of coverage the participants desired inasmuch as most of the material came from only a few of the members (Pinch, 1978; cf. Ivacic, 1978).

These activities have not changed the international media situation much. Media poor countries remain media poor, and media rich countries continue to innovate. Technological developments that are eradicating the old media distinctions may yet facilitate creation of the "information society." Most countries are crafting policies to accommodate them. Although the jury is still out, the NWIO does not seem likely to achieve the aims of the media poor countries (Stevenson, 1988: 75-97, 165-181). Partly this may be because the claims as to the conditions it is meant to remedy are suspect in several respects. A study by three Canadians (Hoskins, Mirus, and Rozeboom, 1989) concluded that the United States does charge market value for its television program exports.[29] Evidence indicates that the United States' share of the world trade in television programs has been declining for almost ten years (Cantor and Cantor, 1992: 101); Shayon's (1977: 41) remarks suggest that the decline might have been setting in even ten year's earlier; and Wildman and Siweks's (1988) analysis highlights several factors that are likely to increase the handicaps that American products will face in world markets. Cantor and Cantor (1990: 323-324), in an earlier assessment of the same issue, wrote that:

> . . . the concept of single-source hegemony applied to the commerce of marketing mass media is outdated and inaccurate. The distribution of American television to major broadcasting systems throughout the world did reach a peak in the early 1970s, but since then, depending on the market involved, its influence has either declined permanently or is in continued flux, varying from year to year [footnote omitted]. There is no denying that U.S.-made television and film entertainment is still very popular in most countries. . . . However, rather than one nation controlling sales worldwide, the world marketplace has become decentralized into overlapping layers of multi-centered regional spheres of activity. American business no longer finds it easy to "dump" products regardless of price [citation omitted]. Instead, U.S. distributors report that they have lost sales to two sources of competition: other countries exporting programs to the same markets, and home-grown production. Because of their more expensive look, there will always be a market for U.S. programs overseas. However, even though the number of stations and outlets to buy them will increase world-wide, each increase in local production and export capability also accelerates the decline of American power in the television marketplace.

Some studies indicate that rather than create wants and dissatisfactions, people everywhere interpret foreign television programs, including those made in the United States, in the context of their own situations (cf. Ang, 1991: 155-165). Still other studies report cases of the development of extremely successful, inexpensive, indigenous alternatives to media imports in countries that might otherwise be very susceptible to media imperialism (Lee, 1980; Rogers and Antola, 1985). More important, they try to identify the factors that underlie these developments. Perhaps the most telling weaknesses of the empirical bases of the concerns blanketed by the cultural imperialism claim, however, are captured in Mowlana's (1985: 66) comment that the research:

> ... has been concerned primarily with the examination of channels and content.... There have been no serious efforts to study precisely who makes what use of which kind of information at the destination level. Likewise, little attempt has been made to carry the research beyond... the media ... to examine the primary source of the message.... The literature on flow ... could only make inferences on probable effect or impact. Less emphasis was placed on exactly what happens to the recipients of information once they are exposed to internal and external messages. Less attention was paid to the dynamics of internal human and societal communication, and to the complexity of culture, in relation to mass media or other technologically mediated messages. Unless these factors are taken into account in a variety of cultural, political and economic settings, we shall have no more than "the conventional wisdom" and guesswork as to the impact and effects of information on individuals, groups and the international system as a whole.

As in most cases, solutions fail if the problem has been incorrectly described or poorly diagnosed.

More important than these matters are the assumptions required to believe that there can be cultural imperialism and then to respond to it. A claim of cultural imperialism rests on beliefs that cultural materials that erode independence are being introduced, that they would not have developed indigenously, and that they are there only by dint of the ill-intentioned plans of a foreign country. Studies of cultural change, however, indicate that foreign cultural material is not accepted unless it fits established ideas and practices of the receiving culture, or promises to meet felt needs. Generally, cultures are not so permeable that anything is acceptable regardless of its impact. Moreover, even attractive foreign materials are likely to appeal only to specific social segments of a country's population (cf. Ogan, 1989b: 242-247). Cultures are valued and protected by members of their societies and would not be so persistent or influential if they were that vulnerable. Relatedly, concern for cultural imperialism seems to imply that, normally, foreign cultural elements would not be incorporated into a culture. Most studies of cultural change, however, suggest that it is normal, that cultural diffusion is a major mechanism in cultural change, and that it accounts for most of the similarities across cultures. It occurs constantly without destroying cultural difference or separation.[30]

If change by diffusion is normal, why the concern with cultural imperialism? For some, it simply may be a reaction to change and to express unhappiness with the loss of long-established and respected practices and values. In that sense it reflects a social conservatism. Currently, however, at the behest of political and cultural leaders, many countries are being urged to develop and protect their domestic cultural industries as a defense against cultural imperialism. Therefore, it is reasonable to ask in whose interests the charge is made. Who promotes the responses and to what end?

In Canada, for example, where American television is often more popular than domestic networks and stations, why is protection of the domestic industry and exclusion of American materials almost a full-time preoccupation of state and cultural elites?[31] The conventional answer—to protect Canadian independence—does generate patriotic support. Nonetheless, despite the long pre-Civil War history of hostility with the United States, Canada has been independent for more than 100 years and there is no evidence of U.S. subversion or even of plans to acquire any Canadian territory. There is no evidence of a surge of Canadian sentiment to merge with the United States just because American media are popular.[32] Admittedly, the United States may want Canada's support in international bodies and Canadian policies consistent with its own. It has wanted Canada's cooperation and collaboration in defense ever since 1867. The Canadian concern for independence probably refers to the economy, in which there is deep interdependence and extensive U.S. control through ownership and trade relations. However, it is not clear that there would be a consensus support throughout the class system for economic warfare for independence or for other measures for freeing the economy from foreign control that many members of Canada's higher social strata would like. Furthermore, the situation is not unusual for neighboring countries, and the balance of trade recently has favored Canada. The facts are that there are cross-national power inequalities and that no nation is completely autonomous in the modern world economy. Both factors may contribute to dissatisfaction with other countries, but neither is sufficient grounds for charging imperialism, let alone cultural imperialism.

If inequality and interdependence by themselves cannot explain the intense concerns about cultural imperialism—and particularly how it impinges on the media and popular culture—in countries like Canada, then what else is relevant? I argue that the concerns of a country's leadership with maintaining the integrity of the state and its domain and their belief in the efficacy of the media for influencing how people feel and behave are central. Every aspect of the phenomenon can be seen in the context of the role of the media in the integration of multiethnic societies. Canada is a country to which all these themes apply.

Since the end of the Seven Years War (the French and Indian War in North America), Canada has been a dual (English-French) society. Until World War II, the arrangement was sustained by a variety of formal and informal understandings about the place of the French and the English. After the war, however, the inequalities and insecurities that inevitably develop between groups that are unequal in size and resources and isolated from each other led to a new, rapid escalation of Quebec separatist sentiments. The federal government responded with a bicultural policy intended to establish equity and increase understanding between the groups. This rather quickly became multiculturalism when other large ethnic groups and indigenous native groups began to agitate for equivalent treatment. In the process of formulating these policies, sensitivity in the federal government to the need for a sense of oneness in the population was renewed. Studies highlighted the facts that textbooks imported from the United States used U.S. rather than Canadian data, history books recounted U.S. rather than Canadian history, magazines were U.S. editions and if edited for the Canadian market inserted only an additional page or two, almost all successful Canadian media personalities moved to the United States to work, and the Canadian media market was dominated by American television, film, radio, and recordings (cf. Ganley, 1982; Hagelin and Janisch, 1984; Miller, 1988; Pendakur, 1988, 1990). Until 1967 and Expo, the country lacked even such integrating symbols as its own flag and national anthem. Its Constitution was embodied in the British North American Act and could only be amended by Parliament in London. Canada, by any measure, has been a country with a state, but not a nation.

Canadian leaders have always understood the situation, and, until Quebec's Quiet Revolution in 1960, had relied on an assortment of accommodative devices and techniques to hold the country together. The bombastic rhetoric about nationhood, loyalty, and patriotism that sometimes erupted on national holidays (usually British) and at times of crisis masked a deeper awareness of an absence of common norms, values, and interests. Even today it is a popular quip that the only thing that Canadians share is the fact that they are not Americans. Thus, it is not surprising that the Aird Commission's report in 1929 stressed the value of a national radio system for "fostering a national spirit and interpreting national citizenship," nor that the theme of not wanting to be dependent on a U.S. radio system permeated the discussions leading to the creation of the CBC, nor that the 1968 Act creating the CRTC referred to the CRTC and CBC as "a single system . . . owned and controlled by Canadians so as to safeguard, enrich, and strengthen the cultural, political, social, and economic fabric of Canada." National integration has been a major justification for every action taken to develop a state-owned public service broadcasting system in Canada. Indeed, during the campaign on the 1980 Quebec Referendum on sovereignty association, some people argued that the CBC should not carry any straight news items on it because to do so would violate its charge to "contribute to the development of national unity." Paradoxically, the 1936 act creating the CBC also provided for a separate French network for Quebec, and the 1968 Act creating the CRTC also mandated a French national television and radio network regardless of population composition. Such actions suggest a schizophrenic national policy on public broadcasting,[33] at one and the same time promoting unity and integration, on the one hand, and promoting projects that foster group autonomy and separate identity, on the other.[34]

Reliance on the media to convert a country to a nation can misfire. Several students of the matter (cf. Norton, 1988; McNulty, 1989; Babe, 1990; Morley, 1992) seem to believe that the chance of failure is extremely high and that the chance of success is comparably low. At a minimum, it is clear that the media need to be used carefully—with almost surgical precision. This requires their strengths and weaknesses for that purpose to be well understood. Ogunade (1982), discussing Nigeria's use of its media to build a sense of nationhood, made several pointed observations about these requisites.[35] He commented, among other things, that:

> . . . utilization of the mass media to promote national integration in a multiethnic nation must be founded on an understanding of the ideological orientation of that country's political culture. (24-25)

> . . . mass media always take the form and coloration of the social and political structures within which they operate. (24)

> ... a nation's political ideology orients its mass media ideology. It gives substance to the system of values which underlies the mass media's construction of reality. Without an ideology, a nation and its mass media have no frame of reference for reflection, no lens through which to see the world, no scales with which to weigh the evidence.... [E]fforts to modernize and expand mass media without parallel efforts to ideologize and indigenize their contents are a waste. There is no neutral or value-free communication since journalistic "objectivity," "impartiality," "balance," and "accuracy" are normally exercised within a political and social system. Thus, no truly neutral or value-free communication can effectively foster national communication (26).

If there is any validity in Ogunade's analysis, one can understand the Canadian concern with cultural imperialism and the media. He suggested by implication—explicitly in the article—that, properly managed, the media can bring together a multiethnic nation that is poorly integrated. When they are being managed for this purpose in exquisite detail (cf. Collins, 1986b; Watson, 1988; Raboy, 1989; Shedd, Wilman, and Burch, 1990) with little visible success and, at the same time, the country is inundated with foreign media products, as has been the case in Canada, it is tempting to conclude that cultural imperialism is the reason for failure. However, Ogunade's remarks would indicate that despite all the effort, Canadian media will not create an integrated unitary country for at least two reasons—the inconsistency between unity and the mosaic and the fact that Canadians subscribe to Western journalistic professional norms. The first has been noted. With respect to the second, Canadians subscribe to Western journalistic norms of objectivity, impartiality, balance, and accuracy and strive to achieve them. Under these conditions, even if American cultural imperialism, real or imagined, were to stop, Canadian media can be expected to continue to disappoint those who rely on them to transform the country into a nation.

These considerations are not taken into account, cultural imperialism continues to be suspected, anger toward the United States is generated, and protectionist measures and steps to build a national culture continue to be taken. It does seem reasonable, therefore, to ask in whose interests the charge is made.[36] The response, if successful, would create a protected market for Canadian cultural products and reenforce the importance of independence. Ultimately, both provide positions in government and the media system from which a few can control many. Therefore, the question as to whose interests are served might be answered by identifying the people who fill these positions. Usually they are people who have occupied similar positions or, if newcomers, people from the same social strata.

Indeed, supporters of protectionist Canadian cultural policies disproportionately include leaders of the economy whose business ventures would benefit from protection and the high-ranking government officials and politicians they help to get elected and appointed, and members of the cultural and educational elites.[37] They are not blue-collar workers or the typical "man in the street." Thus, rather than accepting charges of cultural imperialism at face value, it may be more realistic to consider them a tactic used by an elite to buttress its position. The charge serves them in two ways: (a) it creates a common enemy; solidarity and support for the status quo usually increase when it is believed that the country is threatened, and (b) it justifies the attention given to developing a strong national culture, for, despite any damage caused by suggesting that there is none, a dominant culture expedites rule by increasing predictability.

The Canadian case highlights the complexities that must be grasped to make an informed judgment about charges of cultural imperialism. Barring evidence that the United States or any other exporter of popular culture exports for subversive purposes, or evidence that exposure to imports undermines citizens' desire or ability to remain independent, there is no more reason to consider media exporting to be cultural imperialism than to treat it as an aspect of normal trade among sovereign states.[38] Meyer (1988: 113) on the basis of his study, wrote that ". . . NWIO supporters . . . who want to . . . [claim] that cultural imperialism is one of the effects of the neocolonial flow (of information from the developed to the developing countries), have little or no empirical support on which to stand." Schlesinger (1991: 144-150), after analyzing efforts at European cultural integration, concluded that the UNESCO position on cultural autonomy as an aspect of the NWIO is basically political rhetoric. He observed that:

> The ambiguities of the Unesco discourse, then, are these: the pluralizing tendency, which says all cultures are equal, requires the rejection of culture-identity-as-national-identity, of culture as confined by the nation-state. But the right to distinctiveness, to absolute autonomy, is threatened as soon as "a dialectic between the internal and external" [Schlesinger cites a UNESCO document as the source for the quotation.] is admitted. Therefore the logic of national cultural defence is uneliminable. (145)

In any case, the efforts to prevent the spread of foreign popular culture are unrealistic and doomed to fail. Culture is a distillation of long-established common practices and beliefs that have been legitimized as right and proper by virtue of tradition or warrant by sacred authority. If so, a planned culture is unrealistic and a contradiction in terms. Moreover, people adopt foreign cultural elements not just because there is an active effort at their source to introduce them via mass media, but because they are appealing. To appeal, they must be known, but knowledge does not require the media. Admittedly, the media may expedite exposure to new possibilities, but banning media material does not prevent exposure. There has been cultural borrowing throughout human existence, mass media for little more than 100 years. In the Canada-U.S. case, presumably contact will continue unless the Canadian government stops Canadians from going south during the winter or halts American tourism to Canada. It may not occur to the concerned officials to do so, however, because, as Mowlana (1985: 66) specifically noted, personal exposure and contact are ignored as possible alternative mechanisms to mass media in the studies of information transfer on which concerns about cultural imperialism rest. The emergence of charges of cultural imperialism may say more about the insecurity of domestic regimes than about the motives for media trade.

## THE INFORMATION SOCIETY AND WIRED CITIES

"Information Society" (cf. Lyon, 1988) and "Wired Cities" are popular designations for related developments imminent in modern electronic technology.[39] The first envisions electronic storage of all useful information in some central repository—in most cases a satellite—accessible to eligible users from their own terminals and employs merged satellite and computing technology.[40] The second envisions a combination of monitors with personal computer capabilities and fiber-optic cabling of urban areas—and, eventually, entire countries—that can access both entertainment material, as at present, and a vast range of information and other (e.g., banking, shopping, bill paying) services (Dutton, Blumler, and Kraemer, 1987a). Limited versions of both are operating or have been tried in most of the developed countries (e.g., airline ticket reservation systems, bank records, Videotext, QUBE).[41] The concepts also embody an expectation that their availability and use, as well as the functions they serve, will pervade every area of life. Combined with robotics, they include the indirect accomplishment of physical work. They conjure up science fiction images of a world in which almost all work and personal tasks are done at terminals, in many cases at home, with a minimum of physical activity and contact with others. Without robotics, they capture a sense of the ultimate form of a service economy laced with a multitude of tertiary and quartenary activities. If the technological bases are the media and computing, the structural analog is the library, and the functional analogues are merchandising and retailing.

The development of these systems raises serious domestic and international policy issues for all countries. Policy for domestic development is a subject for serious discussion in almost every developed country but the United States (cf. Wigand, Shipley, and Shipley, 1984; Humphreys, 1986; Dutton and Blumler, 1989). Their global implications are a concern of almost every country, although, again, the United States is an exception at least inasmuch as it is a nonissue for the public.[42] The issues coalesce around national independence and superiority and, therefore, magnify international competition to develop and thus to control hardware and software. The have-not countries foresee a world in which status will depend on control of and access to information. They fear that the present core will continue to dominate because it already controls the hardware and software, and everyone else will have to use their systems to deal with them (cf. Lyon, 1988: 105-122). The core countries also control the data banks that everyone will be using and have the best research and educational systems. Thus, they not only have a head start but have the institutional infrastructure needed to continue their dominance.

Even if nondominant countries are technically able to produce their own hardware (cf. Demac, 1986), most cannot afford to do so at present. If they fall further behind, they are even less likely to be able to do so in the future. Moreover, software for storing and accessing data will have to be compatible with that being used by the current leaders if countries are to participate in global commercial exchange. It is not surprising, then, that the fear of losing independence that countries are attributing to cultural imperialism is being magnified by the prospect of having to rely on the dominant core to store, access, and transfer the information they require to participate in the world economy. Again, it is important to note that even developed countries find it difficult to agree on technical standards for an infrastructure that would permit easy access and exchange among their information societies because the standards that each prefers for its domestic needs often are incompatible (Renaud, 1990).

These concerns are increased further by the possibility that, as data storage grows, satellite storage will be the only feasible alternative. It will be essential if domestic and international trade data at the firm level have to be linked for analyses. Whatever the reasons, it is quite possible that even sensitive domestic data will have to be stored in foreign-controlled facilities. That would raise a host of international policy issues. Does satellite ownership confer the right to assign transponders to clients? What safeguards, if any, can there be to assure controls on access to stored data? Given present inequities and their likely increase, what can be done to help have-not nations develop new hardware or software that might help them achieve some equity and independence? These exemplify the issues that require international agreement.

The issues have been stated as if this will continue to be a world of strong states experienced in negotiating in well-established international systems. That, too, is changing, however. At several points I have noted the weakening of the state and the growth of transnational corporations. They will thrive on satellite data storage and communication. Several already have more resources and are more involved in international economic activities than most countries. By exploiting advancements in transportation and communication, they are escaping state control and acquiring the power to control states. Their intrafirm communication needs have led some to set up private networks that somehow must be excluded from the rules and procedures governing other international communication because of the secret nature of the material (Irwin and Merenda, 1989). Halprin (1989) warned that negotiations over international trade in communications will create numerous unforeseen problems if negotiators forget to distinguish the problems in connecting national telephone networks for private exchanges from trade involving public communications. The development of secured private networks for private corporate use represents the most extreme manifestation of this distinction between private transfer and international exchange and offers perhaps the clearest instance of how TNCs can undermine state sovereignty. If states no longer can set terms for transnational relations in any meaningful way and if they also lose control of international communication facilities, then weaker countries will be even more unable to control their fates.

For most countries, then, an information society on an international scale raises many of the same concerns as cultural imperialism. The disagreements between Canada and the United States in reaching agreement on how to reconcile their different regulatory practices for internal telecommunications so as to expedite cross-border communication in the context of reaching agreement on free trade indicate how difficult it is to achieve unrestricted cross-national flow of information (cf. Aronson and Cowhey, 1988: 153-172). Moreover, the problems are magnified by the possibility that nonstate actors will be in the arena of action but outside the established system of states. They are magnified even more when taken in tandem with the wired city, because the latter could enable groups and individuals to access and establish relations with foreign interests without any domestic knowledge or control of the activity. To understand the implications of a domestic information society in tandem with a wired city environment requires elaborating the wired city concept.

The true wired city is one in which every receiver is interactive and linked to information nodes. The concept joins innovations that have been tried in several countries (e.g., France, Germany, Great Britain, Japan) in varying degree (Dutton, Blumler, and Kraemer, 1987b).[43] In the United States, QUBE, a system for selecting television programs and registering feelings about them while or after viewing, was tested in Columbus, OH (Becker, 1987; Davidge, 1987). Telemarketing promotes items that people can purchase by telephone. Videotext systems, developed primarily in Canada as Telidon and extensively implemented and evaluated as Teletext in Great Britain (Greenberg, 1989), vary. They can include telemarketing, but they also provide a choice of other services including the capacity to get information on such matters as locations, film schedules at theaters, and the weather outlook, to purchase items from select stores, and to register QUBE-like responses to broadcasts or to public-opinion-type questions. The only limits on what is available in wired cities may come from equipment capacity and the constraints of social norms, although Lera (1990) suggested that there are sufficient conflicting pressures arising from the concerns of regulators, market demands, technical requirements, and growth dynamics of the different markets that would be merged to raise serious doubts as to whether the possibilities should be pursued at this time. Given this caveat, then, when everyone in an area is connected, there is, in small scale, the wired city. In large scale it is the wired region or country (cf. Koizumi, 1990). In a whimsical case of language doubling back on itself, Pelton (1990: 87-88) referred to wiring on a world scale as the global electronic village.

The wired city has two major attractions. First, it enables people to do many things at home that otherwise require much more time and energy. It even may have positive environmental side-benefits if it reduces driving and paper consumption. Second, it facilitates democratic participation by permitting people to register their feelings on issues. There are, however, concerns that have been raised wherever wired cities have become a public issue. The most obvious, beside promoting laziness, is the potential centralization of power. Who owns the system if a city can be wired effectively with only one fiber-optic network (cf. Baer, 1989: 165-169)? Who decides what options will be available? Who words opinion questions? Who receives and processes responses from wired homes? Who decides who has access to what? And, if this means that such systems must be monitored carefully, who will the monitors be, how will they be chosen, and will they need monitoring (cf. McQuail, 1987b)? Furthermore, even if steps are taken to assure that operators of these systems are not able to manipulate the systems, user costs can fragment the public by creating an economic barrier that will differentiate subscribers from nonsubscribers on a socioeconomic class basis (cf. Greenberg, 1989: 90-91).

In addition to raising the specters of Big Brother and class polarization, the wired city also may have a deleterious effect on social relations. Opinion polling is not necessarily a democratic boon, particularly if opinions are uninformed and unmediated by discussion. If such polls are taken seriously, the fears of conservative political theorists that the weight of people's unmediated impulses will become the basis for public action may be realized (cf. Gergen, 1990). Socially, the wired city can reduce primary social contact and isolate people at their terminals. Just as the information society raises concerns that it will perpetuate, intensify, and rigidify national inequalities, the control and information processing aspects of the wired city raise concerns that they will have similar effects on status inequalities within societies.

Most countries seem to be avoiding the essentially political and social issues raised by these impending innovations in favor of addressing primarily economic and engineering issues. Discussions focus on such matters as the need for fiber-optic cabling, the size and placement of satellites, whether every structure must be connected to a cable system, the extent of the areas to be cabled, and whether competitive alternative technologies (e.g., dish antennas) can be allowed. The issues with political or social overtones likeliest to be raised publicly include the costs and methods of charging for tying into a wired arrangement and whether to permit competition among private cable operators. Ferguson (1986) noted that the fundamental assumption that the availability of the technology will generate its use is not examined even in countries in which the implications of these applications of the technology are of concern.[44] She pointed out that several countries have made major investments in the infrastructure required by the information society and wired city and have found that they fail to attract subscribers. The result is a waste of resources that might have been invested differently. In any case, the broader issues are not being discussed in the United States. This may be because such video services are not being promoted widely, and that, in turn, may be because it has not seemed profitable to investors. Krasnow and Stern (1988) suggested that investor doubts may arise from regulatory uncertainty. The present predilection of the FCC to let market forces operate because scarcity is so much less of a problem than it was in the early days of telecommunication may create doubts as to what types of systems will win out in a rapidly changing, highly competitive environment. Fiber-optic cabling of the country, or even of large areas, also has not been an issue. Absent state ownership, potential national benefits are not as relevant as economic considerations in the decision process. If wiring a very large country is less feasible and more problematic than wiring a small one, private investment in the project would seem very risky.

## THE STATE AND THE MEDIA

Issues such as privatization, cultural imperialism, and the information society dramatize the extent to which states and the pursuit of state interests can shape and have shaped every facet of social life (Smythe [1986] sees them as the expression of big business rather than state interests). Moreover, a review of the conditions in which states originated and that subsequently affected their development indicates that in almost every country but the United States the interest of states in communication is not idiosyncratic and arbitrary. It reflects a fundamental concern of all states with developing and preserving an infrastructure that enables them to maintain their societies.[45] Because the United States developed in an environment in which it was not pressed to compete with other states for resources and space, it was less burdened by situational constraints and tradition in its formative period. Relative isolation and the minimization of threats are a factor in uniqueness. Their significance already had been demonstrated by the development of the idea of free speech and a free press in England, even if it sometimes is honored there only in the breach. These conditions made it practical for the victorious colonies to consider and eventually to accept a political system in which state participation in the economy was to be minimal.

The absence of a strong state also has deprived Americans of the experience of seeing how a state may play a role in media development that benefits society as a whole. Instead, the premise has been that such matters are best left to the free market, which, it is argued, will provide the best possible outcomes.[46] Early state participation in economic matters tended to be limited to providing funds, land, and monopolies rather than direction, purpose, or guidelines. Rarely were state supported projects monitored. The pattern was to identify a need or legitimize a claim of a need, assure the resources to stimulate action, and withdraw. Regulation came only later. In as recent a case as radio, minimal regulation by the FCC was instituted only several years after the government subsidized the development of the basic technology and, even then, only when the beneficiaries had shown that they could not compete in an orderly fashion.

The three issues discussed here were selected because of both the attention they receive in almost every country but the United States and the unparalleled range and depth of the impact they are likely to have. If innovations continue along present lines, the future well may belong to communication specialists, and Americans are not being prepared to play those roles. The combination of the wired city and information society is likely to change the character of life and the very nature of social contact. We, however, only learn of it, if at all, through Sunday supplement features about people who use personal computers to work at home. The mass media as we know them and their social impact may turn out to be only a 100-year blip in the course of social development, but we treat them as permanent features of the social landscape. Any student of the media and media consumption patterns, though, knows that both always have changed rapidly and drastically. They are likely to change even more drastically with even greater social impact in the foreseeable future. The nature of campaigning for public office in the United States was changed in 1992 when presidential candidates appeared on TV call-in shows and morning newscasts. How much more will it change when commercial television is absorbed by videotext-like systems and there are no talk shows? How will Americans live without newspapers and their advertising?

This discussion has many of the same implications as the prior discussion of American media policy (see Chapter 7). In the United States, public calls for new programs and policies tend to be directed toward epiphenomena and to ignore major issues and opportunities. Earlier I suggested that Americans waste energy and resources in debating control of pornography or children's television rather than considering how to provide early childhood training for a lifetime of media consumption. The same point needs to be made here. A country's role in implementing the world information society is likely to set its place in the world economy for a very long time. That will affect every aspect of its people's lives, for the resolution of the security issues raised by the information society will impinge on the country's autonomy and on its citizens' access to goods and information.

The countries that lead the way in implementing the world information society will have the most to say about the controls that will be adopted to avoid its abuse and also will have an advantage in achieving a desirable quality of life. As for the wired city, cabling has launched it in almost every country. It is only a matter of time until an enterprising American entrepreneur launches a videotext-type service. Because the issues and possible consequences already are known, policy possibilities can be discussed, assessed and, perhaps, even adopted. The subject is ignored. The price Americans pay for thinking of the mass media as somehow separable from society and as entertainment with a simple, direct impact—ideas that will be increasingly difficult to retain with the pending innovations—is excessive concern with relatively limited, passing issues.

Having suggested the prevalence of few and weak policies, it should be noted that a contrary view holds that the United States has a strong media policy. The argument is that the government is committed to protecting American investors' freedom to do as they wish and that this accounts for its insistence on free markets and its unwillingness to enter into international agreements (cf. Mosco, 1979; Roach, 1987; Schiller, 1989b). It expresses one type of state theory.[47] The sketch of the development of the state to its present form with which this discussion began is shaped largely by the other two of what may be considered three types of state theory. One of those two posits a pluralistic society in which the concerns and interests of various groups conflict so that the state must monitor and modulate their relations. To maintain legitimacy, the state cannot operate in the interests of any particular group (although it may often have a bias or tilt). Its primary domestic concern is to monitor the allocation of social goods so as to maintain social order and keep the peace without resorting to repression.

The other of the two extends this argument. It notes that as state responsibilities and the number of technically specialized and skilled functionaries grow, states develop autonomous interests of their own. This implies that sometimes the state is the neutral monitor, as the pluralist version suggests, but that it also may act in ways that seem unrelated to the interests of any group. The rationale is that only the state can deal with other states and with suprasocietal issues (e.g., loss of the ozone layer and greenhouse warming), so only it knows all courses of action and their implications. In addition, given its essential role for society, it also must be prepared to act to sustain itself. From the perspective of either of these two types of state theory, the best that may be said of American state performance vis-à-vis the mass media is that there is monitoring and action when a problem becomes acute; the worst that may be said is that there is almost total, not even benign, neglect.

The third type of theory views the state as an instrument of the ruling class for implementing its rule. Because capitalism causes great disparities in economic and social status to develop, a structure like the state becomes necessary for the capitalist elite to maintain its privileged position. In the United States the elite consists of business leaders and the economically well-to-do, that is, the owners and managers of the largest shares of capital. The media are profit-making enterprises both internationally and nationally, so, it is argued, minimal domestic regulation and participation in international agreements is an intentional state policy that frees capitalists to do whatever they find necessary to maximize profits and maintain rule. Evidence to support this thesis, of course, is difficult to adduce, but its proponents do seek records of discussions and relationships to support the case that inaction or nonparticipation is intentional rather than neglectful (cf. Gitlin, 1979a). The thesis also would imply that, when other groups enter international or national media markets with products that may adversely affect capitalists' market shares or profit, the government will take strong measures to discourage or prevent them from doing so.

Comparative analyses of media policy cannot settle disagreements as to which of the three types of state theory best accounts for the American approach to this issue. It is clear, however, that there are no overt, strong policies and that they have been avoided assiduously in favor of self-regulation when pressure for state intervention has mounted. What policies there are tend to be reactive. The price of avoidance is public ignorance of the emerging big issues and excessive piecemeal attention to specific concerns of particular groups. Strong arguments can be made that successful participatory democracy requires an open, free, responsible media system. The challenge is to meet that need not by waving the banner of a free press but by assuring that there is the type of media system that provides the benefits of a really free press.

## NOTES

1. There is an extensive literature pertinent to these arguments. Most of it is country specific and may be found in the public media as well as the scholarly literature. The empirical base for such claims is to be found in public documents proposing new policies for public media. The MacBride et al. (1980) report, *Many Voices, One World*, and the numerous reports of Canadian Commissions on broadcasting, communication, and cultural policy are archetypal. The data are almost always interpreted as indicating that when commercial popular cultural material is available, they outdraw the materials the public services provide to fulfill their missions. Because the proposals offered usually involve some form of protection and/or reorganization and increased financing of production, the implication is that competition cannot serve the needs that the public service is charged to meet and that it somehow seduces away the very audiences that most require what the public service is charged with providing. Inasmuch as the missions of public services are always couched in terms of the most respectable and defensible goals, the implication is that the competitive materials serve less noble purposes.

2. Wilson's (1988) analysis is summarized in Chapter 6. Its emphases differ slightly from those of Murdock and Golding, although that may be because Wilson dealt with the United States and they are referring largely to Europe and, within Europe, primarily to England (see also Murdock, 1992).
3. The easiest way to clarify what is meant by public broadcasting is to contrast it with private broadcasting. Generally, *private* describes systems in which private owners rely on advertising and other private sources as their main source of financing. In all other systems, the state selects the mechanisms for financing. Blumler, Brynin, and Nossiter (1986) discussed several alternatives on a spectrum ranging from competitive advertising to limited advertising to sponsorship of operations or program production (the predominant source for the more elaborate programs produced for U.S. public broadcasting) to co-production finance to subscription to license fees. The differences among them are not inconsequential, and each rests on a different understanding of the purpose of public service broadcasting. The mechanism that connects financing method to purpose is that each of the former produces an audience of different size with different interests. Purpose includes a desire to reach a specific group with material that they will want for some reason, and mode of finance is geared to that group's ability and willingness to pay in that way. With respect to "advertising supported" systems, it should be noted that many of them restrict the showing of advertisements to station breaks and even to particular time periods. Programs are shown without interruption, even if they were originally produced to accommodate interruptions for advertising. The intent is to deny advertisers access to particular programming and specific audiences. Any impact an advertisement may have is restricted to viewers of the ad and occurs directly through it. It also means that the state's decisions as to who may advertise and how can be made without impacting on programming. Regardless of how public broadcasting is financed, its purpose is to take broadcasting from the open market and preclude *direct* private influence.

The discussion has focused on Europe because that is primarily where the systems that initially mandated nonadvertising financing are located. Browne (1989: 17) succinctly summarized the world distribution of the two types until approximately the mid-1970s by observing that "[a]dvertising is used as the chief means of financing broadcasting in North, Central, and South America and the Caribbean and in the 'non-public systems' of Great Britain, Japan, and Australia. It has been a minor but increasingly important source of support in most of Western Europe and in parts of Africa and Asia since the early 1920s." Canada, which has both a state-supported and private system, certainly belongs in the list of countries with mixed systems, but, perhaps because the public system also permits extensive advertising during programs, Browne may have included it in North America as a country whose entire (i.e., both public and private) system is primarily supported by advertising. In any case, Browne's dichotomy, although it oversimplifies and hides the details of financing of most national systems, highlights a basic underlying distinction. For more detailed discussions of the current financing of individual country broadcasting systems, consult Howell, 1986; Blumler and Nossiter, 1991; and Blumler, 1992a.

4. Proponents of the idea that the state must be involved to assure that the public media are used for the public good have not restricted their attention to broadcasting. Broadcasting happens to have been only the most visible target and, until recently, the most successful effort. In many countries, filmmaking also was targeted for many of the same reasons. Although there are celebrated cases in Nazi (e.g., Triumph of the Will, Mädchen in Uniform) and Soviet (e.g., Battleship Potemkin) cinema, John Grierson's success with the creation of Canada's National Film Board, a state agency dedicated to the production of documentaries intended to improve the skills and knowledge of the Canadian people, if not as well known, is a much more germane example (cf. Evans, 1984, 1991; Aitken, 1990).

5. Although the details of individual public systems vary, these systems were epitomized by the BBC (Burns, 1977; Paulu, 1981; Tunstall, 1983; Briggs, 1985; Scannell, with Cardiff, 1991). According to Hearst (1992: 64), ". . . it was to be the BBC's job to inform, educate, and entertain. No shorter or more literal injunction was ever issued to a broadcasting organization" (cf. Blumler, 1992b). An examination of its well documented early history is particularly instructive with regard to the positions of proponents and opponents of public broadcasting. Obviously, states as such do not create public broadcasting systems. They come into being through legislative and administrative actions that culminate a public debate. In Great Britain, public broadcasting was championed by an elite that also supplied the members of the House of Lords and many of the members of the House of Commons. Hearst (1992: 62) refers to them as ". . . the British opinion-forming classes. . . ." The chief spokesperson for the new Crown Corporation became Lord Rieth, a member of this stratum (Boyle, 1972). Peers (1969, 1979) documented in great detail a similar process in Canada leading to the creation of the CBC (cf. Collins, 1990).

6. There is an important exception to this generalization. During the 1970s, W. Brian Stewart, then a middle-level executive at CBC, conducted a well designed study that suggested that a prime-time national news program combined with extended features might be quite successful. Consequently, CBC put on the air its most popular program, "The National," ten o'clock every weekday evening. Approximately half the program was devoted to straight news reports and half to extended features. The program was almost an immediate success and long predates the McNeil-Lehrer News Hour and the U.S. television networks' love affair with prime-time news magazines. The program had two major appeals to CBC (as do similar programs for American commercial networks): (a) news programs are less expensive to produce than are most forms of entertainment programming, and (b) news programming is likelier than entertainment programming to serve many of the

missions with which CBC is charged. These include being predominantly Canadian in content; contributing to the flow and exchange of regional information; providing a balanced service of information, enlightenment, and entertainment; contributing to the flow and exchange of cultural information; and being extended to all parts of Canada. The program usually drew the largest viewing audience of any nationally broadcast weekday show in the country. Recently the program was moved up an hour and its format changed, with some loss of audience. Nonetheless, what is important is that this case demonstrates that a public broadcasting organization with a primary mission other than maximizing profit *can be* as or more responsive to the public than market-oriented organizations.

7. Perhaps it is more accurate to say that the economic crisis brought to a head or accelerated a process that was already under way in response to pressure from the public for materials that could not be provided under the mandate of public service broadcasting and from entrepreneurs who saw commercial broadcasting as an unexploited profit-making opportunity. Reviews of the end of the public service broadcasting monopolies in Britain (Hearst, 1992) and France (Wolton, 1992: 149) indicate this, and other reports in the volume in which their papers appear affirm the importance of these nonbudgetary factors.

8. Swann (1988: 316) suggested that privatization has been more of an ideologically motivated movement in the United States than in the United Kingdom, where, he argued, it is driven much more by economic considerations.

9. In his analysis of recent British experience, Hearst (1992: 74) observes that, although ". . . the free market ideology behind the 1990 Act was deregulatory in intent, other enactments moved in the other direction." The 1990 Act obligates the Independent Television Commission to award regional franchises to private operators. The ITC and the BBC, which have had the authority and responsibility to police themselves to assure that programming is not offensive and does not wrong members of the public, have no authority to monitor or interfere with private operations. Consequently, at least two new groups have had to be created to serve these roles (cf. Hoffman-Riem, 1986).

10. As an example of the devious ways in which resistance to the end of protectionism may appear, Shorrock (1989: 13) reported some resistance to reducing barriers to telecommunications trade within the region in countries negotiating to establish Europe '92 on the grounds that enlarging the market would invite U.S. and Japanese firms to invade it.

11. Hoffman-Riem (1986: 125) offered a much more precise specification of where state restrictive policies focus. His comments also clarify how these domestic policies can impinge on the international arena:

> . . . [i]t is advisable to differentiate between two distinct functions, namely the production of broadcast programmes, on the one hand, and their distribution to the recipient, on the other. Typically, the

market for broadcasting software has not been the object of state regulation in most Western countries. In this sector an international market has been able to develop without state- or internationally-ordained limitation or restriction. This situation contrasts with that in the sector of the distribution of broadcast programmes. From the very beginning, the broadcasting systems of most countries have been the object of state regulation. In these countries the distribution of programmes does not result from the free play of the market. National regulation has been the obstacle to the extension of the international communications market, which already exists for the function of production, to this sector of distribution.

It is difficult to judge whether countries regulate the market for production because it depends on whether states practice censorship, set standards for consumption of material by different groups, and so on. Moreover, there are indirect but very effective ways in which the state also can control production. In Canada, for example, the state has taken steps to concentrate production domestically and to spread it around the country. Moreover, through Telefilm Canada (formerly the Canadian Film Development Corporation) it participates in film financing, a practice that definitely impacts on what is produced. Among the methods of financing is participation in funding co-productions. Because government participation in financing co-productions has been increasing in many countries, Hoffman-Riem's comment about production may be too extreme.

12. It is pertinent in this regard to note that Renaud (1990: 49), in analyzing recent difficult international negotiations involving the ITU, concluded a discussion of the section of the accord dealing with nonconventional communication needs like those of TNCs by saying that "[w]hile recognizing the full sovereignty of states, special mutual arrangements can be extended for specific communication needs."

13. Cf. Stevenson, 1988: 35-38. In an earlier discussion, Boyd-Barrett (1979) referred to the process as media imperialism. McAnany (1984) has interpreted the development of the Brazilian television industry as an instance of cultural imperialism. He argues that the Brazilian system reproduces the American system because Brazil is committed to privately owned cultural industries financed by whatever legal means its owners choose. The local entrepreneurs chose to emulate the American system. Accordingly, the argument goes, because the system is set up like the American system and the American system is an instrument of capitalist class hegemony within the United States, it can be expected that the Brazilian system will play the same role in Brazil. The mechanism of imperialism, in this case, consists in serving as a model. If McAnany is correct, then cultural imperialism need not be intentional In the discussion that follows, cultural imperialism does not refer to unintentionally serving as a model for other countries to emulate.

14. Colonies also were established for strategic reasons—sometimes to but-

tress the mother country against attack, but more often to protect or service transportation routes to other colonies or trading partners (e.g., Gibraltar, Malta, Singapore, Cape of Good Hope).

15. A case involving communication that is not a very well-masked version of old-fashioned imperialism is that of SOFIRAD, a French government-owned corporation that uses a complex network of holdings in media enterprises in former French colonies and French-speaking countries to promote France's political, cultural, and business interests (Boyd and Benzies, 1983).

16. These were places where raw materials and goods for export were assembled for shipment and imported goods received for distribution.

17. Cf. Smith (1980a: 41-67) for a more complete discussion of the nuances of the concept of cultural dependence.

18. Cf. Beltran and de Cardona's discussion (1979: 60-62) of how Latin American countries have begun to formulate international communication policies intended to protect their interests. Ganley and Ganley reported (1982: 186-192) that developing countries have made a point of joining the INTELSAT consortium. At the time of writing, their memberships outnumbered those of advanced countries, 75 to 30. However, the Ganleys failed to comment on the fact that the developing countries controlled only one-third of the investment shares, the distribution of which is based on use. Demac (1986) identified several developing countries that own their own satellites.

19. On the other hand, after studying the Tanzanian effort to implement development journalism, Nordenstreng (1986) concluded that it was hampered by a lack of professional training among journalists. He realized the risks of professional training, but argued that journalists are citizens and, as citizens, have an obligation to serve their countries as they require. Because there is no such thing as unbiased communication, the country has the right to expect a bias in its behalf. Clearly, the sort of professional training that Nordenstreng urged would not lead journalists to try to satisfy Western professional norms.

20. "As international economic integration expands the impact of domestic public policy is reduced" and "information relating to citizens of one country increasingly is being stored in another" (Melody, 1987: 12). Obviously, the problem is not restricted to Third World countries, although core countries have tried to address it in other ways.

21. Lest the impression be given that this concern applies only to relations among countries, Haight (1984) and others have charged that domestic media policies in the United States are rigged to facilitate the maintenance and even deepening of the subjugation of the lower class.

22. For accounts of the development of the NWIO from its earliest formulations through revisions and final adoption and subsequent implementation, cf. Nordenstreng, 1981; McPhail, 1987b. The classic statement around which the debate raged until final adoption appeared in MacBride et al. (1980), but was available earlier under the authorship of Masmoudi (1979).

23. For descriptions of development journalism that are conditioned by very different professional and political perspectives, cf. Machado, 1982: Meyer, 1988: 17-39; and Stevenson, 1988: 141-145. Although they are not usually labeled as cases of development journalism, Bolivian local radio (Gwyn; 1983; O'Connor, 1990) and the PRC's *People's Daily* (Robinson, 1981) provide good examples of what media would be like in countries practicing development journalism at its best. Tanzania, in contrast, explicitly chose to implement development journalism in an already established system and experienced numerous problems (cf. Nordenstreng, 1986).
24. Negrine (1990) observed that British producers cannot compete successfully in the international television program and film market until they succeed in running a profitable domestic enterprise. Several years earlier, Collins (1986a) reported that British television production did have a satisfactory export business because an 86% British material requirement on domestic television had enabled it to amortize its costs at home. He concurred that British film producers, not being protected, could not enjoy the same success.
25. During the highly politicized struggle over the program, it also led to very negative press coverage of UNESCO in the United States (cf. Giffard, 1989). Consequently, many Americans may have been left with the impression that it is a wasteful organization that has no useful programs, run badly by wild-eyed foreign radicals who oppose everything good that Americans value. Roach (1987) and Schiller (1989b) see this as part of an intentional U.S. policy.
26. This is to be expected, given the parallels between Lenin's view of the role of the press (McNair, 1991: 9-29) and the conception that underlies development journalism (cf. Stevenson, 1988: 35-47).
27. McNair (1991:34) quoted Lenin as having ". . . dismissed the bourgeois notion of press freedom as 'freedom for the rich to publish and for the capitalist to control the newspapers, a practice which, in all countries, even the freest, produced a corrupt press.'" Shayon (1977: 53) used the more restrained phrase, "rhetorical issue," to refer to this interpretation of the free flow of information.
28. The distinction is the same as that discussed in Chapter 5 (127-128).
29. The argument over pricing is complicated by the fact that production costs for films do not vary nearly as much as the income they produce. Hence, in a country with a large domestic market, the cost of production can be covered and even a substantial profit earned before there are any returns from exports. In that case, exports provide almost pure profit and, short of being price gougers, there is no reason to raise prices to the level that would be required if there was still a need to recover costs. Because of the crucial role of domestic market size, if one took as an example a Canadian and an American film, each costing the same to produce, each targeted to the same demographic stratum, each attracting the same percentage of that stratum, and each charging the same admissions price, the Canadian film would have brought in only approximately one-tenth the revenue brought in by the American film.

Ordinarily, then, the Canadian film probably would not yet have returned costs or earned anything on the investment before exports. To cover costs and to earn a profit, export prices would have to be much higher than for an already profitable American film. The same logic applies to printed materials initially produced for a national domestic market. The issue in any such case, though, is whether the price differential for exports represents intentional price manipulation to drive competitors out of a market or reasonable pricing that reflects market differentials.

30. Languages are among the most important factors that protect the integrity of different cultures. Earlier, I noted that it long has been realized that languages do not differ merely by having different vocabularies and rules of grammar, but that they also embody conceptual differences that shape how the world is perceived. Thus, language differences interfere with easy cultural borrowing and assimilation. Negrine suggested (1990), for example, that Europeanization of popular media will not come easily with Europe '92 because of language differences among the members. The concern of English Canadians with building and protecting a national culture is stimulated not just by the presence and availability of the culture of a domineering neighbor, but by the fact that there is no language barrier between the two countries and their cultures.

31. The Canadian case has spawned an immense literature going back at least a century. Some of it addresses the general case, but much of it addresses the issue of independence versus dependence sectorally, that is, military, economy, media, and so on. The most thorough analysis of the issue with respect to the media is found in Collins' book (1990) and earlier, brief summary (1987 [1985]).

32. However, a national study sparked by interest in the consequences of what was then referred to as the Americanization of Canada was conducted in the early 1960s and showed that national support can be eroded (although the study could not really identify the reasons). The June 6, 1964 issue of Maclean's reported that 12% of the respondents strongly favored and 17% favored union with the United States. This 29% is probably the highest level that such sentiments ever have reached in the general public. A much more recent study reported in the July 3, 1989 issue of Maclean's in conjunction with the implementation of the Free Trade Agreement with the United States showed 14% supporting a more sharply drawn option of Canada becoming the 51st state. Other items in the study suggested that national support also had increased. However, the concept of merger has been discussed in Canada since the 1880s and is often referred to as continentalism. It rarely is proposed publicly, usually being reserved for private conversations among politicians, academics, industrialists, and people in the cultural industries. When Dick Collver, a provincial Progressive Conservative Party leader in Saskatchewan, suggested publicly in 1980 that it might be a worthwhile idea to explore, he was forced to resign his position the next day.

33. As noted in the previous chapter, Schlesinger (1991: 137) refers to such logic as a "disjuncture," a much kindlier word.
34. Canadians, in recognition of this apparent conflict, have adopted a notion of the society as a mosaic, that is, an organized, meaningful pattern emerging from and comprised of discrete, identifiable components. The problem with the metaphor is that observers can distance themselves from a mosaic and perceive both its components and overall pattern, but those who comprise the social mosaic cannot do so. Indeed, often they can hardly perceive the pattern of their own sector. The symbol of the mosaic did not originate with the government, but the government has used it subsequently. Schlesinger (1991: 139-141), without referring to a mosaic, identified the same strategy as being used to resolve the problem of creating an integrated "Europe" out of its many diverse cultures. His less than sanguine view of the strategy was conveyed by his reference to it as ". . . a formulaic solution to the tricky problem of actual cultural variation: unity in diversity" (140).
35. Ogunade's comments are pertinent here because Nigeria also is a multiethnic country whose citizens' primary identity is with their ethnic group. It is a country with all of Canada's national integration problems writ large.
36. If the past can be instructive on this point, it is worth noting Noam's (1991: 23) observation that "[t]he strong emphasis on national culture was largely the creation of the nineteenth-century nation-state, part and parcel of the aggressive nationalism for which Europe eventually paid so dearly. The identification of nationhood and culture became part of a justification for external expansion and internal homogenization." Although Noam succinctly expressed much of the argument of this and the preceding chapter in these few lines, he erred on a small but important point already noted. Nation-states create nothing. Their functionaries or those whose interests the functionaries serve do the creating. The issue of whether it is either of the two or both is addressed at the end of this chapter. The relevant point here is that either group comes from an advantaged stratum of the socioeconomic structure. In this regard, Barton (1990: 125-139) identified the leading opponents on the Canadian side of the free-trade debate as intellectuals whose opposition is based on their commitment to the building of a national culture. Globerman (1987: 13-44), on the basis of his analysis, argued that the adoption of protectionist communication policies to expedite the development of a national culture is really a screen for the economic selfishness of the protected industries.
37. Brown's (1986) earlier cited comments on what he referred to as "the policy-planning network" also would suggest this. The role of cultural elites is particularly important not only in Canada but in all countries with significant philosophical commitments to public service broadcasting. Collins (1990), whose judgments are informed by his research in several countries, used Canada as almost an apocryphal case. He called it an exemplary case (xii) and referred to its experience as becoming global (ix). He focused on Canada because "[t]he case of Canadian tele-

vision challenges both classic notions of nationalism that argue for a fit between polity and culture and communication theories that posit a strong influence of television on the identities and behavior of viewers" (xiii). In this analysis I already have called into question the fit between country (the political entity) and nation (the ethnic-cultural entity) and earlier have questioned the "strong effects" model in communication research.

It is appropriate that Collins called into question the application of the strong effects model to national identity and integration because that is one of the major rationales for strong public service broadcasting programs in countries that have them. As already indicated, Canada, aware or not, accepts that rationale. It is pertinent, in this regard, that every edition of the most successful anthology on Canadian mass media (Singer, 1983)—and it has gone through at least three editions—includes both an extract on broadcasting and national unity from Peer's study of the CBC and Elkin's (1983) article, "Communications Media and Identity Formation in Canada." Some academics clearly buy into these ideas.

I have discussed these points to show the wider relevance of the Canadian experience for the issue of whether the interests of elites are central to the emphasis on the role of media, and of popular culture generally, for building national identity and integration. With respect to elites, Collins identified them as primarily middle-class intellectuals who earn their living through symbolic communication (What other kind is there?) and who support policies that would develop and sustain a national culture (1990: 32-37). Schlesinger (1991) said that politicians and intellectuals propose building European unity by using the media to create a European identity and is equally skeptical of that project.

38. Noam (1991: 26-27) predicted, at least for developed countries, that there would be no Americanization of television imports. Rather, his likeliest scenario was cultural homogenization of materials produced by multinationals in which most of the developed countries would participate. His suggestion accords with my observation that imports have to resonate with elements of receiving cultures to be acceptable and potentially influential. If imports simply will be nondomestic productions shaped in part by a society's own representatives, then it is likely that in some respects they will resonate. There can, of course, be questions as to whether specific countries will dominate the multinationals and their products. However, these issues may be secondary inasmuch as tourists and troops stationed overseas already have had homogenizing influences that have brought the cultures of the developed countries closer together. The spread of the bagel throughout the United States after more than a half a century of being restricted to a few major northeastern cities may be instructive on this point.

39. Cf. Dyson and Humphreys (1986: 1-6) for a brief synopsis of all these technologies and how they enable modern media to cross all the national borders in Western Europe. Caron and Taylor (1985: 25) began their discussion of Canadian policy on cable by observing that the alterna-

tives being considered are framed by the larger issue of whether to mesh the national system with the basic North American grid. In an ironic contrast, Collins (1986a: 294-295) noted that the wiring of individual European countries was initially sparked by a belief that it would relieve a chronic channel shortage for over-the-air television that has bedeviled most small European countries struggling to keep their television signals from crossing too many closely neighboring borders. Wiring to support a domestic system has provided an infrastructure for a linked transnational system that can undermine both the conventional media as they were when the countries embarked on wiring and their national distinctiveness. Collins also noted that the basic idea of an information society arose as an adjunct of the concept of postindustrial society and was perceived as a way to make the emerging service-based economies profitable (287-291). He claimed that it began a competition in which too many countries invested too much money to develop their own systems (e.g., Telidon in Canada, Prestel and Teletext in Britain, Télétel/Antiope in France), with the consequent possibility of weakening rather than strengthening their economies (291-294) and undermining well-established, profitable media industries (294-301). Both the idea of the Information Society and the Wired City seem to be conflated in the popular concept of the Information Superhighway that is spreading rapidly throughout the United States.

40. Higman's (1979) discussion referred to an earlier version of the concept that focused on the role of various telecommunications technologies in expanding people's supply of information.
41. Leiss (1989) considered the information society an improbable myth.
42. This is not to imply that observers are unaware of the domestic social problems that also can develop in an information society, for example, inequalities in access (Wilson, 1988; Bates, 1990), centralized control of information (Brooks, 1990) and of the technology that organizes, stores, and conveys it (Schiller, 1987 [1981]), and information overloads (van Cuilenburg, 1987).
43. The authors prepared this paper for their edited volume on policy issues and the results of small-scale experiments on the workings of wired cities in each of these countries.
44. Swann (1988: 315-316) suggested that possibility for the United Kingdom.
45. This phenomenon is well illustrated by Collins' (1986a: 301) observation on unmet consumer demand for broadcasting in Britain: "Broadcasting . . . has not been constrained by a shortage of spectrum capacity in the UK for the limit of spectrum capacity has not yet been reached but rather by a consistent and remarkably enduring series of political and cultural judgements that the national interest is best served by restricting supply of programming to that amount that can be financed and produced indigenously." Caron and Taylor (1985: 69) rendered the point in more general terms in their characterization of European policies on broadcasting while analyzing the issues bearing on Canadian cable policy:

> Most European countries have inherited a centralist tradition in broadcasting. . . . While this approach is certainly familiar to Canadians and is reflected in the philosophy of some of it's [sic] main institutions, it stands strongly in contrast with the prevailing North American model. Centralisation is achieved by restriction, either because of the nature of the technology or through regulation, on the variety of choice available to users. Cable in Canada has been a predominant element in the enlargement of customer choice. Because of its capacity, and hence its voracious appetite, it has exerted a constant pressure on the autonomy of Canadian broadcasting: the country simply is not capable of producing the content required to fill all the available channels and to meet the ever expanding consumer demand. How this expansionist pressure affects traditional European assumptions about the national control of the communication system is a fascinating area of speculation; it is at least doubtful whether policy makers in the European environment really understand the tiger they are grasping by the tail.

With respect to this apparent inconsistency between a general policy commitment to centralization and more specific policies for particular issues, Blatherwick (1987) concluded from his studies that ideologies constrain states in their pursuit of their pragmatic interests in such areas as direct broadcast satellites, transborder data flows, and remote sensing, but do not constrain their choice of tactics to use in international negotiations on these matters. The difference seems to suggest that in the domestic arena, policy consistency can be interpreted as ideological blindness when short-term pragmatic considerations seem to call for deviations from long-term consistent policies. Caron and Taylor's comment suggests that at times the inconsistencies may not be perceived or understood. Collins anticipated that the Thatcher government would introduce ideologically based changes that would be detrimental to the British television production industry. His expectations were realized. This suggests that he and Blatherwick shared the same basic view on the matter, for both premised their analyses on a fundamental state involvement in communication matters.

46. However, studies of such varied events as the development of canals, railways, and schools have shown that the state has played a major role as an investor in the economy throughout the country's history. It also is pertinent in this regard to note that in discussing the long-term consistency in British state policy to maintain a program undersupply by restricting the use of available channels, Collins (1986a: 301) observed that the American government also has created the same situation, but in response to pressures by business interests that profit by having an underserved public rather than to implement cultural policy.

47. The threefold distinction that follows is an amalgam of analyses and distinctions made by such scholars as Miliband, 1969; Stepan, 1978; Held and Krieger, 1984; and Alford and Friedland, 1985.

# 10

# A Sociology of Mass Communication

The pervasive influence of a sociological perspective is evident throughout the entire discussion and accounts for the subtitle, *A Sociology of Mass Communication*. The initial analysis of the communication process was built on the concept of a social act. The model of a communication system is an analog of a social system. The inseparability of the form of a communication system and its components from the larger social environment is a basic premise throughout the last five chapters. The concerns of many Americans about the impact of the media are social concerns, and, finally, the discussion in the preceding two chapters of three major issues that draw the attention of people in other countries to the media but that are relatively neglected in the United States are all intrinsic to the social conditions of modern societies. There is, however, a deeper, more compelling reason for the choice of this title that may not be so obvious.

Because sociology is a critical discipline, much of what I have argued here may be provocative. However, I have chosen a subtitle that reflects that aspect of the discussion in order to reaffirm my belief that a sociological approach to the subject provides a dimension of understanding that other approaches do not. If that is so, then why has the sociology of mass communication or of the media, the product of the process, languished? Indeed, honesty requires admitting that it not only has not flourished but that it is almost a dormant sociological specialty. This is so despite the fact that in its infancy the study of the media was the study of mass communication; the sociological approach was dominant, and many of the leading scholars were sociologists. What has happened since is not surprising. Because the study of mass communication and the media addresses matters of wide interest, it has attracted people from other disciplines who have flooded the field, using other approaches to pursue issues that reflect other concerns. At present the most active people are communication scientists, communication critics, scholars of journalism, political scientists, public policy analysts, cultural studies scholars, film and video scholars, and philosophers and literary critics who provide the underlying rationale for deconstruction and postmodernism. This course of events is not unusual. It has been the experience in many specialties pioneered by sociologists (e.g., public opinion, the family, crime, population, survey research). Sociologists always have considered their discipline to be integrating. If it is, then every aspect of social action and order falls within its province, and none is so uniquely important that it warrants a proprietary claim.

This perspective on the discipline may help explain why it was that in 1948, at the height of his career and still very involved in studying and writing about mass communication, Paul Lazarsfeld almost ignored the field and chose "What Is Sociology?" as the topic of his inaugural lecture as a distinguished visiting scholar at the University of Oslo. In the talk he described sociology as a critical, methodological discipline relevant to any aspect of human groups and behavior. It should not be surprising, then, that unlike other early leaders in the specialty who came from other disciplines, he increasingly neglected the field. As he shifted his scholarly emphases, other sociologists also gave less attention to the topic.[1] Friedson's (1954 [1953]) subsequent critique of the applicability of the concept of mass communication may have been the final blow. In any case, Warren Breed's papers on social factors that influence the activities of journalists were the only pieces in mainline sociological journals from the mid-1950s until Gans, Schudson, Tuchman, and McCormack began publishing their original research and commentary 20 years later. Elihu Katz was the only one of Lazarsfeld's better known students who continued to publish original empirical media research in journals during that long hiatus. Wright (1959) and McQuail's (1969) short syntheses of the field were rare signs of a continuing sociological interest until the resurgence of the mid-1970s.

What, if anything, has been lost by sociologists' neglect of the subject? Largely it is the insights provided by the type of structural approach that is typical of sociological analysis. By not providing sociological analyses in that genre, we appear to condone tacitly the many analyses of the media by scholars, critics, and members of the public who attribute to the media responsibility for almost every aspect of social life that becomes a matter of concern. The prevalent stance on the media is one that implies that such problems never would have developed or would disappear if the media did not exist or somehow were different. A structural approach provides a corrective to this type of thinking in two ways.

First, as I argued at the beginning of the analysis, a structural approach makes it clear that mass communication in a literal sense is impossible, that the referents of the two concepts joined in the term are incompatible, and that it is misleading to use the one to modify the other. The concept of the mass only has meaning within the theory of mass society, although it is, deservedly, a serious concern. The mass society, however, is not a media product. An outcome of a conjunction of several social conditions, it undermines the integrating effects of shared values and norms and isolates people from one another. Inasmuch as it became apparent in the 19th century and concerned 19th-century scholars, it is a pre-media phenomenon. It is true that the factors that heighten mass society conditions can be magnified by the media, and that the media—but not the media alone—are uniquely geared to providing both the impelling, disturbing, novel stimuli that can trigger acting masses and the misleading, persuasive, falsely ameliorating messages that may attract the support of susceptible people in mass society to demagogic social movements. However, the media are not essential to mass society. The conditions favorable to the development of a mass society had developed and instances of socially disruptive mass behavior and of disorganizing demagogic movements were not uncommon prior to there being modern media. Preoccupation with the media obscures the fact that there are other ways to produce and distribute symbolic material.

A structural approach not only reveals the indirect ways in which the mass may relate to communication in those very limited and unusual circumstances in which the otherwise internally contradictory full term has meaning, but it also requires giving attention to the nature of communication. Careful analysis shows communication to be a sequence of related sending and receiving activities that require careful ordering and that, even when it appears natural, impulsive, and simultaneous, always places one participant in a superordinate position, at least temporarily. Thus, for example, when two people begin speaking to one another simultaneously, one must take command and bring order to the process. Or, for a second example, if two people in correspondence write at the same time, letters cross in the mail, information sharing is impaired, and the writers feel frustrated until they agree on an order. Even if participants are satisfied with the experience of communicating with one another, the process is intrinsically unbalanced and generates unequal power.

In brief exchanges this may not be noticed, but, if the process continues, one of the participating roles eventually takes a superordinate position. It usually is the position identified as that of the communicator in the communication system model. Although the power inequality tends to stabilize as communicator superiority and communicatee subordination, the balance may change during the relatively short episodes of action that comprise the process. Usually, however, because receivers seek some sort of satisfaction from playing their role, they must adjust their actions to the activities of a sender, regardless of how they feel about it if they are to have their needs satisfied. In that sense they are dependent. Senders, in contrast, usually feel that they are in control as long as their reasons for playing the role are being satisfied.

Senders, however, also may come to feel that they lack control when they are frustrated by their inability to assure the outcome of their efforts. One reason for this is that outcomes in terms of both understanding and impact depend not just on how communicators construct and send messages, but on receivers' abilities and performances, factors that are beyond the communicator's control. They also may feel that they are not in control because all symbol emission, whether for communication, artistic expression, entertainment, or influence, is indistinguishable and can be misinterpreted by receivers without the proper context. Therefore, communicators also must sustain the proper context if their messages are to be understood as intended, but that, too, may be beyond their control. It is not surprising, then, if speakers sometimes feel that they are casting pearls before swine or if mass communicators, who must maintain audiences to stay in business, sometimes feel that they cannot do as they wish. Despite the many exceptions, though, it is the communicator who usually has the advantage in communication, a process always marked by inequality.

The communication process, then, is fraught with inequalities except for the rare periods in which the participants may understand their mutual dependency. The chronic inequality is particularly germane to whether it is likely that the media will be able to play the information-providing role usually ascribed to them in a democratic society. If people have to be informed in order to be able to make decisions about how to participate, the intrinsic inequality of the communication process suggests that they have to accept a subordinate communicatee role in order to act effectively as equals in a citizen role. Except for situations in which a communicator requires something from a communicatee that will not be given unless the communicatee's information needs are met, why communicators who have an information advantage over the communicatees and may not have the same interests would want to give it up is not clear. The inconsistency between the structural requisites of communication and of democracy is a role contradiction that violates the principle of compatibility required to sustain a communication system.

The impending "Information Superhighway" may change all this if, as promised, the media as we know them disappear, and all possible information is stored in widely accessible repositories. It could be revolutionary in its consequences because it would seem to redefine the dependent role of communicatees. Acquiring the ability to select what is wanted when it is needed would mean that stored material would be converted into information for each person as each person needed it. That would seem to make the communicatee's role ascendant. The conditions for acquiring information would come much closer to matching those appropriate for democracy—ability to choose to participate as an equal rather than as a supplicant. This would be achieved by apparently removing the communicator from the system. However, this scenario is misleading. What we know about the relativity, acquisition, and accumulation of knowledge raises a question as to whether the very idea of "everything" being stored in an accessible place is a fiction. What constitutes "knowledge" of the political, economic, and social spheres, as well as of everyday life, depends on group and individual perspectives. Perhaps even more important is that people will have to know what they do not know and need to know, a skill whose development we have yet to master.

The issue of who decides what is to be stored also is central for an "Information Superhighway." It entails all the uncertainties raised by the *New York Times'* motto, "All the news that's fit to print." Is it "all?" The answer clearly is "No!" if one examines the array of material available in the universe of news sources. And who decides and how is it decided what is "fit" to be printed? Is the unprintable not news? The issues that bedevil current media news also are endemic in the superhighway. Although there may be no apparent communicator, management and decision making are required for both planning and routine operation of data management and access procedures and facilities. Control continues to be a complex systemic process, and policymaking continues to be a difficult challenge. The questions—who decides what is to be stored, what the bill is and how it is to be paid, who has access to what, how the hardware is distributed and maintained, and so on—do not disappear. In fact, because it seems that the communicator has disappeared and the communicatee is in control, the issues are even more critical if members of the public allow themselves to believe that they have been resolved when, in fact, they only have become less visible. The first contribution of a structural approach, then, is that it reveals the power inequalities embedded in communication and, in doing so, raises questions about how effectively the process can serve other purposes.

A second benefit of a structural approach is that it leads to a focus on the elements that distinguish current media from other types of communication systems. These include the large numbers of receivers, the elaborate organization on the sending side and minimal organization on the receiving side, the social and physical distance between senders and receivers and the physical distance among receivers, the absence of direct contact between senders and receivers and among receivers, and the reliance on technology to overcome these constraints. In understanding why media messages can have the significant impact attributed to them, the apparatus may be as important as, if not more important than, anything else. In particular, the features of the apparatus that make the media distinctive include their physical intervention between senders and receivers, the specialized and differentiated character of the equipment of each, the different skills and attributes they require of their users, and the inability of the receiver's equipment to send.

The relatively great expense of sending equipment conveys an aura of special expertise on operators, regardless of whether it is merited. This reenforces the systemic power imbalance in communication. The technology also impedes role reversal. In addition, because senders usually cannot immediately remedy actions that may cause receivers to disengage, senders find it necessary to develop a variety of manipulative techniques to hold receivers. When these techniques are effective, they tend to create addicted, and, therefore, basically weaker, more dependent receivers. These sender skills can be applied in any message construction. Because the content of messages also is determined by the sender and because the high cost of controlling a media enterprise selects out as mass communicators people from a higher economic stratum who share interests, this expertise in shaping and sending enables them to be very effective promoters of their own group interests rather than providers of the array of materials needed by all citizens in a fully participatory democracy. In these several direct and indirect ways, the structural features of the media increase the initial advantages and power of mass communicators and their employers.

Karl Marx understood the advantages of controlling the symbol creation process long before there were contemporary media. In writing that those who control the production of culture control society, he was not assuming a process that requires the media. Similarly, the Nazis mobilized a country behind their cause using demagogic messages and negative propaganda prior to television and other modern media forms. Modern media are not necessary to mislead, manipulate, or create social disorder. The desire to do so and the success of such efforts reflect the social conditions and the potential for power of those in a position to create motivating messages. The media are very efficient for distributing manipulative symbols in populous societies covering large areas (and essential for a modern state to maintain sovereignty over such an area), but they are not essential.

Symbol production for such purposes is not communication by our definition, however, because, given that the primary intention is to influence and that communication is defined on the sender's side by the production and transmission of material to reduce uncertainty, much of the material considered socially deleterious is not communicative. Furthermore, regardless of a sender's intentions, because the receiver's uncertainties and understandings are equally important in determining the outcome of a communication effort, receivers are complicit, to a degree, in the effects of the material that the media deliver. That is only to say that if Germans in the 1930s had been deeply committed to equality and democratic process, they would not have acquiesced to the Nazis' goals or their methods of achieving them.

The insights that derive from a structural approach to mass communication have important policy implications. They suggest that efforts to resolve problems by censoring the media or to pressure the media to become more informational and reliable as an essential step in creating a more equitable and democratic society are misdirected. The structures of mass communication as a process and the media as an institutionalized system are intrinsically inequitable, undemocratic, and noninformational.[2] Communicators behave as they do because of their commitment to their own interests, the demands receivers place on them, and the demands of the larger social environment in which they act. The media fail to meet our expectations as contributors to public knowledge and rationality not only because those that control them may not wish to or because it has not been tried, but for two additional reasons: (a) their intrinsic power imbalances do not suit them for such a role, and (b) the outcome of their performance, in addition to being shaped by what they provide, depends on attracting receivers and on how those receivers perceive the material. This is no defense of the media. It is only to direct attention to the systemic roots of their failure to serve social needs. If we misconstrue the character of what we assume to be the source and consider the media to be an ideal vehicle for making democracy work, we are fated to be disappointed. (See Calhoun [1988, 1992] for a more thoroughly theorized, somewhat similar argument.)

The inappropriateness of the media for socially and politically constructive roles certainly does not mean that they are trivial. As Innis, McLuhan, Meyrowitz, Zaret, and others have noted, any medium reorganizes the established social system of power when it is introduced. The introduction of any new communication medium occasions major social change. As for the mass media, there would be little chance for large countries with large populations to be democratic, participatory polities were it not for the availability of easily accessible systems of communication capable of reaching everyone almost instantly with the same material. Certainly, if in no other respect than accessibility for receiving, up to this time the media are the most equalitarian communication systems available to societies. If they cannot create effective democracy, under the proper circumstances they can play a role in sustaining established democracy. It does not take away from their importance to say that the assumptions that underlie many ideas about what the media do, can do, and should do in a democracy are misconceptions. If we expect the media to provide adequate, unbiased information, we are making a mistake. That is impossible in the best of worlds. If we are concerned that they create violence, we are talking about a marginal effect. We would have violence anyway. The implication of the media being in society rather than acting on society is that it calls into question the idea that *they* are transforming us and, instead, reminds us that they express, as does every aspect of public life, the sorts of values, desires, conflicts, and motivations that we already hold.

The values reflected in our behavior and the problems in modern society would not disappear automatically if modern media were removed. As noted, the various totalitarian political movements of this century were neither invented nor sold by the media, even if the media were used to expedite their causes after they did acquire power. Nineteenth-century Victorians did not need film and television to wallow in pornography and erotica. The media certainly may be guilty of providing distracting alternatives to dissatisfied, unhappy people, but they do not produce the initial unhappiness or dissatisfaction. American students may not learn much in school and they may watch too much television, but the latter does not cause the former. Countries whose students attain better achievement test scores than ours have television; they also could be wasting their time in front of television screens, but they are not. Western film and television may make people in poor, developing countries unhappy, but they are not the cause of their objective situations, nor would their conditions improve if they could not see unattainable alternatives. Modern media by themselves are not responsible for these things.

The popular belief is that the media can be a vehicle for achieving a rational, participatory, informed, democratic society. Although a structural (that is, a sociological) analysis implies that the goal is incompatible with their structure, the nature of communication as a process, and information as an entity, that does not mean that the goal is not laudatory. It simply indicates that use and control of the media for this purpose is not the way to go. Social structure and social process need to be addressed directly. Effective efforts for these purposes require clarity about our values and how they might be changed and promoted. Scholars in cultural studies, postmodernists included, are right to study the media as indicators of the character of our culture because they are part of that culture. The media seem responsible for creating material that shapes culture; they really are giving voice to what already is there. That is the implication of the fact that cultural imperialism only is an issue when "intrusive, foreign" material resonates with the already existing values of the receiving society.

A structural approach is enlightening for American preoccupation with censorship and First Amendment rights because it requires a definition of communication. A clear definition inevitably will highlight the differences between communication and other types of symbolic creation and expression. Traditionally, the determination of the difference has been relegated to the courts, which have established boundaries in the course of rendering decisions about what can and cannot be restricted. However, because analysis of the evolution of modern, participatory government shows that such a system requires free communication to enable its citizens to engage in responsible political behavior, the free and uncontrolled provision and circulation of information pertinent to public issues is justified, regardless of how a court may decide in a case. Such analyses also justify the provision of alternative ideas and opinions as information about positions that might be taken on those issues. They do not justify emotional or misleading or demagogic appeals for political acts. Americans have reached the point of banning and penalizing false advertising. We have not been willing to make similar distinctions between information and political material, on the one hand, and between information and the cultural material that the media convey, on the other.

The rationale that led to a commitment to press freedom, freedom of speech, and the associated First Amendment rights was not meant to apply to all forms of symbolic production. Indeed, at the time, most symbolic production was in the private sphere, and the expression and distribution of symbolic material that did not attack the state's existence was not an issue for the state. Attacks on regimes, of course, were an issue, but only because regimes are the manifestation of the state and because its members want to keep their position. People have a right to produce cultural material in the private sphere, but whether they are permitted to exercise it or share the product is governed by informal social processes. This certainly applies to the mass cultural materials that pervade the media. Although there is no denying that strong conservative forces always have opposed the production and distribution of material that calls the established order into question, it is possible using recent developments in media technology to produce such material but restrict access to it to those who qualify as having a legitimate interest in it. Until now, easy accessibility has made the availability of such material a matter of public interest and, hence, has brought it within the province of the courts. The new media can obviate that situation.

In the meantime, though, news items during the final days of work on this book testify to the extent to which the media and their activities are not oriented to communication in the sense in which the First Amendment was framed. There are gripping reports of a contest between a home shopping television network and a large cable operator for purchase of Paramount Pictures; there is a National Public Radio report on Star Broadcasting Company and its business of providing commercial radio to public high schools (400 already use it) with a stated purpose of fostering in teenagers habits of consumption and brand loyalty; there are reports of conflicts between over-the-air broadcasters and cable system operators as to whether cable systems should pay over-the-air broadcasters for using their signals; and there are reports of people who make off with copies of publications committed to promoting a particular political agenda. The first three cases place the media in the role of influencer and entertainer and the motivating underlying issue in each case is profit—not playing a communicator's role. Only the last case may involve communication, and it is marginal inasmuch as the publications at issue make a point of providing material only from one political perspective. If nothing else, the media, by virtue of their emphasis on entertainment and influence and their neglect of communication, are risking their status as claimants to First Amendment protection for communicators.

It is unlikely that the courts in the United States will stop rendering decisions on free speech and press freedom just because a sociologist proposes definitions to distinguish communication from other forms of symbolic expression and conveyance. Nor is it likely that courts will be swayed by an argument that there was no intention to protect all symbolic production other than informational material and, therefore, that noninformational material is subject to social control without recourse to legal protection. If this position takes hold some day, it is important to understand that the argument does not justify restricting the production of any symbolic material. It may be used by some to justify efforts to restrict the distribution of some noninformational material. Admittedly, the distinction between information and other varieties of symbolic material, the consequences of restricted access for a freedom to express ideas and concepts privately, and the specification of who has a legitimate interest in accessing material whose general distribution has been restricted are all ambiguous issues that will continue to require clarification. However, they are precisely the types of issues that public discussion and the courts are helpful and competent to resolve.

This argument would seem to justify conditional restraints on the distribution and receipt of symbolic expressions. It does not justify any restriction on their production. However, it also should have made it clear that the reasons for needing external controls lie within us. They express our own shortcomings and errors. We have bought into the view that today's media are the press that is to be the beneficiary of the First Amendment. The industry's executives have been perspicacious enough to grab the idea and promote it. Moreover, we have accepted their interpretation of the freedoms of speech and the press as their freedom to engage in symbol production, as well as their corollary claim that this insures the availability of the widest possible variety of information. We have failed to understand that by doing so we have defaulted on our right to be informed. That right is lost because we become oblivious to the fact that free choice means free choice from among only the alternatives the market provides. We seem unaware that free markets can restrict as well as widen choices and that there is no mechanism to assure a wide enough choice. So long as the choices are narrow and media users do not realize it, restrictions on access may not have the deleterious consequences that opponents to controlled access claim. Restrictions would have dire consequences in a system in which the variety of available material was as wide as possible (cf. Keane, 1991; Neuman, 1991).

Our growing concerns about the media are exacerbated by our willingness, on the one hand, to accept uncritically the claim that they are essential to democracy because they monitor the environment and inform the public and, on the other hand, to hold them responsible for every undesirable aspect of contemporary life. In either case, we aggrandize them and become complicit in heightening their status and power. If we were simply to consider the media to be entertainment industries rather than information providers and treat them as providing fictive material, we would behave very differently toward them. We would not rely on them for information or guidance. We would not treat them as trustworthy. We would not see them as some omnipotent entity that rules over us and accounts for everything that concerns us in our society. Not only would we feel free to control them and our consumption of them, but we would be less distracted by what they provide and, perhaps, more able to focus on the communication and information issues that do affect our futures. Moreover, there is no reason to believe that we cannot learn how to produce, transmit, and receive symbolic expression of all kinds with enough facility that we do not feel threatened by or wish to repress any of it. Doing that also makes a right to communicate fully meaningful. Our ability to develop and practice these skills is a function of the sort of society in which we live. We and only we can create that environment. If we get on with these tasks, we can be discriminating and effective participants in public and private communication who do not have to rely on courts to decide what we have a right to distribute and access.

## NOTES

1. This comment is not meant to imply that the activities of one person can account for the status of sociological specialties. This was the period just after the Axis powers had been defeated; there was a great deal of optimism and the problems of mass society—mass communication, alienation, unemployment—no longer seemed as imminent. Instead, the prejudice and discrimination that underlay the Nazis' success in Germany and that plagued race relations in the United States, the emerging international polarization between a Communist-dominated Eastern Europe and China and a capitalist West, and issues integral to the reconstruction that followed a major world depression and war were drawing the attention of social scientists. In addition, the "no effects" position on the role of the media that was dominant at the time well may have contributed to a feeling that mass communication and the media, although interesting and glamorous, did not merit the attention of scholars whose goal was to develop a broader understanding of society. Nevertheless, major figures do attract colleagues to a specialty if their own work in the area is producing seminal contributions to the discipline.
2. Morgan (1989) drew this conclusion about television in particular rather than about the media in general.

# References

Adorno, T. W. and M. Horkheimer
    1972    "The Culture Industry: Enlightenment as Mass Deception." Pp. 120-167 in T. W. Adorno and M. Horkheimer, *Dialectic of Enlightenment*. New York: Seabury.

Afanasiev, Viktor
    1990    [1982] "Some Facts about Pravda." Pp. 212-213 in L. John Martin and Ray Eldon Hiebert (eds.), *Current Issues in International Communication*. New York: Longman.

Aitken, Ian
    1990    *Film and Reform: John Grierson and the Documentary Film Movement*. London: Routledge.

Alford, Robert R. and Roger Friedland
    1985    *Powers of Theory: Capitalism, the State, and Democracy*. New York: Cambridge.

Allen, Irving Lewis
    1977    "Social Integration as an Organizing Principle." Pp. 235-250 in George Gerbner (ed.), *Mass Media Policies in Changing Cultures*. New York: Wiley.

Allen, Robert C.
    1987    *Channels of Discourse*. Chapel Hill: University of North Carolina Press.

Anderson, Alun
    1991    "BA Meets in Plymouth on Dinosaurs' Birthday: Video-Tunneling to School," *Science* 253(September 6): 1090.

Andrews, Edmund L.
    1993    "Educational TV?" *Raleigh News and Observer* March 7: 17A.

Ang, Ien
    1989    "Wanted: Audiences: On the Politics of Empirical Audience Studies." Pp. 96-115 in Ellen Seiter, Hans Borchers, Gabriele Kreutzner, and Eva-Maria Warth (eds.), *Remote Control: Television, Audiences, and Cultural Power*. London: Routledge.
    1991    *Desperately Seeking the Audience*. London: Routledge.

Anger, K.
    1975    *Hollywood Babylon*. New York: Dell.

Argyle, Michael
    1977    "Nonverbal Communication and Language." Pp. 63-78 in George Vesey (ed.), *Communication and Understanding*. Sussex: Harvester.

Arnheim, Rudolf
    1944    "The World of the Daytime Serial." Pp. 34-107 in Paul F. Lazarsfeld and Frank Stanton (eds.), *Radio Research 1942-1943*. New York: Duell, Sloan and Pearce.

Aronson, David and Peter F. Cowhey
    1988    *When Countries Talk: International Trade in Telecommunications Services*. Cambridge, MA: Ballinger.

Associated Press
    1990a    "Videos Not the Same," *Durham Morning Herald* July 11: A2.
    1190b    "Reluctantly, Bush Lets Child Television Act Become Law," *Durham Sun October* 22: 3B.
    1991    "SATs May Continue to Lag, Education Officials Predict," *Durham Herald-Sun* August 28: A1.
    1992    "Group Attempts Overthrow," *Raleigh News and Observer* July 30: 12A.

Atwood, L. Erwin and Stuart J. Bullion
    1982    "News Maps of the World: A View from Asia." Pp. 102-130 in L. Erwin Atwood, Stewart J. Bullion, and Sharon M. Murphy (eds.), *International Perspectives in News*. Carbondale: Southern Illinois University Press.

Audley, Paul
    1983    *Canada's Cultural Industries: Broadcasting, Publishing, Records, and Film*. Toronto: James Lorimer.

Austin, Bruce A.
    1986    "The Film Industry, Its Audience, and New Communication Technologies." Pp. 80-116 in Bruce A. Austin (ed.), *Current Research in Film: Audiences, Economics, and Law*, Vol. 2. Norwood, NJ: Ablex.

Babe, Robert E.
    1990    *Telecommunications in Canada*. Toronto: University of Toronto Press.

Badie, Bertrand and Pierre Birnbaum
1983 *The Sociology of the State* (translated by Arthur Goldhammer). Chicago: University of Chicago Press.

Baer, Walter S.
1989 "New Communications Technologies and Services." Pp. 139-169 in Paula R. Newberg (ed.), *New Directions in Telecommunications Policy*. Durham, NC: Duke University Press.

Bagdikian, Ben H.
1987 *The Media Monopoly*. Boston: Beacon.

Ball-Rokeach, Sandra J. and Kathleen Reardon
1988 "Monologue, Dialogue, and Telelog: Comparing an Emergent Form of Communication with Traditional Forms." Pp. 135-161 in Robert P. Hawkins, John M. Wiemann, and Suzanne Pingree (eds.), *Advancing Communication Science: Merging Mass and Interpersonal Processes*. Sage Annual Reviews of Communication Research, Vol. 16. Newbury Park, CA: Sage.

Barkey, Karen and Sunita Parikh
1991 "Comparative Perspectives on the State." Pp. 523-546 in W. Richard Scott and Judith Blake (eds.), *Annual Review of Sociology*, Vol. 17. Palo Alto, CA: Annual Reviews.

Baron, J. N. and P. C. Reiss
1985 "Same Time, Next Year: Aggregate Analyses of the Mass Media and Violent Behavior," *American Sociological Review* 50(3): 347-364.

Barthes, R.
1968 *Elements of Semiology* (translated by A. Lavers and C. Smith). New York: Hill and Wang.

Barton, Richard L.
1990 *Ties That Blind in Canadian/American Relations: Politics of News Discourse*. Hillsdale, NJ: Erlbaum.

Bassiouni, M. C.
1982 "Media Coverage of Terrorism: The Law and the Public," *Journal of Communication* 32(2): 128-143.

Bates, Benjamin J.
1990 "Information Systems and Society: Potential Impacts of Alternative Structures," *Telecommunications Policy* 14(2): 151-158.

Baudrillard, J.
1981 *The Political Economy of the Sign*. St. Louis: Telos Press.
1988 [1985] "The Masses: The Implosion of the Social in the Media." Pp. 207-219 in *Jean Baudrillard: Selected Writings*, edited with an Introduction by Mark Poster. Stanford, CA: Stanford University Press.

Becker, Boris, Barbara Brewer, Bodie Dickinson, and Rosemary Magee
    1985    "The Influence of Personal Values in Media Preference." Pp. 37-50 in Bruce A. Austin (ed.), *Current Research in Film: Audiences, Economics, and Law*, Vol. 2. Norwood, NJ: Ablex.

Becker, Lee B.
    1982a    "The Mass Media and Citizen Assessment of Issue Importance: A Reflection on Agenda-Setting Research." Pp. 521-536 in D. Charles Whitney, Ellen Wartella, and Sven Windahl (eds.), *Mass Communication Review Yearbook*, Vol. 3. Beverly Hills, CA: Sage.
    1982b    "Print or Broadcast: How the Medium Influences the Reporter." Pp. 145-162 in J. S. Ettema and D. C. Whitney (eds.), *Individuals in Mass Media Organizations: Creativity and Constraint*. Sage Annual Reviews of Communication Research, Vol. 10. Beverly Hills, CA: Sage.
    1987    "A Decade of Research on Interactive Cable." Pp. 102-123 in William H. Dutton, Jay G. Blumler, and Kenneth L. Kraemer (eds.), *Wired Cities*. Boston, MA: G. K. Hall.

Becker, Lee B., Pamela J. Creedon, R. Warwick Blood, and Eric S. Fredin
    1989    "United States: Cable Eases Its Way into the Household." Pp. 291-331 in Lee B. Becker and Klaus Schoenbach (eds.), *Audience Responses to Media Diversification*. Hillsdale, NJ: Erlbaum.

Becker, Lee B. and Klaus Schoenbach
    1989    "When Media Content Diversifies: Anticipating Audience Behaviors." Pp. 1-27 in Lee B. Becker and Klaus Schoenbach (eds.), *Audience Responses to Media Diversification*. Hillsdale, NJ: Erlbaum.

Beckton, Clare F.
    1982    *The Law and the Media in Canada*. Toronto: Carswell.

Bell, Allan
    1991    *The Language of News Media*. Oxford: Basil Blackwell.

Beltran S., Luis Ramiro and Elizabeth Fox de Cardona
    1979    "Latin America and the United States: Flaws in the Free Flow of Information." Pp. 33-64 in Kaarle Nordenstreng and Herbert I. Schiller (eds.), *National Sovereignty and International Communication*. Norwood, NJ: Ablex.

Beniger, James R. and D. Eleanor Westney
    1981    "Japanese and U.S. Media: Graphics as a Reflection of Newspapers' Social Role," *Journal of Communication* 31(2): 14-27.

Bennett, T.
  1982  "Theories of the Media, Theories of Society." Pp. 30-55 in Michael Gurevitch, Tony Bennett, James Curran, and Janet Woollacott (eds.), *Culture, Society, and the Media*. London: Methuen.
Bennett. W. Lance
  1988  *News: The Politics of Illusion*. New York: Longman.
Berelson, Bernard
  1952  *Content Analysis in Communication Research*. Glencoe, IL: Free Press.
Berelson, Bernard and Morris Janowitz
  1966  *Reader in Public Opinion and Communication*, 2nd ed. New York: Free Press.
Berelson, Bernard, P. F. Lazarsfeld and W. N. McPhee
  1954  *Voting: A Study of Opinion Formation in a Presidential Campaign*. Chicago: University of Chicago Press.
Berger, Arthur Asa
  1987 [1982] "Semiological Analysis." Pp. 132-155 in Oliver Boyd-Barrett and Peter Braham (eds.), *Media, Knowledge and Power*. Beckenham, Kent: Croom Helm.
Berkowitz, Dan
  1992  "Who Sets the Media Agenda? The Ability of Policymakers to Determine News Decisions." Pp.81-102 in J. David Kennamer (ed.), *Public Opinion, the Press, and Public Policy*. Westport, CT: Praeger.
Berlo, David K.
  1960  *The Process of Communication*. New York: Holt, Rinehart and Winston.
Beville, Hugh Malcolm, Jr.
  1988  *Audience Ratings: Radio, Television, and Cable*. Hillsdale, NJ: Erlbaum.
Bineham, Jeffrey L.
  1988  "A Historical Account of the Hypodermic Model in Mass Communication," *Communication Monographs* 55: 230-246.
Blatherwick, David E. S.
  1987  *The International Politics of Telecommunications*. Berkeley: Institute of International Studies, University of California.
Blau, Peter M.
  1977  *Inequality and Heterogeneity*. New York: Free Press.
Blumer, Herbert
  1954  "The Crowd, the Public, and the Mass." Pp. 363-379 in Wilbur Schramm (ed.), *The Process and Effects of Mass Communication*. Urbana: University of Illinois Press.

Blumer, Herbert and P. M. Hauser
- 1933 *Movies, Delinquency, and Crime.* New York: Macmillan.

Blumler, Jay G.
- 1992a *Television and the Public Interest: Vulnerable Values in West European Broadcasting.* London: Sage.
- 1992b "Public Service Broadcasting before the Commercial Deluge." Pp. 7-21 in Jay G. Blumler (ed.), *Television and the Public Interest: Vulnerable Values in West European Broadcasting.* London: Sage.
- 1992c "Vulnerable Values at Stake." Pp. 22-42 in Jay G. Blumler (ed.), *Television and the Public Interest: Vulnerable Values in West European Broadcasting.* London: Sage.

Blumler, Jay G., Malcolm Brynin, and T. J. Nossiter
- 1986 "Broadcasting Finance and Programme Quality: An International Review," *European Journal of Communication* 1: 343-364.

Blumler, J. G. and E. Katz
- 1974 *The Uses of Mass Communications: Current Perspectives on Gratifications Research.* Sage Annual Reviews of Communication Research, Vol. 3. Beverly Hills, CA: Sage.

Blumler, Jay G. and T. J. Nossiter
- 1991 *Broadcasting Finance in Transition: A Comparative Handbook.* New York: Oxford University Press.

Bogart, Leo
- 1956 *The Age of Television.* New York: Frederick Ungar.
- 1980 "Editorial Ideals, Editorial Illusions." Pp. 247-266 in Anthony Smith (ed.), *Newspapers and Democracy: International Essays in a Changing Medium.* Cambridge, MA: MIT Press.
- 1989 *Press and Public: Who Reads What, When. Where, and Why in American Newspapers.* Hillsdale, NJ: Erlbaum.
- 1991 *Preserving the Press: How Daily Newspapers Mobilized to Keep Their Readers.* New York: Columbia University Press.

Bollen, K. A. and D. P. Phillips
- 1981 "Suicidal Motor Vehicle Fatalities in Detroit: A Replication," *American Journal of Sociology* 87(2): 404-412.

Boyd, Douglas A. and John Y. Benzies
- 1983 "SOFIRAD: France's International Commercial Media Empire," *Journal of Communication* 33(2): 56-69.

Boyd-Barrett, Oliver
- 1979 "Media Imperialism: towards an international framework for the analysis of media systems. Pp. 116-135 in James Curran, Michael Gurevitch, and Janet Woollacott (eds.), *Mass Communication and Society.* Beverly Hills, CA: Sage.

Boyle, Andrew
    1972    *Only the Wild Wind Will Listen: Reith of the BBC.* London: Hutchinson.
Braman, Sandra
    1989    "Defining Information: An Approach for Policymakers," *Telecommunications Policy* 13(3): 233-242.
Breed, Warren
    1955a   "Newspaper 'Opinion Leaders' and Processes of Standardization," *Journalism Quarterly* 32(Summer): 278-285.
    1955b   "Social Control in the Newsroom: A Functional Analysis," *Social Forces* 33(3): 326-335.
Brenkman, J.
    1979    "Mass Media: From Collective Experience to the Culture of Privatization," *Social Text* 1(1): 94-109.
Breuilly, John
    1985 [1982] *Nationalism and the State.* Chicago: University of Chicago Press.
Briggs, Asa
    1985    *The BBC: The First Fifty Years.* Oxford: Oxford University Press.
Brooks, Harvey
    1990    "Unrecognized Consequences of Telecommunications Technologies." Pp. 17-35 in Sven B. Lundstedt (ed.), *Telecommunications, Values, and the Public Interest.* Norwood, NJ: Ablex.
Brown, Duncan H.
    1986    "Shaping the Communications Culture: The Power of the Policy-Planning Network." Pp. 273-284 in J. Miller (ed.), *Telecommunications and Equity: Policy Research Issues.* New York: North-Holland.
Browne, Donald R.
    1989    *Comparing Broadcast Systems: The Experiences of Six Industrialized Nations.* Ames: Iowa State University Press.
Bryant, Jennings and Richard L. Street, Jr.
    1988    "From Reactivity to Activity and Action: An Evolving Concept and *Weltanschauung* in Mass and Interpersonal Communication." Pp. 162-190 in Robert P. Hawkins, John M. Wiemann, and Suzanne Pingree (eds.) *Advancing Communication Science: Merging Mass and Interpersonal Processes.* Sage Annual Reviews of Communication Research, Vol.16. Newbury Park, CA: Sage.
Budd, Richard W. and Brent D. Ruben
    1988    *Beyond Media: New Approaches to Mass Communication.* New Brunswick, NJ: Transaction.

Burgelman, Jean-Claude
   1986   "The Future of Public Service Broadcasting: A Case Study for a 'New' Communications Policy," *European Journal of Communication* 1: 173-201.

Burns, Tom
   1977   *The BBC: Public Institution and Private World*. London: Macmillan.

Calhoun, Craig
   1988   "Populist Politics, Communications Media and Large Scale Societal Integration," *Sociological Theory* 6(2): 219-241.
   1992   "Introduction: Habermas and the Public Sphere." Pp. 1-48 in Craig Calhoun (ed.), *Habermas and the Public Sphere*. Cambridge, MA: MIT Press.

Campbell, Angus and Charles A. Metzner
   1950   *The Public Use of the Library and Other Sources of Information*. Ann Arbor: Survey Research Center, The University of Michigan.

Cantor, Muriel G. and Joel M. Cantor
   1986a   "Audience Composition and Television Content: The Mass Audience Revisited." Pp. 214-225 in Sandra J. Ball-Rokeach and Muriel G. Cantor (eds.), *Media, Audience, and Social Structure*. Newbury Park, CA: Sage.
   1986b   "Regulation and Deregulation: Telecommunication Policies in the United States." Pp. 84-101 in Marjorie Ferguson (ed.), *New Communication Technologies and the Public Interest*. London: Sage.
   1990   "The Internationalization of TV Entertainment." Pp. 317-324 in Sari Thomas and William A. Evans (eds.), *Studies in Communication*, Vol. 4. Norwood, NJ: Ablex.
   1992   *Prime-Time Television: Content and Control*, 2nd ed. Newbury Park, CA: Sage.

Cantor, Muriel G. and Suzanne Pingree
   1983   *The Soap Opera*. Beverly Hills, CA: Sage.

Cantril, Hadley
   1966   *The Invasion from Mars*. New York: Harper Torchbooks.

Cardiff, David
   1986   "The Serious and the Popular: Aspects of the Evolution of Style in the Radio Talk 1928-1939." Pp. 228-246 in Richard Collins et al. (eds.), *Media, Culture and Society: A Critical Reader*. London: Sage.

Cardiff, David and Paddy Scannell
   1987   "Broadcasting and National Unity." Pp. 157-173 in James Curran, Anthony Smith, and Pauline Wingate (eds.), *Impacts and Influences: Essays on Media Power in the*

*Twentieth Century*. London: Methuen.
Carey, James W.
 1988 *Communication as Culture: Essays in Media and Society.* Boston: Unwin Hyman.
Carmen, I. H.
 1966 *Movies, Censorship, and the Law.* Ann Arbor: University of Michigan Press.
Caron, André and James Taylor
 1985 "Cable Television at the Crossroads: An Analysis of the Canadian Cable Scene." Pp. 47-73 in Ralph M. Negrine (ed.), *Cable Television and the Future of Broadcasting*. New York: St. Martin's.
Carpenter, Edmund S.
 1954 "Certain Media Biases." Pp. 65-74 in E. S. Carpenter, W. T. Easterbrook, H. M. McLuhan, J. Tyrwhitt, and D. C. Williams (eds.), *Explorations: Studies in Culture and Communication*, No. 3. University of Toronto.
Chaffee, Steven H.
 1977 "Mass Media Effects: New Research Perspectives." Pp. 210-241 in D. Lerner and L. Nelson (eds.), *Communication Research—A Half-Century Appraisal*. Honolulu: East-West Center.
 1988 "Differentiating the Hypodermic Model from Empirical Research: A Comment on Bineham's Commentary," *Communication Monographs* 55: 247-249.
Chaffee, Steven H. and John L. Hochheimer
 1985 "The Beginnings of Political Communication Research in the United States: Origins of the 'Limited Effects' Model." Pp. 267-296 in Everett M. Rogers and Francis Balle (eds.), *The Media Revolution in America and Western Europe*. Norwood, NJ: Ablex.
Cherry, Colin
 1978 *On Human Communication*, 3rd edition. Cambridge, MA: MIT Press.
Clippinger, John H.
 1979 "The Hidden Agenda," *Journal of Communication* 29(1): 197-203.
Codding, George A., Jr.
 1979 "International Constraints on the Use of Telecommunications: The Role of the International Telecommunication Union." Pp. 2-37 in L. Lewin (ed.), *Telecommunications: An Interdisciplinary Survey*. Dedham, MA: Artech House.

Cogley, John
    1956    *Report on Blacklisting*, Vol. I (Movies) and Vol. II (Radio-Television). [New York]: The Fund for the Republic, Inc.
Cohen, Ronald
    1978    "Introduction." Pp. 1-20 in Ronald Cohen (ed.), *Origins of the State*. Philadelphia: Institute for the Study of Human Issues.
Coleman, James S.
    1974    *Power and the Structure of Society*. New York: Norton.
Collins, Richard
    1986a   "Broadband Black Death Cuts Queues: The Information Society and the UK." Pp. 287-308 in Richard Collins et al. (eds.), *Media, Culture and Society: A Critical Reader*. London: Sage.
    1986b   "Broadcasting Policy in Canada." Pp. 150-163 in Marjorie Ferguson (ed.), *New Communication Technologies and the Public Interest*. London: Sage.
    1987 [1985] "Canada: Nation-Building Threatened by the US-Dominated Media." Pp. 156-181 in Oliver Boyd-Barrett and Peter Braham (eds.), *Media, Knowledge and Power*. Beckenham, Kent: Croom Helm.
    1990    *Culture, Communication and National Identity: The Case of Canadian Television*. Toronto: University of Toronto Press.
Compaine, B. M., Christopher H. Sterling, Thomas Guback, and J. Kendrick Noble, Jr.
    1982    *Who Owns the Media?* 2nd ed. White Plains, NY: Knowledge Industry Publications.
Comstock, George A.
    1980    *Television in America*. Beverly Hills, CA: Sage.
    1991    *Television and Children*. San Diego: Academic.
Comstock, George A., Stephen Chaffee, Natan Katzman, Maxwell McCombs, and Donald Roberts
    1978    *Television and Human Behavior*. New York: Columbia University Press.
Connell, Ian
    1980    "Television News and the Social Contract." Pp. 129-156 in Stuart Hall et al. (eds.), *Culture, Media, Language: Working Papers in Cultural Studies*. London: Hutchinson.
Connell, Ian and Adam Mills
    1985    "Text, Discourse and Mass Communication." Pp. 26-43 in Teun A. van Dijk (ed.), *Discourse and Communication: New Approaches to the Analysis of Mass Media Discourse and Communication*. Berlin: de Gruyter.

Coulson, David C.
   1988    "Antitrust Laws and Newspapers." Pp. 179-197 in Robert C. Picard, James P. Winter, Maxwell E. McCombs, and Stephen Lacy (eds.), *Press Concentration and Monopoly: New Perspectives on Newspaper Ownership and Operation*. Norwood, NJ: Ablex.

Crane, Rhonda J.
   1992    "TV Technology and Government Policy." Pp. 155-166 in Harvey M. Sapolsky, Rhonda J. Crane, W. Russell Neuman, and Eli M. Noam (eds.), *The Telecommunications Revolution: Past, Present and Future*. London: Routledge.

Crotts, G. Gail and Lawrence M. Mead
   1979    "The FCC as an Institution." Pp. 39-119 in L. Lewin (ed.), *Telecommunications: An Interdisciplinary Survey*. Dedham, MA: Artech House.

Cunningham and Walsh
   1958    *Videotown 1948-1957*. New York: Cunningham and Walsh Publishers.

Curran, James
   1986    "The Impact of Advertising on the British Mass Media." Pp. 309-335 in Richard Collins et al. (eds.), *Media, Culture and Society: A Critical Reader*. London: Sage.

Cutler, Blayne
   1989    "Mature Audiences Only," *American Demographics* 11(10): 20-26.

Cutright, Phillips
   1963    "National Political Development: Its Measurement and Social Correlates." Pp. 569-582 in Nelson W. Polsby, Robert A. Dentler, and Paul A. Smith (eds.), *Politics and Social Life: An Introduction to Political Behavior*. Boston: Houghton Mifflin.

Dale, E.
   1935    *The Content of Motion Pictures*. New York: Macmillan.

Davidge, Carol
   1987    "America's Talk-Back Television Experiment: Qube." Pp. 75-101 in William H. Dutton, Jay G. Blumler, and Kenneth L. Kraemer (eds.), *Wired Cities*. Boston, MA: G. K. Hall.

Davis, Dennis K. and John P. Robinson
   1989    "Newsflow and Democratic Society in an Age of Electronic Media." Pp. 59-102 in George Comstock (ed.), *Public Communication and Behavior*, Vol. 2. San Diego: Academic Press.

DeFleur, Melvin L.
   1966    *Theories of Mass Communication*. New York: David McKay.

DeFleur, Melvin L. and S. Ball-Rokeach
- 1982 *Theories of Mass Communication*, 4th ed. New York: Longman.
- 1989 *Theories of Mass Communication*, 5th ed. New York: Longman.

Delia, Jesse G. and Barbara J. O'Keefe
- 1979 "Constructivism: The Development of Communication in Children." Pp. 157-185 in Ellen Wartella (ed.), *Children Communicating: Media and Development of Thought, Speech, Understanding*. Beverly Hills, CA: Sage.

Demac, Donna A.
- 1986 "Communication Satellites and the Third World." Pp. 35-45 in Michael Traber (ed.), *The Myth of the Information Revolution: Social and Ethical Implications of Communication Technology*. London: Sage.

Deutsch, Karl
- 1966 *Nationalism and Social Communication: An Inquiry into the Foundations of Nationality*. Cambridge, MA: MIT Press.

Dexter, Lewis A. and David M. White
- 1964 *People, Society and Mass Communications*. New York: Free Press.

Doherty, Monika
- 1985 *Epistemic Meaning*. Berlin: Springer-Verlag.

Dominick, Joseph R.
- 1987 "Film Economics and Film Content: 1964-1983." Pp. 136-153 in Bruce A. Austin (ed.), *Current Research in Film: Audiences, Economics, and Law*. Norwood, NJ: Ablex.
- 1990 *The Dynamics of Mass Communication*, 3rd ed. New York: McGraw-Hill.

Douglas, Sara W.
- 1986 *Labor's New Voice: Unions and the Mass Media*. Norwood, NJ: Ablex.

Dreier, Peter
- 1987 [1983] "The Corporate Complaint Against the Media." Pp. 64-80 in Donald Lazere (ed.), *American Media and Mass Culture: Left Perspectives*. Berkeley: University of California Press.

Dua, Hans R.
- 1990 "The Phenomenology of Miscommunication." Pp. 113-139 in Stephen Harold Riggins (ed.), *Beyond Goffman: Studies in Communication, Institution, and Social Interaction*. Berlin: Mouton de Gruyter.

Dunnett, Peter J. S.
    1990    *The World Television Industry: An Economic Analysis.* London: Routledge.
Durkheim, Emile
    1986    "The Concept of the State." Pp. 32-71 in Anthony Giddens (ed.), *Durkheim on Politics and the State,* translated by W. D. Halls. Stanford, CA: Stanford University Press
Dutton, William H.
    1992    "The Ecology of Games in Telecommunications Policy." Pp. 65-88 in Harvey M. Sapolsky, Rhonda J. Crane, W. Russell Neuman, and Eli M. Noam (eds.), *The Telecommunications Revolution: Past, Present and Future.* London: Routledge.
Dutton, William H. and Jay G. Blumler
    1989    "A Comparative Perspective on Information Societies." Pp. 63-88 in Jerry L. Salvaggio (ed.), *The Information Society: Economic, Social, and Structural Issues.* Hillside, NJ: Erlbaum.
Dutton, William H., Jay G. Blumler, and Kenneth L. Kraemer
    1987a    "Continuity and Change in Conceptions of the Wired City." Pp. 3-26 in William H. Dutton, Jay G. Blumler, and Kenneth L. Kraemer (eds.), *Wired Cities.* Boston, MA: G. K. Hall.
    1987b    "A Comparative Analysis." Pp. 456-486 in William H. Dutton, Jay G. Blumler, and Kenneth L. Kraemer (eds.), *Wired Cities.* Boston, MA: G. K. Hall.
Dysinger W. S. and C. A. Ruckmick
    1933    *The Emotional Responses of Children to the Motion Picture Situation.* New York: Macmillan.
Dyson, Kenneth H. F.
    1990    "Luxembourg: Changing Anatomy of an International Broadcasting Power." Pp. 125-147 in Kenneth Dyson and Peter Humphreys (eds.), *The Political Economy of Communications: International and European Dimensions.* London: Routledge.
Dyson, Kenneth H. F. and Peter Humphreys
    1986    *The Politics of the Communications Revolution in Western Europe.* London: Frank Cass.
Eason. David L.
    1988    "On Journalistic Authority: The Janet Cooke Story." Pp. 205-227 in James W. Carey (ed.), *Media, Myths, and Narratives: Television and the Press.* Newbury Park, CA: Sage.
Eco, U.
    1976    *A Theory of Semiotics.* Bloomington: Indiana University Press.

Edgerton, Gary
   1986   "The Film Bureau Phenomenon in America: State and Municipal Advocacy of Contemporary Motion Picture and Television Production." Pp. 204-224 in Bruce A. Austin (ed.), *Current Research in Film: Audiences, Economics, and Law*. Norwood, NJ: Ablex.

Edwards, John
   1984   *Language, Society and Identity*. Oxford: Basil Blackwell in association with André Deutsch.

Eek, Hilding
   1979   "Principles Governing the Use of the Mass Media as Defined by the United Nations and UNESCO." Pp. 173-194 in Kaarle Nordenstreng and Herbert I. Schiller (eds.), *National Sovereignty and International Communication*. Norwood, NJ: Ablex.

Einsiedel, Edna F.
   1988   "The British, Canadian, and U.S. Pornography Commissions and Their Use of Social Science Research," *Journal of Communication* 38(2): 108-121.

Eisenstadt, S.N., with M. Curelaru
   1976   The Form of Sociology: Paradigms in Crises. New York: Wiley.

*Electronic Media*
   1988   "Media Markets Around the World," April 25.

Elias, Norbert
   1991   *The Symbol System* (edited with an introduction by Richard Kliminster). London: Sage.

Elkin, Fred
   1983   "Communications Media and Identity Formation in Canada." Pp. 147-157 in Benjamin D. Singer (ed.), *Communications in Canadian Society*. Don Mills, Ontario: Addison-Wesley.

Elliott, Philip
   1986   "Intellectuals, the 'Information Society' and the Disappearance of the Public Sphere." Pp. 105-115 in Richard Collins et al. (eds.), *Media, Culture, and Society: A Critical Reader*. London: Sage.

Engelkamp, J.
   1983   "Word Meaning and Word Recognition." Pp. 17-33 in T. B. Seiler and W. Wannenmacher (eds.), *Concept Development and the Development of Word Meaning*. Berlin: Springer-Verlag.

Engelman, Ralph
   1987   "From Ford to Carnegie: The Private Foundations and the Rise of Public Television." Pp. 233-242 in Sari Thomas (ed.), *Studies in Communication*, Vol. 3. Norwood, NJ: Ablex.

Evans, Gary
- 1984 *John Grierson and the National Film Board: The Politics of Wartime Propaganda.* Toronto: University of Toronto Press.
- 1991 *In the National Interest: A Chronicle of the National Film Board of Canada from 1949 to 1989.* Toronto: University of Toronto Press.

Evans, Harold
- 1990 "The Norman Conquest: Freedom of the Press in Britain and America." Pp. 189-201 in Simon Serfaty (ed.), *The Media and Foreign Policy.* New York: St. Martin's.

Farace, R. V. and L. Donohew
- 1965 "Mass Communication in National Social Systems: A Study of 43 Variables in 115 Countries," *Journalism Quarterly* 43: 253-261.

Fekete, J.
- 1973 "McLuhancy: Counterrevolution in Cultural Theory," *Telos* 15: 75-123.

Ferguson, Marjorie
- 1986 "The Challenge of Neo-Technological Determinism for Communication Systems, Industry and Culture." Pp. 52-70 in Marjorie Ferguson (ed.), *New Communication Technologies and the Public Interest: Comparative Perspectives on Policy and Research.* London: Sage.

Fisher, Desmond
- 1982 *The Right to Communicate,* Reports and Papers in Mass Communication, No. 94. Paris: Unesco.

Fishman, Mark
- 1982 "News and Nonevents: Making the Visible Invisible." Pp. 219-240 in J. S. Ettema and D. C. Whitney (eds.), *Individuals in Mass Media Organizations: Creativity and Constraint.* Sage Annual Reviews of Communication Research, Vol. 10. Beverly Hills, CA: Sage.

Fiske, John
- 1989 "Moments of Television." Pp. 56-78 in Ellen Seiter, Hans Borchers, Gabriele Kreutzner, and Eva-Maria Warth (eds.), *Remote Control: Television, Audiences, and Cultural Power.* London: Routledge.

Fiske, J. and J. Hartley
- 1978 *Reading Television.* London: Methuen.

Flichy, Patrice
- 1984 "Media Control in France: Conflict between Political and Economic Rationale." Pp. 225-241 in Vincent Mosco and Janet Wasko (eds.), *The Critical Communications Review,* Vol. 2. Norwood, NJ: Ablex.

Foley, Joseph M.
  1990  "Value and Policy Issues in the Marketplace for Broadcast Licenses." Pp. 273-288 in Sven B. Lundstedt (ed.), *Telecommunications, Values, and the Public Interest.* Norwood, NJ: Ablex.
Forman, H. J.
  1935  *Our Movie Made Children.* New York: Macmillan.
Freiman, M. J.
  1984  "Consumer Sovereignty and National Sovereignty in Domestic and International Broadcasting Regulation." Pp. 104-121 in *Cultures in Collision: The Interaction of Canadian and U.S. Television Broadcast Policies (A Canadian-U.S. Conference on Communications Policy).* New York: Praeger.
Friedson, Eliot
  1954  "Communication Research and the Concept of the Mass." Pp. 380-388 in Wilbur Schramm (ed.), *The Process and Effects of Mass Communication.* Urbana: University of Illinois Press.
Gamson, William A.
  1984  *What's News.* New York: Free Press.
Gandy, Oscar H.
  1982  *Beyond Agenda Setting.* Norwood, NJ: Ablex.
Ganley, Gladys D. and Oswald H. Ganley
  1988  "The Political Implications of Videocassette Recording." Pp. 265-291 in Benjamin M. Compaine (ed.), *Issues in New Information Technology.* Norwood, NJ: Ablex.
Ganley, Oswald H.
  1982  "United States-Canada Communications and Information Relationships." Pp. 272-289 in Jorge Reina Schement, Guitierrez, and Marvin S. Sirbu, Jr. (eds.), *Telecommunications Policy Handbook.* New York: Praeger
Ganley, Oswald H. and Gladys D. Ganley
  1982  *To Inform or to Control? The New Communications Networks.* New York: McGraw-Hill.
Gans, H. J.
  1979  *Deciding What's News.* New York: Vintage.
Garnham, Nicholas
  1986  "Contribution to a Political Economy of Mass Communication." Pp. 9-32 in Richard Collins et al. (eds.), *Media, Culture and Society: A Critical Reader.* London: Sage.
  1990 [1979] "The Economics of the US Motion Picture Industry." in Nicholas Garnham (ed.), *Capitalism and Communication: Global Culture and the Economics of Information.* London: Sage.

1992 "The Media and the Public Sphere." Pp. 359-376 in Craig Calhoun (ed.), *Habermas and the Public Sphere*. Cambridge, MA: MIT Press.

Gaunt, Philip
1987 "Developments in Soviet Journalism," *Journalism Quarterly* 64(3): 536-542.

Gerbner, George
1972 "Violence in Television Drama: Trends and Symbolic Functions." Pp. 28-187 in George A. Comstock and Eli A. Rubenstein (eds.), *Television and Social Behavior, Reports and Papers*, Vol. 1, Media Content and Control. Washington, D.C.: U.S. Government Printing Office.
1984 "Political Functions of Television Viewing: A Cultivation Analysis." Pp. 329-343 in Gabrielle Melischek, Karl Erik Rosengren, and James Stappers (eds.), *Cultural Indicators: An International Symposium*. Austrian Academy of Sciences, Philosophical-Historical Series, Vol. 416. Vienna: Austrian Academy of Sciences.
1985 "Mass Media Discourse: Message System Analysis as a Component of Cultural Indicators." Pp. 13-25 in Teun A. van Dijk (ed.), *Discourse and Communication: New Approaches to the Analysis of Mass Media Discourse and Communication*. Berlin: de Gruyter.

Gerbner, George and George Márványi
1984 "The Many Worlds of the World's Press." Pp. 92-102 in George Gerbner and Marsha Siefert (eds.), *World Communications: A Handbook*. New York: Longman.

Gerbner, George and Marsha Siefert
1984 *World Communications: A Handbook*. New York: Longman.

Gergen, David R.
1990 "Diplomacy in a Television Age: The Dangers of Teledemocracy." Pp. 47-63 in Simon Serfaty (ed.), *The Media and Foreign Policy*. New York: St. Martin's.

Gibbs, Graham
1986 "The State in an International Context." Pp. 192-239 in Roger King, *The State in Modern Society*. Chatham, NJ: Chatham House.

Giffard, C. Anthony
1989 *UNESCO and the Media*. White Plains, NY: Longman.

Gifreu, Josep
1986 "From Communication Policy to Reconstruction of Cultural Identity: Prospects for Catalonia," *European Journal of Communication* 1: 463-476.

Giroux, Henry A. and Peter L. MacLaren
　1992　"Media Hegemony: Towards a Critical Pedagogy of Representation." Pp. XV-XXXIV in James Schwoch, Susan Reilly, and Mimi White, *Media Knowledge: Readings in Popular Culture, Pedagogy, and Critical Citizenship*. Albany: State University of New York Press.

Gitlin, Todd
　1977　"Spotlights and Shadows: Television and the Culture of Politics," *College English* 38(8): 789-801.
　1978　"Media Sociology: The Dominant Paradigm," *Theory and Society* 6(2): 205-253.
　1979a　"Prime Time Ideology: The Hegemonic Process in Television Entertainment," *Social Problems* 26(3): 251-266.
　1979b　"News as Ideology and Contested Area: Toward A Theory of Hegemony, Crisis, and Opposition," *Socialist Review* 9(6): 11-54.
　1980　*The Whole World is Watching: Mass Media in the Making and Unmaking of the New Left*. Berkeley: University of California Press.
　1987 [1982]　"Television's Screens: Hegemony in Transition." Pp. 240-265 in Donald Lazere (ed.), in *American Media and Mass Culture: Left Perspectives*. Berkeley: University of California Press.

Globerman, Steven
　1987　*Culture, Governments and Markets*. Vancouver, BC: The Fraser Institute.

Golding, P.
　1979　"Media Professionalism in the Third World: The Transfer of an Ideology." Pp. 291-308 in James Curran, Michael Gurevitch, and Janet Woollacott (eds.), *Mass Communication and Society*. Beverly Hills, CA: Sage.

Goldman, Robert
　1982　"Hegemony and Managed Critique in Prime-Time Television: A Critical Reading of 'Mork and Mindy'," *Theory and Society* 11(3): 363-386.

Goldman, Robert and Arvind Rajagopal
　1991　*Mapping Hegemony: Television News Coverage of Industrial Conflict*. Norwood, NJ: Ablex.

Good, Leslie T.
　1989　"Power, Hegemony, and Communication Theory." Pp. 51-64 in Ian H. Angus and Sut Jhally (eds.), *Cultural Politics in Contemporary America*. New York: Routledge.

Gottdiener, M.
　1985　"Hegemony and Mass Culture: A Semiotic Approach,"

*American Journal of Sociology* 90(5): 979-1001.

Greenberg, Bradley S.
1989 "Teletext in the United Kingdom: Patterns, Attitudes, and the Behavior of Users." Pp.87-103 in Jerry L. Salvaggio and Jennings Bryant (eds.), *Media Use in the Information Age: Emerging Patterns of Adoption and Consumer Use.* Hillsdale, NJ: Erlbaum.

Gross, Larry
1988 "The Ethics of (Mis)representation." Pp. 188-202 in Larry Gross, John Stuart Katz, and Jay Ruby (eds.), *Image Ethics: the Moral Rights of Subjects in Photographs, Film, and Television.* New York: Oxford University Press.

Guback, Thomas H.
1969 *The International Film Industry: Western Europe and America Since 1945.* Bloomington: Indiana University Press.
1977 "The International Film Industry." Pp. 21-40 in George Gerbner (ed.), *Mass Media in Changing Cultures.* New York: Wiley.
1982 "Film as International Business: The Role of American Multinationals." Pp. 336-350 in Gorham Kindem (ed.), *The American Movie Industry: The Business of Motion Pictures.* Carbondale: Southern Illinois University Press.
1987 "Government Financial Support to the Film Industry in the United States." Pp. 88-104 in Bruce A. Austin (ed.), *Current Research in Film: Audiences, Economics, and Law,* Vol. 3. Norwood, NJ: Ablex.

Guback, Thomas and Tapio Varis
1982 *Transnational Communication and Cultural Industries,* Reports and Papers on Mass Communication, No. 92. Paris: UNESCO.

Gunter, Jonathan F.
1978 "An Introduction to the Great Debate," *Journal of Communication* 28(4): 142-156.

Gwyn, Robert J.
1983 "Rural Radio in Bolivia: A Case Study," *Journal of Communication* 33(2): 79-87.

Habermas, Jürgen
1979 *Communication and the Evolution of Society.* Boston: Beacon.

Hachten, William A.
1979 "Policies and Performance of South African Television," *Journal of Communication* 29(3): 62-72.
1987 *The World News Prism: Changing Media, Clashing Ideologies,* 2nd ed. Ames: Iowa State University Press.

Hagelin, Theodore and Hudson Janisch
    1984    "The Border Broadcasting Dispute in Context." Pp. 40-103 in *Cultures in Collision: The Interaction of Canadian and U.S. Television Broadcast Policies (A Canadian-U.S. Conference on Communications Policy)*. New York: Praeger.
Haight, Timothy R.
    1984    "The New American Information Order." Pp. 101-117 in Vincent Mosco and Janet Wasko (eds.), *The Critical Communications Review*, Vol. 2. Norwood, NJ: Ablex.
Hale, F. Dennis
    1988    "Editorial Diversity and Concentration." Pp. 161-176 in Robert C. Picard, James P. Winter, Maxwell E. McCombs, and Stephen Lacy (eds.), *Press Concentration and Monopoly: New Perspectives on Newspaper Ownership and Operation*. Norwood, NJ: Ablex.
Hall, Laurence S.
    1979    "ControllIng Public Communications: Theory and Practice for Human Management of Electric Literature." Pp. 169-201 in Timothy R. Haight (ed.), *Telecommunications Policy and the Citizen: Public Interest Perspectives on the Communications Act Rewrite*. New York: Praeger.
Hall, Stuart
    1977    "Culture, the Media, and the 'Ideological' Effect." Pp. 315-345 in James Curran, Michael Gurevitch, and Janet Woollacott (eds.), *Mass Communication and Society*. Beverly Hills, CA: Sage.
    1980    "Encoding/decoding." Pp. 128-138 in Stuart Hall et al. (eds.), *Culture, Media, Language: Working Papers in Cultural Studies*. London: Hutchinson.
Hallin, Daniel C.
    1987    "We Keep America on Top of the World." Pp. 9-41 in Todd Gitlin (ed.), *Watching Television*. New York: Pantheon.
Halloran, James D.
    1986    "The Social Implications of Technological Innovations in Communication." Pp. 46-63 in Michael Traber (ed.), *The Myth of the Information Revolution: Social and Ethical Implications of Communication Technology*. London: Sage.
Halprin, Albert
    1989    "What Will the Liberlised Telecommunications Market in Europe Mean to the USA?" Pp. 193-204 in David Shorrock (ed.), *European Communications: Technologies and Regulations of the Single Market*. London: Blenheim Online.
Haralovich, Mary Beth
    1985    "Film Advertising, the Film Industry, and the Pin-Up: The

Industry's Accommodations to Social Forces in the 1940s." Pp. 127-164 in Bruce A. Austin (ed.), *Current Research in Film: Audiences, Economics, and Law,* Vol. 1. Norwood, NJ: Ablex.

Harrison, Randall and Paul Ekman
 1977 "TV's Last Frontier: South Africa." Pp. 189-196 in George Gerbner (ed.), *Mass Media Policies in Changing Cultures.* New York: Wiley.

Hart, David J.
 1980 "Changing Relationships between Publishers and Journalists: An Overview." Pp.268-285 in Anthony Smith (ed.), *Newspapers and Democracy: International Essays in a Changing Medium.* Cambridge, MA: MIT Press.

Hartley, Eugene L. and Ruth E. Hartley
 1952 *Fundamentals of Social Psychology.* New York: Knopf.

Haslett, Beth and Alison Alexander
 1988 "Developing Communication Skills." Pp. 224-252 in Robert P. Hawkins, John M. Wiemann, and Suzanne Pingree (eds.), *Advancing Communication Science: Merging Mass and Interpersonal Processes.* Sage Annual Reviews of Communication Research, Vol.16. Newbury Park,CA: Sage.

Hays, Will
 1955 *Memoirs.* Garden City, NY: Doubleday.

Hearold, Susan
 1986 "A Synthesis of 1043 Effects of Television on Social Behavior." Pp. 65-133 in George Comstock (ed.), *Public Communication and Behavior,* Vol. 1. Orlando: Academic Press.

Hearst, Stephen
 1992 "Broadcast Regulation in Britain." Pp. 61-78 in Jay G. Blumler (ed.), *Television and the Public Interest: Vulnerable Values in West European Broadcasting.* London: Sage.

Heath, Stephen and Gillian Skirrow
 1986 "An Interview with Raymond Williams." Pp. 3-17 in Tania Modleski (ed.), *Studies in Entertainment: Critical Approaches to Mass Culture.* Bloomington: Indiana University Press.

Heeter, Carrie
 1989 "Implications of New Interactive Technologies for Conceptualizing Communication." Pp. 217-235 in Jerry L. Salvaggio and Jennings Bryant (eds.), *Media Use in the Information Age: Emerging Patterns of Adoption and Consumer Use.* Hillsdale, NJ: Lawrence Erlbaum.

Heeter, Carrie and Bradley S. Greenberg
 1988 *Cableviewing.* Norwood, NJ: Ablex.

Held, David and Joel Krieger
    1984    "Theories of the State: Some Competing Claims." Pp. 1-20 in Stephen Bornstein, David Held, and Joel Krieger (eds.), *The State in Capitalist Europe: A Casebook*. London: Allen and Unwin.

Heller, Scott
    1991    "7,000 Students Protest Michigan State U. Decision to Offer Required History Course Using Television," *The Chronicle of Higher Education* October 16: A47-A48.

Heritage, John C., Steven Clayman, and Don H. Zimmerman
    1988    "Discourse and Message Analysis: The Micro-Structure of Mass Media Messages." Pp. 77-109 in Robert P. Hawkins, John M. Wiemann, and Suzanne Pingree (eds.), *Advancing Communication Science: Merging Mass and Interpersonal Processes*. Sage Annual Reviews of Communication Research, Vol. 16. Newbury Park,CA: Sage.

Herman, Edward S. and Noam Chomsky
    1988    *Manufacturing Consent*. New York: Pantheon.

Higman, Howard
    1979    "The Information Society." Pp. 219-234 in L. Lewin (ed.), *Telecommunications: An Interdisciplinary Survey*. Dedham, MA: Artech House.

Hill, Harold E.
    1979    "Broadcast Control and Regulation." Pp. 147-180 in L. Lewin (ed.), *Telecommunications: An Interdisciplinary Survey*. Dedham, MA: Artech House.

Hixson, Richard
    1989    *Mass Media and the Constitution: An Encyclopedia of Supreme Court Decisions*. New York: Garland.

Hoffman-Riem, Wolfgang
    1986    "Law, Politics and the New Media: Trends in Broadcasting Regulation." Pp.125-146 in Kenneth H. F. Dyson and Peter Humphreys (eds.), *The Politics of the Communications Revolution in Western Europe*. London: Frank Cass.

Horton, Donald and R. Richard Wohl
    1956    "Mass Communication and Para-Social Interaction: Observations on Intimacy at a Distance," *Psychiatry* 19(3): 215-229.

Horwitz, Robert Britt
    1989    *The Irony of Regulatory Reform: The Deregulation of American Telecommunications*. New York: Oxford University Press.

Hoskins, Colin, Rolf Mirus, and William Rozeboom
    1989    "U.S. Television Programs in the International Market: Unfair Pricing?" *Journal of Communication* 39(2): 55-75.

Howell, W. J., Jr.
　1986　*World Broadcasting in the Age of the Satellite: Comparative Systems, Policies, and Issues in Mass Telecommunication.* Norwood, NJ: Ablex.

Hulett, J. Edward
　1966　"A Symbolic Interactionist Model of Human Communication," *Audiovisual Communications Review* 14(Spring): 15-33.

Humphreys, Peter
　1986　"Legitimating the Communications Revolution: Governments, Parties and Trade Unions in Britain, France and West Germany." Pp. 163-194 in Kenneth H. F. Dyson and Peter Humphreys (eds.), *The Politics of the Communications Revolution in Western Europe.* London: Frank Cass.

Ihde, Don
　1982　"The Technological Embodiment of Media." Pp. 54-72 in Michael J. Hyde (ed.), *Communication Philosophy and the Technological Age.* University: University of Alabama Press.

Innis, Harold A.
　1951　*The Bias of Communication.* Toronto: University of Toronto Press.

Irwin, Manley R. and Michael J. Merenda
　1989　"Corporate Networks, Privatization and State Sovereignty," *Telecommunications Policy* 13(4): 329-335.

Ivacic, Pero
　1978　"The Flow of News: Tanjug, the Pool, and the National Agencies," *Journal of Communication* 28(4): 157-162.

Janowitz, Morris
　1952　*The Community Press in an Urban Setting.* Glencoe, IL: Free Press.
　1975　"Professional Models in Journalism," *Journalism Quarterly* 52(4): 618-626, 662.

Jansen, Sue Curry
　1988　*Censorship: The Knot That Binds Power and Knowledge.* New York: Oxford.

Jarvie, Ian
　1985　"Suppressing Controversial Films: From Objective Burma to Monty Python's Life of Brian." Pp. 181-196 in Bruce A. Austin (ed.), *Current Research in Film: Audiences, Economics, and Law*, Vol. 1. Norwood, NJ: Ablex.

Jefferson, Mark
　1939　"The Law of the Primate City," *Geographical Review* 29(2): 226-232.

Jensen, Joli
   1990   *Redeeming Modernity: Contradictions in Media Criticism.* Newbury Park, CA: Sage.

Johnson, F. Craig and George R. Klare
   1962   "Feedback: Principles and Analogies," *Journal of Communication* 12 (September): 150-159.

Johnson, Wendell
   1953   "The Fateful Process of Mr. A. Talking to Mr. B.," *Harvard Business Review* 31(January-February): 49-56.

Johnstone, John, E. L. Slawiski, and W. W. Bowman
   1973   "The Professional Values of American Newsmen," *Public Opinion Quarterly* 36(Winter): 522-540.

*Journal of Communication*
   1979   "UNESCO's Mass Media Declaration: A Forum of Three Worlds" 29(2): 186-189,192-199.

Jowett, Garth S.
   1985   "Giving Them What They Want: Movie Audience Research Before 1950." Pp. 19-35 in Bruce A. Austin (ed.), *Current Research in Film: Audiences, Economics, and Law,* Vol. 1. Norwood, NJ: Ablex.

Jowett, Garth S. and James M. Linton
   1980   *Movies as Mass Communication.* Beverly Hills, CA: Sage.

Jowett, Garth S. and Victoria O'Donnell
   1986   *Propaganda and Persuasion.* Newbury Park, CA: Sage.

Kamiss, Phyllis C.
   1991   *Making Local News.* Chicago: University of Chicago Press.

Kasza, Gregory J.
   1988   *The State and the Mass Media in Japan, 1918-1945.* Berkeley: University of California Press.

Katz, Elihu
   1957   "The Two-Step Flow of Communication: An Up-To-Date Report on an Hypothesis," *Public Opinion Quarterly* 21(Spring): 61-78.
   1978   "Of Mutual Interest," *Journal of Communication* 28(2): 133-141.
   1979   "Cultural Continuity and Change: Role of the Media." Pp. 65-81 in Kaarle Nordenstreng and Herbert I. Schiller (eds.), *National Sovereignty and International Communication.* Norwood, NJ: Ablex.

Katz, Elihu and Paul F. Lazarsfeld
   1955   *Personal Influence.* Glencoe, IL: Free Press.

Keane John
   1991   *The Media and Democracy.* Cambridge, MA: Blackwell.
   1992   "The Crisis of the Sovereign State." Pp. 16-33 in Marc

Raboy and Bernard Dagenais (eds.), *Media, Crisis, and Democracy: Communication and the Disruption of Social Order*. London: Sage.

Kellner, D.
　1979　"TV, Ideology, and Emancipatory Popular Culture," *Socialist Review* 9(3): 13-53.
　1981　"Network Television and American Society: Introduction to a Critical Theory of Television," *Theory and Society* 10(1): 31-62.
　1987 [1983] "Public Access Television: Alternative Views." Pp. 610-618 in Donald Lazere (ed.), *American Media and Mass Culture: Left Perspectives*. Berkeley: University of California Press.

Kerner, Irving J.
　1979　"Telecommunications and the Constitution: Speech and Privacy." Pp. 183-215 in L. Lewin (ed.), *Telecommunications: An Interdisciplinary Survey*. Dedham, MA: Artech House.

King, Roger
　1986　*The State in Modern Society*. Chatham, NJ: Chatham House.

Klapp, Orrin
　1986　*Overload and Boredom: Essays on the Quality of Life in the Information Society*. New York: Greenwood.

Klapper, J. T.
　1960　*The Effects of Mass Communication*. Glencoe, IL: Free Press.

Klopfenstein, Bruce C.
　1989　"The Diffusion of the VCR in the United States." Pp. 21-39 in Mark R. Levy (ed.), *The VCR Age: Home Video and Mass Communication*. Newbury Park, CA: Sage.

Koizumi, Tetsunori
　1990　"Telecommunications Technology and Social Change: The Japanese Experience." Pp. 217-226 in Sven B. Lundstedt (ed.), *Telecommunications, Values, and the Public Interest*. Norwood, NJ: Ablex.

Krasnow, Erwin G., Lawrence D. Longley, and Herbert A. Terry
　1982　*The Politics of Broadcast Regulation*, 3rd ed. New York: St. Martin's.

Krasnow, Erwin G. and Jill Abelhouse Stern
　1988　"The New Video Marketplace: A Regulatory Identity Crisis." Pp.45-143 in Benjamin M. Compaine (ed.), *Issues in New Information Technology*. Norwood, NJ: Ablex.

Kubey, Robert and Mihaly Csikszentmihalyi
　1990　*Television and the Quality of Life: How Viewing Shapes Everyday Experience*. Hillsdale, NJ: Erlbaum.

Lacy, Stephen and Todd F. Simon
- 1993 *The Economics and Regulation of United States Newspapers.* Norwood, NJ: Ablex.

Lang, K. and G. E. Lang
- 1953 "The Unique Perspective of Television: A Pilot Study," *American Sociological Review* 18(1): 3-12.

Langer, Suzanne K.
- 1948 *Philosophy in a New Key.* New York: Mentor.

Lasswell, Harold O.
- 1948 "The Structure and Function of Communication in Society." Pp. 37-51 in Lyman Bryson (ed.), *The Communication of Ideas.* New York: Harper.

Lazarsfeld, Paul F.
- 1941 "Remarks on Administrative and Critical Communications Research," *Studies in Philosophy and Social Science* 9(1): 2-16.
- 1948 "Communications Research and the Social Psychologist." Pp. 218-273 in W. Dennis (ed.), *Current Trends in Social Psychology.* Pittsburgh: University of Pittsburgh Press.

Lazarsfeld, Paul F., B. Berelson and H. Gaudet
- 1944 *The People's Choice: How the Voter Makes Up His Mind in a Presidential Campaign.* New York: Duell, Sloan and Pearce.

Lazarsfeld, Paul F. and Patricia L. Kendall
- 1948 *Radio Listening in America.* New York: Prentice-Hall.

Lazarsfeld, Paul F. and Robert K. Merton
- 1943 "Studies in Radio and Film Propaganda," *Transactions of the New York Academy of Science*, Series 2 6: 58-79.
- 1948 "Mass Communication, Popular Taste and Organized Social Action." Pp. 95-118 in Lyman Bryson (ed.), *Communication of Ideas.* New York: Harper.

Lazarsfeld, Paul F. and H. D. Schneider
- 1949 "Research for Action." Pp. 73-108 in P. Lazarsfeld and F. N. Stanton (eds.), *Communication Research 1948-1949.* New York: Harper.

Lazere, Donald
- 1987 "Conservative Media Criticism: Heads I Win, Tails You Lose." Pp. 81-94 in Donald Lazere (ed.), *American Media and Mass Culture: Left Perspectives.* Berkeley: University of California Press.

Le Duc, Don R.
- 1979 "The Common Market Film Industry: Beyond Law or Economics," *Journal of Communication* 29(1): 44-55.

Lee, Chin-Chuan
  1980  *Media Imperialism Reconsidered: The Homogenizing of Television Culture.* Beverly Hills, CA: Sage.
Leff, Leonard J. and Jerold L. Simmons
  1990  *The Dame in the Kimono: Hollywood, Censorship, and the Production Code from the 1920s to the 1960s.* New York: Grove Weidenfeld.
Leff, Mark Hugh
  1984  *The Limits of Symbolic Reform: The New Deal and Taxation.* Cambridge: Cambridge University Press.
Leiss, William
  1989  "The Myth of the Information Society." Pp. 282-298 in Ian H. Angus and Sut Jhally (eds.), *Cultural Politics in Contemporary America.* New York: Routledge.
Lent, John A.
  1975  "The Price of Modernity," *Journal of Communication* 25(2): 128-135.
Lera, E.
  1990  "Conflicts in the Development of Broadband Communications," *Telecommunications Policy* 14(4): 283-289.
Levinson, Paul
  1984  "The Human Option: Media, Evolution and Rationality as Checks on Media Determinism." Pp. 231-237 in Sari Thomas (ed.), *Studies in Communication,* Vol. 1. Norwood, NJ: Ablex.
Liebert, Robert M. and Joyce Sprafkin
  1988  *The Early Window: Effects of Television on Children and Youth.* New York: Pergamon.
Liebes, Tamar and Elihu Katz
  1988  "Dallas and Genesis: Primordiality and Seriality in Popular Culture." Pp. 113-125 in James W. Carey (ed.), *Media, Myths, and Narratives: Television and the Press.* Newbury Park, CA: Sage.
Lindstrom, Paul B.
  1989  "Home Video: The Consumer Impact." Pp. 40-49 in Mark R. Levy (ed.), *The VCR Age: Home Video and Mass Communication.* Newbury Park, CA: Sage.
Link, Henry C. and Hopf, Harry Arthur
  1946  *People and Books: A Study of Reading and Book-Buying Habits.* New York: Book Industry Committee of the Book Manufacturers' Institute.
Lipset, Seymour Martin
  1959  "Some Social Requisites of Democracy: Economic Development and Political Legitimacy," *American Political Science Review* 53: 169-105.

Litman, Barry Russell
  1979 *The Vertical Structure of the Television Broadcasting Industry: The Coalescence of Power.* East Lansing: Division of Research, Graduate School of Business Administration, Michigan State University.

Locksley, Gareth
  1987 "Direct Broadcast Satellites: The Media-Industrial Complex in the UK and Europe," *Telecommunications Policy* 11(2): 193-207.

Lowenthal, Leo
  1944 "Biographies in Popular Magazines." Pp. 507-548 in Paul F. Lazarsfeld and Frank Stanton (eds.), *Radio Research 1942-1943.* New York: Duell, Sloan and Pearce.
  1984 *Literature and Mass Culture: Communication in Society,* Vol. 1. New Brunswick, NJ: Transaction.

Lowery, S. and M. L. DeFleur
  1988 *Milestones in Mass Communication Research,* 2nd ed. New York: Longman.

Luhmann, Niklas
  1990a "Meaning as Sociology's Basic Concept." Pp.21-79 in *Essays on Self-Reference.* New York: Columbia University Press.
  1990b "The Improbability of Communication." Pp. 86-98 in *Essays on Self-Reference.* New York: Columbia University Press.
  1990c "Modes of Communication and Society." Pp. 99-106 in *Essays on Self-Reference.* New York: Columbia University Press.

Lull, James
  1990 [1980] "The Social Uses of Television." Pp. 28-48 in *Inside Family Viewing: Ethnographic Research on Television's Audiences.* London: Routledge.
  1990 [1982] "A Rules Approach to the Study of Television and Society." Pp. 62-85 in *Inside Family Viewing: Ethnographic Research on Television's Audiences.* London: Routledge.

Lundberg, F.
  1936 *Imperial Hearst.* New York: Equinox Cooperative Press.

Lundstedt, Sven B. and Michael W. Spicer
  1990 "Latent Policy and the Federal Communications Commission." Pp. 289-297 in Sven B. Lundstedt (ed.), *Telecommunications, Values, and the Public Interest.* Norwood, NJ: Ablex.

Lyon, David
  1988 *The Information Society: Issues and Illusions.* Cambridge: Polity.

MacBride, Sean, et al.
  1980 *Many Voices, One World.* London, New York, Paris: Kogan Paul, Unipub, and UNESCO

MacDougald, Duncan, Jr.
1941 "The Popular Music Industry." Pp. 65-109 in Paul F. Lazarsfeld and Frank N. Stanton (eds.), *Radio Research 1941*. New York: Duell, Sloan and Pearce.

Machado, Jose A. Mayobre
1982 "Is Development News?" Pp. 13-21 in L. Erwin Atwood, Stewart J. Bullion, and Sharon M. Murphy (eds.), *International Perspectives in News*. Carbondale: Southern Illinois University Press.

Madrid, Javier Esteinou
1986 "Means of Communication and Construction of Hegemony." Pp. 112-124 in Rita Atwood and Emile G. McAnany (eds.), *Communication and Latin American Society: Trends in Critical Research, 1960-1985*. Madison: University of Wisconsin Press.

Maley, S. W.
1980 "Telecommunications Systems." Pp. 391-462 in L. Lewin (ed.), *Telecommunications: An Interdisciplinary Survey*. Dedham, MA: Artech House.

Mann, Michael
1988 [1984] "The Autonomous Power of the State: its Origins, Mechanisms and Results." Pp. 1-32 in *States, War and Capitalism*. Oxford: Basil Blackwell.

Marchetti, Gina
1986 "Subcultural Studies and the Film Audience: Rethinking the Film Viewing Context." Pp. 62-79 in Bruce A. Austin (ed.), *Current Research in Film: Audiences, Economics, and Law*, Vol. 2. Norwood, NJ: Ablex.

Martin, L. John and Anju Grover Chaudhary
1983 *Comparative Mass Media Systems*. New York: Longman.

Maruyama, Magoroh
1980 "Information and Communication in Poly-Epistemological Systems." Pp. 28-40 in Kathleen Woodward (ed.), *The Myths of Information: Technology and Post-Industrial Culture*. Madison, WI: Coda.

Masmoudi, Mustapha
1979 "The New World Information Order," *Journal of Communication* 19(2): 172-198.

Masterman, Len
1987 [1980] "Television, Film and Media Education." Pp. 374-400 in Oliver Boyd-Barrett and Peter Braham (eds.), *Media, Knowledge and Power*. Beckenham, Kent: Croom Helm.

Matta, Fernando Reyes
1979 "The Latin American Concept of News," *Journal of*

*Communication* 29(2): 164-171.

McAnany, Emile G.
1978 "Does Information Really Work?" *Journal of Communication* 28(1): 84-90.
1984 "The Logic of Cultural Industries in Latin America: The Television Industry in Brazil." Pp. 185-208 in Vincent Mosco and Janet Wasko (eds.), *The Critical Communications Review*, Vol. 2. Norwood, NJ: Ablex.

McCombs, Maxwell E.
1988 "Concentration, Monopoly, and Content." Pp. 129-137 in Robert C. Picard, James P. Winter, Maxwell E. McCombs, and Stephen Lacy (eds.), *Press Concentration and Monopoly: New Perspectives on Newspaper Ownership and Operation.* Norwood, NJ: Ablex.

McCombs, Maxwell E. and Donald Shaw
1972 "The Agenda-Setting Function of Mass Media," *Public Opinion Quarterly* 36(Summer): 176-187.

McDonald, Frederick J.
1961 "Motivation and the Communication Processes," *Audiovisual Communications Review* 9(September-October): 57-67.

McGuire, William J.
1986 "The Myth of Massive Media Impact: Savagings and Salvagings." Pp. 173-257 in George Comstock (ed.), *Public Communication and Behavior*, Vol. 1. Orlando: Academic Press.

McLaughlin, Margaret L.
1984 *Conversation: How Talk Is Organized.* Beverly Hills, CA: Sage.

McLeod, Jack M. and S. Hawley
1964 "Professionalization Among Newsmen," *Journalism Quarterly* 41(3): 529-539.

McLeod, Jack M., Gerald M. Kosicki, and Zhongdang Pan
1991 "On Understanding and Misunderstanding Media Effects." Pp. 235-266 in James Curran and Michael Gurevitch (eds.), *Mass Media and Society.* London: Edward Arnold.

McLeod, Jack M. and Byron Reeves
1980 "On the Nature of Media Effects." Pp. 17-54 in Stephen B. Withey and Ronald P. Abeles (eds.), *Television and Social Behavior: Beyond Violence and Children.* Hillsdale, NJ: Erlbaum.

McLuhan, H. M.
1962 *The Gutenberg Galaxy: The Making of Typographic Man.* Toronto: University of Toronto Press.
1964 *Understanding Media: The Extensions of Man.* New York: McGraw-Hill.

1967 The Medium is the Message. New York: Bantam.
McNair, Brian
    1991 *'Glasnost,' 'Perestroika' and the Soviet Media.* London: Routledge.
McNulty, Jean
    1989 "Broadcasting Policy in the Canadian Context: The Significance of Ideas about Technology and Nation-Building," *Canadian Issues* 10(6): 5-27.
McPhail, Thomas L.
    1987a "Contemporary Canadian Communication Issues: An Alternative Plan." Pp. 262-277 in Sari Thomas (ed.), *Studies in Communication*, Vol. 3. Norwood, NJ: Ablex.
    1987b *Electronic Colonialism: The Future of International Broadcasting and Communication*, revised 2nd ed. Newbury Park, CA: Sage.
McPhail, Thomas L. and Brenda M. McPhail
    1990 *Communication: The Canadian Experience.* Toronto: Copp Clark Pitman.
McQuail, Denis
    1969 *Toward a Sociology of Mass Communications.* London: Macmillan.
    1977 "The Influence and Effects of Mass Media." Pp. 70-94 in James Curran, Michael Gurevitch, and Janet Woollacott (eds.), *Mass Communication and Society.* Beverly Hills, CA: Sage.
    1984 *Mass Communication Theory: An Introduction.* Beverly Hills, CA: Sage.
    1985 "Sociology of Mass Communications," *Annual Review of Sociology* 11: 93-111.
    1986a "Is Media Theory Adequate to the Challenge of New Communication Technologies?" Pp. 1-17 in Marjorie Ferguson (ed.), *New Communication Technologies and the Public Interest.* London: Sage.
    1986b "Policy Perspectives for New Media in Europe." Pp. 122-136 in Marjorie Ferguson (ed.), *New Communication Technologies and the Public Interest.* London: Sage.
    1987a *Mass Communication Theory: An Introduction*, 2nd ed. London: Sage.
    1987b "Research on New Communication Technologies: Barren Terrain or Promising Arena?" Pp. 431-445 in William H. Dutton, Jay G. Blumler, and Kenneth L. Kraemer (eds.), *Wired Cities.* Boston, MA: G. K. Hall.
Melischek, Gabrielle, Karl Erik Rosengren, and James Stappers (eds.)
    1984 *Cultural Indicators: An International Symposium.* Austrian Academy of Sciences, Philosophical-Historical Series, Vol.

416. Vienna: Austrian Academy of Sciences.

Melody, William H.
- 1987 "UK Research on Implications of Information and Communication Technologies," *Telecommunications Policy* 11(1): 11-19.

Melody, William H., H. L. Salter, and P. Heyer
- 1981 *Culture, Communication, and Dependency: The Tradition of H. A. Innis.* Norwood, NJ: Ablex.

Melody, William H. and Rohan Samarajiva
- 1986 "Canada's Contradictions on the New International Information Order." Pp. 160-167 in Jörg Becker, Göran Hedebro, and Leena Paldán (eds.), *Communication and Domination: Essays to Honor Herbert I. Schiller.* Norwood, NJ: Ablex.

Mendelsohn, Harold
- 1966 *Mass Entertainment.* New Haven, CT: College and University Press.

Merton Robert K.
- 1946 *Mass Persuasion.* New York: Harper.
- 1949 *Social Theory and Social Structure.* Glencoe, IL: Free Press.

Metcalfe, Stan
- 1986 "Information and Some Economics of the Information Revolution." Pp. 37-51 in Marjorie Ferguson (ed.), *New Communication Technologies and the Public Interest.* London: Sage.

Meyer, Timothy P. and Anne Hexamer
- 1982 "The Use and Abuse of Media Effects Research in the Development of Telecommunications Social Policy." Pp. 222-235 in Jorge Reina Schement, Guitierrez, and Marvin S. Sirbu, Jr. (eds.), *Telecommunications Policy Handbook.* New York: Praeger.

Meyer, William H.
- 1988 *Transnational Media and Third World Development: The Structure and Impact of Imperialism.* New York: Greenwood.

Meyrowitz, J.
- 1985 *No Sense of Place.* New York: Oxford.
- 1990 "Redefining the Situation: Extending Dramaturgy into a Theory of Social Change and Media Effects." Pp. 65-98 in Stephen Harold Riggins (ed.), *Beyond Goffman: Studies on Communication, Institution, and Social Interaction.* Berlin: Mouton de Gruyter.

Miliband, Ralph
- 1969 *The State in Capitalist Society: An Analysis of the Western System of Power.* New York: Basic.

Miller, James
   1990    "France Confronts the New Media: Issues in National Communication and Cultural Policy." Pp. 325-341 in Sari Thomas (ed.), *Studies in Communication*, Vol. 4. Norwood, NJ: Ablex.

Miller, Robert E.
   1988    "The Canadian Feature Film Conundrum: 1894-1967." Pp. 125-146 in Bruce A. Austin (ed.), *Current Research in Film: Audiences, Economics, and Law*, Vol. 4. Norwood, NJ: Ablex.

Miyamoto, S. Frank
   1959    "The Social Act: Re-examination of a Concept," *Pacific Sociological Review* 2(Fall): 51-55.

Moley, R.
   1945    *The Hays Office*. Indianapolis: Bobbs-Merrill.

Montgomery, Kathryn C.
   1982    "Special Interest Groups and the Networks: A Case Study of Pressure and Access." Pp. 241-254 in Jorge Reina Schement, Guitierrez, and Marvin S. Sirbu, Jr. (eds.), *Telecommunications Policy Handbook*. New York: Praeger.
   1989    *Target: Prime Time: Advocacy Groups and the Struggle over Entertainment Television*. New York: Oxford University Press.

Morgan, Kenneth
   1989    "A View from Abroad: The Experience of the Voluntary Press Council." Pp. 135-151 in Everette E. Dennis, Donald M. Gillmor, and Theodore L. Glasser (eds.), *Media Freedom and Accountability*. New York: Greenwood.

Morgan, Michael
   1989    "Television and Democracy." Pp. 240-253 in Ian H. Angus and Sut Jhally (eds.), *Cultural Politics in Contemporary America*. New York: Routledge.

Morley, David
   1989    Changing Paradigms in Audience Studies." Pp. 16-43 in Ellen Seiter, Hans Borchers, Gabriele Kreutzner, and Eva-Maria Warth (eds.), *Remote Control: Television, Audiences, and Cultural Power*. London: Routledge.
   1992    "Electronic Communities and Domestic Rituals: Cultural Consumption and the Production of European Collective Identities." Pp. 65-83 in Michael Skovmand and Kim Christian Schrøder (eds.), *Media Cultures: Reappraising Transnational Media*. London: Routledge.

Morrison, David
   1978    "The Beginnings of Modern Mass Communication Research," *European Journal of Sociology* 19(2): 347-359.

Mosco, Vincent
- 1979 "Who Makes U.S. Government Policy in World Communications?" *Journal of Communication* 29(1): 158-164.
- 1984 "Home Sweet Factory: Perspectives on Mass Society." Pp. 104-120 in Sari Thomas (ed.), *Studies in Communication*, Vol. 1. Norwood, NJ: Ablex.
- 1988 "Toward a Theory of the State and Telecommunications Policy," *Journal of Communication* 38(1): 107-124.

Mowlana, Hamid
- 1985 *International Flow of Information: A Global Report and Analysis*, Reports and Papers on Mass Communication, No. 99. Paris: UNESCO.
- 1990 *The Passing of Modernity*. White Plains, NY: Longman.

Murdock, Graham
- 1984 "The 'Privatization' of British Communications." Pp. 265-290 in Vincent Mosco and Janet Wasko (eds.), *The Critical Communications Review*, Vol. II. Norwood, NJ: Ablex.
- 1992 "Citizens, Consumers, and Public Culture." Pp. 17-41 in Michael Skovmand and Kim Christian Schrøder (eds.), *Media Cultures: Reappraising Transnational Media*. London: Routledge.

Murdock, Graham and P. Golding
- 1977 "Capitalism, Communication, and Class Relations." Pp. 12-43 in James Curran, Michael Gurevitch, and Janet Woollacott (eds.), *Mass Communication and Society*. Beverly Hills, CA: Sage.
- 1989 "Information Poverty and Political Inequality: Citizenship in the Age of Privatized Communications" *Journal of Communication* 39(3): 180-195.

Negrine, Ralph
- 1990 "British Television in an Age of Change." Pp. 148-170 in Kenneth Dyson and Peter Humphreys (eds.), *The Political Economy of Communications: International and European Dimensions*. London: Routledge.

Nelson, Jenny L.
- 1989 "Limits of Consumption: An Ironic Revision of Televisual Experience." Pp. 152-163 in Herbert W. Simons (ed.), *Rhetoric in the Human Sciences*. London: Sage.

Neuman, W. Russell
- 1991 *The Future of the Mass Audience*. New York: Cambridge University Press.

Neuman, W. Russell, Marion R. Just, and Ann N. Crigler
- 1992 *Common Knowledge: News and the Construction of Political Meaning*. Chicago: University of Chicago Press.

Newcomb, Horace
　1988　"One Night of Prime Time: An Analysis of Television's Multiple Voices." Pp. 88-112 in James W. Carey (ed.), *Media, Myths, and Narratives*. Newbury Park, CA: Sage.
Newcomb, Theodore M.
　1953　"An Approach to the Study of Communicative Acts," *Psychological Review* 60(November): 393-404.
Nillesen, A. B. and J. G. Stappers
　1987　"The Government as Communicator: A Dutch Dilemma," *European Journal of Communication* 2: 491-512.
Noam, Eli
　1991　*Television in Europe*. New York: Oxford University Press.
Nordenstreng, Kaarle
　1981　*The Mass Media Declaration of UNESCO*. Norwood, NJ: Ablex.
　1986　"Tanzania and the New Information Order: A Case Study of Africa's Second Struggle." Pp. 177-191 in Jörg Becker, Göran Hedebro, and Leena Paldán (eds.), *Communication and Domination: Essays to Honor Herbert I. Schiller*. Norwood, NJ: Ablex.
Nordenstreng, Kaarle and Tapio Varis
　1974　*Television Traffic—A One-Way Street*, Reports and Papers on Mass Communication, No. 70. Paris: UNESCO.
Norton, R. D.
　1988　"Continental Restructuring: U.S.-Canadian Comparisons." Pp. 7-16 in David L. McKee (ed.), *Canadian-American Economic Relations: Conflict and Cooperation on a Continental Scale*. New York: Praeger.
O'Connor, Alan
　1990　"The Miners' Radio Station in Bolivia: A Culture of Resistance," *Journal of Communication* 40(1): 102-111.
Ogan, Christine
　1989a　"The Effect of New Technologies on Communication Policy." Pp. 43-58 in Jerry L. Salvaggio and Jennings Bryant (eds.), *Media Use in the Information Age: Emerging Patterns of Adoption and Consumer Use*. Hillsdale, NJ: Erlbaum.
　1989b　"The Worldwide Cultural and Economic Impact of Video." Pp. 230-251 in Mark R. Levy (ed.), *The VCR Age: Home Video and Mass Communication*. Newbury Park, CA: Sage.
Ogunade, Adelumola
　1982　"Mass Media and National Integration in Nigeria." Pp. 22-32 in L. Erwin Atwood, Stewart J. Bullion, and Sharon M. Murphy (eds.), *International Perspectives in News*. Carbondale: Southern Illinois University Press.

Owen, Bruce M. and Steven S. Wildman
  1992   *Video Economics.* Cambridge, MA: Harvard University Press.
Parenti, M.
  1986   *Inventing Reality: The Politics of the Mass Media.* New York: St. Martin's.
Park, Robert Ezra
  1955 [1923]   "Natural History of the Newspaper." Pp. 89-104 in *Society.* Glencoe, IL: Free Press.
Parsons, Talcott and Winston White
  1960   "The Mass Media and the Structure of American Society," *Journal of Social Issues* 16(3): 67-77.
Paulu, Burton
  1981   *Television and Radio in the United Kingdom.* Minneapolis: University of Minnesota Press.
Peatman, John Gray
  1944   "Radio and Popular Music." Pp. 335-393 in Paul F. Lazarsfeld and Frank N. Stanton (eds.), Radio Research 1942-1943. New York: Duell, Sloan and Pearce.
Peers, Frank
  1969   *The Politics of Canadian Broadcasting, 1920-1951.* Toronto: University of Toronto Press.
  1979   *The Public Eye: Television and the Politics of Canadian Broadcasting, 1952-1968.* Toronto: University of Toronto Press.
Pelton, Joseph N.
  1990   "Coping with Telepower." Pp. 81-99 in Sven B. Lundstedt (ed.), *Telecommunications, Values, and the Public Interest.* Norwood, NJ: Ablex.
Pendakur, Manjunath
  1986   "Canadian Feature Films in the Chicago Theatrical Market, 1978-1981: Economic Relations and Some Public Policy Questions." Pp. 186-203 in Bruce A. Austin (ed.), *Current Research in Film: Audiences, Economics, and Law,* Vol. 2. Norwood, NJ: Ablex.
  1988   "Internationalization of the Canadian Film Industry." Pp. 147-169 in Bruce A. Austin (ed.), *Current Research in Film: Audiences, Economics, and Law,* Vol. 4. Norwood, NJ: Ablex.
  1990   *Canadian Dreams and American Control: The Political Economy of the American Film Industry.* Detroit: Wayne State University Press.
Peters, C. C.
  1933   *Motion Pictures and Standards of Morality.* New York: Macmillan.

Peters, John Durham and Eric W. Rothenbuhler
   1989   "The Reality of Construction." Pp. 11-27 in Herbert W. Simons (ed.), *Rhetoric in the Human Sciences*. London: Sage.
Peterson, R. C. and L. L. Thurstone
   1933   *Motion Pictures and Social Attitudes of Children*. New York: Macmillan.
Phillips, David P.
   1977   "Motor Vehicle Fatalities Increase Just After Publicized Suicide Stories," *Science* 196: 1464-1465.
   1979   "Suicide, Motor Vehicle Fatalities, and the Mass Media: Evidence Toward A Theory of Suggestion," *American Journal of Sociology* 84(5): 1150-1174.
   1982   "The Impact of Fictional Television Stories in U. S. Adult Fatalities: New Evidence on the Effect of the Mass Media on Violence," *American Journal of Sociology* 87(6): 1340-1359.
   1986   "The Found Experiment: A New Technique for Assessing the Impact of Mass Media Violence on Real-World Aggressive Behavior." Pp. 259-307 in George Comstock (ed.), *Public Communication and Behavior*, Vol. 1. Orlando: Academic Press.
Phillips, Joseph D.
   1982   "Film Conglomerate Blockbusters: International Appeal and Product Homogenization." Pp. 325-335 in Gorham Kindem (ed.), *The American Movie Industry: The Business of Motion Pictures*. Carbondale: Southern Illinois University Press.
Picard, Robert G.
   1989   *Media Economics: Concepts and Issues*. Newbury Park, CA: Sage.
Pinch, Edward T.
   1978   "The Flow of News: An Assessment of the Non-Aligned News Agencies Pool," *Journal of Communication* 28(4): 163-171.
Poggi, Gianfranco
   1978   *The Development of the Modern State: A Sociological Introduction*. Stanford, CA: Stanford University Press.
   1990   *The State: Its Nature, Development and Prospects*. Stanford, CA: Stanford University Press.
Pool, Ithiel deSola, Wilbur Schramm, Frederick W. Frey, Nathan Maccoby, and Edwin B. Parker (eds.)
   1973   *Handbook of Communication*. Chicago: Rand McNally.
Postman, Neal
   1985   *Amusing Ourselves to Death*. New York: Penguin.
Potts, Timothy C.
   1977   "The Place of Structure in Communication." Pp. 99-115 in

George Vesey (ed.), *Communication and Understanding*. Sussex: Harvester.

Pratt, Steven
   1991   "TV still Prime Time Culprit, Rebellion One Way Out," *Durham Herald-Sun* September 18: B2.

Raboy, Marc
   1989   "Canada's Broadcasting Policy Debate." Pp. 41-54 in Deborah C. Poff (ed.), *Canadian Issues*. Ottawa and Montreal: International Council for Canadian Studies and The Association for Canadian Studies.

Rachlin, Allan
   1988   *News as Hegemonic Reality: American Political Culture and the Framing of News Accounts*. New York: Praeger.

Rafaeli, Sheizaf
   1988   "Interactivity: From New Media to Communication." Pp. 110-134 in Robert P. Hawkins, John M. Wiemann, and Suzanne Pingree (eds.) *Advancing Communication Science: Merging Mass and Interpersonal Processes*. Sage Annual Reviews of Communication Research, Vol.16. Newbury Park,CA: Sage.

Renaud, Jean-Luc
   1990   "The Role of the International Telecommunication Union: Conflict, Resolution and the Industrialized Countries." Pp. 33-57 in Kenneth Dyson and Peter Humphreys (eds.), *The Political Economy of Communications: International and European Dimensions*. London: Routledge.

Riley, John W., Jr. and Matilda White Riley
   1959   "Mass Communication and the Social System." Pp. 537-578 in Robert K. Merton, Leonard Broom, and Leonard S. Cottrell, Jr. (eds.), *Sociology Today: Problems and Prospects*. New York: Basic.

Riley, Matilda White and John W. Riley, Jr.
   1954 [1951]   "A Sociological Approach to Communications Research." Pp. 389-401 in Wilbur Schramm (ed.), *The Process and Effects of Mass Communication*. Urbana: University of Illinois Press.

Roach, Colleen
   1987   "The U.S. Position on the New World Information and Communication Order," *Journal of Communication* 37(4): 36-51.

Robinson, Deanna Campbell
   1981   "Changing Functions of Mass Media in the People's Republic of China," *Journal of Communication* 31(4): 58-73.

Rogers, Everett M.
   1978   "The Rise and Fall of the Dominant Paradigm," *Journal of Communication* 18(1): 64-69.

1985 "The Empirical and Critical Schools of Communication Research." Pp. 219-235 in Everett M. Rogers and Francis Balle (eds.), *The Media Revolution in America and Western Europe*. Norwood, NJ: Ablex.

Rogers, Everett M. and Livia Antola
1985 "Telenovelas, A Latin American Success Story," *Journal of Communication* 35(4): 24-35.

Rosenau, Pauline Marie
1992 *Post-Modernism and the Social Sciences: Insights, Inroads, and Intrusions*. Princeton, NJ: Princeton University Press.

Rosengren, K. E., L. A. Wenner, and P. Palmgreen (eds.)
1985 *Media Gratifications Research: Current Perspectives*. Beverly Hills, CA: Sage.

Rowland, W. D., Jr.
1982 "The Struggle for Self-Determination: Public Broadcasting, Policy Problems, and Reform." Pp. 71-97 in Jorge Reina Schement, Guitierrez, and Marvin S. Sirbu, Jr. (eds.), *Telecommunications Policy Handbook*. New York: Praeger.
1983 *The Politics of TV Violence*. Beverly Hills, CA: Sage.

Rowland, W. D., Jr. and Michael Tracey
1990 "Worldwide Challenges to Public Service Broadcasting," *Journal of Communication* 40(2): 7-27.

Ruud, Charles A.
1979 "Limits on the 'Freed' Press of 18th- and 19th-Century Europe," *Journalism Quarterly* 56(3): 521-530.

Samarajiva, Rohan and Peter Shields
1990 "Value Issues in Telecommunications Resource Allocation in the Third World." Pp. 227-253 in Sven B. Lundstedt (ed.), *Telecommunications, Values, and the Public Interest*. Norwood, NJ: Ablex.

Saxer, Ulrich
1992 "Television in a Small Multicultural Society: The Case of Switzerland." Pp. 130-146 in Jay G. Blumler (ed.), *Television and the Public Interest: Vulnerable Values in West European Broadcasting*. London: Sage.

Scannell, Paddy, with David Cardiff
1991 *A Social History of British Broadcasting*. Oxford: Blackwell.

Schiller, Herbert I.
1979 "Transnational Media and National Development." Pp. 21-32 in Kaarle Nordenstreng and Herbert I. Schiller (eds.), *National Sovereignty and International Communication*. Norwood, NJ: Ablex.
1982 "Sources of Opposition to U.S. Information Supremacy." Pp.

258-271 in Jorge Reina Schement, Guitierrez, and Marvin S. Sirbu, Jr. (eds.), *Telecommunications Policy Handbook*. New York: Praeger.

1987 [1981] "The Infrastructure of the "Information Society'." Pp. 183-193 in Oliver Boyd-Barrett and Peter Braham (eds.), *Media, Knowledge and Power*. Beckenham, Kent: Croom Helm.

1989a "The Privatization and Transnationalization of Culture." Pp. 317-332 in Ian H. Angus and Sut Jhally (eds.), *Cultural Politics in Contemporary America*. New York: Routledge.

1989b "Is There a United States Information Policy?" Pp. 287-311 in William Preston,Jr., Edward S. Herman, and Herbert I. Schiller, *Hope and Folly: the United States and Unesco, 1945-1985*. Minneapolis: University of Minnesota Press.

Schlesinger, Philip
1991 *Media, State and Nation: Political Violence and Collective Identities*. London: Sage.

Schoenbach, Klaus and Lee B. Becker
1989 "The Audience Copes with Plenty: Patterns of Reactions to Media Changes." Pp. 353-366 in Lee B. Becker and Klaus Schoenbach (eds.), *Audience Responses to Media Diversification*. Hillsdale, NJ: Erlbaum.

Schramm, Wilbur
1954a "Procedures and Effects of Mass Communication." Pp. 112-138 in Nelson B. Henry (ed.), *Mass Media and Education: The Fifty-third Yearbook of the National Society for the Study of Education*, Part II. Chicago: University of Chicago Press.

1954b *The Process and Effects of Mass Communication*. Urbana: University of Illinois Press.

1964 *Mass Media and National Development: The Role of Information in the Developing Countries*. Stanford, CA: Stanford University Press.

1967 "Communication and Change." Pp. 5-32 in Daniel Lerner and William Schramm (eds.), *Communication and Change in the Developing Countries*. Honolulu: East-West Center Press.

1971 "The Nature of Communication Between Humans." Pp. 1-53 in W. Schramm and D. F. Roberts (eds.), *The Process and Effects of Mass Communication*, rev. ed. Urbana: University of Illinois Press.

1973 *Men, Messages, and Media: A Look at Human Communication*. New York: Harper and Row.

Schramm, Wilbur and William E. Porter
1982 *Men, Women, Messages, and Media: Understanding Human Communication*, 2nd ed. New York: Harper and Row.

Schramm, Wilbur and W. Lee Ruggels
   1967   "How Mass Media Systems Grow." Pp. 57-75 in Daniel Lerner and Wilbur Schramm (eds.), *Communication and Change in the Developing Countries*. Honolulu: East-West Center Press.

Schudson, Michael
   1986   "The Menu of Media Research." Pp. 43-50 in Sandra J. Ball-Rokeach and Muriel G. Cantor (eds.), *Media, Audiences, and Social Structure*. Newbury Park, CA: Sage.
   1988   "What Is A Reporter?: The Private Face of Journalism." Pp. 228-245 in James W. Carey (ed.), *Media, Myths, and Narratives: Television and the Press*. Newbury Park, CA: Sage.

Schwoch, James
   1990   *The American Radio Industry and Its Latin American Activities*. Urbana: University of Illinois Press.

Schwoch, James, Susan Reilly, and Mimi White
   1992   *Media Knowledge: Readings in Popular Culture, Pedagogy, and Critical Citizenship*. Albany: State University of New York Press.

Scott, William T.
   1990   *The Possibility of Communication*. Berlin: Mouton de Gruyter.

Sears, D. O.
   1968   "The Paradox of De Facto Selective Exposure Without Preferences for Supportive Information." Pp. 777-787 in R. P. Abelson et al. (eds.), *Theories of Cognitive Consistency*. Chicago: Rand McNally.

Sears, D. O. and J. L. Freedman
   1967   "Selective Exposure to Information: A Critical Review," *Public Opinion Quarterly* 31(2): 194-213.

Seiter, Ellen, Hans Borchers, Gabriele Kreutzner, and Eva-Maria Warth
   1989   "Introduction." Pp. 1-16 in Ellen Seiter, Hans Borchers, Gabriele Kreutzner, and Eva-Maria Warth (eds.), *Remote Control: Television, Audiences, and Cultural Power*. London: Routledge.

Selznick, Philip
   1951   "Institutional Vulnerability in Mass Society," *American Journal of Sociology* 56(4): 320-331.

Serfaty, Simon
   1990   "The Media and Foreign Policy." Pp. 1-16 in Simon Serfaty (ed.), *The Media and Foreign Policy*. New York: St. Martin's.

Service, Elman R.
   1978   "Classical and Modern Theories of the Origins of Government." Pp. 21-33 in Ronald Cohen (ed.), *Origins of the State*. Philadelphia: Institute for the Study of Human Issues.

Seton-Watson, Hugh
   1977   *Nations and States.* Boulder, CO: Westview.
Severin, W. J. and J. W. Tankard
   1979   *Communication Theories: Origins, Methods, Uses.* New York: Hastings.
Severin, W. J. with J. W. Tankard
   1988   *Communication Theories: Origins, Methods, Uses*, 2nd ed. New York: Longman.
Seymour-Ure, Colin
   1987   "Media Policy in Britain: Now You See It, Now You Don't," European *Journal of Communication* 2: 269-288.
Shannon, Claude E. and Warren Weaver
   1949   *The Mathematical Theory of Communication.* Urbana: University of Illinois Press.
Shaw, Donald and Maxwell E. McCombs
   1977   *The Emergence of Political Issues: The Agenda-Setting Function of the Press.* St. Paul, MN: West.
Shayon, Robert Lewis
   1977   "Television International." Pp. 41-55 in George Gerbner (ed.), *Mass Media in Changing Cultures.* New York: Wiley.
Shedd, M. S., Elizabeth A. Wilman, and R. Douglas Burch
   1990   "An Economic Analysis of Canadian Content Regulations and a New Proposal," *Canadian Public Policy* 16(1): 60-72.
Shils, Edward A.
   1951   "The Study of the Primary Group." Pp. 44-69 in Daniel Lerner and Harold D. Lasswell (eds.), *The Policy Sciences.* Palo Alto: Stanford University Press.
   1963   "The Theory of Mass Society." Pp. 30-47 in Philip Olson (ed.), *America as a Mass Society.* Glencoe, IL: Free Press.
Shimanoff, Susan B.
   1980   *Communication Rules: Theory and Research.* Beverly Hills, CA: Sage.
Shoemaker, Pamela J. and Stephen D. Reese
   1991   *Mediating the Message: Theories of Influence on Mass Media Content.* New York: Longman.
Shorrock, David
   1989   "Europe—Towards 1992." Pp. 1-17 in David Shorrock (ed.), *European Communications: Technologies and Regulations of the Single Market.* London: Blenheim Online.
Shuttlesworth, F. K. and M. A. May
   1933   *The Social Conduct and Attitudes of Movie Fans.* New York: Macmillan.
Siebert, Fred S., Theodore Peterson, and Wilbur Schramm
   1956   *Four Theories of the Press: The Authoritarian, Libertarian,*

*Social Responsibility, and Soviet Concepts of What the Press Should Be and Do.* Urbana: University of Illinois Press.

Simmel, George
  1950  *The Sociology of George Simmel.* Glencoe, IL: Free Press.

Simonet, Thomas
  1987  "Conglomerates and Content: Remakes, Sequels, and Serials in the New Hollywood." Pp. 154-162 in Bruce A. Austin (ed.), *Current Research in Film: Audiences, Economics, and Law,* Vol. 3. Norwood, NJ: Ablex.

Singer, Benjamin D.
  1970  *Black Rioters: A Study of Social Factors and Communication in the Detroit Riot.* Lexington, MA: Heath Lexington.
  1983  *Communications in Canadian Society.* Don Mills, Ontario: Addison-Wesley.

Skocpol, Theda
  1985  "Bringing the State Back In: Strategies of Analysis in Current Research." Pp. 3-37 in Peter B. Evans, Dietrich Rueschemeyer, Theda Skocpol (eds.), *Bringing the State Back In.* Cambridge: Cambridge.

Smith, Anthony
  1980a  *The Geopolitics of Information: How Western Culture Dominates the World.* New York: Oxford.
  1980b  *Goodbye Gutenberg: The Newspaper Revolution of the 1980s.* New York: Oxford.

Smith, Anthony D.
  1983  *State and Nation in the Third World.* New York: St. Martin's.
  1986  "State-Making and Nation-Building." Pp. 228-263 in John A. Hall (ed.), *States in History.* Oxford: Basil Blackwell.

Smith, Joel
  1954  *Organization of the Farm and Mass Communication.* Unpublished doctoral dissertation, Northwestern University.

Smith, Joel, Robert C. Bealer, and Francis M. Sim
  1962  "Communication and the 'Consequences' of Communication," *Sociological Inquiry* 32(Winter): 10-15.

Smythe, Dallas W.
  1986  "An Historical Perspective on Equity: National Policy on Public and Private Sectors in the United States." Pp. 21-30 in J. Miller (ed.), *Telecommunications and Equity: Policy Research Issues.* Amsterdam: North-Holland.

Sparkes, Vernon M. and Jeffrey P. Delbel
  1989  "United States: Changing Perceptions of Television." Pp. 333-352 in Lee B. Becker and Klaus Schoenbach (eds.), *Audience Responses to Media Diversification.* Hillsdale, NJ: Erlbaum.

Spitzer, Matthew L.
- 1986 *Seven Dirty Words and Six Other Stories: Controlling the Content of Print and Broadcast.* New Haven, CT: Yale University Press.

Starker, Steven
- 1989 *Evil Influences: Crusades Against the Mass Media.* New Brunswick, NJ: Transaction.

Stepan, Alfred
- 1978 *The State and Society: Peru in Comparative Perspective.* Princeton, NJ: Princeton University Press.

Stevenson, Robert L.
- 1988 *Communication, Development, and the Third World: The Global Politics of Information.* New York: Longman.

Straubhaar, Joseph D. and Carolyn Lin
- 1989 "A Quantitative Analysis of the Reasons for VCR Penetration Worldwide." Pp. 125-145 in Jerry L. Salvaggio and Jennings Bryant (eds.), *Media Use in the Information Age: Emerging Patterns of Adoption and Consumer Use.* Hillsdale, NJ: Erlbaum.

Swann, Dennis
- 1988 *The Retreat of the State: Deregulation and Privatization in the UK and US.* Ann Arbor: University of Michigan Press.

Szecskö, Tamas
- 1977 "The Development of a Socialist Communication Theory." Pp. 223-234 in George Gerbner (ed.), *Mass Media Policies in Changing Cultures.* New York: Wiley.

Thayer, Lee
- 1968 *Communication and Communication Systems in Organizations, Management, and Interpersonal Relations.* Homewood, IL: Irwin.
- 1988 "On the Mass Media and Mass Communication: Notes Toward A Theory." Pp. 52-83 in Richard W. Budd and Brent D. Ruben (eds.), *Beyond Media: New Approaches to Mass Communication.* New Brunswick, NJ: Transaction.

Thomas, George M. and John W. Meyer
- 1984 "The Expansion of the State." Pp. 461-482 in Ralph H. Turner (ed.), *Annual Review of Sociology*, Vol. 10. Palo Alto, CA: Annual Reviews.

Thorburn, David
- 1988 "Television as an Aesthetic Medium." Pp. 48-66 in James W. Carey (ed.), *Media, Myths, and Narratives: Television and the Press.* Newbury Park, CA: Sage.

Tichenor, Philip J., George A. Donohue, and Clarice N. Olien
- 1980 *Community Conflict and the Press.* Beverly Hills, CA: Sage.

Times Mirror Center for People and the Press
  1990 *The American Media: Who Reads, Who Watches, Who Listens, Who Cares.* Washington: Times Mirror Center for People and the Press.
Trauth, Denise M. and John L. Huffman
  1985 "Public Nuisance Laws: A New Mechanism for Film Censorship." Pp. 197-207 in Bruce A. Austin (ed.), *Current Research in Film: Audiences, Economics, and Law*, Vol. 1. Norwood, NJ: Ablex.
Tuchman, G.
  1972 "Objectivity as Strategic Ritual: An Examination of Newsmen's Notions of Objectivity," *American Journal of Sociology* 77(4): 660-679.
  1978 *Making News: A Study in the Construction of Reality.* Glencoe, IL: Free Press.
  1983 "Consciousness Industries and the Production of Culture," *Journal of Communication* 33(3)330-341.
  1988 "Mass Media Institutions." Pp. 601-626 in Neil J. Smelser (ed.), *Handbook of Sociology.* Newbury Park, CA: Sage.
Tunstall, Jeremy
  1983 *The Media in Britain.* New York: Columbia University Press.
  1986 *Communications Deregulation: The Unleashing of America's Communications Industry.* Oxford: Blackwell.
Turow, J.
  1984a *Media Industries: The Production of News and Entertainment.* New York: Longman.
  1984b "Unconventional Programs on Commercial Television: An Organizational Perspective." Pp. 77-95 in Sari Thomas (ed.), *Studies in Communication*, Vol. 1. Norwood, NJ: Ablex.
Ungerer, Herbert
  1989 "Promoting European Communications: The Role of the European Community." Pp. 165-176 in David Shorrock (ed.), *European Communications: Technologies and Regulations of the Single Market.* London: Blenheim Online.
van Cuilenberg, Jan J.
  1987 "The Information Society: Some Trends and Implications," *European Journal of Communication* 2: 105-121.
van Dijk, Teun A.
  1985 "Introduction: Discourse Analysis in (Mass) Communication Research." Pp. 1-9 in Teun A. van Dijk (ed.), *Discourse and Communication: New Approaches to the Analysis of Mass Media Discourse and Communication.* Berlin: de Gruyter.

Varis, Tapio
- 1984a "The International Flow of Television Programs," *Journal of Communication* 34(1): 143-152.
- 1984b "Global Traffic in Television Programming." Pp. 144-152 in George Gerbner and Marsha Siefert (eds.), *World Communications: A Handbook*. New York: Longman.
- 1985 *International Flow of Television Programmes*, Reports and Papers on Mass Communication, No. 100. Paris: UNESCO.

Waldman, Diane
- 1988 "The Justice Department versus the National Film Board of Canada: An Update and Analysis." Pp. 170-187 in Bruce A. Austin (ed.), *Current Research in Film: Audiences, Economics, and Law*, Vol. 4. Norwood, NJ: Ablex.

Ward, Ken
- 1989 *Mass Communications in the Modern World*. London: Macmillan.

Wartella E. and B. Reeves
- 1985 "Historical Trends in Research on Children and Media: 1900-1960," *Journal of Communication* 35(2): 118-133.

Wasko, J.
- 1981 "The Political Economy of the American Film Industry," *Media, Culture, and Society* 3(2): 135-153.
- 1982 *Movies and Money: Financing the American Film Industry*. Norwood, NJ: Ablex.
- 1985 "Hollywood, New Technologies and International Banking." Pp. 101-110 in Bruce A. Austin (ed.), *Current Research in Film: Audiences, Economics, and Law*, Vol. 1. Norwood, NJ: Ablex.
- 1986 [1978] "D. W. Griffith and the Banks: A Case Study in Film Financing." Pp. 31-42 in Paul Kerr (ed.), *The Hollywood Film Industry*. London: Routledge and Kegan Paul.

Watson, William G.
- 1988 *National Pastimes: The Economics of Canadian Leisure*. Vancouver, BC: The Fraser Institute.

Weaver, David Hugh, Judith M. Buddenbaum, and Jo Ellen Fair
- 1985 "Press Freedom, Media, and Development, 1950-1979: A Study of 134 Nations," *Journal of Communication* 35(2): 104-117.

Weaver, David Hugh, Doris A. Graber, Maxwell E. McCombs, and Chaim H. Eyal
- 1981 *Media Agenda-Setting in a Presidential Election: Issues, Images, and Interest*. New York: Praeger.

Webster, James G.
- 1989 "Television Audience Behavior: Patterns of Exposure in the New Media Environment." Pp. 197-216 in Jerry L. Salvaggio

and Jennings Bryant (eds.), *Media Use in the Information Age: Emerging Patterns of Adoption and Consumer Use.* Hillsdale, NJ: Lawrence Erlbaum.

Weimann, G.
1983 "The Theater of Terror: Effects of Coverage," *Journal of Communication* 33(1): 38-45.

Westergaard, J.
1979 "Power, Class, and the Media." Pp. 95-115 in James Curran, Michael Gurevitch, and Janet Woollacott (eds.), *Mass Communication and Society.* Beverly Hills, CA: Sage.

Westley, Bruce H. and Malcolm S. MacLean, Jr.
1966 "A Conceptual Model for Communications Research." Pp. 80-87 in Alfred Smith (ed.), *Communication and Culture.* New York: Holt, Rinehart and Winston.

Wigand, Rolf T., Carrie Shipley, and Dwayne Shipley
1984 "Transborder Data Flow, Informatics, and National Policies," *Journal of Communication* 34(1): 153-175.

Wildman, Steven S. and Stephen E. Siwek
1988 *International Trade in Films and Television Programs.* Cambridge, MA: Ballinger.

Wilensky, Harold L.
1966 "Mass Society and Mass Culture." Pp. 293-327 in Bernard Berelson and Morris Janowitz (eds.), *Reader in Public Opinion and Communication,* 2nd ed. New York: Free Press.

Wilhoit, G. Cleveland and H. DeBock (eds.)
1981 *Mass Communication Review Yearbook,* Vol. 2. Beverly Hills, CA: Sage.

Williams, Raymond
1977 *Marxism and Literature.* Oxford: University Press.
1987 [1986] "Human Communication and Its History." Pp. 32-48 in Oliver Boyd-Barrett and Peter Braham (eds.), *Media, Knowledge and Power.* Beckenham, Kent: Croom Helm.

Williams, Tanis McB.
1986 *The Impact of Television: A Natural Experiment in Three Communities.* New York: Academic.

Williamson, J.
1978 *Decoding Advertisements: Ideology and Meaning in Advertising.* London: Marion Boyers.

Wilson, Kevin G.
1988 *Technologies of Control: The New Interactive Media for the Home.* Madison: University of Wisconsin Press.

Winkler, J. K.
1928 *W. R. Hearst: An American Phenomenon.* New York: Simon and Schuster.

Wise, George
  1992 "Everyday Objects." *Science* 256(May 15): 1037-1038.
Wober, J. Mallory
  1988 *The Use and Abuse of Television: A Social Psychological Analysis of the Changing Screen.* Hillsdale, NJ: Erlbaum.
  1989 "The U.K.: The Constancy of Audience Behavior." Pp. 91-107 in Lee B. Becker and Klaus Schoenbach (eds.), *Audience Responses to Media Diversification.* Hillsdale, NJ: Erlbaum.
Wober, J. Mallory and Barrie Gunter
  1988 *Television and Social Control.* New York: St. Martin's Press.
Wolton, Dominique
  1992 "Values and Normative Choices in French Television." Pp. 147-160 in Jay G. Blumler (ed.), *Television and the Public Interest: Vulnerable Values in West European Broadcasting.* London: Sage.
Wright, Charles R.
  1959 *Mass Communication: A Sociological Perspective.* New York: Random House.
  1986a *Mass Communication: A Sociological Perspective*, 3rd ed. New York: Random House.
  1986b "Mass Communication Rediscovered: Its Past and Future in American Sociology." Pp. 22-33 in Sandra J. Ball-Rokeach and Muriel G. Cantor (eds.), *Media, Audience, and Social Structure.* Newbury Park, CA: Sage.
Wrong, Dennis H.
  1979 *Power: Its Forms, Bases, and Uses.* New York: Harper and Row.
Zaret, David
  1980 "Ideology and Organization in Puritanism," *Archives Européenes de Sociologie* 21(1): 83-115.
  1985 *The Heavenly Contract: Ideology and Organization in Pre-Revolutionary Puritanism.* Chicago: University of Chicago Press.
  1992 "Religion, Science, and Printing in the Public Spheres in Seventeenth-Century England." Pp. 212-235 in Craig Calhoun (ed.), *Habermas and the Public Sphere.* Cambridge, MA: MIT Press.

# Author Index

Adrono, T.W., 151, *323*
Afanasiev, V., 255, *323*
Aitken, I., 261n, 300n (4), *323*
Alexander, A., 214, *337*
Alford, R.R., 297n, 309n (47), *323*
Allen, I.L., 147, *323*
Allen, R.C., 152n, 161n (17), *323*
Anderson, A., 7, *323*
Andrews, E.L., 194, *323*
Ang, I., 39, 107, 154n, 161n (18), 180, 198, 284, *324*
Anger, K., 168, *324*
Antola, L., 284, *361*
Argyle, M., 46n, 59n (8), *324*
Arnheim, R., 155, *324*
Aronson, D., 292, *324*
Associated Press, 116, 146, 188, 224, *324*
Atwood, L.E., 255, *324*
Audley, P., 166, *324*
Austin, B.A., 2, 112, 117, *324*

Babe, R.E., 239, 287, *324*
Baer, W.S., 293, *325*
Badie, B., 227n, 260n (8), *325*
Bagdikian, B.H., 44, 102, 105, 166, 167, 177, *325*
Ball-Rokeach, S.J., 3, 17n, 29n (9), 88n, 128n (1), 142, *325, 334*
Barkey, K., 226, *325*
Baron, J.N., 144n, 160n (11), *325*
Barthes, R., 175, *325*
Barton, R.L., 223, 273, 288n, 306n (36), *325*
Bassiouni, M.C., 179, *325*
Bates, B.J., 291n, 308n (42), *325*
Baudrillard, J., 33, 139n, 159n (2), *325*
Bealer, R.C., 17, 33, *365*
Becker, B., 77n, 85n (10), *326*
Becker, L.B., 109, 111, 112, 143, 149, 174, 198, 293, *326, 362*
Beckton, C.F., 245, *326*
Bell, A., 64, 213, *326*
Beltran, S.L.R., 277n, 303n (18), *326*
Beniger, J.R., 126n, 129n (9), *326*
Bennett, T., 175, *327*
Bennett, W.L., 144, 150, 156, *327*
Benzies, J.Y., 275n, 303n (15), *328*
Berelson, B., 12, 142n, 160n (7), *327, 348*

Berger, A.A., 175, *327*
Berkowitz, D., 177, *327*
Berlo, D.K., 35, 82, 142, *327*
Beville, H.M., Jr., 107, *327*
Bineham, J.L., 140, 142, *327*
Birnbaum, P., 227n, 260n (8), *325*
Blatherwick, D.E.S., 241, 295n, 308-309n (45), *327*
Blau, P.M., 78, 85n (11), *327*
Blood, R.W., 109, 111, *326*
Blumer, H., 133, 142n, 159n (5), 222, *327, 328*
Blumler, J.G., 147, 247, 251n, 263n (25), 267n, 268n, 290, 291, 293, 299-300n (3), 300n (5), *328, 335*
Bogart, L., 12, 101, 112, 113, 169, 174, *328*
Bollen, K.A., 144, *328*
Borchers, H., 180, 363, *364*
Bowman, W.W., 174, *346*
Boyd, D.A., 275n, 303n (15), *328*
Boyd-Barett, O., 275n, 302n (13), *328*
Boyle, A., 268n, 300n (5), *329*
Braman, S., 21n, 29n (10), *329*
Breed, W., 77n, 85n (10), 173, *329*
Brenkman, J., 144, *329*
Breuilly, J., 235n, 261n (14), *329*
Brewer, B., 77n, 85n (10), *326*
Briggs, A., 268n, 300n (5), *329*
Brooks, H., 146, 291n, 308n (42), *329*
Brown, D.H., 172, 183n, 186n (8, 9), 289n, 306n (37), *329*
Browne, D.R., 210, 267n, 299n (3), *329*
Bryant, J., 148, 170n, 186n (6), *329*
Brynin, M., 267n, 299n (3), *328*
Budd, R.W., 17n 29n (9), *329*
Buddenbaum, J.M., 246, *368*

Bullion, S.J., 255, *324*
Burch, R.D., 288, *364*
Burgelman, J-C., 274, *330*
Burns, T., 268n, 300n (5), *330*
Calhoun, C., 318, *330*
Campbell, A., 112, *330*
Cantor, J.M., 2, 148, 283, *330*
Cantor, M.G., 2, 12, 148, 283, *330*
Cantril, H., 135, *330*
Cardiff, D., 98n, 128n (3), 147, 234n, 258, 261n (13), 268n, 300n (5), *330-331, 361*
Carey, J.W., 4, 12, 14, 23, 91, 141, 144n, 160n (9), *331*
Carmen, I.H., 168, *331*
Caron, A., 290n, 294n, 307n (39), 308n (45), *331*
Carpenter, E.S., 74, *331*
Chaffee, S.H., 142, 142n, 143, 148n, 160n (8, 13), *331, 332*
Chaudhary, A.G., 166, 247, *351*
Cherry, C., 4, 54, *331*
Chomsky, N., 44, *344*
Clayman, S., 171, *344*
Clippinger, J.H., 248, *331*
Codding, G.A., Jr., 248, *331*
Cogley, J., 124n, 129n (8), *332*
Cohen R., 225n, 260n (6), *332*
Coleman, J.S., 32, 180, 227, *332*
Collins, R., 212, 242, 268n, 281, 285n, 288, 289n, 290n, 295n, 300n (5), 304n, (24), 305n, (31), 306-307n (37), 307-308n (39), 308n (45), 309n (46), *332*
Compaine, B.M., 166, *332*
Comstock, G.A.12, 109n, 129n (6), 142, 143, *332*
Connell, I., 44, 175, *332*
Coulson, D.C., 167, *333*
Cowhey, P.F., 292, *324*
Crane, R.J., 223, *333*
Creedon, P.J., 109, 111, *326*

Crigler, A.N., 233, *356*
Crotts, G.G., 193n, 217n (2), *333*
Cunningham and Walsh, 144, *333*
Curelaru, 25, *336*
Curran, J., 155, *333*
Cutler, B., 112, *333*
Cutright, P., 246, *333*
Csikszentmihalyi, M., 119, 213, *347*

Dale, E., 142n, 159n (5), *333*
Davidge, C., 293, *333*
Davis, D.K., 77n, 85n (10), *333*
DeBock, H., 143, *369*
de Carepmq. E.F., 227n, 303n (18), *326*
DeFleur, M.L., 3, 12, 17n, 29n (9), 142, 142n, 159n (5), *333, 334, 350*
Delbel, J.P., 109, 112, *365*
Delia, J.G., 34, 171, *334*
Demac, D.A., 277n, 291, 303n (18), *334*
Deutsch, K., 235, 265, *334*
Dexter, L.A., 12, *334*
Dickinson, B., 77n, 85n (10), *326*
Doherty, M., 73, *334*
Dominick, J.R., 102, 112, 166, *334*
Donohew, L., 126n, 129n (8), *337*
Donohue, G.A., 14, 127, *366*
Douglas, S., 166, *334*
Dreier, P., 171, *334*
Dua, H.R., 37n, 42, 58n (2), *334*
Dunnett, P.J.S., 247, *335*
Durkheim, E., 225n 260n (6), *335*
Dutton, W.H., 222, 223, 290, 291, 293, *335*
Dysinger, W.S., 142n, 159n (5), *335*
Dyson, K.H.F., 247, 270, 290n, 307n (39), *335*

Eason, D.L., 8n, 28n (1), *335*

Eco, U., 175, *335*
Edgerton, G., 95, *336*
Edwards, J., 64, *336*
Eek, H., 281, *336*
Einsiedel, E.F., 222, *336*
Eisenstadt, 25, *336*
Ekman, P., 141, *343*
Electronic Media, 246n, 263n (18), *336*
Elias, N., 64n, 84n (3), *336*
Elkin, F., 289, 306n-307n (37), *336*
Elliott, P., 9, 111, *336*
Engelkamp, J., 33, *336*
Engelman, R., 141n, 159n (3), *336*
Evans, G., 267n, 300n (4), *337*
Evans, H., 222n, 245, 260n (4), *337*
Eyal, C., 143, *368*

Fair, J.E., 246, *368*
Farace, R.V., 126n, 129n (8), *337*
Fekete, J., 144n, 160n (10), *337*
Ferguson, M., 294, *337*
Fisher, D., 248, *337*
Fishman, M., 174, *337*
Fiske, J., 108, 169, 175, *337*
Flichy, P., 268, *337*
Foley, J.M., 193, *338*
Forman, H.J., 142n 159n (5), *338*
Freden, E.S., 109, 111, *326*
Freedman, J.L., 3, 12, 142, *363*
Freiman, M.J., 154, 169, 259, *338*
Frey, W.F., 12, *359*
Friedland, R., 297n, 309n (47), *323*
Friedson, E., 3, 138, 312, *338*

Gamson, W.A., 12, *338*
Gandy, O.H., 149, 176, 286, *338*
Ganley, G.D., 7, 277, *338*
Ganley, O.H., 7, 277, *338*
Gans, H.J., 44, 174, *338*
Garnham, N., 10n, 14, 28n (2),

273, *338-339*
Gaudet, H., 142n, 160n (7), *348*
Gaunt, P., 255, *339*
Gerbner, G., 150n, 160n (15), 166, 175, 255, *339*
Gergen, D.R., 294, *339*
Gibbs, G., 241, *339*
Giffard, C. A., 282n, 304n (25), *339*
Gifreu, J., 236n, 261n (15), *339*
Giroux, H.A., 213, *340*
Gitlin, T., 12n, 13-14, 28n (3), 141, 142n, 160n (8), 175, 198n, 217n (3), 298, *340*
Globerman, S., 288n, 306n (36), *340*
Golding, P., 166, 174, 184, 266-267, 279, *340, 356*
Goldman, R., 13, 175, *340*
Good, L.T., 13, *340*
Gottdiener, M., 175, *340-341*
Graber, D.A., 143, *368*
Greenberg, B.S., 108, 111, 293, 294, *341, 343*
Gross, L., 177, *341*
Guback, T.H., 165n, 166, 186n (4), 247, 258n, 264n (29), 281, *332, 341*
Gunter, B., 150n, 160n (15), 163, *370*
Gunter, J.F., 248, *341*
Gwyn, R.J., 280n, 304n (23), *341*

Habermas, J., 34, 62n, 84n (1), *341*
Hachten, W.A., 141, 210, 252, *341*
Hagelin, T., 286, *342*
Haight, T.R., 280n, 303n (21), *342*
Hale, F.D., 167, *342*
Hall, L.S., 196, 197, *342*
Hall, S., 175, *342*
Hallin, D.C., 144, 156, *342*

Halloran, J.D., 112, *342*
Halprin, A., 292, *342*
Haralovich, M.B., 168, 175, *342-343*
Harrison, R., 141, *343*
Hart, D.J., 173, *343*
Hartley, E.L., 82, *343*
Hartley, J., 175, *337*
Hartley, R.E., 82, *337*
Haslett, B., 214, *337*
Hauser, P.M., 142n, 159n (5), *328*
Hawley, S., 174, *352*
Hays, W., 168, *343*
Hearold, S., 157, *343*
Hearst, S., 251n, 263n (23), 268n, 272n, 300n (5), 301n (7, 9), *343*
Heath, S., 133, 139, *343*
Heeter, C., 33, 108, 111, *343*
Held, D., 297n, 309n (47), *344*
Heller, S., 7, *344*
Heritage, J.C., 171, *344*
Herman, E.S., 44, *344*
Hexamer, A., 191, *354*
Heyer, P., 144n, 160n (9), *354*
Higman, H., 146, 290n, 308n (40), *344*
Hill, H.E., 164n, 186n (2), *344*
Hixson, R., 201, 202, *344*
Hochheimer, J.L., 142n, 160n (8), *331*
Hoffman-Riem, W., 268, 272n, 274, 274n, 301n (9, 11), *344*
Hopf, H.A., 112, *349*
Horkheimer, M., 142n, 160n (8), *323*
Horton, D., 98, *344*
Horwitz, R.B., 188n, 190, 193n, 196, 217n (1, 2)), *344*
Hoskins, C., 283, *344*
Howell, W.J., Jr., 166, 210, 247, 251n, 264n (25), 267n, 300n (3), *345*
Huffman, J.L., 168, *367*

Hulett, J.E., 83, *345*
Humphreys, P., 222n, 347, 259n (1), 290n, 291, 301n (39), *335, 345*
Ihde, D., 110,, *345*
Innis, H.A., 144, *345*
Irwin, M.R., 292, *345*
Ivacic, P., 283, *345*
Janisch, H., 286, *342*
Janowitz, M., 12, 127, 174, 327, *345*
Jansen, S.C., 16, 64n, 84n (3), 181, 196, *345*
Jarvie, I., 167, *345*
Jefferson, M., 276, *345*
Jensen, J., 158n, 161n (19), *346*
Johnson, F.C., 68, *346*
Johnson, W., 83, *346*
Johnstone, J., 174, *346*
Journal of Communication, 282, *346*
Jowett, G.S., 12, 141n, 159n (4), 169, *346*
Just, M.R., 233, *356*

Kamiss, P.C., 182, *346*
Kasza, G.J., 249n, 263n (21), *346*
Katz, E., 138, 142, 147, 148, 241, 279, *328, 346, 349*
Katzman, N., 142, 143, *332*
Keane, J., 9, 152, 232, 258n, 264n (28), 274, 321, *346-347*
Kellner, D., 151, 175, 184, *347*
Kendall, P.L., 12, 112, *348*
Kerner, I.J., 201, 204n, 217n (5), *347*
King, R., 227, 260n (8), *347*
Klapp, O., 71, 72, *347*
Klapper, J.T., 12, 143-144, 147, *347*
Klare, G.R., 68, *346*
Klofpenstein, B.C., 109, 116, *347*
Koizumi, T., 223, 293, *347*
Kosicki, G.M., 141, *352*

Kraemer, K.L., 290, 293, *335*
Krasnow, E.G., 195, 294, *347*
Kreutzner, G., 180, *363*
Krieger, J., 297n, 309n (47), *344*
Kubey, R., 119, 213, *347*

Lacy, S., 107, 129n (5), *348*
Lang, G.E., 170, *348*
Lang, K., 170, *348*
Langer, S.K., 42, *348*
Lasswell, H.O., 12, *348*
Lazarsfeld, P.F., 12, 45, 80n, 85n (14), 112, 138, 139, 141, 141n, 142, 142n, 143, 148n, 151, 159n (4), 160n (7, 13), *327, 346, 348*
Lazere, D., 171, *348*
Le Duc, D.R., 241n, 261n (17), *348*
Lee, C.-C., 284, *349*
Leff, L.J., 190, *349*
Leff, M.H., 168n, 186n (5), *349*
Leiss, W., 290n, 308n (41), *349*
Lent, J.A., 281, *349*
Lera, E., 293, *349*
Levinson, P., 152n, 161n (16), *349*
Liebert, R.M., 150, 166, 183n, 186n (8), *349*
Liebes, T., 148, *349*
Lin, C., 246, *366*
Lindstrom, P.B., 109, *349*
Link, H.C., 112, *349*
Linton, J.M., 12, *346*
Lipset, S.M., 246, *349*
Litman, B.R., 167, *350*
Locksley, G., 223, 241n, 261n (17), 273, *350*
Longley, L.D., 195, *347*
Lowenthal, L., 4, 8,23, 155, *350*
Lowery, S., 142n, 159n (5), *350*
Luhmann, N., 4, 15n, 16, 21, 23, 29n (7), 43, 43n, 44, 55n, 59n (6, 7), 60n (12), 146, 265, *350*

Lull, J., 24, 46n, 59n (8), 148n, 160n (14), *350*
Lundberg, F., 141, *350*
Lundstedt, S.B., 190, *350*
Lyon, D., 223n, 260n (5), 290, 291, *350*
MacBridge, S., 266n, 280n, 281, 298n (1), 303n (22), *350*
MacDougald, D., Jr., 155, *351*
MacLean, M.S., Jr., 82, *369*
MacLaren, P.L., 213, *340*
Machado, J.A.M., 278, 290n, 304n (23), *351*
Maccoby, N., 12, *359*
Madrid, J.E., 14, 19, *351*
Magee, R., 77n, 85n (10), *326*
Maley, S.W., 66n, 84n (5), *351*
Mann, M., 225n, 226, 227n, 260n (6, 8), *351*
Marchetti, G., 116, *351*
Martin, L.J., 166, 247, *351*
Maruyama, M., 25, *351*
Márványi, G., 255, *339*
Masmoudi, M., 280n, 303n (22), *351*
Masterman, L., 214, *351*
Matta, F.R., 279, *351-352*
May, M.A., 142n, 159n (5), *364*
McAnany, E.G., 275n, 277, 302n (13), *351*
McCombs, M.E., 142, 143, 167, 279, *332, 352, 364, 368*
McDonald, F.J., 55, *352*
McGuire, W.J., 143, 157, *352*
McLaughlin, M.L., 24, 64, *352*
McLeod, J.M., 144, 174, *352*
McLuhan, H.M., 144, 152, *352-353*
McNair, B., 255, 282n, 304n (26, 27), *353*
McNulty, J., 210, 239, 287, *353*
McPhail, B.M., 210, 252, *353*
McPhail, T.L., 210, 252, 273, 280n, 303n (22), *353*
McPhee, W.N., 142n, 160n (7), *327*
McQuail, D., 4, 12, 17n, 29n (9), 138n, 147, 159n (1), 165, 171, 274, 293, 312, *353*
Mead, L.M., 193n, 217n (2), *333*
Melischek, G., 150n, 160n (15), *353-354*
Melody, W.H., 144n, 160n (9), 280, 280n, 303n (20), *354*
Mendelsohn, H., 12, *354*
Merenda, M.J., 292, *345*
Merton, R.K., 45, 80n, 85n (14), 139, 142, 143, 151, *348, 354*
Metcalfe, S., 103, *354*
Metzner, C.A., 112, *330*
Meyer, J.W., 226, *361*
Meyer, T.P., 191, *354*
Meyer, W.H., 210, 278, 280n, 289, 304n (23), *354*
Meyrowitz, J., 8, 15n, 29n (6), 80n, 85n (13), 144, 145, 150, 152, *354*
Miliband, R., 226, 297n, 309n (47), *354*
Miller, J., 274, *355*
Miller, R.E., 286, *355*
Mills, A., 175, *332*
Mirus, R., 283, *344*
Miyamoto, S.F., 34, *355*
Moley, R., 168, *355*
Montgomery, K.C., 171, 172, *355*
Morgan, K., 317n, 322n (2), *355*
Morgan, M., 220, *355*
Morley, D., 9, 18, 116, 170n, 186n (6), 287, *355*
Morrison, D., 12n, 28n (3), *355*
Mosco, V., 3, 212n, 217n (6), 223, 297, *356*
Mowlana, H., 62, 87-88, 97, 125, 176, 219, 247, 275, 281, 284, 290, *356*
Murdock, G., 166, 184, 266-267,

267n, 268, 299n (2), *356*
Negrine, R., 241n, 261n (17), 281n, 285n, 304n (24), 305n (30), *356*
Nelson, J.L., 109n, 129n (6), *356*
Neuman, W.R., 233, 321, *356*
Newcomb, H., 148, 169, *357*
Newcomb, T.M., 35, *357*
Nillesen, A.B., 243, *357*
Noam, E., 273, 288n, 289n, 306n (36), 307n (38), *357*
Noble, J.K.N., Jr., 166, *332*
Nordenstreng, K., 247, 279n, 280, 280n, 281, 303n (19, 22), 304n (23), *357*
Norton, R.D., 239, 267n, 287, 300n (3), *357*
Nossiter, T.J., 247, 267n, 299n (3), *328*

O'Connor, A., 280n, 304n (23), *357*
O'Donnell, V., 141n, 159n (4), *346*
O'Keefe, B.J., 34, 171, *334*
Ogan, C., 270, 285, *357*
Ogunade, A., 236, 287, 287n, 306n (35), *357*
Olien, C.N., 14, 127, *366*
Owen, B.M., 107, 129n (5), *358*

Palmgreen, P., 148, *361*
Pan, Z., 144, *352*
Parenti, M., 143, *358*
Parikh, S., 226, *325*
Park, R.E., 127, *358*
Parker, E.B., 12, *359*
Parsons, T., 138, *358*
Paulu, B., 268n, 300n (5), *358*
Peatman, J.R., 155, *358*
Peers, F., 268n, 300n (5), *358*
Pelton, J.N., 293, *358*
Pendakur, M., 222n, 239, 257n, 259n (3), 264n (27), 286, *358*
Peters, C.C., 142n, 159n (5), *358*

Peters, J.D., 17, *359*
Peterson, R.C., 142n, 159n (5), 252, *359*
Peterson, T., 210, *364-365*
Phillips, D.P., 144, 157, 328, *359*
Phillips, J.D., 139, 222, *359*
Picard, R.G., 107n, 129n (5), *359*
Pinch, E.T., 283, *359*
Pingree, S., 12, *333*
Poggi, G., 227n, 230, 241, 260n (8), *359*
Pool, I. de S., 12, *359*
Porter, W.E., 112, *362*
Postman, N., 45, 65n, 84n (4), 144, 150, 179n, 186n (7), *359*
Potts, T.C., 33, *359-360*
Pratt, S., 145, *360*

Raboy, M., 288, *360*
Rachlin, A., 13-14, 174, 215, *360*
Rafaeli, S., 63n, 84n (2), *360*
Rajagopal, A., 13, *340*
Reardon, K., 88n, 128n (1), *325*
Reese, S.D., 165n, 186n (3), *364*
Reeves, B., 142n, 144, 159n (5), *352*
Reilly, S., 214n, 217n (7), *363*
Renaud, J.-L., 248, 274n, 280, 291, 302n (12), *360*
Reeves, B., 142n, 144, 159n (5), *368*
Reiss, P.C., 144n, 160n (11), *325*
Riley, J.W., Jr., 82, 127, *360*
Riley, M.W., 82, 127, *360*
Roach, C., 282n, 297, 304n (25), *360*
Roberts, D., 142, 143, *332*
Robinson, D.C., 252n, 264n (26), 280, 304n (23), *360*
Robinson, J.P., 77n, 85n (10), *333*
Rogers, E.M., 14, 277, 284, *360-361*
Rosenau, P.M., 27n, 30n (11), *361*

Rosengren, K.E., 148, 150n, 160n (15), *353-354, 361*
Rothenbuhler, E.W., 17, *359*
Rowland, W.D., Jr., 141, 191, 267, *361*
Rozeboom, W., 283, *344*
Ruben, B.D., 17n, 29n (9), *329*
Ruckmick, C.A., 142n, 159n (5), *335*
Ruggels, W.L., 246, *363*
Ruud, C.A., 249, *361*

Salter, H.L., 144n, 160n (9), *354*
Samarajiva, R., 278, 280, *354, 361*
Saxer, U., 271, *361*
Scannell, P., 147, 234n, 257, 201n (13), 268n, 300n (5), *330-331, 361*
Schiller, H., 223n, 251n, 257n, 260n (5), 263n (24), 282n, 291n, 304n (25), 308n (42), *361-362*
Schlesinger, P., 152, 200, 217n (4), 222, ,234, 241n, 261n (17), 287n, 289, 289n, 297, 306-307n (33, 34, 37), *362*
Schneider, H.D., 141n, 159n (4), *348*
Schoenbach, K., 109, 112, 149, 198, *326, 362*
Schramm, W., 12, 71, 82, 112, 142, 210, 246, 252, *359, 362-363, 364-365*
Schudson, M., 77n, 85n (10), 174, *363*
Schwoch, J., 214n, 217n (7), 270, *363*
Scott, W.T., 17, 24, 33, 42, 44, 54n, 55n, 60n (11, 12), *363*
Sears, D.O., 3, 12, 142, *363*
Seiter, E., 180, *363*
Selznick, P., 134, *363*
Serfaty, S., 152, 200n, 217n (4), 222, *363*
Service, E.R., 241, *363*
Seton-Watson, H., 226, 234, 234n, 261n (14), *364*
Severin, W.J., 142, *364*
Seymour-Ure, C., 248, *364*
Shannon, C.E., 43n, 59n (5), 70n, 71, 72, 82, *364*
Shaw, D., 143, 352, *364*
Shayon, R.L., 285n, 283, 304n (27), *364*
Shedd, M.S., 288, *364*
Shields, P., 278, *361*
Shils, E.A., 138, *364*
Shimanoff, S.B., 24, *364*
Shipley, C., 241n, 248, 261n (16), 291, *369*
Shipley, D., 241n, 248, 261n (16), 291, *369*
Shoemaker, P.J., 165n, 261n (17), 273n, 301n (10), *364*
Shorrock, D., 241n, 261n (17), 273n, 301n (10), *364*
Shuttlesworth, F.K., 142n, 159n (5), *364*
Siebert, F.S., 210, 252, *364-365*
Siefert, M., 166, *339*
Sim, F., 17, 33, *365*
Simmel, G., 78n, 85n (11), *365*
Simmons, J.L., 168n, 186n (5), *349*
Simon, T.F., 107, 129n (5), *348*
Simonet, T., 167, *365*
Singer, B., 139, 289n, 306-307n (37), *365*
Siwek, S.E., 247, 273, 283, *369*
Skirrow, G., 133, 139, *343*
Skocpol, T., 226, *365*
Slawiski, E.L., 174, *346*
Smith, A., 152n, 161n (16), 277n, 303n (17), *365*
Smith, A.D., 232, 235, 275, *365*
Smith, J., 17, 33, 80n, 85n (14), 98, 127, *365*

## Author Index

Smythe, D.W., 173, 295, *364*
Sparkes, V.M., 109, 112, *365*
Spicer, M.W., 190, *350*
Spitzer, M.L., 196, *366*
Sprafkin, J., 150, 166, 183n, 186n (8), *349*
Stappers, J.G., 150n, 160n (15), 243, *353-354, 357*
Starker, S., 163, 171, *366*
Stepan, A., 297n, 309n (47), *366*
Sterling, C.H., 166, *332*
Stern, J.A., 294, *347*
Stevenson, R.L., 210, 275n 278, 280n, 282n, 283, 302n (13), 303n (23), 304n (26), *366*
Straubhaar, J.D., 246, *366*
Street, R.L., Jr., 148, 170n, 186n (6), *329*
Swann, D., 272n, 294n, 301n (8), 308n (44), *366*
Szecskö, T., 14n, 29n (5), *366*

Tankard, J.W., 142, *364*
Taylor, J., 290n, 294n, 307n (39), 308n (45), *331*
Terry, H.A., 195, *347*
Thayer, L., 5, 12, 24, 25, 35, 42, 43n, 46n, 53n, 58n (9), 59n (4, 5, 10), 65n, 84n (4), 77n, 85n (10), 143, 153, *366*
Thomas, G.M., 226, *366*
Thorburn, D., 124, 143, 166, *366*
Thurstone, L.L., 142n, 159n (5), *359*
Tichenor, P.J., 14, 127, *366*
Times Mirror Center for People and the Press, 112, *367*
Tracey, M., 267, *361*
Trauth, D.M., 168, *367*
Tuchman, G., 14, 27, 44, 142, 148, 149, 152, 174, *367*
Tunstall, J., 185, 268n, 300n (5), *367*
Turow, J., 70n, 84n (7), 171, 175, *367*

Ungerer, H., 272, *367*
van Cuilenberg, J., 146, 291n, 308n (42), *367*
van Dijk, T.A., 175, *367*
Varis, T., 247, 281, *341, 357, 368*
Waldman, D., 257n, 264n (27), *368*
Ward, K., 4, 7, 13n, 29n (4), 35, 140, 142m, 160n (6), 164n, 168, 185n (1), 198, 199, 200, 241n, 250n, 255, 261n (16), 263n, (22), *368*
Wartella, E., 142n, 159n (5), *368*
Warth, E.-M., 180, *363*
Wasko, J., 12, 166, *368*
Watson, W.G., 288, *368*
Weaver, D.H., 143, 246, *368*
Weaver, W., 43n , 59n (5), 70, 71, 72, 82, *364*
Webster, J.G., 108, 116, 118, *368-369*
Weimann, G., 179, *369*
Wenner, L.A., 148, *361*
Westergaard, J., 175, *369*
Westley, B.H., 82, *369*
Westney, D.E., 126n, 129n (9), *326*
White, M., 214n, 217n (7), *363*
White, D.M., 12, *334*
White, W., 138, *358*
Wigand, R.T., 241n, 248, 261n (16), 291, *369*
Wildman, S.S, 107, 129n (5), 247, 273, 283, *358, 369*
Wilensky, H.L., 138, *369*
Wilhoit, G.C., 143, *369*
Williams, R., 175, *369*
Williams, T. McB., 144, *369*
Williamson, J., 175, *369*
Wilman, E.A., 288, *364*
Wilson, K.G., 25, 119, 184, 185, 267n, 291n, 299n (2), 308n

(42), *369*
Winkler, J.K., 141, *369*
Wise, G., 224, *370*
Wober, J.M., 107, 110n, 112, 119, 129n (7), 150n, 160n (15), 163, 171, 180, *370*
Wohl, R.R., 98, *344*
Wolton, D., 272n, 301n (7), *370*

Wright, C.R., 12, 17n, 29n (9), 142, 312, *370*
Wrong, D.H., 179, *370*
Zaret, D., 232, *370*
Zimmerman, D.H., 191, *344*

# Subject Index

activity-passivity, 66-8, 148, 177-178, 178, 191, 206
advertising, 3, 103, 104, 105, 118, 153-157, 178
Africa, 226, 236, 239, 299-300n (3)
agenda setting, 176-177, 192
Agnew, Spiro, 172
apparatus (*also see* communication system), 62, 64-65, 65, 67, 69, 84n (2), 91-92, 109, 115-119, 120, 123, 132, 170, 178, 179, 183-184, 206-207
  communicator's cost, indebtedness, financing, 95, 121, 166, 177
  effects, consequences, 115, 118-119, 144-145, 160-161n (16), 177, 184
  innovations, change, xx-xxi, 3, 5, 95, 96, 109, 118, 120, 124, 125, 160-161n (16), 165, 166, 183, 184, 223, 248-249
  receivers' costs, 117, 121, 122, 124
  skills, knowledge required, 8, 103, 117-118, 170, 171, 179, 206
Asia, 226, 239, 299-300n (3)
audience (*also see* intended audience, mass), xiii, 6, 53, 76, 107-108, 111, 112, 112-113, 114, 124, 138, 156-157, 272
  behavior, 3, 98-99, 108-111, 138, 155-156
  composition, demographics, 53, 111, 114, 115, 119-120, 124, 138, 154-155, 204
  defined, 107, 108
  relation to control, 168-170, 177-178, 179-180
  research, research methods, measurement methods, xix, 107-108, 112, 113
  size, ratings, 53, 68, 112-114
  skill, knowledge, 109, 111, 117, 119-120
  structure, 5, 110-112, 129n (6)
audiovisual media, electronic media, radio and television,

broadcasting, 4, 96-97, 122, 123, 173, 183, 190, 193, 194, 196, 198, 206, 221, 223, 242, 245, 247, 251, 256, 260n (5), 261n (13), 262n (18), 264n (25), 268, 269, 270, 271, 272, 273, 279, 283, 298n (1), 300n (4), 300n (5), 301-302n (11), 306-307n (37), 308-309n (45)
BBC, 245, 261n (13), 263n (23), 268-269, 271, 272, 273, 301n (9)
Bealer, Robert, 33, 58
Belgium, 227, 271
Blumer, Herbert, 4
books, 9, 117, 247, 268, 282, 287
Brazil, 237n (13)
Breed, Warren, 312
Canada, 7, 160n (9), 202, 212, 227, 262n (13), 236-239, 245, 246, 256-257, 262n (18), 264n (25), 271, 272, 274, 286-290, 293-294, 299-300n (3), 300n (4), 300n (5), 300-301n (6), 301-302n (11), 304-305n (29), 305n (31), 306n (34), 306-307n (37), 307-308n (39), 308-309n (45).
Canadian-U.S. relations, 223, 228, 273-274, 286, 293, 305n (30), 305n (32)
capacity, 75-77, 85n (9), 175
Caribbean, 226, 299-300n (3)
censorship, 16, 165, 168, 178, 181, 195, 242, 249-250
China (People's Republic of China), 264n (26), 323n (1)
cinema (see film)
colonialism, imperialism, 241-242, 244, 249, 276, 276-278, 302-303n (14), 303n (15), 306n (36)
communicatee (also see audience, receiver, communication system), 62, 64, 91, 95, 107, 115, 170, 176-177, 184, 213-214
role performance, 66, 79, 96, 153, 170, 186n (6)
skills, knowledge, 96, 122, 170-171, 177, 213-214, 217-218n (7)
communicating act (see communication act)
communication, xiii, xiv, xviii, xix, 2-4, 9, 14-19, 22-25, 33-37, 40, 41, 43, 45, 48, 50, 51, 54, 55, 60n (12), 122, 123, 152-154, 170, 201-204
analysis of, 38-42, 56, 59n (8)
and society, and state, x, xviii-xix, 224, 225-226
definition, problems in defining, 4, 25-26, 33, 34, 34-35, 50, 55, 62
norms, rules, 15, 35, 127, 167, 201
relation to information, learning, 33, 42, 43, 51, 58n (3), 59n (6), 59n (7)
relation to symbolic expression, 33, 203
structural inequalities, 314-317
successful communication, xiii, 34, 37, 38, 44, 48, 50-51, 61, 170
uncertainties in studying, xiii, xv, xvi, 37-38, 58n (2)
work, 22-23, 43, 53, 54
communication (communicating) act, xiii, 34. 37, 37-38, 39-40, 41, 41-42, 42, 48, 50, 50-51, 55, 88, 92
communication episode, xiii, 38, 43-44, 50, 52, 53, 56-57
communication system (also see communicator, communicatee, apparatus, symbol system), xiii, 4, 23-24, 24, 51, 56, 61,

# Subject Index 383

72, 80-81, 82-83, 84n (1), 87-92, 92, 126, 128n (1), 153, 216, 220, 246-247
components, elements, 62-66, 192
defined, 57-58, 62
exogenous conditions, forces, context, 58, 62, 125-128, 129n (8), 166, 168, 171-172, 172-173, 179, 180, 181-182, 192, 214-215, 219, 288-9
model, minimum conditions, 62, 87-88, 88-91, 92
sociological analysis of, 24, 55, 75, 81, 131
types, generality, 88-91, 126
communicator (*also see* sender, communication system), 16, 33, 62, 64, 91, 95, 97, 100-102, 123, 166-167, 170, 171, 180-181, 184, 203, 206, 207
relation to policy, 207-209
role performance, 66, 79, 96, 153, 202-203
skills, 44, 57, 72, 76, 170-171, 171, 202-203
compatibility (*also see* capacity), 23-24, 77-81, 85n (11), 85n (13), 122, 126, 205
defined, 77
of communicator and communicatee, 23-24, 77, 79, 122
relation to communication systems, xxii, 23-24, 80-81, 95, 316
conglomerates, 104, 105, 167-168, 177, 178, 207, 216
consuming media, 129n (6)
act, senses employed, 52, 110, 112-113, 119, 129n (7), 147, 150
conditions of consumption, 109, 115, 116, 122, 124
consuming unit, 110-112, 116

cost of consumption, 109, 117, 128n (2)
locus of consumption, 109, 115-117
social conventions, norms, 109, 111, 115
time of consumption, 109-110, 113, 116
variations among media, 108-112
control, process of control (*also see* censorship, deregulation, power), xvii, 9-10, 10, 95, 96, 126, 132-133, 163-185, 186n (4), 186n (8), 186n (9), 188, 264n (29), 316-317, 321-323
conflict over, 172-175
consumer sovereignty, audience pressure, 169, 188, 258-259, 264n (29), 272
defined, 164
diffusion of, distributed, as a field of forces, xvii, 106-107, 115, 164-165, 175-176, 177, 177-178, 179, 182, 192, 194-195, 205, 269
interactive, dynamic process, 9-10, 126, 166-172, 172-173, 182-183, 186n (3), 191
market-state alternatives, relationship, xxi, 168-169, 173, 196, 200, 212
public standards, public opinion, public pressure, pressure groups, 126, 163-164, 167, 168, 171, 178, 181-182, 183, 188-189, 196-197, 199-200, 200, 267
relation to meaning, 175-178
relation to policy, 164, 182-185, 188-189, 191-193, 197-200
self-control, self-regulation, 163, 167, 188, 197-200, 207,

211
  state control, measures, regulation, 7, 20-22, 103, 126, 167, 178, 179, 181, 186n (4), 188, 271
  tactics, 179-182, 205-206, 214-215
  trade associations, industry codes, 166, 168, 178, 200, 207, 208, 211-212
  variations in, 165, 172, 178-182, 193-194, 205
conversation, 82, 88, 243-244
Cooley, Charles Horton, ix
countries, nations, societies, ethnic groups, cultures, 231, 232, 235, 236, 244, 258, 285-286, 290-291
  ethnic heterogeneity in country, state, 228, 234, 235-236, 261n (15), 298, 306n (34), 306n (35), 306-7n (37)
  expansion of society, inclusion of groups in society, extension of citizenship, 227, 230, 233, 240, 244, 260-261n (10)
  relation of country, state to nation, 234, 234-236, 236-239, 244, 288
critical theory, ix, 13, 14, 198
cultural imperialism, 254, 284-285, 302n (13), 303n (17)
  arguments contradicting the claim, 284-291, 304-305n (29)
  NWIO, and related responses, 221, 241, 248, 256, 264n (27), 281-284, 290, 303n (22)
  supporters of charge, reasons for belief in, 280, 283, 286, 289, 289-290, 306n (36)
cultural production, 13-15, 203-204

demographics *(also see* audience)

developing, ex-colonial, peripheral, third world countries, 278, 279, 285, 303n (20)
  and international news, professional journalism, 279-280, 303n (19)
  development journalism, 241, 304n (23), 304n (26)
  development requirements, strategies, 278-279, 279-280, 303n (18)
  impact of foreign media, media imports, 278, 282, 303n (15)
domestic communication, media policies, 223, 234, 250, 258, 259, 261n (17), 274, 275, 289, 301-302n (11), 308-309n (45), 309n (46)

Ehrlich, Howard, 58
elites, and media policy, 258, 289-290, 298-299, 301n (5), 306-307n (37), 307n (38)
Ellison, Chris, xxiv
entertainment, recreation, 8, 14-15, 15-19, 53, 117, 150-151, 156, 186n (7), 207, 298
  contrast to information, vii, 14-15, 20, 21, 96-97, 149-150
  defined, 21-22

feedback, 68-70, 72, 95, 120-122, 122, 124, 132
film, xviii, 4, 6, 9, 12, 14, 15, 22, 25, 95, 98, 99, 99-100, 102, 103, 105-106, 106, 113, 114, 115-116, 120, 121, 122, 123, 124, 128n (2), 140, 142, 143, 166, 168, 178, 186n (4), 186n (5), 193-194, 198, 206-211, 221, 246, 247, 250, 268, 282, 284, 287, 300n (4), 304n (24), 319, *see* Hays Office
  audience, audience behavior, 110-114, 138, 208, 249
films, xii, 4, 9, 114, 121, 142,

## Subject Index

246, 247
financing, xii, 246-247, 264n (29), 301-302n (11), 304-305n (29)
Hollywood films, xii, 171, 185
organization of industry, 99-100, 105-106, 169, 246, 251, 257, 259-260n (3), 262n (18), 282, 301-302n (11)
theaters, screens, 109, 110, 111, 112-116, 247, 262n (18)
France, 225, 227, 233, 242, 258, 260-261n (10), 261n (15), 262n (18), 264n (25), 267, 271, 275, 294, 301n (7), 303n (15), 307-308n (39)

Gans, Herbert, 312
gestures, 93, 119
Germany (also East Germany), 227, 232, 249, 257, 264n (25), 271, 294, 300n (4), 303n (1), 318
Glasgow, Margaret, xxiv
Glennie, Beth, xxiv
Goffman, Irving, 29
governments, regimes, 226-227
relation to state, 226
rule, 224, 225, 227-228, 228, 228-229, 232, 234, 244
rule and communication, 226, 244-245, 249-250
tactics for building support, acceptance, addressing weakness, 231, 232-234, 249
Great Britain (also England, United Kingdom), 7, 189, 212, 227, 232, 242-243, 245, 250, 251, 257, 260n (4), 264n (25), 271, 272, 282-283, 294, 299-300n (3), 300n (5), 301n (7), 301n (8), 301n (9), 304n (24), 307-308n (39), 308n (44), 308-309n (45), 309n (46)

Grierson, John, 300
Halsted, Donald, 58
Harkness, James, 58
Hays Office, 168, see Film
Hearst, William Randolph, 9, 141
hegemony, 13, 149, 172-175, 284-285
Heston, Charlton, 116
history of media development, xxi, 136, 137, 166, 197-199
humor, irony, 15-16, 16, 53
Huxley, Aldous, 147

imitation, 139, 142, 144, 148, 158, 160n (11)
individualism, 201-204
influence, 15-19, 20, 131-132, 138, 205-206
information (also see noninformation), 14-15, 15, 29n (7), 34, 43, 44, 44-45, 46, 48-49, 49, 53, 54
contrast to entertainment, xiii, 14-15, 96-97, 149-150
defined, 21, 29n (10), 43
irrelevant, repetitive, redundant, 43, 45, 54, 123
relation to learning, communication, 42, 43, 50, 58n (3), 59n (6), 59n (7)
Information Society, Wired Cities (and the Information Superhighway), 146, 219, 260n (5), 292, 292-293, 293, 307-308n (39), 308n (41), 308n (43), 316-317
domestic policy concerns, issues, responses 260n (5), 294-295, 297-298, 308n (42)
relation to cultural imperialism, 281, 292, 293
societal impact, social effects, 291-292, 294, 294-295
technological bases, structure,

## Subject Index

issues, 284, 291, 292, 294, 295, 307-308n (39)
Innis, Harold, 318
intended audience, targeted groups (*also see* audience, receivers), 3, 32, 34, 39, 107, 108, 113, 120, 121, 123, 124, 138, 180, 183, 206
   relation to actual audience, 39, 48, 105, 206
interact (various types), 40, 41, 43, 46, 48, 55, 57, 61
international agreements, cooperation, organizations
   issues, points of contention, 281-282, 283-284, 304n (25)
   ITU, WARC, 248, 281-282, 302n (12)
   UNESCO, 221, 247, 248, 262n (19), 264n (27), 282, 282-283, 304n (25), 290
international communication standards, ideals (*also see* United States), 220
   press freedom, standards of professional journalism, 221, 232, 283, 304n (27)
internationalization, regional markets, globalization, global economy, world system, 220, 221, 241, 257-258, 258-259, 259, 259-260n (3), 263-264n (24), 264n (28), 275, 281, 282, 286, 292, 297, 307n (38)
   effect on national media policies, 241, 257-259, 261n (17), 270, 273-274
Iran, 7
Italy, 232, 245, 249, 262n (18), 264n (25)

Japan, 223, 263n (21), 294, 299-300n (3), 301n (10)
journalism, journalists, professional norms, 128n (4), 248, 280, 281, 289, 299-300n (27), 313

Katz, Elihu, 312
Kornberg, Allan, xxiv
Kresse, Kevin, xxiv

language (*also see* symbol system, meaning), 16, 23, 42, 64, 84n (3), 84n (4), 123, 202, 305n (30)
Lasswell, Harold, 12, 13, 140, 186
Latin America, South America, 226, 239, 271, 299-300n (3), 303n (18)
Lazarsfeld, Paul, F., xvii, 12, 128, 312
Lerner, Daniel, 126
lies, lying, 44
Lippman, Walter, ix, 186
Luxembourg, 271

magazines, periodicals, 6, 9, 13, 14, 15, 24, 95, 96, 98, 99, 101, 104-105, 109-114, 115, 120, 121, 128n (2), 137, 155, 165, 169, 193, 208, 246, 247, 256, 268, 287
Malagasy Republic (*also* Madagascar), 224, 225
Marxist scholars, scholarship, x, xii, 13, 14, 229, 255, 283
mass (*also see* audience), 2-3, 3, 4, 69, 114, 133-140, 158, 314
   defined, 4, 133-134
mass communication, ix, x, xi, xiii-xiv, xviii, xx, 2, 3, 24, 26, 31-32, 32, 33, 47, 65, 69, 74, 86, 88, 111, 114, 124, 179, 314
   characteristics, xix-xx, 24, 111, 124, 133, 183
   contradiction in terms, improbability, xvii, xxi-xxii, 2-3, 3, 5, 110-111, 135

## Subject Index

defined, 31, 32
legacies for media, for control, 5-10, 17, 28n (2), 95-96, 183
organization, complex organization, bureaucratic organization, monopolies, big business as source 31, 32, 39, 97, 133, 180, 184, 215-216
personalizing tactics, 97-99
relation to media, xii, xvii, 3, 5, 26, 32, 50
social role, effects, 131-159, 212
systems, 88, 91-92, 92, 92-105
mass communication scholarship, xii, xvii-xviii, 10-15, 27-28, 28n (3), 29n (5), 139-140, 141-143, 159n (4), 185-186n (1), 313, 323n (1)
mass media (*see* media)
mass society, 3, 4-5, 134-140, 314
relation to mass media, 136, 136-137, 314
Mayer, Louis, B., 9
mathematical communication theory, 59n (5)
McCormack, Thelma, xxiv, 312
McLuhan, Marshall, 318
Mead, George Herbert, xxii, 33, 34, 58n (3), 59n (7)
Mead, Margaret, 126
meaning, xiii, 15, 16, 23, 29n (7), 33, 34, 123, 285
of significant symbols, 33, 43, 64
media (*also see* film, magazines, newspapers, print, radio, telecommunications, television), 5, 6, 6-7, 8, 11, 18-19, 48, 50, 53, 54, 62, 69, 72, 76, 84n (4), 95, 95-96, 114, 123, 136-137, 141-142, 159n (2), 161n (18)
and hegemony, 13, 149, 172-175, 302n (13)
and social context, societal context, community context, xvii, 113, 132, 165-166, 173-175, 182, 222, 252-4, 255, 256, 262n (18)
as legacy of mass communication, 5-10, 95-96
beliefs about, knowledge of, images of, evaluations of, xxi, 8, 96-97, 103, 127, 141, 159n (3), 163, 255, 287
content, 145-147
control, 9, 9-10, 169-185, 320
differences among, 96-97, 118, 120-125
mystique, 8, 65-66, 103, 115
ownership, owners' interests, entrepreneurship, business interests, 9, 96, 103-104, 128-129n (5), 166, 166-167, 168, 177, 178-179, 197, 198, 321
public-private character, xx-xxi, 110, 110-111, 165, 184, 199-200, 206
relation to advertising, 154-157, 198
relation to communication, xiii-xiv, 17, 50, 152, 152-153, 207
relation to mass communication, xiii, xvii, 5-6, 26, 32, 50, 97
relation to mass society, 136, 136-137, 138-140
relation to society, 10, 14, 127, 132-133, 158, 174, 297-298
social consequences, social role, 10, 11, 52, 148-152, 158-159, 198, 303n (21), 319-320
sociological analysis of, ix-x, xi-xii, xiv, 11, 111, 127
structure, 145-147, 179, 317
styles, genres, 110, 125, 128n

(3), 155-157
system, social systems, social institution, ix, 3, 4, 11, 26, 32, 52, 62, 95-97, 125, 127, 132
voluntarism, 51, 67, 124
media effects, consequences, xviii, 8, 11, 13, 131-159, 160n (13), 161n (17), 267, 306-307n (37)
   causes, sources, mechanisms, 142, 143-147, 157-158, 163-164, 267, 297-298
   cultivation effects, 149-150, 160n (15)
   hypodermic effects model, 140, 142, 143, 160n (6)
   negative consequences, evaluation as negative, 141, 143, 147, 151-152, 158, 164, 179, 184, 314
   "no effects," "limited effects" model, 142, 157, 157-158, 160n (8), 323n (1)
   relation to social role, 148-152, 160n (14)
media materials, products, 8, 10, 108, 109-110, 121, 123, 124-125, 128n (2)
media organizations, 97, 99, 103, 106-107
   financing, income, revenue, profit, 103, 105, 154-155, 155, 198-199, 207
   personnel functions, 97, 103, 103-104, 105
   size, structure, 99-100, 102-107
media research, 13-15, 70, 84n (6), 112, 180, 259n (2)
mediated relationships, xi, 8, 17, 23, 31, 110-111, 111, 115, 128n (1), 175
Merton, Robert, K., ix, xviii

message, 43, 51, 53, 60, 73-75, 98, 123, 124-125, 169
metaphor, 38, 54, 84n (8)
Meyrowitz, Joshua, 318
Milton, John, 232
misinformation, 44, 45
motion pictures (*see* film)
movies (*see* film)

narcotizing dysfunction, 45
news, 44, 96, 109, 110, 112, 114, 121, 144, 150, 171, 243, 250, 268, 271, 279-280, 282, 288, 300-301n (6), 316
   and entertainment, 28n (1), 156, 186n (7), 281
newspapers, 4, 6, 13, 14, 24, 85n (10), 88, 95-96, 98, 99, 100-101, 104, 104-105, 106, 108-114, 115, 119-120, 121, 127, 128n (2), 137, 165, 167, 169, 173, 173-174, 182, 193, 246, 247, 255, 256, 262n (18), 268, 304n (27)
noise, 70-71, 109, 122-123, 124
noncommunication, 37
   defined, 34
noninformation (*also see* information), 54, 56-58, 58, 60n (11)
   relation to information, 43, 53, 54, 57
   types of, 43, 53, 54, 59-60n (10)

Orwell, George, 146, 147
Paine, Tom, 232
Paley, William, 9
Park, Robert, ix
policy, policies, 7, 163-164, 182-183, 185, 187-216, 217n (1), 223, 248, 318-319
   conflicts, contradictions, lack of consistency, 196-197, 234, 288, 306n (33), 308-309n (45)

## Subject Index 389

locus of, 192-193, 193-197
policy implementation, enforcement, programs, 188, 189, 190, 190-191, 191-192, 192-193, 193-197, 204
policy making, formulation process, 188, 189-197, 223, 248
relation to control, 164, 182-185, 188, 189, 191-193, 197-200
resistance to, neglect of policy, 201-204, 297-298
targets, 204-209
United States uniqueness, 187, 189, 196, 197, 212-213, 222, 223, 225, 236, 292
postmodernist analysis, xiii, xiv-xvi, 14, 25, 29n (10), 30n (11), 166n (15)
potentially interactive situations, 38, 40, 45, 47, 48, 50, 51, 52, 56-58
power (*also see* control), 65, 115, 178-179, 179
distributed, xvii, 103, 115, 166-172
imbalances among elements, social distance, xxii, 32, 103, 111, 122, 175, 176, 177, 178, 183, 184-185, 205
print media, xviii, 2, 6, 8, 28, 96, 96-97, 98, 99, 109-111, 123, 125, 143, 152, 178, 206, 210-211, 233, 244, 245, 250, 251, 256, 257, 268, 304-305n (29)
privatization, deregulation, 178, 183, 185, 190, 221, 264n (25), 268, 270, 273
rationale, economic philosophy, 196, 212, 273
protectionist, exclusionary national policies, trade restraints, 221, 223, 245, 258-259, 264n (27), 274, 283, 301n (10), 302n (12)
public broadcasting, 242, 245, 267-273, 298n (1), 301n (7)
assumptions, philosophy supporting, 267-268, 306-307n (37)
financial mechanisms, sources of and level of support, advertising, 270, 271, 272-273, 299-300n (3)
functions, role, 267-268, 299n (2), 300n (4)
reasons for decline, lack of public support, interest, 269-270, 270-275, 275

radio, xviii, 6, 8, 9, 13, 24, 88, 97, 98, 99, 102, 103, 104, 114, 119, 120, 121, 122, 123, 135, 140, 141-142, 142, 143, 152, 155-156, 156, 166, 168, 169, 173, 182, 207, 210, 224, 225, 245, 246, 247, 250, 250-251, 257, 261n (13), 262n (18), 263n (22), 271, 272, 273, 278, 287, 296, 304n (23), 321
audience, audience behavior, 109-114
radios, receivers, technology, 7, 115, 119, 144, 165, 198, 206, 224, 245, 250, 263n (23)
receiver (*also see* communicatee, audience), xiii, 16, 32, 33, 34, 38, 39, 40, 42, 49, 50, 54, 107, 110, 122, 123, 153, 215
power, 178, 208-209, 215
unintended, 38, 48, 183
unorganized, 32, 107, 215
work, 53, 98-99, 109, 118
redundancy, 72-73, 95, 123-124, 124-125
Rieth, Lord, 300
role reversal (*also see* role

changes), 31-32, 62, 123-124
Rose, Dina, xxiv
Rushing, Beth, xxiv
Sapir, Edward, ix, 126
Schramm, Wilbur, 12
Schudson, Michael, 312
semiotics, semiotic analysis, 14, 169, 175-176
sender (*also see* communicator), 40, 43, 46, 49, 53, 54
   defined, 38
   intentions, xiii, 15-16, 19, 32, 34, 35, 38, 39, 40, 41, 43, 153
sending act, 31, 40, 41, 46
Sherkat, Darren, xxiv
significant symbol, 33, 64
Sim, Francis, 58
Sindlinger Polls, 138
soap operas, 141-142, 144, 155
social act, 34, 37, 62
social action (*also see* communication), 29n (6), 34
social convention
   defining potentially communicative situations, 47, 49, 51
   norms, values, 46, 126, 127, 167, 178, 179, 181, 188, 189, 191
social institution, 26-27
social process, 26-27
social system, 26, 26-27, 61, 62
society, 146, 151, 172, 296
sociology of mass communication, xviii-xix, 16, 28, 77, 128, 131-132, 167, 312-323
Spain, 227, 232, 261n (15)
state, 219, 223, 224-239, 240, 242, 260n (6), 275, 293, 296
   and communication, media policy, xvii, 20-22, 165, 191, 217n (6), 219, 234, 241, 243-244, 251-257, 259n (1)
   definition, nature of the state, 225, 226,, 227, 227-228, 234, 240
   development of states, 226-234, 242-243, 260n (8, 9), 261n (12, 14)
   functions, roles, responsibilities, 165, 188, 189, 226, 227, 228, 229, 234, 239-240, 241-242, 249-250
   internal-external focus, 226, 228, 234, 239-240, 260n (7), 288
states and media, xvii, 219, 239-244, 246-251, 296-299
   building and maintaining control, rule, order, integration, mobilization, the public good, 224, 226, 234, 239, 261n (12, 13), 279, 288-289, 296
   building and maintaining national identity, national culture, solidarity, 227, 234, 236, 258, 269, 274, 288
   changing public-private line and state interest in media, 184, 240, 243-244, 249, 251, 267, 269
   communication policy, media policy, 193-197, 217n (4), 225, 235, 261n (16)
   media control measures (financing, licensing), 225, 246, 250, 251, 256-257, 268, 273
   media development, xxi, 232-233, 244-245, 250-251, 263n (23)
   public-private line, state and civil society, 221, 251, 264n (25), 268-269, 271, 273, 300n (46)
symbol system (*also see* language, communication sys-

# Subject Index 391

tem), 62, 65, 67, 68, 91, 110, 119-120, 126, 129n (9)
symbolic expression, production, transmission, 12, 16, 17-19, 123, 318
   relation to communication, 43, 49, 50, 314, 318
   relation to information, 15, 16, 320-321

Tanzania, 303n (19), 304n (23)
technological innovation, 6, 198, 217n (3), 248-249, 259
telecommunications, xxi, 6, 9-10, 118, 165, 185, 190, 193, 239, 242, 248, 259, 281, 308n (40)
television, x, xiv, xx, 2, 6, 7, 9, 13, 14, 15, 24, 27, 59n (8), 96, 97, 98, 106, 108, 112, 113, 114-119, 121, 120, 121, 122, 123, 124, 133, 143, 144, 145-146, 150, 150-151, 151, 160n (15), 161n (17), 165, 169, 178, 184, 186n (8), 194, 198, 206, 207, 208, 210, 221, 245, 246, 251, 257, 259-260n (3), 282, 284, 286, 287, 294, 297, 300-301n (6), 301n (9), 304n (24), 306-307n (37), 307n (38), 308-309n (45), 318, 319
   audience, audience behavior, 108, 108-115, 138, 146, 150-151
   cable, cable networks, cable systems, 5, 7, 96, 99, 101-102, 103-104, 108, 112-113, 114, 115, 118, 120, 124, 151, 321
   television networks, network television, 24, 99, 102, 104, 105, 107, 113, 114, 120, 121, 167, 185, 196, 221, 273, 288, 300-301n (6), 321
   television news, 8, 121, 150, 152, 223
   television programming styles, mode of presentation, 84n (7), 96, 124, 150-151, 156-157, 170-171, 186n (4), 196, 259n (2), 284, 297
   television stations, channels, local television, 98, 99, 102, 104, 114, 120, 121, 170, 173. 247, 262n (18), 272, 307-308n (39)
text, xiii, xv, xvi, xix, 73, 111, 144-145, 169
Thompson, John, xxiv
transmission, transport view of communication, 3, 4, 13-15, 48-49, 152, 185, 203-204
Tuchman, Gaye, 312
types of national media systems, media policies, 251-257
   discrepancies between ideal and reality, 247-248, 254-257, 262n (20)
   relativity of national perspectives, media, differences in systems, 245, 247, 255

United States, 179, 186n (2), 187-188, 194, 202, 233, 242-243, 260-261n (10), 262n (18), 282-283, 296, 301n (10)
   Constitution, First Amendment, 165, 187-188, 189, 204, 205, 232, 320
   dominance in media, as a media exporter, media imperialist, 222, 269-270, 304-305n (29)
   FCC, 151, 190, 192-193, 193-194, 195, 196, 217n (2)
   free enterprise, market economy, relation of state to economy, 189, 196, 200, 201, 296
   freedom of speech, free press,

freedom of information, 165, 179, 184. 185, 187, 189, 193, 196, 201, 203, 217n (5), 260n (4), 296, 320, 321-323

media policies, policy issues, involvement of state in policy, 248, 264n (27), 295-296, 296, 297, 298, 298-299

private ownership, private entrepreneurship, private property rights, 165, 189, 196, 256

role in media development, 220, 224, 245, 250, 263n (22)

uniqueness, bias, 219, 236, 247, 251, 256, 269, 295, 296

Union of South Africa, 141

U.S.S.R. (also Russia), 226, 236, 271, 300n (4)

VCRs, 7, 9, 112, 113, 116-117, 246

War of the Worlds, 13, 135, 140, 144

Wells, H.G., 13

Whorf, Benjamin, ix, 126

Wright, Charles, xxiv

Yugoslavia, 227, 236

Zaret, David, 318